Phillip T Sandhurst

The Table Book of Art

A history of art in all countries and ages

Phillip T Sandhurst

The Table Book of Art
A history of art in all countries and ages

ISBN/EAN: 9783337427214

Printed in Europe, USA, Canada, Australia, Japan

Cover: Foto ©ninafisch / pixelio.de

More available books at **www.hansebooks.com**

TABLE BOOK OF ART

A

HISTORY OF ART

IN

ALL COUNTRIES AND AGES

EDITED BY

P. T. SANDHURST, Ph. D.

SUPERBLY ILLUSTRATED

BY

THE FINEST ENGRAVINGS ON STEEL AND WOOD

"*Art is long, and Life is fleeting.*"

NEW YORK:

R. WORTHINGTON, PUBLISHER

1880

ALL RIGHTS RESERVED

INTRODUCTION.

HAT is Art? We owe, what we consider the best definition, to one who never meddled with paints, or marble, yet who helped on the cause of art in his day with an energy of practice and a blaze of enthusiasm which has rarely been equalled before or since. This was Benvenuto Cellini, the immortal jeweller of the sixteenth century, and he says in effect that the aim of art is "to produce a representation of a beautiful human figure, with correctness of design and in a graceful attitude." If we approve this definition, and keep it in mind, it will greatly simplify our estimate of the men and works we shall have to discuss in the present work—The History of Art.

But, "What is the history of painting to me?" may be the remark of a worthy citizen whose eye lights on the title-page of our history: "I leave all that to artists, to picture-dealers and their customers, and perhaps to a few young ladies who are learning to sketch." Softly, my good sir; with your leave, it may be possible to show that a great many more people than you think for are gifted by nature with a capacity for deriving enjoyment from Art; and that their indifference, it may be, to it is due quite as much to want of opportunity, as to inaptitude. Who can have failed to notice the intense delight children take in harmonious combinations of colors? How catching is a broad grin reflected from a Teniers, or a Van der Meer, to the eye of a holiday gazer! Part of this natural accessibility to Art-influence is the undefined but often acute pleasure felt by very simple people in contemplating a beautiful landscape, or a beautiful face; the feeling after something better, brighter, lovelier than their earthly surroundings; something of what the poet describes as—

> "The desire of the moth for the star,
> Of the night for the morrow,
> The devotion to something afar
> From the sphere of our sorrow."

It is not altogether impossible that our worthy citizen himself may have undergone something of this kind, long ago perhaps, when he was younger, less prosperous, and less careworn. There is no doubt that the mind is more open to such impressions in the days of sweet youth; unless, indeed, they take such lasting root there, as to preserve the mind in perpetual youth, amidst the decay and death of nature.

It is not only as a source of intellectual pleasure that painting has a high value; it is as a means of quickening the intelligence, of stimulating the imagination; in a word, of cultivating the mind. Education is often regarded as equivalent to the acquisition of knowledge; a far more important part of true education is awaking the mind to activity, is rousing it to think. What, on a large scale, the recovery of Greek and Roman literature effected for European forethought centuries ago, Art is capable of doing for each separate mind. It awakes the dormant faculties; it is the wine of life, vivifying, lightening, and strengthening.

In the following pages the endeavor has been made to give a succinct history of Art.

> "I bless thee, promethean Muse
> And hail thee, Brightest of the Nine!"
> —*Thomas Campbell.*

The writers of all periods have furnished the materials from which this synopsis has been garnered; and chiefly is the Editor indebted to Miss Tytler and M. Viardot, who in their turn had gathered almost entirely from their predecessors.

THE TABLE BOOK OF ART.

CHAPTER I.

CLASSIC GREEK SCHOOL.

ANY writers," says Vasari, "have asserted that Painting and Sculpture originated with the Egyptians; others attribute to the Chaldeans the discovery of the bas-relief, and give to the Greeks the invention of painting: for my own part, I hold that a knowledge of Drawing, the creative principle of all art, has existed since the beginning of the world."

From remains that are left to the present day, we know that the people of Egypt, Phœnicia, and Assyria, of Persia, India, and China, were all acquainted with the art of painting, but it was always symbolical and as an accessory to Architecture. We find fresco paintings as decorations of walls and pillars, manuscripts on papyrus ornamented with coloured figures, and mummy cases covered with hieroglyphics; but no movable Pictures, in our present acceptation of that term, have come down to us, nor have any been mentioned by the early historians of those Eastern nations.

It is not till the fifth century before Christ that we have any record of Painting as a fine art by itself, and then it must have quickly reached to the highest eminence. It is to Athens that we must give the glory of its birth-place, though, by a fatality ever to be deplored, no work of the famous Greek painters remains to the present day.

In spite of the ravages made by time and many generations of barbarians, Architecture and Sculpture have left monuments numerous and magnificent enough to enable us to judge of the state of both these arts in Greece. The master-pieces of two thousand years ago continue to excite at once the delight and despair of the student. We can still see the ruins of the Parthenon and the temple of Theseus at Athens, and of the temple of Neptune at Pæstum. The museums of Italy are full of beautiful relics of Greek statuary. At Paris are the *Venus of Melos, Diana the Huntress*, the *Gladiator*, the *Achilles*. Munich possesses the marbles of Ægina, and London the fragments of Pheidias from the Parthenon. But Painting, using more fragile materials, has not been able to survive the tempests which entirely engulfed ancient civilization, and threw back the human mind, like another Sisyphus, from the heights it had attained, to the humble commencement of a new road, which it has had to re-mount by a long and painful way. The style of painting adopted by the ancients is, strictly speaking, almost unknown to us, but we can arrive at some estimate of its merits by evident analogies and indications.

And firstly, Painting occupied, in the esteem of the people of antiquity, the same place that it now holds, relatively to other arts, in public opinion; and the names of Apelles, Zeuxis, Parrhasius, Polygnotus, Aristides, Pamphilus, Timanthes, Nicomachus, are no less great, no less illustrious as painters than those of Pheidias, Alcamenes, Polycletus, Praxiteles, Myron, Lysippus, as sculptors, or than those of Hippodamus, Ictinus, and Callicrates, as architects.

This high esteem in which the ancient painters were held by their contemporaries is shown again clearly in the value which their works commanded. If it be true that a marble statue, made by an inferior artist, was currently worth $2,500 of our money in that Rome where statues, as Pliny says, were more numerous than the inhabitants, where Nero brought five hundred, *in bronze*, from the temple of Delphi alone, and from the soil of which had been dug—in the time of the Abbé Barthélemy—more than seventy thousand; if it be true that for the *Diadumenos*, Polycletus was paid a hundred talents ($108,000), and that Attalus in vain offered the inhabitants of Cnidus to pay all their debts in exchange for the *Venus* of Praxiteles,—the other productions of high art, of which Athens acquired a monopoly, must have risen to a value which in our days can scarcely be believed. According to the uniform testimony of Plutarch and Pliny, who would have been contradicted if they had asserted falsehoods or exaggerations, Nicias refused for one of his pictures sixty talents ($65,000), and made a present of it to the town of Athens; Cæsar paid eighty talents ($86,500) for the two pictures by Timomachus, which he placed at the entrance to the temple of Venus Genetrix; a picture by Aristides, which was called the *Beautiful Bacchus*, was sold for one hundred talents ($108,000); and when the town of Sicyon was laden with debts which its revenues were not sufficient to pay, the pictures which belonged to the public were sold, and the produce of these works sufficed to discharge the amount.

Enough has been said to show that the painting of the ancients was held by them in equal esteem with their sculpture and their architecture; it follows that the excellence of the remains of the two latter arts proves, at the same time, the excellence of the former. Certainly, if in future ages our civilization were to perish under fresh invasions of barbarians, and that, to make it known to a new generation born in after ages, there only remained parts of St. Peter's at Rome and of the Venetian palaces, with some of the statues which adorn them—would not the men of those future times—seeing in what esteem we hold Leonardo, Raphael and Titian, Rubens, Velazquez and Rembrandt—think that the lost works of these painters must have been equal to the works still preserved of Bramante and Michael Angelo, Palladio and Sansovino?

But there also remain to us some descriptions of pictures in default of the pictures themselves; and, yet more than this, some fragments of ancient paintings have been found, which confirm this reasoning, and leave no doubt as to the excellence of the art which these precious remains represent. Passing over the

THE CUMÆAN SIBYL.
From the original painting by Michael Angelo.

detailed eulogies of Cicero and Quintilian, we have the descriptions which Pausanias gives of the paintings in the Pœcile at Athens, and of the Lesche of the Cnidians at Delphi; those which Pliny gives of the pictures of *Venus* and of *Calumny*, by Apelles, and of *Penelope*, by Zeuxis, and that which Lucian gives of *Helen the Courtesan*, also by Zeuxis. The painted vases, both of Etruscan and of Greek manufacture, must be included among the actual remains of ancient pictorial art. Such again are the arabesques in the baths of Titus, discovered under the church of San Pietro in Vincula, at the time of the excavations ordered by Leo X.; the frescoes found in the sepulchre of the Nasos; those in the pagan catacombs; and more recently the frescoes of Herculaneum and Pompeii, which, although merely decorations of ordinary citizens' houses in little towns, fifty leagues from Rome, are of great importance. There are also monochrome designs on marble and stone, for example, *Theseus killing the Centaur* and the *Ladies playing at the game of talus* (huckle-bones), wonderful compositions, traced on marble with a red pigment, which Pliny calls *cinnabaris indica*, both in the museum at Naples.

Examples of Greek and Greco-Roman mosaics also remain; amongst others the beautiful mosaic found at Pompeii in the "*House of the Faun*," so called because it had already yielded the charming little *Dancing Faun*, the pride of the cabinet of bronzes: both are in the same museum at Naples. This mosaic, the most important vestige of the painting of the ancients which has come down to us, cannot be otherwise than the copy of a picture; probably of one of the Greek pictures brought to Rome after the conquest of Greece, not impossibly of one by Philoxenus of Eretria, a pupil of Nicomachus, who is, indeed, known to have painted, for King Cassander, one of the battles of Alexander against the Persians. The mosaic formed the pavement of the *triclinium* (dining-room). Surrounded by a sort of frame, it contains twenty-five persons and twelve horses, of nearly the size of life, and thus forms a real historical picture. It certainly represents one of the battles of Alexander against the Persians, and probably the victory of Issus, for the recital of Quintus Curtius (lib. iii.) agrees perfectly with the work of the painter.

If the original picture, of which this mosaic was a copy, were of Greek origin, the painter and historian must have drawn from the same traditions; if of Roman origin, the artist must have described on his panel the details given by the historian of Alexander.

A study of the various remains to which reference has been made, shows first, that the painters of antiquity knew how to treat all subjects, mythology, history, landscape, sea-pieces, animals, fruit, flowers, costume, ornament, and even caricature; and also that, while treating great subjects and embracing vast compositions, they knew how to attain a perfect order, a happy arrangement of groups, various planes, foreshortenings, chiaroscuro, movement, action, expression by gesture and by countenance, all the qualities in short of high painting, which the people of modern times have usually denied to the ancients.

The works of the best known of the Greek painters have been described by Herodotus, Aristotle, Pausanius, Lucian, Plutarch and Pliny; and mentioned by many other classic writers.

DIONYSIUS of Colophon, one of the earliest of the Greek painters whose names have been handed down to us, was probably born about B. C. 490; it is known that he lived in the time of Pericles. Aristotle and Plutarch both speak of his works as being forcible and full of spirit. He was probably a good portrait painter (Ανθρωπογραφος), as Aristotle says, "Polygnotus painted men better than they are; Dionysius as they are." Ælian (a Roman author of the third century), says that Dionysius and Polygnotus painted similar subjects—Polygnotus in large, and Dionysius in small. Whether the writer referred to the style of the painters or the size of their pictures, it is difficult to determine.

POLYGNOTUS, a native of the island of Thaos, was known as a painter in Athens in B. C. 460. His principal pictures were: In the Lesche, an open hall at Delphi, *The Taking of Troy; The Return of the Greeks;* and the *Ulysses visiting the Shades:* —fully described in seven chapters by Pausanias. In the porch at Athens, called the Pœcile, in which he painted the *Destruction of Troy.*—For this work it is said he would not receive payment, and consequently the Public Council gave him a house in Athens, and made him a guest of the state at the public expense.—In the temple of the Dioscuri at Athens, *The Marriage of the daughter of Leucippus;* and in the temple of Minerva at Platæa, *Ulysses after the slaughter of the suitors of Penelope.* It is said that Polygnotus first used the yellow earth found in the silver mines, and a purple colour prepared from the husks of grapes. Aristotle speaks of him as "the painter of noble characters," and Pliny says he was the first who gave expression to the features.

It seems probable that the style of painting of the celebrated artists of these days was extremely simple—and very like the best class of decorative art upon the Greek vases in the Louvre and the British Museum.

PANÆNUS of Athens was the brother of the great sculptor Pheidias; so Pliny tells us. Strabo seems to think he was the nephew.

He was one of the earliest of the Greek painters, though younger than Polygnotus and Micon by some few years. Panænus's most celebrated picture was the *Battle of Marathon*, in the Pœcile at Athens. This picture contains the *Iconies*, or portraits of celebrated generals (both of the Athenians and the barbarians); these could not have been portraits from life, for the picture was not painted till at least thirty years after the battle. Panænus painted several pictures on the throne and on the wall round the throne of the Olympian Jupiter. The subjects of some of these were: *Atlas supporting Heaven and Earth; Theseus and Pirithous;* allegorical figures of *Greece* and *Salamis; The Combat of Hercules with the Nemean Lion;* and several other historical subjects. The Pœcile was built by Cimon B. C. 470, therefore supposing Panænus to have painted his great picture ten years after its erection, we may take B. C. 460 to have been about the most important period of his life. Nothing certain is known either of his birth or death.

PARRHASIUS, born about B. C. 470, was instructed in the art of painting by his father. He was a native of Ephesus, but removed early in life to Athens, where he became by far the greatest artist of his time. He compared the works of Polygnotus, Apollodorus, and Zeuxis, and adopted from each that quality which he most admired. Parrhasius was by no means ignorant of the excellence of his own works. He took for himself the title of the Elegant, and called himself the Prince of Painters. Pliny says, and not without reason, that he was "the most insolent and most arrogant of artists." Parrhasius excelled especially in outline, form, and expression. Among the principal works of this artist may be mentioned his *Allegorical figure of the Athenian People;* a *Theseus* (it was probably this picture that gained for him his citizenship at Athens); a *Naval commander in his armour;* *Meleager;* *Hercules and Perseus;* *Castor and Pollux;* *Archigallus* (bought by the Emperor Tiberius for 60,000 sesterces, $50,000), and many portraits of warriors. Pliny says that in a competition with Timanthes of Cythnos he painted *The Contest of Ajax and Ulysses;* and that when the award was given to his rival, he said to his friends, "It is not I who should complain, but the son of Telamon, who has a second time become a victim to the folly of his judges." Parrhasius became so rich that at last he would not sell his pictures, saying that no price was sufficient for their value.

Pliny also tells us that Zeuxis acknowledged his painting of *Grapes* to be beaten by the *Curtain* of Parrhasius. It is related by Seneca that he selected a very old man from among the captives that Philip of Macedon had brought home from Olynthus, and crucified him, in order to see the true expression of pain, as a model for his *Prometheus Chained.* This story, even if true, could not refer to this Parrhasius, as he would have been about 120 years of age, if living, when Philip took Olynthus. The last record we have of Parrhasius is about B.C. 400.

ZEUXIS, one of the most celebrated painters of ancient times, was probably born between B.C. 460 and B.C. 450, in one of the cities named Heraclea; Pliny fixes the time at B.C. 400, but this is apparently too late a date, for he was at the height of his renown in the reign of Archelaus, which was from B.C. 413 until B.C. 399 (Diodorus Siculus). Lucian terms Zeuxis the greatest painter of his time, but he was unquestionably surpassed by Parrhasius, who was his contemporary. The excellence of Zeuxis's painting is noticed by several ancient writers, among whom may be mentioned Aristotle, Quintilian, and Cicero. One of the most celebrated of Zeuxis's pictures is *The Family of Centaurs,* the original of which was lost at sea. Lucian graphically describes a copy of it which he saw at Athens; but even this picture was surpassed by his celebrated *Helen the Courtesan,* which he painted for the city of Croton, and which, according to Ælian, he exhibited at a fixed charge. Other famous works by him are: *The Infant Hercules strangling the serpent;* *Jupiter in the assembly of the Gods;* *Penelope bewailing the absence of her husband;* *Menelaus mourning the fate of Agamemnon;* an *Athlete;* under which he wrote, "It is easier to find fault than to imitate;" and a *Cupid crowned with roses.* It is related of Zeuxis that he wore a mantle with his name woven in gold on the border. Ælian records that on one occasion he reproved Megabyzus, a high-priest of Diana, who while on a visit to the artist's studio, showed such palpable ignorance of any knowledge of art, that the boys whom the artist employed to mix his colours, laughed at him; whereupon Zeuxis quietly remarked, "While you were silent, these boys admired you for the richness of your dress and the number of your servants; but now that you disclose your ignorance they cannot refrain from laughter." Plutarch relates this same story of Apelles and Megabyzus, and Pliny of Apelles and Alexander. The story told by Pliny of Zeuxis deceiving the birds with a picture of ripe grapes, at which they came to peck, and of being himself deceived by a painting of a curtain so ably imitated by Parrhasius that Zeuxis asked him to draw it aside, is often quoted. Zeuxis also painted a picture of a *Boy with Grapes*, which likewise deceived the birds, but the artist was not entirely satisfied with it, for he justly remarked, "Had the boy been painted as well as the grapes the birds would have been afraid to come near them." It is said that Zeuxis amassed such a large fortune by the sale of his pictures that he would not sell any more. He gave his picture of *Pan* to Archelaus, and his *Alcmena* to the town of Agrigentum. The place and date of Zeuxis's death are unknown. Sillig remarks—with justice—that he must have died before the 106th Olympiad (B. C. 355), for in that year Isocrates, in his oration, praised Zeuxis, which he would not have done had the painter been then living.

MICON, a contemporary and fellow-worker with Polygnotus, was born about B. C. 450. He excelled in painting horses, which are generally introduced into his pictures. In the celebrated Colonnades of the Pœcile, Micon painted *The Battle of the Amazons*, and assisted Panænus in *The Battle of Marathon*, in which he painted the Persians larger than the Greeks; for this, it is said, he was fined half-a-talent (about $500). He also painted battle-pictures in the temple of Theseus; and assisted Polygnotus with his work in the temple of the Dioscuri. Micon painted horses with such truth to nature, that the only fault an Athenian art critic named Simon could find with them was that he had given lashes to their under eyelids.

APOLLODORUS, a native of Athens, lived about B. C. 430. It is said that he was the first to introduce light and shade into his pictures; for this reason he was called the "shadow painter." He must have been surpassed in this branch of painting by Zeuxis, for he complains that the latter had robbed him of his art. The line, "It is easier to find fault than to imitate," which Zeuxis wrote under a picture of an athlete, is attributed by Plutarch to Apollodorus.

EUPOMPUS, a native of Sicyon, was more famous as the founder of the school of Sicyon, which Pamphilus, his pupil, afterwards more fully established, than as a painter. One of his principles was, that man should be represented as he ought to appear, not as he really is (Pliny). The period of Eupompus is sufficiently certain from the fact that he taught Pamphilus, who flourished from about B. C. 388 to B. C. 348.

TIMANTHES of Cythnos lived about B. C. 400. His paintings were especially admired for their expression and reality of representation. Though Timanthes was undoubtedly one of the greatest painters of his time, only five of his works are mentioned by writers of antiquity. Pliny mentions him with great praise; he says of his painting, "Though in execution he was always excellent, the execution is

TABLE OF CONTENTS

INTRODUCTION . . . .
LIST OF ILLUSTRATIONS . . . .

CHAPTER I.
CLASSIC GREEK ART . . . .
GRECO-ROMAN SCHOOL . . . .

CHAPTER II.
PAINTING IN THE MIDDLE AGES . . . .

CHAPTER III.
EARLY ITALIAN ART . . . .

CHAPTER IV.
EARLY FLEMISH ART . . . .

CHAPTER V.
EARLY SCHOOLS OF ITALIAN ART . . . .

CHAPTER VI.
LIONARDO DA VINCI—MICHAEL ANGELO—RAPHAEL—TITIAN . . . .

CHAPTER VII.
GERMAN ART.—ALBRECHT DÜRER . . . .

CHAPTER VIII.
LATER ITALIAN ART . . . .

CHAPTER IX.
CARRACCI—GUIDO RENI—DOMENICHINO—SALVATOR ROSA . . . . .

CHAPTER X.
RUBENS—REMBRANDT—TENIERS, (FATHER AND SON), ETC. . . . . .

CHAPTER XI.

SPANISH ART.—VELASQUEZ, MURILLO, ETC. 88

CHAPTER XII.

FRENCH ART.—NICOLAS POUSSIN—CLAUDE LORRAINE, ETC. 102

CHAPTER XIII.

THE FOREIGN SCHOOL OF ENGLAND.—HOLBEIN, VAN DYCK, ETC. 109

SECOND PART.—MODERN PAINTERS.

CHAPTER I.

ENGLISH ART.—THORNHILL—HOGARTH—REYNOLDS, ETC. 123

CHAPTER II.

TURNER—WILKIE—HAYDON—ETTY—CONSTABLE, ETC. 143

CHAPTER III.

FRENCH ART.—VIEN—DAVID—ISABEY—INGRES, ETC. 154

CHAPTER IV.

MODERN GERMAN ART.—OVERBECK, CORNELIUS, ETC. 165

CHAPTER V.

MULREADY—DYCE—MACLISE—PHILLIP—LANDSEER, ETC. 170

CHAPTER VI.

THE AMERICAN SCHOOL.—WEST—COPLEY—STUART, ETC. 191

CHAPTER VII.

CONCLUSION.—CONTEMPORARY ART IN EUROPE. 212

DESCRIPTION OF THE STEEL AND WOOD ENGRAVINGS. 227

INDEX 242

ENGRAVINGS ON STEEL.

ARTIST.	SUBJECT.	PAGE.
1. Allom, Thomas	*Constantinople*	198
2. Bellangé, J. L. H.	*The Old Soldier and Family*	190
3. Berghem, Nicholas	*The Wayside Fountain*	22
4. Burnet, John	*The Dancing Dolls*	102
5. Callcott, Sir Augustus	*Crossing the Stream*	142
6. Collins, William	*The Old Farm Gate*	134
7. Compte-Calix, F. C.	*Youth and Age*	214
8. Delaroche, Paul	*The Young Princes in the Tower*	70
9. Frith, W. P.	*The Beau's Stratagem*	126
10. Gainsborough, Thomas	*The Village Beau*	54
11. Hart, James	*A Watering Place*	158
12. Ingres, Jean A. D.	*The Slave and her Slave*	118
13. Landseer, Sir Edwin	*Caught*	182
14. Leslie, Charles R.	*Taming of the Shrew*	62
15. Lewis, E. D.	*Scene on the Schuylkill*	230
16. Mount, W. S.	*Noon-day Rest*	86
17. Nicol, Erskine	*Kept In*	166
18. Raphael	*The Cartoons*	6
19. Reynolds, Sir Joshua	*The Coquette*	46
20. Richter, H.	*The Tight Shoe*	230
21. Rothermel, P. T.	*January and May*	206
22. Scheussele, Christen	*Daniel Webster at Shakespeare's Tomb*	94
23. Schopin, Henri Frederick	*Paul and Virginia*	222
24. Sully, Thomas	*Bedfellows*	110
25. Tayler, Frederick	*The Young Chief's First Ride*	174
26. Terburg, G.	*Refreshment*	14
27. Tschaggeny, C.	*The Cow Doctor*	150
28. Trumbull, John	*The Declaration of Independence*	38
29. West, Benjamin	*Christ Healing the Sick*	30
30. White, J. B.	*General Marion and the British Officer*	78
31. Wilkie, Sir David	*The Blind Fiddler*	Frontispiece

ENGRAVINGS ON WOOD.

	ARTIST.	SUBJECT.	PAGE.
32.	ANGELO, MICHAEL	The Cumean Sibyl	2
33.	BOUGHTON, G. H.	The Return of the Mayflower	202
34.	BRETON, JULES	The Eve of St. John's Day	186
35.	BURR, JOHN	The Peddler	122
36.	CABANEL, ALEX	The Annunciation	218
37.	CARAVAGGIO, M. A.	The Card-players	42
38.	CHALON, A. B.	Hunt the Slipper	90
39.	CONSTABLE, JOHN	The Wheatfield	66
40.	DAVID, J. L.	The Death of Socrates	130
41.	DORÉ, GUSTAVE	Alexander Weeping over the Dying Darius	226
42.	DÜRER, ALBERT	Samson and the Lion	18
43.	FAED, THOMAS	Jeanie Deans and the Duke of Argyle	82
44.	FORTUNY, MARIANO	Prayer in an Arab Mosque	146
45.	FOSTER, BIRKET	A Race up the Hill	114
46.	GÉRÔME, J. L.	Begging Monk at the Door of a Mosque	170
47.	HAYDON, BENJAMIN	Quintus Curtius	58
48.	HERMANN, LEO.	A Pause in the Argument	234
49.	HOGARTH, WILLIAM	Marriage à la Mode	50
50.	KÆMMERER, M.	At the Seashore	234
51.	LINNELL, JOHN	Sunshine	106
52.	LEWIS, J. F.	The Arab Scribe	154
53.	LEYS, HENRI (BARON)	Luther Singing in the Streets of Eisenach	162
54.	MEISSONIER, J. L. E.	The Flute-player	234
55.	REMBRANDT	Adolphus de Guildre Threatening his Father	34
56.	ROBERTS, DAVID	Interior of the Greek Church, Constantinople	98
57.	ROSENTHAL, TOBY	Elaine	178
58.	RUBENS	The Descent from the Cross	26
59.	TITIAN	Titian's Daughter	10
60.	STAMMEL, E.	The Connoisseur	194
61.	SCHEFFER, ARY	The Temptation on the Mount	138
62.	SCHREYER, A.	Horses alarmed by Wolves	210
63.	TURNER, J. M. W.	The Wreck of the Minotaur	74

invariably surpassed by the conception." The pictures by this painter of which we read were: a *Sleeping Cyclops*; *The Stoning of Palamedes*; *The Contest of Ajax and Ulysses* (for which picture he was declared victor against Parrhasius in a competition at Samos); *The Sacrifice of Iphigenia* (with which he defeated in competition Colotes of Teos—an otherwise unknown artist).

There is no other painting of ancient times which has been the subject of so much criticism as this, on account of the concealment of the face of Agamemnon. Ancient writers have given it unlimited praise, but modern critics have questioned its excellence and called it a trick. The fifth and last work known to us was the picture of a *Hero* in the Temple of Peace at Rome.

NICIAS, a native of Athens, was probably born about B.C. 370, for we hear that Praxiteles employed him to colour his statues about B.C. 350. He refused sixty talents ($65,000) offered him by Ptolemy I. of Egypt, for his famous picture *Nexuia* or *The Region of the Shades*, and gave it to his native town, Athens. Ptolemy assumed the title of king in B.C. 306, when Nicias would be about sixty-four years of age, and consequently likely to be rich and have a reputation, and able to refuse the enormous sum offered by the king. Pliny doubts very much whether the painter of the *Nexuia* and the assistant of Praxiteles can be the same. Pausanias tells us that Nicias was the most excellent animal painter of his time. It is true that he was very studious, even to absent-mindedness, for Ælian tells us that he frequently forgot to take his meals. His picture of *Nemea sitting on a lion* is one of the most famous of his works. Nicias wrote on this picture that he had painted it in encaustic. Nicias also painted the interiors of tombs, notably that of the high-priest Megabyzus.

PAMPHILUS, a native of Amphipolis, lived from about B.C. 388 to B.C. 348. He studied under Eupompus of Sicyon, and helped to establish the style of painting which Eupompus had begun, and which was eventually perfected by Euphranor, Apelles, and Protogenes. Pamphilus, Pliny tells us, was himself a man skilled in all sciences: *omnibus literis eruditus*. He occupied himself more with the theory of art and with teaching others, than with actual painting. He founded a school at Sicyon, the admission to which was one talent ($1080). Pliny says that Apelles and Melanthius both paid the fee, and studied at this school, and that Pausias received instruction in encaustic painting from Pamphilus. The sons of the Greek nobles attended the school, and Painting at this time occupied the first place among the liberal arts. Slaves were not allowed to use the *cestrum* or *graphis*. Four pictures only by this artist are recorded: *The Heraclidæ* (mentioned by Aristophanes); *The Battle of Phlius*; *Ulysses on the raft*; and a *Family Portrait* (Pliny).

EUPHRANOR, born in the Isthmus of Corinth, is called by Pliny "the Isthmian." He was contemporary with Apelles, and flourished from about B.C. 360 to B.C. 320. He was celebrated as a sculptor as well as a painter, and the same author tells us that he was "in all things excellent." He was chiefly famous as a portrayer of *Gods and Heroes*. Like Pausias and Aristides of Thebes, he painted in encaustic. Three of his most celebrated pictures were at Ephesus: *A Group of Philosophers in consultation*; *A Portrait of a General*; and *The feigned madness of Ulysses*. But his most celebrated works were, *The Twelve Gods*, and a *Battle of Mantinea*, painted in the Keramicus at Athens.

THEON, a native of Samos, lived about B. C. 350. He was much admired for the gracefulness of his painting. Pliny mentions two of his works: *Orestes in the act of killing his mother;* and *Thamyris playing the cithara.* Ælian describes *A youthful Warrior hastening to meet the foe.*

ATHENION, a pupil of Glaucion of Corinth, and a native of Maronea in Thrace, was probably a contemporary of Nicias, and painted about the year B. C. 330. Among other works, he executed a *Portrait of Phylarchus*, the historian, and *Achilles discovered by Ulysses disguised as a girl.* Pliny tells us that, had Athenion lived to maturity, no artist would have been worthy to be compared to him.

PAUSIAS, a native of Sicyon, was a fellow-student with Apelles and Melanthius in the school of Pamphilus, and consequently we may place his date at about B. C. 350. He was fond of small pictures, but occasionally painted large ones. He was the first to bring the use of encaustic to perfection. Pausias was celebrated for his foreshortening, especially to be remarked in a picture—*The Sacrifice of an Ox*—which in the time of Pliny was in the Hall of Pompey. He introduced the decorative ceiling painting, afterwards common, consisting of single figures, flowers, and arabesques (Müller). A portrait of this maiden, with a garland called the $\Sigma\tau\epsilon\varphi\alpha\nu\eta\pi\lambda\omicron\kappa\omicron\varsigma$, or *Garland Wreather*, was reckoned one of his best paintings. He also painted a picture of a boy, called '$H\mu\epsilon\rho\iota\omicron\varsigma$, because it was executed in a single day, in order to silence the reproaches of his rivals who said he was a slow painter.

NICOMACHUS, a native of Thebes, lived from about B. C. 360 to B. C. 300. He was the most celebrated of all Greek painters for quickness of execution. In illustration of this Pliny mentions the decorations of the monument erected to the honour of the poet Telestes by Aristratus, the tyrant of Sicyon, which were completed in a few days in order to fulfil the contract that they should be ready by a certain date. A few of the best pictures of Nicomachus were: a *Victory* in a quadriga; *Apollo and Diana*, a *Cybele* and a *Scylla.* Stobæus relates that Nicomachus, hearing some one remark that he saw no beauty in the *Helen* of Zeuxis, observed, "Take my eyes and you will see a goddess." He had several scholars, the principal of whom was his brother Aristides. The unfinished picture of the *Tyndaridæ* by this artist was valued more highly than any of his completed works.

MELANTHIUS was one of the most careful painters of the Sicyonic school. Pliny mentions that he paid the talent—the price of admission—and studied in the school of Pamphilus. He shared with his instructor, according to Quintilian, the honour of being the most renowned among the Greeks for composition.

We also learn from Plutarch that Aratus, wishing to make a present to Ptolemy, sent him pictures by Melanthius and Pamphilus worth 150 talents ($162,000). Melanthius lived in the fourth century B. C.

PROTOGENES was born at Caunus in Caria (according to Suidas, the Greek historian, he was born at Xanthus in Lycia, but Pausanias and Pliny are both in favour of Caunus). He was a contemporary and friend of Apelles, and was at the height of his fame in B. C. 332. Protogenes was by no means a prolific painter, for, as Quintilian says, "excessive carefulness was his predominating idea." He is said by Ælian to have taken seven years to complete his most celebrated picture, *The Rhodian hero Ialysus and his dog.* Apelles greatly admired this picture. A tale is related that Protogenes, after trying in vain for a long time to represent the foam at the dog's mouth, to his own satisfaction, in a fit of anger and disgust threw his sponge at the animal's head, and thus by accident obtained in a second that which many hours of labour had been unable to acquire. Pliny tells us that the renown of this picture was so great, that Demetrius Poliorcetes, when besieging Rhodes in B. C. 304, refrained from setting fire to that part of the town in which Protogenes lived, for fear of damaging the picture. It is said that Apelles gave Protogenes fifty talents for each picture that he found in his studio, and thus made the fortune of this artist, who was, Pliny tells us, in very needy circumstances. All ancient writers agree in praising his works.

APELLES was a native of the little island of Cos in the Ægean Sea. Neither the date of his birth nor death is known, but he was at the height of his fame in the year B. C. 332. He studied chiefly under the Macedonian painter Pamphilus, at Sicyon, and was a most indefatigable worker. He frequently painted figures of *Venus;* he also painted many portraits of *Alexander the Great,* who, it is said, would not sit to any other artist. He received four talents ($4300), for a portrait of this monarch wielding a thunderbolt, which he painted on the walls of the Temple of Diana at Ephesus. A picture of *Venus Anadyomene* was valued at 100 talents ($108,000). This was one of the most famous of all the Greek paintings; the goddess was represented as rising from the sea, wringing from her hair the water which fell in a silver shower around her. A story is related of him which is said to have given rise to the well-known saying, "A shoemaker should not go beyond his last." Apelles exhibited a finished picture, and concealed himself near by in order to hear the criticisms which he rightly imagined would be made upon it. A shoemaker found fault with a defect in a sandal, which Apelles accordingly rectified; on another occasion the shoemaker, encouraged by the success of his former remark, began to criticise the leg: upon this the artist, coming forth from his hiding-place, angrily told him to keep to his trade. Once, it is said, when Alexander visited Apelles, and remained unmoved before an equestrian portrait, his horse neighed at the sight of the charger represented in the painting: "Your horse," said the artist to the king, "knows more about pictures than you do." Apelles wrote a work on painting which has unfortunately been lost. He is said to have been the original author of the well-known saying, "*Nulla dies sine lineâ.*"

ARISTIDES, who was a native of Thebes, was born about B. C. 330. He was a brother and pupil of Nicomachus, and contemporary with Apelles. He excelled in painting battle pictures; one of his most celebrated was *The Capture of a City,* in which the expression of a dying woman and her infant was much admired: Alexander the Great took this picture to Macedonia. Aristides also painted a *Battle with the Persians*, in which there were one hundred figures; this was purchased for a large sum by Mnason of Elatea. Attalus, king of Pergamus, bought a picture by Aristides, *A Sick Man on his Bed*, for 100 talents (about $108,000), and Pliny says that Lucius Mummius refused more than 200 talents for a *Father Bacchus* which he captured at the siege of Corinth. Many of the best paintings of Aristides were sent to Rome with the rest of the plunder from the cities of Greece. An unfinished picture of *Iris* was the most highly valued.

ASCLEPIODORUS was contemporary with Aristides and Apelles. He painted twelve figures, representing the twelve Gods, and sold them to Mnason the tyrant of Elatea for five talents ($5,400) each.

PHILOXENUS, a native of Eretria, and a pupil of Nicomachus, was renowned for the rapidity of his execution. Nothing is known concerning the dates of his birth or death. He probably painted his famous picture of the *Battle of Alexander and Darius*, by order of Cassander, king of Macedon, shortly after B.C. 315, in which year Cassander succeeded in driving Polysperchon out of Macedon, and certainly not later than B.C. 296, for in that year Cassander died. It is not improbable that the mosaic representing the *Battle of Issus*, found in the "*House of the Faun*" at Pompeii in 1831, is a reproduction of this picture, for Darius and Alexander are the most conspicuous figures. Only one other work by Philoxenus is mentioned by Pliny. It is a representation of *Three Satyrs Feasting*. Pliny also tells us that Philoxenus discovered various methods of facilitating execution in painting.

TIMOMACHUS, a native of Byzantium, was imagined by many to have been contemporary with Julius Cæsar, from a statement to that effect by Pliny ("Julii Cæsaris ætate"). Durand thinks that *ætate* is an addition of the copyist. This seems quite within the bounds of possibility, for Pliny himself, speaking of him elsewhere, mentions him among the ancient and renowned painters of Greece. Timomachus was probably a contemporary of Nicias, and consequently lived about B.C. 300. His most celebrated pictures, *Ajax brooding over his misfortunes*, and *Medea meditating the destruction of her children*, were bought by Julius Cæsar for the enormous sum of eighty Attic talents ($86,500), and placed in the temple of Venus Genetrix. Ovid alludes to them in his "Tristia":

> "Utque sedet vultu fassus Telamonius iram,
> Inque oculis facinus barbara Mater habet."

Pliny says that the picture of Medea was not completed, yet it was more admired than any of the finished works of the same artist. The fact that the picture was left unfinished proves beyond a doubt that Timomachus did not sell it himself to Julius Cæsar, and therefore was not likely to have been his contemporary. Pliny mentions among other works by this artist an *Orestes*, *Iphigenia in Tauris*, and a celebrated picture of a *Gorgon*.

TIMANTHES of Sicyon (?) is only known to us by his picture of the *Battle of*

TITIAN'S DAUGHTER.

Pellene, in Arcadia, in which Aratus defeated the Ætolians in B.C. 240. He was contemporary with Aratus, who lived from B.C. 271 to B.C. 213. He was probably a native of Sicyon, though nothing certain is known either of the date or place of his birth.

NEACLES, probably a native of Sicyon, painted about the year B.C. 250. Pliny, who mentions him with praise, tells us of two pictures by him, a *Venus*, and a *Battle between the Persians and the Egyptians on the Nile*. In the latter, he introduced an ass drinking in the stream, and a crocodile, in order that the river might not be mistaken for the sea. It is also related of Neacles that by painting over the figure and introducing a palm-tree in its stead, he managed to save the *Portrait of Aristratus* by Melanthius and Apelles, from the fury of Aratus.

GRECO-ROMAN SCHOOL.

From Athens let us now pass to Rome. Ashamed of being in all matters of taste the disciples of the conquered Greeks, the Romans boasted of having a national school of painting, although the ancient religious law of the Latins was, like that of the Hebrews, hostile to images. Their writers pretended that about the year A. U. C. 450, a member of the illustrious family of Fabius, surnamed Pictor, who derived his name from his profession, had executed paintings in the Temple of Health. They cited also, in the following century, a certain dramatic poet, named Pacuvius, a nephew of the old Ennius, who had himself painted the decorations of his theatre; as did also, a hundred years later, Claudius Pulcher. It is related, besides, that Lucius Hostilius exhibited in the Forum, a picture where he had represented himself advancing to the assault of Carthage, which obtained him so much popularity that he was named consul the following year. All this appears as doubtful as the tales of Livy about the foundation of Rome. What is certain is that, when they penetrated as conquerors into Greece, the Romans showed neither taste for, nor knowledge of, the arts. They began, like true barbarians, by breaking the statues and tearing the pictures. At last, Metellus and Mummius stopped the stupid fury of the soldiers, and sent pell-mell to Rome whatever they found in the temples of Greece, without, however, having any true idea of the value of these precious spoils. This Lucius Mummius, who placed in the temple of Ceres the celebrated *Bacchus* of Aristides, was so ignorant, that after the siege of Corinth, he threatened those who conveyed to Rome the pictures and statues taken in that town, that if they lost the pictures, they must replace them!

The Romans, imitating their neighbours the Etruscans, whose industry and arts they borrowed, became great architects, and especially great engineers: they constructed roads, highways, bridges, aqueducts, which, surviving their empire, still excite our astonishment and admiration. But their only knowledge of the arts of painting and sculpture was through the works of the Greeks. Still more: at Rome itself there were scarcely any artists but the Greeks, who had gone, like grammarians and schoolmasters, to practise their profession in the capital of the world. It was a Greek painter, Metrodorus of Athens, who came to Rome to execute for the triumph of Paulus Æmilius the paintings of the Procession of the victorious general. Transplanted out of their country, reduced to the condition of artisans, the Greek artists had no longer at Rome those original inspirations which independence and dignity alone can give. They formed there a school of imitation, which could not but alter and deteriorate. Architecture, being necessary to the great works commanded by the emperors, was everywhere held in honour: so also was Sculpture, which provided the new temples with statues of the deified Cæsars. But Painting, reduced to decorate the interior of houses, became a kind of domestic art, a simple trade.

At the same time that the Romans prohibited their slaves from becoming painters, they disdained to recognize the art as worthy of being followed by themselves. It is true that amongst their painters is mentioned a certain Turpilius, belonging to the equestrian order; but he lived at Verona. Quintus Pedius, the son of a consul, is also cited; but he was dumb from his birth; and to enable his family to allow him to learn painting as an amusement, the express permission of Augustus was required. The painter Amulius, who has left some reputation, worked without taking off the toga (*pingebat semper togatus*—Pliny), in order not to be confounded with foreigners, and to preserve the dignity of a Roman citizen. The consequent decadence of the art of painting was inevitable. By degrees the Romans came to prefer richness to beauty, the precious metals to simple colours. Pompey exhibited his portrait made of pearls; and Nero proposed to gild the bronze *Alexander* of Lysippus; after having caused himself to be represented in a portrait one hundred and twenty feet high. In short, Painting, losing all nobility and all character, was reduced to the decoration of the interior of houses, in a style in accordance with such a degraded taste.

The most important of the Roman painters of this period that have been mentioned by the classic writers were:—

FABIUS PICTOR, one of the sons of Marcus Fabius Ambustus the consul, was called *Pictor* because he painted various objects in the Temple of the Goddess of Health, in B.C. 304. Pliny and Livy both mention these works, which existed until the destruction of the temple in the reign of Claudius.

MARCUS PACUVIUS, a native of Brundusium, was born about B.C. 219. He was a nephew of Ennius the epic poet, and, though renowned as a painter, was more celebrated for his poems. Pliny mentions paintings by him in the Temple of Hercules at Rome; he also tells us that Pacuvius was the last to paint "*honestis manibus.*" He died at Tarentum in the ninetieth year of his age, which, if the date of his birth be correct, would be about B.C. 130. He wrote an epitaph on himself which runs as follows:—

"Adolescens, tamenetsi properas, te hoc saxum rogat, uti ad se adspicias, deinde quod scriptum est, legas. Hic sunt poetæ Pacuvii Marci sita ossa. Hoc volebam, nescius ne esses; vale."

METRODORUS, a distinguished painter and philosopher, was born at Athens (?) about B.C. 200. When Paulus Æmilius had defeated the Greeks in B.C. 168, he ordered the Athenians to send him their best artist, to perpetuate his triumph, and their most renowned philosopher, to educate his sons. The Athenians paid Metrodorus the extraordinary honour of declaring that he was both their best artist and their most renowned philosopher; and it is said that Æmilius was quite satisfied. The painting of this Triumph must have been a most stupendous undertaking, for in the procession, which is partly described by Plutarch, there were no less than 250 wagons containing Greek works of art, called by Livy *simulacra pugnarum picta*. The spectacle lasted the entire day. Metrodorus, though a Greek, well deserves a mention among the Roman School, as he painted at Rome, and very likely helped to introduce a better style of painting among the Romans.

LAIA or LALA, of CYZICUS, a female artist, lived about B.C. 100, and was especially renowned for her portrait painting.

CLAUDIUS PULCHER, lived about B.C. 100, and is said to have painted decorations for theatres. There is little else known of him.

LUDIUS, the painter, lived in the time of Augustus. Pliny tells us he "invented the art of decorations for the walls of apartments, whereon he scattered country houses, porticoes, shrubs, thickets, forests, hills, ponds, rivers, banks—in a word, all that fancy could desire." Paintings of this kind have been discovered at Pompeii and Herculaneum and elsewhere. They are very beautiful, though it must be admitted they are but imitations of the Greek works which had preceded them.

DIONYSIUS of Rome lived about the time of the first Roman Emperors. Pliny tells us that he was a very prolific painter, so much so, in fact, that his pictures filled whole galleries. Pliny also calls him $Ἀνθρωπογράφος$, because he painted figure subjects only.

CHAPTER II.

PAINTING IN THE MIDDLE AGES.

N our last chapter we spoke of the gulf which apparently separates modern from ancient pictorial art. It may perhaps be possible, by taking up the links of the broken chain of tradition, to trace a connection, however slight, between the two periods.

Constantine removed the seat of the empire from Rome to Byzantium, precisely at the period to which we have come. This great event obliges us to divide the history of art into two parts. We shall follow it first in the Eastern Empire, until the taking of Constantinople; then we shall find it once more in Italy.

After having enthroned Christianity, Constantine set himself to decorate his new capital—to make it another Rome. He built churches, palaces, baths; he carried objects of art from Italy, and he was followed by the artists to whom proximity to the court was a necessity of existence. As it happened at Rome under Augustus, who boasted of having found a city of brick and left it of marble, so architecture quickly grew at Byzantium to be the first of the arts. Painting, although occupying an inferior position, was not abandoned. The Emperor Julian, to show at once his tastes, his talents, and his success, caused himself to be painted crowned by Mercury and Mars; we know, too, that Valentinian, who prided himself on his caligraphy, was also a painter and sculptor.

To avenge themselves for the Pagan reaction attempted by Julian the Apostate, the Christians began to destroy many of the vestiges of antiquity anterior to Christ—temples, books, and works of art. "Eager to destroy all that might recall Paganism, the Christians," says Vasari, "destroyed not only the wonderful statues, the sculptures, the paintings, the mosaics, and the ornaments of the false gods, but also the images of the great men which decorated the public edifices."

Under the Emperor Theodosius the Great, in the fourth century, the fatal sect of Iconoclasts (breakers of images) arose. This was the signal for a fresh destruction of statues and ancient pictures. However, if the column of Theodosius—the worthy rival of that of Trajan—testifies to the cultivation of the arts of design, the writings of St. Cyril, who lived in the time of that emperor, furnish irrefragable proofs of it.

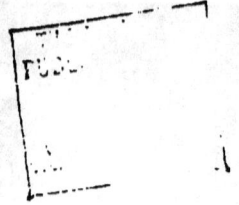

In the sixth of the ten books which he wrote against the Emperor Julian, one chapter has for its motto: "Our paintings teach piety" (*nostræ picturæ pietatem docent.*) In it he entreats painters to teach children temperance, and women chastity. In his book against the *Anthropomorphites*, the same St. Cyril supports the opinion of the artists of his time, who believed that they must make Jesus "the least beautiful of the children of men." It is remarkable that on this question—whether our Blessed Lord should have in His images the beauty that charms and recalls His celestial origin, or the deformity which the extreme humility of His mission seems to require—the Church has never decided. The Fathers, as well as the Schoolmen, have always been divided on this point. The opinion that Jesus should not be beautiful, sustained by St. Justin, St. Clement, St. Basil, and St. Cyril, was then most generally received. Celsus, the Pagan physician, triumphed at it. "Jesus was not beautiful," said he: "then he was not God." The most eminent of the Fathers, St. Gregory of Nyssa, St. Jerome, St. Augustine, and St. Chrysostom, vainly sustained the contrary opinion. Vainly again, in the twelfth century, did St. Bernard affirm that, as the new Adam, Jesus surpassed even the angels in beauty. The greater number of theologians, down to Saumaise and the Benedictines, Pouget and Delarue, in the last century, reproached painters with having taken too much license in ascribing physical beauty to Him of whom the prophet Isaiah said, "He hath no form nor beauty that we should desire Him."

In any case, the writings of the Fathers suffice to prove that Christian paintings were till the seventh or eighth century very common. They frequently assumed allegorical forms. Jesus was represented, as well as His mission and sacrifice, under the features of Daniel in the den of lions; of Jonah swallowed by the whale; of the Good Shepherd carrying back to the fold the lost sheep; of Orpheus charming the animals; of the Submissive Lamb; and of the Phœnix rising from its ashes. It was the Council of Constantinople, held in A.D. 692, which ordered artists to abandon emblems, and to return to the painting of Sacred History. Taste, however, continued to change more and more, to the detriment of painting. That only was considered beautiful which was rich. When marble seemed too poor a material for sculpture, when statues were made of porphyry, of silver, or gold, they could no longer be contented with pictures on panels. Painting existed, no doubt, for it is stated that the portraits of the emperors were sent into the provinces at their accession; for example, with Eudoxia, the wife of Arcadius, when she took the title of Augusta, in 395. And Theodosius II., who erected, in 425, a sort of university at Constantinople, cultivated painting, like Valentinian. But the more brilliant mosaic, often formed of precious materials, was preferred for the decoration of temples and palaces. Later—at the time of the sanguinary disturbances which accompanied and followed the reign of Zeno (A.D. 474 to A.D. 491)—painting was prostituted to the lowest employment to which it could descend, serving to trace those coarse and strange figures used as talismans, abraxas, and amulets of all sorts, which had become fashionable amongst a superstitious people.

It is known that Justinian ordered great works in architecture. He caused a new temple (St. Sophia) to be erected to The Divine Wisdom, by the architects

Anthemius of Tralles and Isidorus of Miletus, and was called, like Adrian, *Reparator orbis*. It was at this period, and precisely on the occasion of these architectural constructions, that the complete triumph of mosaic over painting took place. Procopius says positively, that to ornament certain rooms of the emperor's palace, they employed instead of fresco or painting in encaustic, brilliant mosaics in coloured stones, which commemorated the victories and conquests of the imperial arms. From that time mosaic was held in honour, and dethroning true painting, it became especially the art of the Greeks of the Eastern empire. With them taste was becoming depraved, and their works, as well as their actions and character, showed great debasement of mind. Architectural art, corrupted by oriental taste, was seldom anything but a confused prodigality of capricious ornaments. Statuary, no less degenerated and strange, created only small images in metal, or even mixtures of metals; and Painting itself became merely a working with enamels and precious stones, with chasings in gold and silver.

After Justinian, the bitter theological quarrels led to civil wars; and whilst Mahomedanism, itself iconoclastic, grew up almost in the vicinity of the holy places, the sect of the Iconoclasts, still increasing, finished by ascending the throne in the person of Leo the Isaurian (A. D. 726). The other Leo, the Armenian, and Michael the Stammerer, joined themselves to the same party, which carried their proceedings against their opponents to such a point, that Theophilus, the son of Michael, caused a monk named Lazarus to be burned, in A. D. 840, as punishment for having painted sacred subjects. At last Basil the Macedonian, an enemy to the iconoclastic party and its excesses, re-established in A. D. 867 the worship of images, and restored to the arts their free exercise. It seems that either old artists must have been preserved from the proscription, which, indeed, had only alighted on religious images, or new artists must have speedily arisen; since historians tell us that Basil, the greatest constructor of edifices after Constantine and Justinian, had in his palaces so many pictures representing the battles he had gained and the towns he had taken, that the porticoes, the walls, the ceilings, and the pavements were covered by them. Delivered from the Iconoclasts, the Arts of design could take breath again, and continued to flourish unchecked to the time of the Crusades, at the end of the eleventh century.

Everyone knows that these great armed migrations threw Europe as much on Constantinople as on Antioch or Jerusalem; and that in 1204 the capital of the Eastern Empire was carried by assault by the Crusaders, under Baldwin of Flanders. In the sack of this town the *Jupiter Olympius* by Pheidias, the *Juno of Samos* by Lysippus, and other great works of antiquity, perished at the same time with a number of works of art which a fashion in bad taste had laden with precious ornaments. But after the brief division of the Grecian empire between the French and the Venetians, and after the establishment of the Genoese and Pisans in the Bosphorus, when a more regular state succeeded to the disorders of conquest, the communication of ancient Greek art to the western nations commenced. The monuments of that art were then much better preserved at Byzantium than at Rome, which had been so many times sacked by the barbarians. At the same time with the ancient, a new art was also communicated, that of the modern Greeks, who had their architecture, their statuary, their frescoes, and their mosaics. Then, after the expulsion of the Crusaders and the destruction of their ephemeral empire, Michael Palæologus, who raised for one moment the Greek empire, also restored some life to the fine arts, and amongst them painting was not forgotten.

This prince had his principal victories depicted in his palace, and placed a portrait of himself in St. Sophia. After Michael, the empire was occupied almost exclusively with resistance to its enemies until the time of Mahomed II., who carried Constantinople by assault, on the 29th May, 1453. Arts and letters then alike took refuge in Italy, where we shall resume their history from the reign of Constantine the Great.

Between the translation of the seat of empire to Byzantium and the taking of Rome by Odoacer and the discontented mercenaries in A. D. 476, there is little to relate beyond the attacks and the invasions of barbarians. We must then start from their conquest of Rome. It is known with what frightful disasters this was accompanied, and how many inestimable objects perished in the reiterated pillages that Rome had to undergo. During the short rule of the first hordes from the north, a deep slumber seemed to have fallen on all the works of intellect, and the only productions of this sad period which can be considered as in any way belonging to painting are some mosaics serving as pavements in the halls of the bath-rooms.

At last the Goths appeared, drove out the nations which had preceded them, and founded an empire. Their appearance in Italy was a deliverance, as it was also in Spain, for in both peninsulas they showed the same mildness of manners, the same spirit of justice, order, and of conservatism. Unfortunately for Italy, their rule was of shorter duration there than in Spain. The great Theodoric—great at least until his old age—who had attached to himself Symmachus, Boethius, and Cassiodorus, stopped the ravages as much as he could, and took every care to preserve the monuments of antiquity. "Having had the happiness," to adopt his own expression, "to find at Rome a nation of statues and a troop of bronze horses," he had several buildings erected to receive them. We are surprised to find this barbarian recommending the imitation of the ancients to his architect Aloisius, whom he had made a Count (*comes*), and whom he called *your sublimity*, and especially urging him, by a rare instinct of good taste, to make the new buildings to agree with the old ones. His worthy minister, Cassiodorus, himself cultivated painting, at all events that of the time. He relates in his "Epistolæ," that he took pleasure in enriching the manuscripts of the monastery he had founded in Calabria, with ornaments painted in miniature. Bede, who had, it is asserted, seen these figures and ornaments of the manuscripts of Cassiodorus, says, that nothing could be more carefully executed or more perfect. Unfortunately all these works afterwards perished, and nothing of this period has been preserved to us but mosaics.

The Goths, "closely resembling the Greeks," says their historian Jornandes, did not stand long against the civil wars which broke out after the death of Theodoric;

the attacks of the Romans from Byzantium, conducted by Narses; and those of the fresh tribes which precipitated themselves across the Alps from the North.

In the middle of the sixth century, the Lombards, under Alboin, made themselves masters of Italy. The dominion of these new conquerors was continually disturbed by intestine quarrels, and contested by the exarchs of Ravenna, acting as lieutenants of the emperor at Constantinople. In such a situation, when feudal anarchy was beginning to people Italy with petty tyrants, the arts could be but feebly cultivated. However, the king, Antharis, who had become a Christian to please his wife Theodelinda (as Clovis had at the prayers of Clotilda), caused churches to be built or repaired, which he decorated with sculptures and paintings. Then Theodelinda herself, when a widow and queen, founded the celebrated residence of Monza, near Milan. We find in the writings of the Lombard Warnefridus of Aquileia, known by the name of Paul the Deacon, a minute description of the paintings in the Palace of Monza, which recorded the exploits of the Lombard armies. From these pictures, which were before his eyes, he described all the accoutrements of his fellow-countrymen, or rather of his ancestors, for he lived two centuries later. Luitprand continued the work of Theodelinda. An enemy to the Iconoclasts, he began, by the advice of Gregory III., to decorate the churches with frescoes and mosaics.

The removal of the imperial court, in the first place, and then the rule of the barbarians—now become Christians and devotees—had given great importance to the bishops of Rome. Under cover of the long wars between the Lombard kings and the exarchs of Ravenna, the popes founded their temporal power, acquired territory, and became sovereigns. This circumstance was fortunate for the arts, which found in them natural protectors, and Rome, restored by the papacy, became the centre and the capital of art. In spite of the approach of Attila, whom St. Leo stopped at the gates of the holy city—in spite of the pillage to which Genseric, less awed than the fierce king of the Huns, delivered it—we see the successive labours of the popes for the restoration of Rome begun and continued. Before leaving that ancient capital of the world, Constantine had built the old St. Peter's, the old St. Paul's, St. Agnes, and St. Lawrence. The popes decorated these churches magnificently, and we may mention principally the great work of St. Leo, who caused the whole series of popes from St. Peter to himself to be painted on the wall of the basilica of St. Paul. This work, begun in the fifth century, has lasted to our own day, having been spared in the great fire which destroyed the greater part of that edifice in 1824; and Lanzi justly quotes it in proof of the assertion with which he begins his book: "That Italy was not without painters, even during the dark ages, appears not only from history, but from various pictures that have resisted the attacks of time. Rome still retains some of very ancient date."

In the "Liber Pontificalis," Anastasius the librarian, or whoever else may be the author of that book, gives a very complete detail of the sculpture, the carving, and the works in gold and silver in the churches founded by Constantine. As for the paintings, of which he also speaks, they have all perished except the mosaics and frescoes in the Christian catacombs. But Anastasius speaks of the new kind of painting, which was just becoming fashionable, in those times when metals alone

SAMSON AND THE LION.
(From the original painting by Albert Durer.)

were considered valuable; I mean painting in embroidery, that is to say, worked with gold and silver threads on silk stuffs. He speaks among other things of a chasuble of Pope Honorius I., A.D. 625, the embroidery on which represented the *Deliverance of St. Peter* and the *Assumption of the Virgin*.

The art of embroidery had been brought from the East by the Greeks of Byzantium. It was known to the ancient Greeks, even from the earliest times, as is evidenced by the tapestry of Penelope, wherein figures were represented in different colours. It was also known to the Romans, according to Cicero's allusion when reproaching Verres with his thefts in Sicily ("neque ullam picturam, neque in tabula, neque *textili* fuisse"). In the time of St. John Chrysostom (fourth century), the toga of a Christian senator contained as many as six hundred figures, which made the eloquent orator say with grief, "All our admiration is now reserved for goldsmiths and weavers." It was especially in Italy that the art of embroidery gained ground. It is enough to mention the famous tapestry of the Countess Matilda, that celebrated friend of Gregory VII., who reigned over Tuscany, Modena, Mantua, and Ferrara, from 1076 to 1125, and who by her donations so largely added to the "Patrimony of St. Peter."

When Charlemagne, after having destroyed the Lombard kingdom, was crowned, at Rome, Emperor of the West, there was a moment of great hope for the arts. What might not have been expected from the powerful protection of a prince who understood—though without possessing it—the advantages of science, who collected around his person the Lombard Paul the Deacon, Peter of Pisa, Paulinus of Aquileia, the English Alcuin, and his pupil Eginhard? But continued military expeditions left him too little leisure to permit him to give an impulse to arts which would have required his whole care and time. Charlemagne only caused some bas-reliefs, mosaics, and illuminated manuscripts to be executed for his much-loved church of Aachen (Aix-la-Chapelle). But the popes, tranquil in Italy under his protection, took the part he could not fulfil. Adrian I., who praises in his letters the works of painting ordered by his predecessors, caused a picture of *Feeding the poor* to be painted on the walls of St. John Lateran; and his successor, Leo III., had the *Preaching of the Apostles* represented in fresco in the gallery of the *triclinium* at the palace of the Lateran, the vaulted roof of which was decorated in mosaic.

It was in the eleventh century,—after that terrible year 1000, which it had been generally expected would bring the end of the world, during that period when, favoured by the ever-reviving quarrels between the emperors and the popes, the Italian republics, Venice, Florence, Genoa, Pisa, and Siena, were in process of formation, and when the Normans regaining Sicily from the Arabs, were establishing an empire in the south of Italy,—that we see clearly how to take up the links of the traditional chain, and find the first symptoms of the future revival. It is to this time that the different images of the Virgin, which have been attributed to St. Luke, the paintings also in the vaults of the Duomo of Aquileia, of Santa Maria Prisca at Orvieto, the *Madonna delle Grazie*, and the *Madonna di Tressa*, in the cathedral of Siena, all belong. At the same period, and even before the crusades, an intercourse was begun between the artists of the Eastern Empire and those of Italy. This had become very important to the latter, after such a long interruption in the practice of art. Many Greek paintings were then brought from Constantinople and Smyrna, amongst others a *Madonna*, which is at Rome in Sta. Maria in Cosmedin, and another *Madonna* in the Camerino of the Vatican, which is said by Lanzi to be the best work of the Byzantines in Italy, both in regard to its painting and its state of preservation. It was also in the eleventh century that the Venetians sent for Greek workers in mosaic, to whom we owe the large mosaics in the singular and quite oriental basilica of St. Mark's at Venice. Other Greek workers in mosaic were invited to Sicily, and many were found already there, in the twelfth century, by the Norman William the Good, when he built his celebrated cathedral of Monreale.

Then at last national art awoke in Italy, and after the long period of obscurity which we call the dark ages, the first streaks of light were seen announcing the dawn of a new civilization soon to arise on the world. And yet this was not because the country was either peaceful or prosperous. The quarrels of the Emperor Otho IV. and the Pope Innocent III. had revived the hatred of the Guelph and the Ghibelline factions. Under Frederick II. the league of the Lombard towns, the claims of Gregory IX. and Innocent IV. kept up the incessant war between the empire and the papacy. But in the midst of these conflicts, not only of words, but also of arms, and in which every one wished to prove that he had right as well as might on his side, intellect had thrown off its drowsiness, and the human mind once more moved forward. Notwithstanding his reverses, Frederick II. contributed much to this movement. He was a clear-sighted prince, learned for his period, and had gathered around him a polite and elegant court. King of the Two Sicilies, as well as emperor of Germany, he almost constantly resided in Italy. He composed verses in the vulgar idiom, and caused a number of Greek or Arabian books to be translated into Latin. He erected several palaces, which he delighted in decorating with columns and statues. The medals of his reign are of a style and finish till then forgotten since ancient times. Lastly, he had books of his own composition illuminated with miniature paintings, the execution of which he himself directed and superintended. The princes of the house of Anjou followed his example, and the popes would not yield to the emperor in art any more than in the rest of their pretensions. The sovereign pontiffs of this age, Honorius III., Gregory IX., Innocent IV., Nicholas IV., caused the porticoes and the immense galleries of their churches to be ornamented with frescoes and mosaics.

By a result scarcely perhaps to be expected, even the agitation of the period fostered an increased growth of all the sciences, and also especially of art. The republics, the free cities, the small states, all the fragments of divided Italy, in everything disputed pre-eminence with each other. Each wished to triumph over its rival by the importance of its establishments and the beauty of the works of its artists. Again, the rulers whom the greater number of these states had chosen, or those who had raised themselves to be masters, each considering himself a new Pericles, and forestalling the Medici, wished, whilst he flattered the vanity of his fellow-citizens, at the same time to occupy their attention and to satisfy their wishes. We can understand what this double sentiment, this double want, must have produced. From it there resulted indeed vast cathedrals, sumptuous monasteries, grand palaces, and halls. From the same cause sprang up a universal taste, a spirit of emulation, a passionate ardour, all the stimulating qualities of a noble labour performed publicly, which, while it seeks, is at the same time rewarded by the public approval. When in A. D. 1294, Florence decreed the erection of her cathedral, the podestà of the seignory was enjoined " to trace the plan of it with the most sumptuous magnificence, so that the industry and power of man shall never invent and undertake anything more vast or beautiful ; inasmuch as no one ought to put his hand to the works of the community with any less design than to make them correspond with the lofty spirit which binds the souls of all the citizens into one single, united, identical will." Who is it that holds such magnificent and haughty language? Was it Pericles giving orders to Ictinus and Pheidias for the erection of the temple to the virgin daughter of Zeus? No. It was simply the seignory of Florence;—but Florence was then a modern Athens.

Having succinctly given the history of art in general through the events and changes of political revolutions, it remains for us to trace the particular history of the various processes which form the links between ancient and modern art.

CHAPTER III.

EARLY ITALIAN ART.

HE Lives of the most excellent Painters, Sculptors and Architects by Vasari, the first historian of Italian Art, opens with CIMABUE, but we believe that Vasari gave this distinction to Cimabue because he was like himself, a Florentine. If art implies the blending of modern thought and knowledge with the pure spirit of the antique, then Nicola Pisano is the real reviver of art in Italy. He was born in 1204, and as sculptor and architect exercised immense influence on the art of his own century, and made classic feeling a possession of his countrymen for all time. It is vain, however, after three centuries of recognition, to alter the order of names occurring in a book which has exercised the ingenuity of almost as many annotators and critics as the "Divine Comedy" itself.

Art fell but did not expire with the Roman empire. On the contrary, when sustenance ceased in one quarter it turned to another, and found in the Christian Church a patron who made it the special vehicle for the propagation of her doctrines, and whose fostering care surpassed that of the Cæsars. The art culminated, perhaps, in the long and glorious reign of Justinian, 527-565; but Roman influence and tradition did not cease to be active till the eighth or ninth century. It was restored and carried on by artists from the East during the tenth, eleventh, and twelfth centuries, as the rising wealth of cities enabled their rulers to import the technically skilled hands of Byzantium.

Art, then, like truth, has never in the darkest night of history been without a torch-bearer; and whether reflected on the broad bosom of the Euphrates or the Nile, on the streamlet of the Illissus, or on the yellow waters of the Tiber, its light has been borne safely along, till now in Cimabue it meets the approaching dawn of intellectual life and freedom.

Italian art existed in small beginnings, in the gorgeous but quaintly formal or fantastic devices of illuminated missals, and in the stiff spasmodic efforts of here and there an artist spirit such as the old Florentine Cimabue's, when a great man heralded a great epoch. But first we should like to mention the means by which art then worked. Painting on board and on plastered walls, the second styled painting

in fresco, preceded painting on canvas. Colours were mixed with water or with size, egg, or fig-juice—the latter practices termed *tempera* (in English in distemper) before oil was used to mix colours. But painters did not confine themselves then to painting with pencil or brush, else they might have attained technical excellence sooner. It has been well said that the poems of the middle ages were written in stone; so the earlier painters painted in stone, in that mosaic work which one of them called—referring to its durability—"painting for eternity;" and in metals. Many of them were the sons of jewellers or jewellers themselves; they worked in iron as well as in gold and silver, and they were sculptors and architects as well as painters, engineers also, so far as engineering in the construction of roads, bridges, and canals, was known in those days. The Greek knowledge of anatomy was well-nigh lost, so that drawing was incorrect and form bad. The idea of showing degrees of distance, and the management of light and shade, was feebly developed. Even the fore-shortening of figures was so difficult to the old Italian painters that they could not carry it into the extremities, and men and women seem as if standing on the points of their toes. Landscape-painting did not exist farther than that a rock or a bush, or a few blue lines, with fishes out of proportion prominently interposed, indicated, as on the old stage, that a desert, a forest, or a sea, was to play its part in the story of the picture. So also portrait-painting was not thought of, unless it occurred in the likeness of a great man belonging to the time and place of the painter, who was the donor of some picture to chapel or monastery, or of the painter himself, alike introduced into sacred groups and scenes; for pictures were uniformly of a religious character, until a little later, when they merged into allegorical representations, just as one remembers that miracle plays passed into moral plays before ordinary human life was reproduced. Until this period, what we call dramatic expression in making a striking situation, or even in bringing the look of joy or sorrow, pleasure or pain, into a face, had hardly been attained.

Perhaps you will ask, what merit had the old paintings of the middle ages to compensate for so many great disadvantages and incongruities? Certainly before the time we have reached, they have, with rare exceptions, little merit, save that fascination of pathos, half-comic, half-tragic, which belongs to the struggling dawn of all great endeavours, and especially of all endeavours in art. But just at this epoch, art, in one man, took a great stride, began, as we shall try to show, to exert an influence so true, deep, and high that it extends, in the noblest forms, to the present day, and much more than compensates to the thoughtful and poetic for a protracted train of technical blunders and deficiencies.

GIOVANNI GAULTHERI or CIMABUE, infused life into the old school from which he sprang. He was to reanimate old and worn-out types, to soften the harshness of a degenerate school, and to shed over barbarous times the poetry of sentiment and colour.

He was born in Florence in 1240, and was living in 1302, when he was engaged on a mosaic in the Duomo of Pisa. The date of his death is unknown, but it occurred at Florence, and he was buried in the Church of Santa Maria del Fiore.

He early discovered a bias for art, and the circumstances of his family and the time were entirely in his favour. Florence and other Italian cities gave employment to many Greek artists at the time the youthful Cimabue was most keenly perceptive, and his own style, as a natural consequence, was founded on the Byzantine. The number of those Greek artists, it may be well to remember, had, since the beginning of the century, largely increased; and it was the conquest of Constantinople by the Latins in 1204 which extended and made more frequent this intercourse between the Greeks and the Latins. In the early Christian ages there was grandeur as well as severity in Byzantine art; but in Cimabue's time it had become, in spite of its technique, altogether debased; his greatest service to art consisted in abandoning much of the uncouth manner of the Byzantines, and turning, like ancient Greeks, to nature. His great picture, the *Madonna*, which he painted as an altar-piece for the Church of Santa Maria Novella, in Florence, was the largest picture painted down to these times, and the work, says Vasari, "was an object of much admiration to the people."

Great was the industry of Cimabue; and his work on the cathedrals and convents of Pisa and Florence are mementoes revered as foundation-pictures of Christian art.

GIOTTO, known also as Magister Joctus, was born in 1276 near Florence. We dare say many have heard one legend of him, and we mean to tell the legends of the painters, because even when they are most doubtful they give the most striking indications of the times and the light in which painters and their paintings were regarded by the world of artists, and by the world at large; but so far as we have heard this legend of Giotto has not been disproven. The only objection which can be urged against it, is that it is found preserved in various countries, of very different individuals—a crowning objection also to the legend of William Tell. Giotto was a shepherd boy keeping his father's sheep and amusing himself by drawing with chalk on a stone the favourites of the flock, when his drawings attracted the attention of a traveller passing from the heights into the valley. This traveller was the well-born and highly-esteemed painter Cimabue, who was so delighted with the little lad's rough outlines, that getting the consent of Giotto's father, Cimabue adopted the boy, carried him off to the city of Florence, introduced him to his studio, and so far as man could supplement the work of God, made a painter of the youthful genius. We may add here a later legend of Giotto. Pope Boniface VIII. requested specimens of skill from various artists with the view to the appointment of a painter to decorate St. Peter's. Giotto, either in impatient disdain, or to show a careless triumph of skill, with one flourish of his hand, without the aid of compass, executed a perfect circle in red chalk, and sent the circle as his contribution to the specimens required by the Pope. The audacious specimen was accepted as the most conclusive, Giotto was chosen as the Pope's painter for the occasion, and from the incident arose the Italian proverb "round as the o of Giotto." Giotto was the friend of Dante, Petrarch, and Boccaccio, especially of Dante, to whom the grandeur of some of the painter's designs has been vaguely enough attributed. The poet of the "Inferno" wrote of his friend :

> "—— Cimabue thought
> To lord it over painting's field; and now
> The cry is Giotto's, and his name eclipsed."

Petrarch bequeathed in his will a Madonna by Giotto and mentioned it as a rare treasure of art. Boccaccio wrote a merry anecdote of his comrade the painter's wit, in the course of which he referred with notable plain-speaking to Giotto's "flat currish" plainness of face.

The impression handed down of Giotto's character is that of an independent, high-spirited man, full of invention, full of imagination, and also, by a precious combination, full of shrewdness and common sense; a man genial, given to repartee, and at the same time not deficient in the tact which deprives repartee of its sting. While he was working to King Robert of Naples, the king, who was watching the painter on a very hot day, said, with a shrug, "If I were you, Giotto, I would leave off work and rest myself this fine day." "And so would I, sire, if I were *you*," replied the wag.

We need scarcely add that Giotto was a man highly esteemed and very prosperous in his day; one account reports him as the head of a family and the father of four sons and four daughters. We have purposely writen first of the fame, the reputed character, and the circumstances of Giotto before we proceed to his work. This great work was, in brief, to breathe into painting the living soul which had till then—in mediæval times—been largely absent. Giotto went to Nature for his inspiration, and not content with the immense innovation of superseding by the actual representation of men and women in outline, tint, and attitude, the rigid traditions of his predecessors, he put men's passions in their faces—the melancholy looked sad, the gay glad. This result, to us so simple, filled Giotto's lively countrymen, who had seldom seen it, with astonishment and delight. They cried out as at a marvel when he made the commonest deed even coarsely life-like, as in the case of a sailor in a boat, who turned round with his hand before his face and spat into the sea; and when he illustrated the deed with the corresponding expression, as in the thrill of eagerness that perceptibly pervaded the whole figure of a thirsty man who stooped down to drink.

Giotto's work did not end with himself; he was the founder of the earliest worthy school of Italian art, so worthy in this very glorious idealism, that, as we have already said, the men whose praise is most to be coveted, have learned to turn back to Giotto and his immediate successors, and, forgetting and forgiving all their ignorance, crudeness, quaintness, to dwell never wearied, and extol without measure these oldest masters' dignity of spirit, the earnestness of their originality, the solemnity and heedfulness of their labour.

The last example of Giotto's, is the one which of all his works is most potent and patent in its beauty, and has struck, and, in so far as we can tell, will for ages strike, with its greatness multitudes of widely different degrees of cultivation whose intellectual capacity is as far apart as their critical faculty. We mean the matchless *Campanile or bell-tower* "towering over the Dome of Brunelleschi" at Florence, formed of coloured marbles—for which Giotto framed the designs, and even executed with his own hands the models for the sculpture. Of this great example the Emperor Charles V. said, "the Campanile ought to be kept under glass."

It is known that Giotto, together with his friend Dante, died before this—Giotto's last great work—was finally constructed by Giotto's pupil, Taddeo Gaddi, and that therefore neither of the friends could have really looked on "Giotto's Tower," though Italian Ciceroni point out, and strangers love to contemplate, the very stone on which "Grim Dante" sat and gazed with admiration in the calm light of evening on the enduring memorial of the painter.

Giotto died in the year 1336 or 1337, and was buried with suitable honours by a city, which, like the rest of the nation, has magnified its painters amongst its great men, in the church of Santa Maria del Fiore, where his master Cimabue had been buried. Lorenzo de' Medici afterwards placed over Giotto's tomb his effigy in marble.

ANDREA ORCAGNA, otherwise known as Andrea di Cione, one of a brotherhood of painters, was born in Florence about 1315. His greatest works are in the Campo Santa of Pisa.

This wonderful "holy field" is a grand legacy, so far as dilapidation, alas, will let it be, of the old painters. Originally a place of burial, though no longer used as such, it is enclosed by high walls and an arcade, something like the cloisters of a cathedral or college running round, and having on the north and east sides chapels where masses for the dead were celebrated. The space in the centre was filled with earth brought from the Holy Land by the merchant ships of Pisa. It is covered with turf, having tall cypress-trees at the corners, and a little cross in the centre. The arcade is pierced with sixty-two windows, and contains on its marble pavement hundreds of monuments—among them the Greek sarcophagi studied by Nicola Pisano. But the great distinction of the Campo Santa (of which there are many photographs) are the walls opposite the windows of the arcade painted with Scriptural subjects by artists of the fourteenth and fifteenth centuries, for the decoration of the walls was continued at intervals, during two hundred years. The havoc wrought by time and damp has been terrible; not only are the pictures faded and discoloured, but of the earliest only mutilated fragments, " here an arm and there a head," remain. Giotto's illustrations of the book of Job have thus perished. Still Orcagna's work has partially escaped, and left us indications of what it was in his and its youth, when Michael Angelo and Raphael did not disdain to borrow from it in design and arrangement.

One of Orcagna's altar-pieces, that of *The Coronation of the Virgin*, containing upwards of a hundred figures, and with the colouring still rich, is in the English National Gallery. As an architect, Orcagna designed the famous Loggia de' Lanzi of the grand ducal palace at Florence.

Now we must take you back to the bronze gates of the Baptistery in their triumphant completion nearly a hundred years after the first gate was executed by Andrea Pisano. We should have liked, but for our limits, to tell in full the legend of the election of Lorenzo Ghiberti, the step-son of a goldsmith, and skilled in chasing and enamelling, to design the second gate; when yet a lad of twenty-three, how he and two other young men, one of them still younger than Ghiberti, were declared the most promising competitors in the trial for the work; how the last two voluntarily

THE DESCENT FROM THE CROSS.
From the original painting by Rubens.

withdrew from the contest, magnanimously proclaiming Lorenzo Ghiberti their superior; how all the three lived to be famous, the one as a founder in metal, the others as an architect and a sculptor, and remained sworn brothers in art till death.

LORENZO GHIBERTI has left us an expression of the feeling with which he set about his task, an expression so suggestive that, even had we no other indication, it is enough to stamp the true and tender nature of the man. He prepared for his achievement "with infinite diligence and love"—the words deserve to be pondered over. He took at least twenty-two years to his work, receiving for it eleven hundred florins. He chose his subjects from the life and death of the Lord, working them out in twenty panels, ten on each side of the folding doors, and below these were eight panels containing full-length figures of the four evangelists and four doctors of the Latin Church, with a complete border of fruit and foliage, having heads of prophets and sibyls interspersed. So entire was the satisfaction the superb gate gave, that Lorenzo was not merely loaded with praise, he received a commission to design and cast a third and central gate which should surpass the others, that were thenceforth to be the side entrances.

For his second gate Lorenzo Ghiberti repaired to the Old Testament for subjects, beginning with the creation and ending with the meeting of Solomon and the Queen of Sheba, and represented them in ten compartments enclosed in a rich border of fruit and foliage, with twenty-four full-length figures of the Hebrew heroes and prophets, clearly and delicately designed and finished, occupying corresponding niches. This crowning gate engaged the founder upwards of eighteen years—forty-nine years are given as the term of the work of both the gates.

Michael Angelo called these gates "worthy to be the gates of Paradise," and they are still one of the glories of Florence. Casts of the gates are to be found in the Academy of Fine Arts at Philadelphia, and in the Corcoran Gallery, Washington, D. C.

A little village boy learned to draw and model from Ghiberti's gates. He in his turn was to create in the Brancacci Chapel of the Church of the Carmine at Florence a school of painters scarcely less renowned and powerful in its effects than that produced by the works in the Campo Santo. You will find the Italian painters not unfrequently known by nicknames, quite as often by their father's trades as by their father's surnames, and still oftener by the town which was their place of birth or nurture. This Tommaso Guido, or Maso de San Giovanni (from his village birthplace), was commonly called MASACCIO, short for Tomasaccio, "hulking Tom," as we have heard it translated, on account of his indifferent, slovenly habits. We think there is a tradition that he entered a studio in Florence as a colour boy, and electrified the painter and his scholars, by *brownie* like freaks of painting at their unfinished work, in their absence, better than any of his masters, and by the dexterity with which he perpetrated the frolic of putting the facsimile of a fly on one of the faces on the easels. His end was a tragic conclusion to such light comedy. At the age of twenty-six, he quitted Florence for Rome so suddenly that he left his frescoes unfinished. It was said that he was summoned thither by the Pope. At Rome, where little or nothing of Masaccio's life is known, he died shortly afterwards, not without a suspicion of his having been poisoned.

There is a tradition—not very probable under the circumstances—that Masaccio is buried, without name or stone, under the Brancacci Chapel. Be that as it may, he very early rose to eminence, surpassing all his predecessors in drawing and colouring, and he combined with those acquirements such animation and variety of expression in his characters, that it was said of him "he painted souls as well as bodies," while his invention was not less bold and fresh.

It is difficult to indicate Masaccio's pictures because some of them have been repainted and destroyed. As to those in the Brancacci Chapel from the life of St. Peter, (with the exception of two,) considerable confusion has arisen as to which are Masaccio's, and which belong to his scholar Filippino Lippi. The fresco which Masaccio left unfinished, that of the Apostles Peter and Paul raising a dead youth (from traditional history), was finished by Lippi. In the fresco of Peter baptizing the converts, generally attributed to Masaccio, there is a lad who has thrown off his garments, and stands shivering with cold, whose figure, according to authority, formed an epoch in art. Lionardo da Vinci, Michael Angelo, Andrea del Sarto, Fra Bartolommeo, all studied their art in this chapel. Raphael borrowed the grand figure of St. Paul preaching at Athens in one of the cartoons, from one of Masaccio's or Filippo Lippi's frescoes. Masaccio's excellence as an artist, reached at an immature age, is very remarkable.

FRA FILIPPO LIPPI was born in Florence, probably in 1412. This artist, according to Vasari, was one who disgraced his profession in his private life; but many doubts have since been thrown on the story, which may be briefly thus related. Left an orphan at an early age, Lippi was placed by an aunt—Mona Lappaccia by name—in the Carmelite Convent del Carmine when eight years old. He soon displayed great talent and liking for painting, and the prior wisely allowed him to follow his favourite amusement as a profession.

In 1432, at about the early age of twenty, on leaving the convent, Lippi gave up the frock,—so says Vasari,—and during a pleasure excursion from Ancona, he and his companions were taken prisoners by Moorish pirates, and carried slaves to Barbary. After eighteen months' captivity Lippi drew a portrait of his owner with charcoal on a white wall, which excited so much wonder and admiration among the Moors, that his master, after getting him to execute several works in colour, sent him safely back to Italy. He landed at Naples, where he stayed only a few months, and then returned to Florence. In 1458, while employed in painting at the Convent of Santa Margherita, he carried off Lucrezia Buti—a young Florentine lady, who was being educated by the nuns—and who was afterwards the mother of Filippino Lippi.

No evidence has been found of his reputed stay at Ancona, his capture by pirates, or his residence in Naples, at which town he is supposed to have landed on his return from Barbary. When he left the Convent of the Carmelites in 1432, he does not appear to have given up the frock, for later in life he signs himself "Frater Filippus," and in the register of his death in the Carmine Convent, he is called "Fr. Filippus." As regards the tale of Lucrezia, it is not likely that a monk who had led a scandalous life would have been appointed chaplain of a nunnery in Florence, and rector of San Quirico at Legnaia, both of which facts are now certain; therefore it is better to give Lippi the benefit of the doubt, especially as everything which has since been discovered tends to show the fallacy of Vasari's statements regarding him, and nothing has been found to corroborate them. It is supposed by some that Filippino Lippi was an adopted son of this artist.

In the Convent del Carmine, Filippo Lippi is said to have studied under Masaccio, who was at that time employed in the chapel of the convent, but it is more probable that he studied more from the pictures of that master than from the artist himself. He painted frescoes both in the church and convent, and amongst others the *Confirmation of the Rules of the Carmelites*, in the cloisters; these are no longer in existence; those in the church were destroyed by fire in 1771. Lippi painted frescoes in Prato from 1456 to 1464, with numerous interruptions. He died at Spoleto—it is supposed of poison administered by Lucrezia's friends (Vasari)—October 8th, 1469. He was buried in the Cathedral of Spoleto, and a marble monument was erected over his grave by Filippino Lippi, at the desire and the cost of Lorenzo de' Medici.

We have come to the last and probably the best appreciated of the early Italian painters. FRA ANGELICO DA FIESOLE, the gentle devout monk whom Italians called "*Il Beato*," the Blessed, and who probably did receive the distinction of beatification, a distinction only second in the Roman Catholic Church to that of canonization. He was born at the lovely little mountain-town of Fiesole near Florence, 1387, and his worldly name, which he bore only till his twenty-first year, was Guido Petri de Mugello. In his youth, with his gift already recognized, so that he might well have won ease and honour in the world, he entered the Dominican Convent of St. Mark, Florence, for what he deemed the good and peace of his soul. He seldom afterwards left it, and that only as directed by his convent superior, or summoned by the Pope. He was a man devoid of personal ambition, pure, humble, and meek. When offered the Archbishopric of Florence as a tribute to his sanctity, he declined it on account of his unworthiness for the office. He would not work for money, and only painted at the command of his prior. He began his painting with fasting and prayer. Believing himself inspired in his work, he steadfastly refused to make any alteration in the originals. It is said that he was found dead at his easel with a completed picture before him. It is not wonderful, that from such a man should come one side of the perfection of that idealism which Giotto had begun. Fra Angelico's angels, saints, Saviour, and Virgin are more divinely calm, pure, sweet, endowed with a more exulting saintliness, a more immortal youth and joy, and a more utter self-abnegation and sympathetic tenderness than are to be found in the saints and the angels, the Saviour and the Virgin of other painters. Neither is it surprising that Fra Angelico's defects, besides that of the bad drawing which shows more in his large than in his small pictures, are those of a want of human knowledge, power, and freedom. His wicked— even his more earthly-souled characters, are weak and faulty in action. What should the reverent and guileless dreamer know, unless indeed by inspiration, of the rude conflicts, the fire and fury of human passions intensified in the malice and anguish of devils? But Fra Angelico's singular successes far transcend his failures. In addition to the sublime serenity and positive radiance of expression which he could impart to his heads, his notions of grouping and draping were full of grace, sometimes of splendour and magnificence. In harmony with his happy temperament and fortunes, he was fond of gay yet delicate colours "like spring flowers," and used a profusion of gold ornaments which do not seem out of keeping in his pictures. The most of Fra Angelico's pictures are in Florence—the best in his own old convent of St. Mark, where he lovingly adorned not only chapter-hall and court, but the cells of his brother friars. A crucifix with adoring saints worshipping their crucified Saviour is regarded as his master-piece in St. Mark's. A famous coronation of the Virgin, which Fra Angelico painted for a church in his native town, and which is now in the Louvre, Paris, is thus described by Mrs. Jameson: "It represents a throne under a rich Gothic canopy, to which there is an ascent of nine steps; on the highest kneels the Virgin, veiled, her hands crossed on her bosom. She is clothed in a red tunic, a blue robe over it, and a royal mantle with a rich border flowing down behind. The features are most delicately lovely, and the expression of the face full of humility and adoration. Christ, seated on the throne, bends forward, and is in the act of placing the crown on her head; on each side are twelve angels, who are playing a heavenly concert with guitars, tambourines, trumpets, viols, and other musical instruments; lower than these, on each side, are forty holy personages of the Old and New Testament; and at the foot of the throne kneel several saints, male and female, among them St. Catherine with her wheel, St. Agnes with her lamb, and St. Cecilia crowned with flowers. Beneath the principal picture there is a row of seven small ones, forming a border, and representing various incidents in the life of St. Dominic."

CHAPTER IV.

EARLY FLEMISH ART.

N the Low Countries painting had very much the same history that it had in Italy, but the dates are later, and there may be a longer interval given to each stage of development. Religious painting, profuse in symbolism, with masses of details elaborately worked in, meets us in the first place. This style of painting reached its culmination, in which it included (as it did not include in its representation in the Italian pictures) many and varied excellencies, among them the establishment of painting in oil in the pictures of the Flemish family of painters—the Van Eycks.

Before going into the little that is known of the family history of the Van Eycks, we should like to call attention to the numerous painter families in the middle ages. What a union, and repose, and happy sympathy of art-life it indicates, which we appear to have lost in the restlessness and separate interests of modern life. The Van Eycks consisted of no less than four members of a family, three brothers, Hubert, John, and Lambert, and one sister, Margaret, devoted, like her brothers, to her art. There is a suggestion that they belonged to a small village of Limburg called Eyck, and repaired to Bruges in order to pursue their art. Hubert was thirty years older than John, and it is said that he was a serious-minded man as well as an ardent painter, and belonged to the religious fraternity of our Lady of Ghent. He died in 1426. John, though of so much consideration in his profession as to be believed to be "the Flemish painter" sent by Duke Philip the Good of Flanders and Burgundy with a mission to Portugal to solicit the hand of a princess in marriage, is reported to have died very poor in 1449, and has the suspicion attached to him of having been a lover of pleasure and a spendthrift. Of Lambert, the third brother, almost nothing is known; indeed, the fact of his existence has only lately come to light. Margaret lived and died unmarried, and belonged, like her brother Hubert, to the religious society of our Lady of Ghent. She died about 1432.

The invention of painting in oil, for which the Van Eycks are commonly known, was not literally that of mixing colours with oil, which was occasionally done before their day. It was the combining oil with resin, so as to produce at once a good varnish, and avoid the necessity of drying pictures in the sun, a bright thought, which may stand in the same rank with the construction, by James Watt, of that valve which rendered practicable the application of steam to machinery. The thought, occasioned by the cracking of a picture in tempera exposed to the sun, is due to Hubert Van Eyck.

The great picture of the Van Eycks, which was worked at for a number of years by both Hubert and John, and, as some reckon, touched by the whole family, is the *Adoration of the Lamb*, at St. Bavon's, Ghent.

Hubert Van Eyck died while this work was in progress, and it was finished by his brother John six years after Hubert's death. When one thinks of the intense application and devotion which such a work costs, and recalls the bronze gates of St. John that occupied Lorenzo Ghiberti forty-nine years, and when we occasionally hear reports of large paintings which were begun and ended in so many days—even so many hours, one can better understand what is the essential difference between the works of the early and the later painters, a difference which no skill, no power even can bridge over. John Van Eyck, who had lived late enough to have departed from the painting of sacred pictures alone, so that he left portraits and an otter hunt among his works, is three times represented in the National Gallery of England, in three greatly esteemed portraits, one a double portrait, believed to be the likenesses of the painter and his wife, standing hand in hand with a terrier dog at their feet.

GOSSAERT, called DE MABUSE from his native town of Mabeuze, sometimes signing his name Joannes Malbodius, followed in the steps of the Van Eycks, particularly in his great picture of the *Adoration of the Kings*, which is at Castle Howard, the seat of the Earl of Carlisle. Mabuse was in England and painted the children of Henry VII. in a picture, which is at Hampton Court. There is a picture in the palace of Holyrood, Edinburgh, which has been attributed to Mabuse. It represents on the sides of a triptych or diptych (somewhat like a folding screen) James III. and his queen with attendants. The fur on the queen's dress displays already that marvellous technical skill for which Flemish painting is so celebrated.

HANS MEMLING belonged to Bruges. There is a tradition of him, which is to a certain extent disproven, that he was a poor soldier relieved by the hospital of St. John, Bruges, and that in gratitude he executed for the hospital the well-known reliquary of St. Ursula. However it might have originated, this is the most noted work of a painter, who was distinguished frequently by his minute missal-like painting (he was also an illuminator of missals), in which he would introduce fifteen hundred small figures in a picture two feet eight inches, by six feet five inches in size, and work out every detail with the utmost niceness and care. The reliquary, or "chasse," is a wooden coffer or shrine about four feet in length, its style and form those of a rich Gothic church, its purpose to hold an arm of the saint. The whole exterior is covered with miniatures by Memling, nearly the whole of them giving incidents in the legendary history of St. Ursula, a "virgin princess of Brittany," or of England, who, setting out with eleven thousand virgins—her companions, her lover, and an escort of knights on a pilgrimage to Rome, was, with her whole company, met and murdered, by a horde of heathen Huns, when they had reached Cologne, on their return. Our readers may be aware that the supposed bones of the virgins and St. Ursula form the ghastly adornment of the church founded in her honour at

Cologne. It is absolutely filled with bones, built into the walls, stowed under the pavement, ranged in glass cases about the choir. Hans Memling's is a pleasanter commemoration of St. Ursula.

QUINTIN MATSYS, the blacksmith of Antwerp, was born at Louvain about 1460. Though he worked first as a smith, he is said by Kugler to have belonged to a family of painters, which somewhat takes from the romance, though it adds to the probability of his story. Another painter in Antwerp having offered the hand and dowry of his daughter—beloved by Quintin Matsys—as a prize to the painter who should paint the best picture in a competition for her hand, the doughty smith took up the art, entered the lists, and carried off the maiden and her portion from all his more experienced rivals. The vitality of the legend is indicated by the inscription on a tablet to the memory of Quintin Matsys in the Cathedral, Antwerp. The Latin inscription reads thus in English:

" 'Twas love connubial taught the smith to paint."

Quintin Matsys lived and died a respected burgher of Antwerp, a member of the great Antwerp painters' guild of St. Luke. He was twice married, and had thirteen children.

Whatever might have been his source of inspiration, Quintin Matsys was an apt scholar. His *Descent from the Cross*, now in the Museum, Antwerp, was *the* "Descent from the Cross," and *the* picture in the Cathedral, until superseded by Rubens' master-piece on the same subject. Still Quintin Matsys' version remains, and is in some respects an unsurpassed picture. There is a traditional grouping of this Divine tragedy, and Quintin Matsys has followed the tradition. The body of the Lord is supported by two venerable old men—Joseph of Arimathea and Nicodemus—while the holy women anoint the wounds of the Saviour; the Virgin swooning with grief is supported by St. John. The figures are full of individuality, and their action is instinct with pathos. For this picture Quintin Matsys—popular painter as he was —got only three hundred florins, equivalent to $125.00 (although, of course, the value of money was much greater in those days). The Joiners' Company, for whom he painted the *Descent from the Cross*, sold the picture to the city of Antwerp for five times the original amount, and it is said Queen Elizabeth offered the city nearly twenty times the first sum for it, in vain.

Quintin Matsys painted frequently half-length figures of the Virgin and Child, an example of which is in the National Gallery. He excelled in the "figure painting" of familiar subjects, then just beginning to be established, affording a token of the direction which the future eminence of the Flemish painters would take. One of his famous pictures of this kind is *The Misers*, in the Queen's collection at Windsor. Two figures in the Flemish costume of the time, are seated at a table; before them are a heap of money and a book, in which one is writing with his right hand, while he tells down the money with his left. The faces express craft and cupidity. The details of the ink-horn on the table, and the bird on its perch behind, have the Flemish graphic exactness.

CHAPTER V.

IN EARLY SCHOOLS OF ITALIAN ART.

E have come to the period when Italian art is divided into many schools—Paduan, Venitian, Umbrian, Florentine, Roman, Bolognese, &c., &c. With the schools and their definitions we do not mean to meddle, except it may be to mention to which school a great painter belonged. Another difficulty meets us here. We have been trying so far as we could to give the representative painters in the order of time. We can no longer follow this rule strictly, and the grouping of this chapter is made on the principle of leading our readers up by some of the predecessors who linked the older to the later Italian painters, and by some of the contemporaries of these later painters, to that central four, Lionardo da Vinci, Michael Angelo, Raphael, and Titian, who occupy so great a place in the history of art.

In the brothers Bellini and their native Venice, we must first deal with that excellence of colouring for which the Venitian painters were signally noted, while they comparatively neglected and underrated drawing. A somewhat fanciful theory has been started, that as Venice, Holland, and England have been distinguished for colour in art, and as all those States are by the sea, so a sea atmosphere has something to do with a passion for colour. Within more reasonable bounds, in reference to the Venitians, is the consideration that no colouring is richer, mellower, more exquisitely tinted than that which belongs to the blue Italian sky over the blue Adriatic, with those merged shades of violet, green, and amber, and that magical soft haze which has to do with a moist climate.

The two brothers Gentile and Gian or John Bellini, the latter the more famous of the two, were the sons of an old Venitian painter, with regard to whom the worthy speech is preserved, that he said it was like the Tuscans for son to beat father, and he hoped, in God's name, that Giovanni or Gian would outstrip him, and Gentile, the elder, outstrip both. The brothers worked together and were true and affectionate brothers, encouraging and appreciating each other.

Gentile was sent by the Doge at the request of the Sultan—either Mahommed II. or Bajazet II., to Constantinople, where Gentile Bellini painted the portrait of the

ADOLPHUS DE GUILDRE THREATENING HIS FATHER.

Sultan and the Sultana his mother, now in the British Museum. The painter also painted the head of John the Baptist in a charger as an offering—only too suitable—from him to the Grand Turk. The legend goes on to tell that in the course of the presentation of the gift, an incident occurred which induced Gentile Bellini to quit the Ottoman Court with all haste. The Sultan had criticized the appearance of the neck in John the Baptist's severed head, and when Gentile ventured to defend his work, the Sultan proceeded to prove the correctness of his criticism, by drawing his scimitar and cutting off at a stroke the head of a kneeling slave, and pointing to the spouting blood and the shrinking muscle, gave the horrified painter a lesson in practical anatomy. On Gentile's return from the East, he was pensioned by his State, and lived on painting, till he was eighty years of age, dying in 1501.

Gian Bellini is said to have obtained by a piece of deceit, which is not in keeping with his manly and honourable character, the secret, naturally coveted by a Venitian, of mixing colours with resin and oil. A Venitian painter had brought the secret from Flanders, and communicated it to a friend, who, in turn, communicated it to a third painter, and was murdered by that third painter for his pains, so greedy and criminal was the craving, not only to possess, but to be as far as possible the sole possessor of, the grand discovery. Gian Bellini was much less guilty, if he were really guilty. Disguised as a Venitian nobleman, he proposed to sit for his portrait to that Antonella who first brought the secret from Flanders, and while Antonella worked with unsuspicious openness, Gian Bellini watched the process and stole the secret.

Gian Bellini lived to the age of ninety, and had among his admirers the poet Ariosto and Albrecht Dürer. The latter saw Gian Bellini in his age, and said of him, when foolish mockers had risen up to scout at the old man, and his art now become classic, " He is very old, but he is still the best of our painters." Gian Bellini had illustrious pupils, including in their number Titian and Giorgione.

The portraits of Gentile and Gian, which are preserved in a painting by Gian, show Gentile fair-complexioned and red-haired, and Gian with dark hair.

Gian Bellini is considered to have been less gifted with imagination than some of his great brother artists; but he has proved himself a man of high moral sense, and while he stopped short at the boundary between the seen and the unseen, it is certain he must still have painted with much of "the divine patience" and devout consecration of all his powers, and of every part of his work, which are the attributes of the earliest Italian painters. When he and his brother began to paint, Venitian art had already taken its distinctive character for open-air effects, rich scenic details in architecture, furniture and dress (said to be conspicuous in commercial communities), and a growing tendency to portraiture. Gian went with the tide, but he guided it to noble results. His simplicity and good sense, with his purity and dignity of mind, were always present. He introduced into his pictures "singing boys, dancing cherubs, glittering thrones, and dewy flowers," pressing the outer world into his service and that of religious art. It is said also that his Madonnas seem "amiable beings imbued with a lofty grace;" while his saints are "powerful and noble forms." But he never descended to the paltry or the vulgar. He knew from the depths of his own soul how to invest a face with moral grandeur. Especially in his representations of our Saviour Gian Bellini "displays a perception of moral power and grandeur seldom equalled in the history of art." The example given is that of the single figure of the Lord in the Dresden Gallery, where the Son of God, without nimbus, or glory, stands forth as the "ideal of elevated humanity."

The greater portion of Gian Bellini's pictures remain in the churches and galleries of Venice. But the first great work at which the two brothers in their youth worked in company—the painting of the Hall of Council in the palace of the Doge, with a series of historical and legendary pictures of the Venitian wars with the Emperor Frederick Barbarossa (1177), including the Doge Ziani's receiving from the Pope the gold ring with which the Doge espoused the Adriatic, in token of perpetual dominion over the sea—was unfortunately destroyed by fire in 1577. Giovanni Bellini's greatest work, now at St. Salvatore, is Christ at Emmaus, with Venitian senators and a Turkish dragoman introduced as spectators of the risen Lord.

No praise can exceed that bestowed on Gian Bellini's colouring for its intensity and transparency. "Many of his draperies are like crystal of the clearest and deepest colour," declares an authority; and another states "his best works have a clear jewel brightness, an internal gem-like fire such as warms a summer twilight. The shadows are intense and yet transparent, like the Adriatic waves when they lie out of the sun under the palace bridges."

Portrait-painting, just beginning, was established in Venice, its later stronghold, by Gian Bellini. His truthful portrait of the Doge Loredano, one of the earliest of that series of Doges' portraits which once hung in state in the ducal palace, is now in the National Gallery in London.

Of Gentile Bellini, whose work was softer, but less vigorous than his brother's, the best painting extant is that at Milan of St. Mark preaching at Alexandria, in which the painter showed how he had profited by his residence at Constantinople in the introduction of much rich Turkish costume, and of an animal unknown to Europe at the time—a camelopard.

LUCA D'EGIDIO DI VENTURA, called LUCA SIGNORELLI, and sometimes LUCA DA CORTONA, was born at Cortona in 1441 (?)—some writers say in 1439. He was a pupil of the celebrated Pietro della Francesca, with whom he worked at Arezzo in 1472. Luca was one of the competitors for the prize offered by Pope Sixtus IV. for paintings in the Sistine Chapel in 1480, and his *History of Moses* is worthy of great praise. In 1484 he returned to Cortona, which he afterwards made his home. His native city still possesses several of his works; a *Deposition from the Cross*, and a *Last Supper* are in the Cathedral. In 1484 Luca painted the altar-piece in the Cappella Sant' Onofrio in the Cathedral of Perugia; it represents a *Madonna enthroned* with saints. The design, though hard, is full of power, and displays a beautiful conception of the subject; this picture may justly be considered one of Signorelli's masterpieces. In Siena he painted frescoes in the Convent of Monte Uliveto and in the Petrucci Palace. In Volterra altar-pieces by his hand still exist. The most famous of all Signorelli's paintings are the frescoes of the *Last Judgment* in the chapel of San Brizio in the Cathedral of Orvieto. This great work was commenced in 1447 by

Fra Angelico, who executed the figure of Christ and the attendant saints and angels. After waiting a considerable time for Perugino, the authorities engaged Signorelli to finish it. By the contract, which is dated April 5th, 1499, Signorelli undertook to complete the ceiling for 200 ducats and the walls for 600 ducats, besides free lodgings and two measures of wine, and two quarters of corn per month. The ceiling was finished in 1500, but the date of the completion of the walls is not known, though, judging from the time Signorelli took to execute the ceiling, it was probably about 1503. The frescoes comprise the *History of the Antichrist; the Resurrection of the Dead; Hell* and *Paradise*. Great power and vigour are displayed in these paintings, especially in the naked figures and the foreshortening.

The exact date of his death is unknown, but he was still living in 1524.

ANDREA MANTEGNA was born near Padua. He was the son of a farmer. His early history, according to tradition, is very similar to that of Giotto. Just as Cimabue adopted Giotto, Squarcione, a painter who had travelled in Italy and Greece, and made a great collection of antiques, from which he taught in a famous school of painters, adopted Andrea Mantegna at the early age of ten years. It was long believed that Mantegna, in the end, forfeited the favour of his master by marrying Nicolosa Bellini, the sister of Gentile and Gian Bellini, whose father was the great rival of Squarcione; and farther, that Mantegna's style of painting had been considerably influenced by his connection with the Bellini. Modern researches, which have substituted another surname for that of Bellini as the surname of Andrea Mantegna's wife, contradict this story.

Andrea Mantegna, a man of much energy and fancy, entered young into the service of the Gonzaga lords of Mantua, receiving from them a salary of $150 a year and a piece of land, on which the painter built a house, and painted it within and without—the latter one of the first examples of artistic waste, followed later by Tintoret and Veronese, regardless of the fact that painting could not survive in the open air of Northern Italy.

Andrea Mantegna had his home at Mantua, except when he was called to Rome to paint for the Pope, Innocent VIII. An anecdote is told by Mrs. Jameson of this commission. It seems the Pope's payments were irregular; and one day when he visited his painter at work, and his Holiness asked the meaning of a certain allegorical female figure in the design, Andrea answered, with somewhat audacious point, that he was trying to represent *Patience*. The Pope, understanding the allusion, paid the painter in his own coin, by remarking in reply, "If you would place Patience in fitting company, you would paint Discretion at her side." Andrea took the hint, said no more, and when his work was finished not only received his money, but was munificently rewarded.

Andrea Mantegna had two sons and a daughter. One of his sons painted with his father, and, after Andrea Mantegna's death, completed some of his pictures.

Andrea Mantegna's early study of antique sculpture moulded his whole life's work. He took great delight in modelling, in perspective, of which he made himself a master, and in chiaro-scuro, or light and shade. Had his powers of invention and grace not kept pace with his skill, he would have been a stiff and formal worker; as it was, he carried the austerity of sculpture into painting, and his greatest work, the "Triumph of Julius Cæsar," would have been better suited for the chiselled frieze of a temple than it is for the painted frieze of the hall of a palace. Yet he was a great leader and teacher in art, and the true proportions of his drawing are grand, if his colouring is harsh. Mantegna's "Triumph of Julius Cæsar" is in England at Hampton Court, having been bought from the Duke of Mantua by Charles I. These cartoons, nine in number, are sketches in water-colour or distemper on paper fixed on cloth. They are faded and dilapidated, as they well may be, considering the slightness of the materials and their age, about four hundred years. At the same time, they are, after the cartoons of Raphael (which formed part of the same art collections of Charles I.), perhaps the most valuable and interesting relic of art in England.

The series of the "Triumph" contain the different parts, originally separated by pillars, of a long and splendid procession. There are trumpeters and standard bearers, the statues of the gods borne aloft, battering-rams and heaps of glittering armour, trophies of conquest in huge vases filled with coin, garlanded oxen, and elephants. The second last of the series, presents the ranks of captives forming part of the show, rebellious men, submissive women, and unconscious children—a moving picture. In the last of the series comes the great conqueror in his chariot, a youth in the crowd following him, carrying his banner, on which is inscribed Cæsar's notable despatch, "Veni, vidi, vici;" "I came, I saw, I conquered."

Another of Mantegna's best pictures is in distemper—in which, and on fresco, Mantegna chiefly painted,—and is in the Louvre, Paris. It is the Madonna of Victory, so called from its being painted to commemorate the deliverance of Italy from the French army under Charles VIII., a name which has acquired a sardonic meaning from the ultimate destination of the picture. This picture—which represents the Virgin and Child on a throne, in an arbour of fruit and flowers, between the archangels, Michael and St. Maurice, in complete armour, with the patron saints of Mantua and the infant St. John in the front, and the Marquis Ludovico of Mantua and his wife, Isabella D'Este, kneeling to return thanks—was painted by Mantegna at the age of seventy years; and, as if the art of the man had mellowed with time, it is the softest and tenderest of his pictures in execution. A beautiful Madonna of Mantegna's, still later in time, is in the National Gallery of England.

DOMENICO GHIRLANDAJO was properly Domenico Bicordi, but inherited from his father, a goldsmith in Florence, the by-name of Ghirlandajo or Garland-maker—a distinctive appellation said to have been acquired by the elder man from his skill in making silver garlands for the heads of Florentine women and children. Domenico Ghirlandajo worked at his father's craft till he was twenty-four years of age, when, having in the mean time evinced great cleverness in taking the likenesses of the frequenters of Ghirlandajo the elder's shop, the future painter abandoned the goldsmith's trade for art pure and simple. He soon vindicated the wisdom of the step which he had taken by giving proofs of something of the strength of Masaccio, united with a reflection of the feeling of Fra Angelico.

Ghirlandajo was summoned soon to Rome to paint in the Sistine Chapel, after-

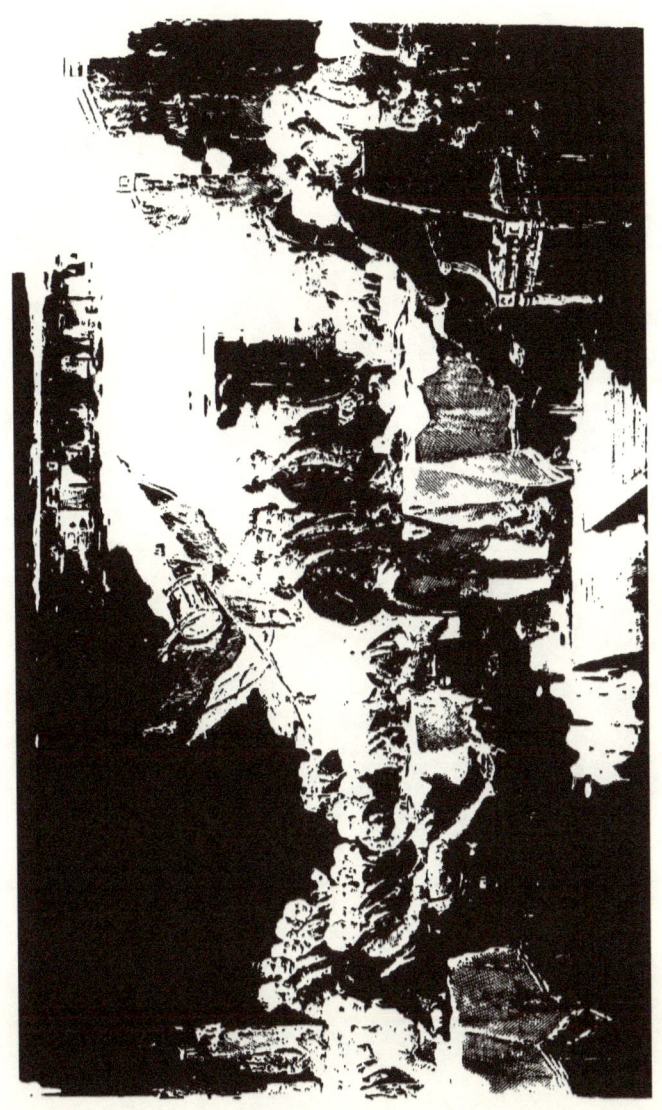

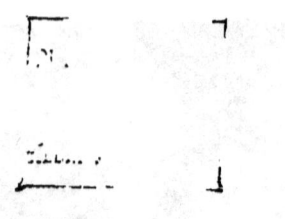

wards to be so glorious; but his greatest works were done in the prime of his manhood, in his native city, Florence, where he was chosen as the teacher of Michael Angelo, who was apprenticed to Ghirlandajo for three years.

While still in the flower of his age and crowned with golden opinions, being, it is said, with effusion, "the delight of his city," Ghirlandajo died after a short illness.

In Ghirlandajo's time Florence had reached her meridian, and her citizens outvied each other in the magnificence of their gifts to their fair mother city. Ghirlandajo was fitted to be their painter; himself a generous-spirited artist, in the exuberance of life and power, he wished that his fellow-citizens would give him all the walls of the city to cover with frescoes. He was content with the specified sum for his painting, desiring more the approbation of his employers than additional crowns. His genius lying largely in the direction of portrait painting, he introduced frequently the portraits of contemporaries, causing them to figure as spectators of his sacred scenes. One of these contemporaries thus presented, was Amerigo Vespucci, who was to give his name to our continent. Another was a Florentine beauty, a woman of rank, Ginevra de Benci.

Ghirlandajo was lavish in his employment of rich Florentine costumes and architecture. He even made the legends of the saints and the histories of the Bible appear as if they had happened under the shadow of Brunelleschi's duomo and Giotto's campanile, and within sound of the flow of the Arno. In the peculiar colouring used in fresco Ghirlandajo excelled.

He painted a chapel for a Florentine citizen, Francesco Sasetti, in the church of the Trinità, Florence, with scenes from the life of St. Francis. Of these, the death of St. Francis, surrounded by the sorrowing monks of his order, with the figures of Francesco Sasetti and his wife, Madonna Nera, on one side of the picture, is considered the best. As a curious illustration of the modernizing practice of Ghirlandajo, he has painted an old priest at the foot of the bier, chanting the litanies for the dying, with spectacles on his nose, the earliest known representation of these useful articles.

Ghirlandajo painted during four years the choir of the church of Santa Maria Novella, Florence, for one of the great Florentine benefactors, Giovanni Tornabuone, and there are to be seen some of Ghirlandajo's finest frescoes from the history of John the Baptist and the Virgin.

A Madonna and Child with angels in the English National Gallery is attributed to Ghirlandajo.

FRANCESCO FRANCIA, or IL FRANCIA, was born at Bologna, and was the son of a carpenter, whose surname was Raibaloni, but Francesco assumed the name of his master, a goldsmith, and worked himself at a goldsmith's trade till he was forty years of age. Indeed he may be said never to have relinquished his connection with the trade, and certainly he was no more ashamed of it than of his calling as a painter, for he signed himself indiscriminately "goldsmith" and "painter," and sometimes whimsically put "goldsmith" to his paintings, and "painter" to his jewellery. He was a famous designer of dies for coins and medals, and it is quite probable, as a countryman of his own has sought to prove, that he was the celebrated type-cutter, known as "Francesco da Bologna." But it is with Francesco "*pictor*" that we have to do.

Though he only began to prosecute the painter's art in middle age, he rose with remarkable rapidity to eminence, was the great painter of Lombardy in his day, rivalling Squarcione, Mantegna's teacher in his school, which numbered two hundred scholars, and becoming the founder of the early Bolognese school of painters.

Francia is said to have been very handsome in person, with a kindly disposition and an agreeable manner. He was on terms of cordial friendship with Raphael, then in his youth, and thirty years Il Francia's junior. Il Francia addressed an enthusiastic sonnet to Raphael, and there is extant a letter of Raphael's to Il Francia, excusing himself for not sending his friend Raphael's portrait, and making an exchange of sketches, that of his *Nativity* for the drawing of Il Francia's *Judith;* while it was to Il Francia's care that Raphael committed his picture of St. Cecilia, when it was first sent to Bologna. These relations between the men and their characters throw discredit on the tradition that Il Francia died from jealous grief caused by the sight of Raphael's *St. Cecilia.* As Il Francia was seventy years of age at the time of his death, one may well attribute it to physical causes. Il Francia had at least one son, and another kinsman, painters, whose paintings were so good as to be occasionally confounded with those of Il Francia.

Il Francia is thought to have united, in his works, a certain calm sedateness and frank sincerity to the dreamy imaginativeness of some of his contemporaries. His finest works are considered to be the frescoes from the life of St. Cecilia in the church of St. Cecilia at Bologna.

FRA BARTOLOMMEO. We come to a second gentle monk, not unlike Fra Angelico in his nature, but far less happy than Fra Angelico, in having been born in stormy times. Fra Bartolommeo, called also Baccio della Porta, or Bartholomew of the gate, from the situation of his lodgings when a young man, but scarcely known in Italy by any other name than that of Il Frate, or the Friar, was born near Florence, and trained from his boyhood to be a painter. In his youth, however, a terrible public event convulsed Florence, and revolutionized Baccio della Porta's life. He had been employed to paint in that notable Dominican convent of St. Mark, where Savonarola, its devoted friar, was denouncing the sins of the times, including the profligate luxury of the nobles and the degradation of the representatives of the Church. Carried away by the fervour and sincerity of the speaker, Baccio joined the enthusiasts who cast into a burning pile the instruments of pride, vanity, and godless intellect denounced by the preacher. Baccio's sacrifice to the flaming heap of splendid furniture and dress, and worldly books, was all his designs from profane subjects and studies of the undraped figure. A little later Savonarola was excommunicated by the Pope and perished as a martyr; and Baccio, timid from his natural temper, distracted by doubt, and altogether horror-stricken, took a monk's vows, and entered the same convent of St. Mark, where for four years he never touched a pencil.

At the request of his superior Fra Bartolommeo painted again, and when Raphael visited Florence, and came with all his conquering sweetness and graciousness to greet the monk in his cell, something of Il Frate's old love for his art, and delight in its exercise, returned. He even visited Rome, but there his health failed him, and the great works of Lionardo, Michael Angelo, and Raphael, when he compared his own with theirs, seemed to crush and overwhelm him. But he painted better for his visit to Rome, even as he had painted better for his intimacy with Raphael. Nay, it is said Raphael himself painted better on account of his brotherly regard for, and confidence in, Fra Bartolommeo.

Fra Bartolommeo died aged forty-eight years. Among his best pupils was a nun of St. Catherine's, known as Suor Plautilla.

ANDREA VANUCCHI, commonly called Andrea del Sarto, from the occupation of his father, who was a tailor (in Italian, *sarto*), was born at Florence in 1488. He was first a goldsmith, but soon turned painter, winning early the commendatory title of " Andrea senza errori," or "Andrea the Faultless." His life is a miserable and tragic history. In the early flush of his genius and industry, with its just crown of fame and success, he conceived a passion for a beautiful but worthless woman, whom, in spite of the opposition of his friends, he married. She rendered his home degraded and wretched, and his friends and scholars fell off from him. In disgust he quitted Florence, and entered the service of Francis I. of France; but his wife, for whom his regard was a desperate infatuation, imperiously summoned him back to Florence, to which he returned, bringing with him a large sum of money, entrusted to him by the king for the purchase of works of art. Instigated by his wife, Andrea del Sarto used this money for his, or rather her, purposes, and dared not return to France. Even in his native Florence he was loaded with reproach and shame. He died of the plague at the age of fifty-five years, according to tradition, plundered and abandoned in his extremity by the base woman for whom he had sacrificed principle and honor. We may read the grievous story of Andrea del Sarto, written by one of the greatest of England's modern poets, Robert Browning.

As may be imagined, Andrea del Sarto's excellence lay in the charm of his execution. His works were deficient in earnestness and high feeling, and some will have it, that, evilly haunted as he was, he perpetually painted in his Madonnas the beautiful but base-souled face of the woman who ruined him. Andrea del Sarto's best works are in Florence, particularly in the cloisters of the convent of the Annunziata. In the court of the same convent is his famous *Riposo* (or rest of the Holy Family on their way to Egypt), which is known as the "*Madonna of the Sack*," from the circumstance of Joseph in the picture leaning against a sack. This picture has held a high place in art for hundreds of years.

PIETRO DI VANUCCIO, called PERUGINO, was born at Citta della Pieve, near Perugia, in 1446. He went to Florence when very young, and, Vasari says, was so poor, that he slept in a chest for lack of a bed. He studied under Verrocchio, and won such fame, that he was soon in a position to open a school, where the uncles of Raphael, Simone Ciarla and Bartolommeo Santi, brought him the child who was, soon afterwards, to become the glory of his age. Perugino counted also among his disciples Pinturicchio, Il Bacchiata, Lo Spagna, Gerino da Pistoia, and that Andrea Luigi of Assisi, surnamed l'Ingegno, who at eighteen was, according to Vasari, called the rival of Raphael, but who became blind before he had attained the age for great works, or rather, as documentary evidence seems to indicate, who left art for civic employment.

Perugino was one of the first painters sent for to Rome by Sixtus IV., who intrusted him with a part of the paintings to decorate the chapel which bears the name of that pontiff (the Sistine). He has left in it one of his largest and most beautiful frescoes, *St. Peter receiving the keys*. In Florence there is, in the Pitti Palace, a magnificent *Entombment;* at Rome, in the Museum of the Vatican, a *Resurrection*, in which he has, it is said, introduced his much loved pupil, while still a youth, under the form of the sleeping soldier, and himself under that of the soldier who is running off in fear; and at Naples there is, in the Museum degli Studj, an *Eternal Father* between four cherubim. For a long time the Louvre possessed only a simple sketch by Perugino, the *Combat of Chastity and Love*, painted in distemper,—although dated 1505,—because, (as Perugino himself says in the letter sent with it), a picture by Andrea Mantegna, to which his was to be a pendant, was painted by the same process; a remarkable proof of the persistent employment of distemper long after the generally-spread knowledge of oil-painting. But the Louvre now boasts pictures more worthy of Perugino, a *Nativity*, a *Virgin in Glory* worshipped by St. Rosa, St. Catherine, and two Angels, and lastly, a *Madonna and Child* between St. Joseph and St. Catherine, remarkable for the reverential style, charming grace, and exquisite colour. At Caen, in Normandy, there is a *Marriage of the Virgin*, with a temple in the background, which, it is said, Raphael copied in his celebrated *Sposalizio*.

If however we wish to know Perugino well, out of Italy, we must see his pictures in Germany and in England. And first, there are at Berlin two *Madonnas* with landscape backgrounds. Notwithstanding the care taken to assign them to Raphael when still in the school of Perugino, there seems no doubt that they are both the work of Perugino himself. At Vienna, at the Belvedere Gallery, Perugino holds the first place in the Roman hall; his *Madonna with Saints*, dated 1493, is one of his largest and most admirable compositions. It is to be regretted that it should have been cleaned and touched up so often. Munich is still richer than either Vienna or Berlin. It possesses a half-length *Madonna* standing out from a clear sky; a *Virgin adoring the Infant Saviour*, and the *Appearance of the Virgin to St. Bernard;* two angels accompany the mother of the Saviour, and two saints are with St. Bernard. These three remarkable works, in perfect preservation, and of large size for easel-pictures by Perugino, attain the utmost excellence of his style, so sweet, so tender, so certain to soften and to charm the beholder. The *Appearance of the Virgin to St. Bernard* is a surpassingly beautiful picture, and Raphael himself has, in the simple religious style, achieved nothing finer. It is before the paintings of Perugino that we see clearly how much a pupil owes to his master, and that the truth of the saying is verified, that a great genius is only a complete summary of his forerunners and contemporaries.

In London, the National Gallery can show with pride the *Virgin and Infant Christ with St. John* purchased of the late Mr. Beckford; and a fine picture which Vasari declares to be a chef-d'œuvre of the old master of Perugia; it is a triptych painted originally for the Carthusian Convent, near Pavia, purchased from Duke Melzi of Milan: in the centre is the *Virgin adoring the Infant Christ;* to the left, the *Archangel Michael* in full armour; to the right, the *Archangel*

THE CARD-PLAYERS.

Raphael holding the young Tobias by the hand. (A study, supposed to be by Raphael, for this portion of the triptych, is now in the Randolph Gallery at Oxford.) Vasari is right; it would be difficult to find in all the works of Perugino anything superior to this. It is in perfect preservation, and unites in itself every kind of beauty. Several parts of this triple picture—for example, the young Tobias, or the group of the Madonna and Child—resemble the earliest works of Raphael to such a degree that many have supposed that the master must have been helped by the pupil, who would be thus in part the painter of this masterpiece. It is however probable that this picture belongs to a more advanced period of his life, when Perugino, who survived his pupil four years, might have profited by example, and improved his primitive style under the influence of Raphael. Vanuccio would thus have ceased to be the master of Raphael, and have become his disciple. This mutual help, this mutual teaching, producing a reaction in style, is often seen in the history of art; and at the same time the same phenomenon—if we may so call it—was taking place at Venice between Bellini and Giorgione. In the South Kensington Museum, on the south-east staircase, is a fresco by Perugino—which has been transferred to canvas—representing the *Adoration of the Shepherds*. It was originally painted for the church at Fontignano. Perugino died, wealthy and much honoured, at Castello di Fontignano, in 1524.

CHAPTER VI.

LIONARDO DA VINCI,—MICHAEL ANGELO,— RAPHAEL—TITIAN.

E have arrived at the triumph of art, not, indeed, in unconsciousness and devotion, but in fulness and completeness, as shown in the works of four of the greatest painters and men whom the world ever saw. Of the first, Lionardo da Vinci, born at Vinci in the neighbourhood of Florence, 1452, it may be said that the many-sidedness which characterized Italians—above all Italians of his day—reached its height in him. Not only was he a painter, a sculptor, an architect, and engineer, but also one of the boldest speculators of the generation which gave birth to Columbus, and was not less original and ingenious than he was universally accomplished—an Admirable Crichton among painters. There is a theory that this many-sidedness is a proof of the greatest men, indicating a man who might have been great in any way, who, had his destiny not found and left him a painter, would have been equally great as a philosopher, a man of science, a poet, or a statesman. It may be so; but the life of Lionardo tends also to illustrate the disadvantage of too wide a grasp and diffusion of genius. Beginning much and finishing little, not because he was idle or fickle, but because his schemes were so colossal and his aims so high, he spent his time in preparation for the attainment of an excellence which constantly eluded him. Lionardo was the pioneer, the teacher of others, rather than the performer of his own dreams; and the life of the proud, passionate man was in many respects a life of failure and mortification. This result might, in a sense, have been avoided; but Lionardo, great as he was, proved also one of those unfortunate men whose noblest efforts are met and marred by calamities which could have hardly been foreseen or prevented.

Lionardo da Vinci was the son of a notary, and early showed a taste for painting as well as for arithmetic and mathematics. He was apprenticed to a painter, but he also sedulously studied physics. He is said, indeed, to have made marvellous guesses at truth, in chemistry, botany, astronomy, and particularly, as helping him in his art, anatomy. He was, according to other accounts, a man of noble person, like

Ghirlandajo. And one can scarcely doubt this who looks at Lionardo's portrait painted by himself, or at any engraving from it, and remarks the grand presence of the man in his cap and furred cloak; his piercing wistful eyes; stately outline of nose; and sensitive mouth, unshaded by his magnificent flowing beard.

He was endowed with surprising bodily strength, and was skilled in the knightly exercises of riding, fencing, and dancing. He was a lover of social pleasure, and inclined to indulge in expensive habits. While a lad he amused himself by inventing machines for swimming, diving, and flying, as well as a compass, a hygrometer, &c. &c. In a combination from the attributes of the toads, lizards, bats, &c. &c., with which his studies in natural history had made him familiar, he painted a nondescript monster, which he showed suddenly to his father, whom it filled with horror. But the horror did not prevent the old lawyer selling the wild phantasmagoria for a large sum of money. As something beyond amusement, Lionardo planned a canal to unite Florence with Pisa (while he executed other canals in the course of his life), and suggested the daring but not impossible idea of raising *en masse*, by means of levers, the old church of San Giovanni, Florence, till it should stand several feet above its original level, and so get rid of the half-sunken appearance which destroyed the effect of the fine old building. He visited the most frequented places, carrying always with him his sketch-book, in which to note down his observations; he followed criminals to execution in order to witness the pangs of despair; he invited peasants to his house and told them laughable stories, that he might pick up from their faces the essence of comic expression. A mania for truth—alike in great and little things—possessed him.

Lionardo entered young into the service of the Gonzaga family of Milan, being, according to one statement, chosen for the office which he was to fill, as the first singer in *improvisatore* of his time (among his other inventions he devised a peculiar kind of lyre). He showed no want of confidence in asserting his claims to be elected, for after declaring the various works he would undertake, he added with regard to painting—" I can do what can be done, as well as any man, be he who he may." He received from the Duke a salary of five hundred crowns a year. He was fourteen years at the court of Milan, where, among other works, he painted his *Cenacolo*, or "Last Supper," one of the grandest pictures ever produced. He painted it, contrary to the usual practice, in oils upon the plastered walls of the refectory of the Dominican convent, Milan. The situation was damp, and the material used proved so unsuitable for work on plaster, that, even before it was exposed to the reverses which in the course of a French occupation of Milan converted the refectory into a stable, the colours had altogether faded, and the very substance of the picture was crumbling into ruin.

The equestrian statue of the old Duke of Milan by Lionardo excited so much delight in its first freshness, that it was carried in triumph through the city, and during the progress it was accidentally broken. Lionardo began another, but funds failed for its completion, and afterwards the French used the original clay model as a target for their bowmen.

Lionardo returned to Florence, and found his great rival, Michael Angelo, already in the field. Both of the men, conscious of mighty gifts, were intolerant of rivalry. To Lionardo especially, as being much the elder man, the originator and promoter of many of the new views in art which his opponent had adopted, the competition was very distasteful, and to Michael Angelo he used the bitter sarcasm which has been handed down to us, "I was famous before you were born."

Nevertheless Lionardo consented to compete with Michael Angelo for the painting in fresco of one side of the council-hall, by the order of the gonfaloniere for the year. Lionardo chose for his subject a victory of the Florentines over the Milanese, while Michael Angelo took a scene from the Pisan campaigns. Not only was the work never done (some say partly because Lionardo *would* delay in order to make experiments in oils) on account of political troubles, but the very cartoons of the two masters, which all the artists of the day flocked to see, have been broken up, dispersed, and lost; and of one only, that of Michael Angelo, a small copy remains, while but a fragment from Lionardo's was preserved in a copy made by Rubens.

Lionardo went to Rome in the pontificate of Leo X., but there his quarrel with Michael Angelo broke out more violently than ever. The Pope too, who loved better a gentler, more accommodating spirit, seemed to slight Lionardo, and the great painter not only quitted Rome in disgust, but withdrew his services altogether from ungrateful Italy.

At Pavia Lionardo was presented to Francis I. of France, who, zealous in patronizing art, engaged the painter to follow Francis's fortunes at a salary of seven hundred crowns a year. Lionardo spent the remainder of his life in France. His health had long been declining before he died, aged sixty-seven years, at Cloux, near Amboise. He had risen high in the favour of Francis. From this circumstance, and the generous, chivalrous nature of the king, there doubtless arose the tradition that Francis visited Lionardo on his death-bed; and that, while in the act of gently assisting him to raise himself, the painter died in the king's arms. Court chronicles do their best to demolish this story, by proving Francis to have been at St. Germain on the day when Lionardo died at Cloux.

Lionardo was never married, and he left what worldly goods he possessed to a favourite scholar. Besides his greater works, he filled many MS. volumes, some with singularly accurate studies and sketches, maps, plans for machines, scores for music (three volumes of these are in the Royal Library at Windsor), and some with writing, which is written—probably to serve as a sort of cipher—from right to left, instead of from left to right. One of his writings is a valuable "Treatise" on painting; other writings are on scientific and philosophic subjects, and in these Lionardo is believed to have anticipated some of the discoveries which were reached by lines of close reasoning centuries later.

Lionardo's genius as a painter was expressed by his uniting, in the very highest degree, truth and imagination. He was the shrewdest observer of ordinary life, and he could also realize the higher mysteries and profounder feelings of human nature. He drew exceedingly well. Of transparent lights and shadows, he was the greatest master; but he was not a good colourist. His works are very rare, and many which are attributed to him are the pictures of his scholars, for he founded one of the great

schools of Milan or Lombardy. There is a tradition that he was, as Holbein was once believed to be, ambidextrous, or capable of using his left hand as well as his right, and that he painted with two brushes—one in each hand. Thus more than fully armed, Leonardo da Vinci looms out on us like a Titan through the mists of centuries, and he preaches to us the simple homily, that not even a Titan can command worldly success; that such men must look to higher ends as the reward of their travail, and before undertaking it they must count the cost, and be prepared to renounce the luxurious tastes which clung to Leonardo, and which were not for him or for such men as he was.

Lionardo's great painting was his *Last Supper*, of which, happily, good copies exist, as well as the wreck of the picture itself. The original is now, after it is too late, carefully guarded and protected in its old place in the Dominican convent of the Madonna della Grazia, Milan. The assembled company sit at a long table, Christ being seated in the middle, the disciples forming two separate groups on each side of the Saviour. The gradations of age are preserved, from the tender youth of John to the grey hairs of Simon; and all the varied emotions of mind, from the deepest sorrow and anxiety to the eager desire of revenge, are here portrayed. The well-known words of Christ, "One of you shall betray me," have caused the liveliest emotion. The two groups to the left of Christ are full of impassioned excitement, the figures in the first turning to the Saviour, those in the second speaking to each other,—horror, astonishment, suspicion, doubt, alternating in the various expressions. On the other hand, stillness, low whispers, indirect observations, are the prevailing expressions in the groups on the right. In the middle of the first group sits the betrayer; a cunning, sharp profile, he looks up hastily to Christ, as if speaking the words, "Master, is it I?" while, true to the Scriptural account, his left hand and Christ's right hand approach, as if unconsciously, the dish that stands before them.

A sketch of the head of Christ for the original picture, which has been preserved on a torn and soiled piece of paper at Brera, expresses the most elevated seriousness, together with Divine gentleness, pain on account of the faithless disciple, a full presentiment of his own death, and resignation to the will of the Father. It gives a faint idea of what the master may have accomplished in the finished picture.

During his stay at Florence Lionardo painted a portrait of Ginevra Benci; and a still more famous portrait by Lionardo was that of Mona Lisa, the wife of his friend Giocondo. This picture is also known as *La Jaconde*. We wish to call attention to it because it is the first of four surpassingly beautiful portraits of women which four great painters gave in succession to the world. The others, to be spoken of afterwards, are Raphael's *Fornarina*, Titian's *Bella Donna*, and Rubens' *Straw Hat*. About the original of *La Jaconde* there never has been a mystery such as there has been about the others. At this portrait the unsatisfied painter worked at intervals for four years, and when he left it he pronounced it still unfinished. *La Jaconde* is now in the Louvre in an utterly ruined condition, yet a judge says of it that even now "there is something in this wonderful head of the ripe southern beauty, with its airy background of a rocky landscape, which exercises a peculiar fascination over the mind."

The fragment of the cartoon in which Lionardo competed with Michael Angelo, may be held to survive in the fine painting by Rubens called *the Battle of the Standard*.

MICHAEL ANGELO BUONARROTI, born at Castel Caprese near Arezzo in Tuscany, 1475, is the next of these universal geniuses, a term which we are accustomed to hold in contempt, because we have only seen it exemplified in parody. After Lionardo, indeed, Michael Angelo, though he was also painter, sculptor, architect, engineer, poet, musician, might almost be regarded as restricted in his pursuits, yet still so manifold was he, that men have loved to make a play upon his name and call him " Michael the angel," and to speak of him as of a king among men.

Michael Angelo was of noble descent, and though his ancient house had fallen into comparative poverty, his father was mayor or podesta of Chiusi, and governor of the castle of Chiusi and Caprese. Michael Angelo was destined for the profession of the law, but so early vindicated his taste for art, that at the age of thirteen years he was apprenticed to Ghirlandajo. Lorenzo the Magnificent was then ruling Florence, and he had made a collection of antique models in his palace and gardens, and constituted it an academy for young artists. In this academy Michael Angelo developed a strong bias for sculpture, and won the direct patronage of the Medici.

To this period of his life belong two characteristic anecdotes. In a struggle with a fellow-student, Michael Angelo received a blow from a mallet in his face, which, breaking bone and cartilage, lent to his nose the rugged bend,

" The bar of Michael Angelo."

An ill-advised member of the Medician house, while entertaining a party of guests during a snow-storm, sent out the indignant artist to make a snow man within sight of the palace windows. These anecdotes bear indirectly on the ruling qualities of Michael Angelo—qualities so integral that they are wrought into his marble and painted on his canvas—proud independence and energy.

Before going farther we wish to guard against a common misapprehension of Michael Angelo—that he was a haughty, arrogant man, absolutely narrow in his half-idolatrous, half-human worship of art. Michael Angelo was severe in place of being sweet; he was impatient of contradiction; he was careless and scornful of ceremony; and in his very wrath at flattery and hypocrisy, he was liable to sin against his own honesty and sincerity. But he was a man with a lofty sense of duty and a profound reverence for God. He was, unlike Lionardo, consistently simple, frugal, and temperate, throughout his long life. If he held up a high standard to others, and enforced it on them with hardness, he held up a higher standard to himself, and enforced it on himself more hardly still. He was a thoroughly unworldly man, and actions which had their root in unworldliness have been ascribed unjustly to a kind of Lucifer pride. Greed, and the meanness of greed, were unknown to him. He worked for the last ten years of his life (under no less than five different Popes) at his designs for St. Peter's, steadfastly refusing pay for the work, saying that he did it for the honour of God and his own honour. He made many enemies and suffered from their enmity, but I cannot learn that, except in one instance, he was guilty of dealing an unworthy blow at his opponents. He was generous to his scholars, and without jealousy of them, suffering them to use his designs for their own purposes. He said, "I have no friends, I need none, I wish for none;" but that was in feeling himself "alone before Heaven;" and of the friends whom he did possess, he loved them all the more devotedly and faithfully, because they were few in number.

One need only be told of his love for his old servant Urbino, whom he presented with two thousand crowns to render him independent of service; and when the servant was seized with his last illness Michael Angelo nursed him tenderly, sleeping in his clothes on a couch that he might be ready to attend his patient. When his cares were ended, Michael Angelo wrote to a correspondent—"My Urbino is dead—to my infinite grief and sorrow. Living, he served me truly; and in his death he taught me how to die. I have now no other hope than to rejoin him in Paradise."

Of Michael Angelo's more equal friendship with Vittoria Colonna we hope our readers will read at leisure for themselves. No nobler, truer friendship ever existed. It began when the high-born and beautiful, gifted, and devout Marchesa de Pescara—most loyal of wives and widows, was forty-eight, and Michael Angelo sixty-four years of age. After a few years of privileged intercourse and correspondence, which were the happiest years in Michael Angelo's life, it ended for this world when he stood mourning by her lifeless clay. "I was born a rough model, and it was for thee to reform and re-make me," the great painter had written humbly of himself to his liege lady.

Italy, in Michael Angelo's time, as Germany in Albert Dürer's, was all quickened and astir with the new wave of religious thought which brought about the Reformation. Ochino and Peter Martyr, treading in the footsteps of Savonarola, had preached to eager listeners, but "in Italy men did not adopt Lutheranism, though they approached it;" and in all the crowd of great Italian artists of the day, Michael Angelo shows deepest traces of the conflict—of its trouble, its seriousness, its nobleness. He only, among his brethren, acted out his belief that the things of the world sank into insignificance before those thoughts of God and immortality which were alone fully worthy of the soul. And it was, as to a religious work for which he was fitted, that he at last gave himself up to the raising of St. Peter's. We shall have next in order the life of a man who had all the winning qualities which Michael Angelo wanted, but we shall hardly, through the whole range of history, find a nobler man than Michael Angelo.

After his first visit to Rome, 1496, Michael Angelo executed his colossal statue of David. In 1503 he entered into the competition with Lionardo for the painting of one end of the Council-hall, in Florence, which has been already mentioned. For this object he drew as his cartoon, "Pisan soldiers surprised while bathing by a sudden trumpet call to arms." The grand cartoon, of which only a small copy exists, was said to have been torn to pieces as an act of revenge by a fellow-sculptor, whom Michael Angelo had offended.

Michael Angelo was invited to Rome by Julius II. in 1504 to aid in erecting the unapproachable monument which the Pope projected raising for himself. Then commenced a series of contentions and struggles between the imperious and petulant Pope and the haughty, uncompromising painter, in which the latter certainly had the best of it. At one time in the course of the quarrel, Michael Angelo departed from Rome without permission or apology, and stoutly refused to return, though followed hotly by no less than five different couriers, armed with threats and promises, and urged to make the reparation by his own gonfaloniere. At last a meeting and a reconciliation between Michael Angelo and the Pope were effected at Bologna. Michael Angelo designed for Pope Julius II. not only the statue of Pope Julius at Bologna, which was finally converted into a cannon, and turned against the very man whose effigy it had originally presented, but also for that tomb which was never completed, the famous figure of Moses seated, grasping his beard with one hand.

While employed at the tomb, Michael Angelo, then in his fortieth year, was desired by the Pope to undertake the decoration of the ceiling of the Sistine Chapel. Here, again, the hand of an enemy is said to have been at work. Michael Angelo, with the first place as a sculptor, was inexperienced in fresco painting; while Raphael, who was taking the place of Lionardo as Michael Angelo's most formidable rival (yet whom it is said Michael Angelo pointed out as the fittest painter of the ceiling), and who was then engaged in painting the Vatican chambers, had already achieved the utmost renown. It was anticipated by secret hostility, so records tradition, that Michael Angelo would fail signally in the unaccustomed work, and that his merit as an artist would pale altogether before that of Raphael's. We need hardly write how entirely malice was balked in the verdict to which posterity has set its seal.

Michael Angelo brought artists from Florence to help him in his great undertaking, for over the chapel, whose walls had already been painted by older artists—among them Ghirlandajo, was an enormous vault of 150 feet in length by 50 in breadth, which Michael Angelo was required to cover with designs representing the Fall and Redemption of Man. But the painter was unable to bear what seemed to him the bungling attempts of his assistants; so dismissing them all and destroying their work, he shut himself up, and working in solitude and secrecy, set himself to evolve from his own inner consciousness the gigantic scenes of a tremendous drama. In 22 months (or, as Kugler holds, in three years, including the time spent on the designs) he finished gloriously the work, the magnitude of which one must see to comprehend. On All Saints' Day, 1512, the ceiling was uncovered, and Michael Angelo was hailed, little though he cared for such clamorous hailing, as a painter indeed. For this piece of work Michael Angelo received 3000 crowns.

Pope Julius died, and was succeeded by Leo X. of the Medician house, but, in spite of early associations as well as of mother country, Michael Angelo was no more acceptable to the Pope—a brilliantly polished, easy-tempered man of the world, who filled the chair of St. Peter's, than Lionardo had been. Leo X. greatly preferred Raphael, to whom all manner of pleasantness as well as of courteous deference was natural, to the two others. At the same time, Leo employed Michael Angelo, though it was more as an architect than as a painter, and rather at Florence than at Rome. At Florence Michael Angelo executed for Pope Clement VII., another Medici, the

MARRIAGE À LA MODE.
(From the original painting by Wm. Hogarth.)

mortuary chapel of San Lorenzo, with its six great statues, those of the cousins Lorenzo de Medici and Giuliano de Medici, the first called by the Florentines "Il Pensiero," or "Pensive Thought," with the four colossal recumbent figures named respectively the Night, the Morning, the Dawn, and the Twilight.

In 1537 Michael Angelo was employed by his fellow-citizens to fortify his native city against the return of his old patrons the Medici, and the city held out for nine months.

Pope Paul III., an old man when elected to the popedom, but bent on signalizing his pontificate with as splendid works of art as those which had rendered the reigns of his predecessors illustrious, summoned Michael Angelo, now grown old, being upwards of sixty years, and though reluctant to accept the commission to finish the decoration of the Sistine Chapel, painted on the wall, at the upper end, "The Last Judgment." The picture is forty-seven feet high by forty-three wide, and it occupied the painter eight years. It was during its progress that Michael Angelo entered on his friendship with Vittoria Colonna.

For the chapel called the Paolina or Pauline Chapel Michael Angelo also painted less-known frescoes, but from that time he devoted his life to St. Peter's. He had said that he would take the old Pantheon and "suspend it in air," and he did what he said, though he did not live to see the great cathedral completed. His sovereign, the Grand Duke of Florence, endeavoured in vain with magnificent offers to lure the painter back to his native city. Michael Angelo protested that to leave Rome then would be "a sin and a shame, and the ruin of the greatest religious monument in Christian Europe." Michael Angelo, like Lionardo, did not marry; he died at Rome in 1563, in his eighty-ninth year.

His nephew and principal heir, by the orders of the Grand Duke of Florence, and it is believed according to Michael Angelo's own wish, removed the painter's body to Florence, where it was buried with all honours in the church of Santa Croce there.

The traits which recall Michael Angelo personally to us, are the prominent arch of the nose, the shaggy brows, the tangled beard, the gaunt grandeur of a figure like that of one of his prophets.

Michael Angelo's will was very simple. "I bequeath my soul to God, my body to the earth, and my possessions to my nearest relations."

While Michael Angelo lived, one Pope rose on his approach, and seated the painter on his right hand, and another Pope declined to sit down in his painter's presence; but the reason given for the last condescension, is that the Pope feared that the painter would follow his example. And if the Grand Duke Cosmo uncovered before Michael Angelo, and stood hat in hand while speaking to him, we may have the explanation in another assertion, that "sovereigns asked Michael Angelo to put on his cap, because the painter would do it unasked."

The solitary instance in which Michael Angelo is represented as taking an unfair advantage of an antagonist, is in connection with the painter's rivalry in his art with Raphael. Michael Angelo undervalued the genius of Raphael, and was disgusted by what the older man considered the immoderate admiration bestowed on the younger. A favourite pupil of Michael Angelo's was Sebastian Del Piombo, who being a Venitian by birth, was an excellent colourist. For one of his pictures—the very "Raising of Lazarus" now in the National Gallery, London, which the Pope had ordered at the same time that he had ordered Raphael's "Transfiguration"—it is rumoured that Michael Angelo gave the designs and even drew the figures, leaving Sebastian the credit, and trusting that without Michael Angelo's name appearing in the work, by the help of his drawing in addition to Sebastian's superb colouring, Raphael would be eclipsed, and that by a painter comparatively obscure.

The unwarrantable inference that the whole work was that of one painter, constituted a stratagem altogether unworthy of Michael Angelo, and if it had any existence, its getting wind disappointed and foiled its authors. When the story was repeated to Raphael, his sole protest is said to have been to the effect that he was glad that Michael Angelo esteemed him so highly as to enter the lists with him.

In the decoration of the Sistine Chapel the pictures from the Old Testament, beginning from the altar, are—

1. The Separation of Light and Darkness.
2. The Creation of the Sun and Moon.
3. The Creation of Trees and Plants.
4. The Creation of Adam.
5. The Creation of Eve.
6. The Fall and the Expulsion from Paradise.
7. The Sacrifice of Noah.
8. The Deluge.
9. The Intoxication of Noah.

The lower portion of the ceiling is divided into triangles, occupied by the Prophets and Sibyls in solemn contemplation, accompanied by angels and genii. Beginning from the left of the entrance, their order is:—

1. Joel.
2. Sibylla Erythræa.
3. Ezekiel.
4. Sibylla Persica.
5. Jonah.
6. Sibylla Libyca.
7. Daniel.
8. Sibylla Cumæa.*
9. Isaiah.
10. Sibylla Delphica.

Near the altar are:
Right, The Deliverance of the Israelites by the Brazen Serpent.
Left, The Execution of Haman.
Near the entrance are:
Right, Judith and Holofernes.
Left, David and Goliath.

Michael Angelo was thirty-nine years of age when he painted the ceiling of the Sistine. When he began to paint the "Day of Judgment" he was above sixty years of age, and his great rival, Raphael, had already been dead thirteen years.

The picture of the "Day of Judgment," with much that renders it marvellous and awful, has a certain coarseness of conception and execution. The moment chosen

* See Illustration.

is that in which the Lord says, "Depart from me, ye cursed," and the idea and even attributes of the principal figure are taken from Orcagna's oil painting in the Campo Santo. But with all Michael Angelo's advantages, he has by no means improved on the original idea. He has robbed the figure of the Lord of its transcendent majesty; he has not been able to impart to the ranks of the blessed the look of blessedness which "Il Beato" himself might have conveyed. The chief excellence of the picture is in the ranks of the condemned, who writhe and rebel against their agonies. No wonder that the picture is sombre and dreadful.

A comparison and a contrast have been instituted between Michael Angelo and Milton, and Raphael and Shakespeare. There may be something in them, but, as in the case of broken metaphors, they will not bear being pushed to a logical conclusion or picked to pieces. The very transparent comparison which matches Michael Angelo with his own countryman, Dante, is after all more felicitous and truer. Michael Angelo with Lionardo are the great chiefs of the Florentine School.

RAPHAEL SANZIO, or Santi of Urbino, the head of the Roman School, was one of those very exceptional men who seem born to happiness, to inspire love and only love, to pass through the world making friends and disarming enemies, who are fully armed to confer pleasure while almost incapable of either inflicting or receiving pain. To this day his exceptional fortune stands Raphael's memory in good stead, since for one man or woman who yearns after the austere righteousness and priceless tenderness of Michael Angelo, there are ten who yield with all their hearts to the gay, sweet gentleness and generosity of Raphael. No doubt it was also in his favour as a painter, that though a man of highly cultivated tastes, "in close intimacy and correspondence with most of the celebrated men of his time, and interested in all that was going forward," he did not, especially in his youth, spend his strength on a variety of studies, but devoted himself to painting. While he thus vindicated his share of the breadth of genius of his country and time, by giving to the world the loveliest Madonnas and Child-Christs, the most dramatic of battle-pieces, the finest of portraits, his noble and graceful fertility of invention and matchless skill of execution were confined to and concentrated on painting. He did not diverge long or far into the sister arts of architecture and sculpture, though his classic researches in the excavations of Rome were keen and zealous (a heap of ruins having given to the world in 1504 the group of the Laocoon), so that a writer of his day could record that "Raphael had sought and found in Rome another Rome."

Raphael was born in the town of Urbino, and was the son of a painter of the Umbrian School, who very early destined the boy to his future career, and promoted his destination by all the efforts in Giovanni Santi's power, including the intention of sending away and apprenticing the little lad to the best master of his time, Perugino, whom we have already described. Raphael's mother died when he was only eight years of age, and his father died when he was no more than eleven years, before the plans for his education were put into action. But no stroke of outward calamity, or loss—however severe, could annul Raphael's birthright of universal favour. His stepmother, the uncles who were his guardians, his clever and perverse master, all joined in a common love of Raphael and determination to promote his interests.

Raphael at the age of twelve years went to Perugia to work under Perugino, and remained with his master till he was nearly twenty years of age. In that interval he painted industriously, making constant progress, always in the somewhat hard, but finished, style of Perugino, while already showing a predilection for what was to prove Raphael's favourite subject, the Madonna and Child. At this period he painted his famous *Lo Sposalizio* or the "Espousals," the marriage of the Virgin Mary with Joseph, now at Milan. In 1504 he visited Florence, remaining only for a short time, but making the acquaintance of Fra Bartolommeo and Ghirlandajo, seeing the cartoons of Lionardo and Michael Angelo, and from that time displaying a marked improvement in drawing. Indeed nothing is more conspicuous in Raphael's genius in contra-distinction to Michael Angelo's, than the receptive character of Raphael's mind, his power of catching up an impression from without, and the candour and humility with which he availed himself unhesitatingly of the assistance lent him by others.

Returning soon to Florence, Raphael remained there till 1508, when he was twenty-five years, drawing closer the valuable friendships he had already formed, and advancing with rapid strides in his art, until his renown was spread all over Italy, and with reason, since already, while still young, he had painted his *Madonna of the Goldfinch*, in the Florentine Gallery, and his *La Belle Jardinière*, or Madonna in a garden among flowers, now in the Louvre.

In his twenty-fifth year Raphael was summoned to Rome to paint for Pope Julius II. Our readers will remember that Michael Angelo, in the abrupt severity of his prime of manhood, was soon to paint the ceiling of the Sistine Chapel for the same despotic and art-loving Pope, who had brought Raphael hardly more than a stripling to paint the "*Camere*" or "*Stanze*" chambers of the Vatican.

The first of the halls which Raphael painted (though not the first in order) is called the *Camera della Segnatura* (in English, signature), and represents Theology, Poetry, Philosophy, with the Sciences, Arts, and Jurisprudence. The second is the *Stanza d' Eliodoro*, or the room of Heliodorus, and contains the grandest painting of all, in the expulsion of Heliodorus from the Temple of Jerusalem (taken from Maccabees), the Miracle of Bolsena, Attila, king of the Huns, terrified by the apparition of St. Peter and St. Paul, and St. Peter delivered from prison. The third stanza painted by Raphael is the *Stanza dell' Incendio* (the conflagration), so called from the extinguishing of the fire in the Borgo by a supposed miracle, being the most conspicuous scene in representations of events taken from the lives of Popes Leo III. and IV.; and the fourth chamber, which was left unfinished by Raphael, and completed by his scholars, is the *Sala di Constantino*, and contains incidents from the life of the Emperor Constantine, including the splendid battle-piece between Constantine and Maxentius. At these chambers, or at the designs for them, Raphael worked at intervals, during the popedoms of Julius II., who died in the course of the painting of the Camere, and Leo X., for a period of twelve years, till Raphael's death in 1520, after which the *Sala di Constantino* was completed by his scholars.

Raphael has also left in the Vatican a series of small pictures from the Old Testament, known as Raphael's Bible. This series decorates the thirteen cupolas of

the "Loggie," or open galleries, running round three sides of an open court. Another work undertaken by Raphael should have still more interest for us. Leo X., resolving to substitute woven for painted tapestry round the lower walls of the interior of the Sistine Chapel, commanded Raphael to furnish drawings to the Flemish weavers, and thence arose eleven cartoons, seven of which have been preserved, have become the property of England, and are the glory of the Kensington Museum. The subjects of the cartoons* in the seven which have been saved, are *The Death of Ananias, Elymas the Sorcerer struck with Blindness, The Healing of the Lame Man at the Beautiful Gate of the Temple, The Miraculous Draught of Fishes, Paul and Barnabas at Lystra, St. Paul Preaching at Athens,* and *The Charge to St. Peter.* The four cartoons which are lost were, *The Stoning of St. Stephen, The Conversion of St. Paul, Paul in Prison,* and *The Coronation of the Virgin.*

In these cartoons figures above life-size were drawn with chalk upon strong paper, and coloured in distemper, and Raphael received for his work four hundred and thirty gold ducats (about $3,200), while the Flemish weavers received for their work in wools, silk, and gold, fifty thousand gold ducats. The designs were cut up in strips for the weavers' use, and while some strips were destroyed, the rest lay in a warehouse at Arras, till Rubens became aware of their existence, and advised Charles I. to buy the set, to be employed in the tapestry manufactory established by James I. at Mortlake. Taken to England in the slips which the weavers had copied, the fate of the cartoons was still precarious. Cromwell bought them in Charles I.'s art collection, and Louis XIV. sought, but failed, to re-buy them. They fell into farther neglect, and were well-nigh forgotten, when Sir Godfrey Kneller recalled them to notice, and induced William III. to have the slips pasted together, and stretched upon linen, and put in a room set apart for them at Hampton Court, whence they were transferred, within the last ten years, for the greater advantage of artists and the public, to Kensington Museum.

The woven tapestries for which the cartoons were designed had quite as chequered a career. In the two sacks of Rome by French soldiers, the tapestries were seized, carried off, and two of them burnt for the bullion in the thread. At last they were restored to the Vatican, where they hang in their faded magnificence, a monument of Leo X. and of Raphael. An additional set of ten tapestry cartoons were supplied to the Vatican by Raphael's scholars.

Raphael painted for the Chigi family in their palace, which is now the Villa Farnesina, scenes from the history of Cupid and Psyche, and the Triumph of Galatea, subjects which show how the passion for classical mythology that distinguishes the next generation, was beginning to work. To these last years belong his *Madonna di San Sisto,* so named from its having been painted for the convent of St. Sixtus at Piacenza, and his last picture, the *Transfiguration,* with which he was still engaged when death met him unexpectedly.

Raphael, as the Italians say, lived more like a "*principe*" (prince) than a "*pittore*" (painter). He had a house in Rome, and a villa in the neighbourhood, and on his

* See Engraving on Steel.

death left a considerable fortune to his heirs. There has not been wanting a rumour that his life of a principe was a dissipated and prodigal life; but this ugly rumour, even if it had more evidence to support it, is abundantly disproven by the nature of Raphael's work, and by the enormous amount of that work, granting him the utmost assistance from his crowd of scholars. He had innumerable commissions, and retained an immense school from all parts of Italy, the members of which adored their master. Raphael had the additional advantage of having many of his pictures well engraved by a contemporary engraver named Raimondi.

Like Giotto, Raphael was the friend of the most distinguished Italians of his day, including Count Castiglione, and the poet Ariosto. He was notably the warm friend of his fellow-painters both at home and broad, with the exception of Michael Angelo. A drawing of his own, which Raphael sent, in his kindly interchange of such sketches, to Albert Dürer, is preserved at Nüremberg. The sovereign princes of Italy, above all Leo X., were not contented with being munificent patrons to Raphael, they treated him with the most marked consideration. The Cardinal Bibbiena proposed the painter's marriage with his niece, ensuring her a dowry of three thousand gold crowns, but Maria di Bibbiena died young, ere the marriage could be accomplished; and Raphael, who was said to be little disposed to the match, did not long survive her. He caught cold, as some report, from his engrossing personal superintendence of the Roman excavations; and, as others declare, from his courtly assiduity in keeping an appointment with the Pope, was attacked by fever, and died on his birth-day, April 6th, 1520, having completed his thirty-seventh year.

All Rome and Italy mourned for him. When his body lay in state, to be looked at and wept over by multitudes, his great unfinished picture of the *Transfiguration* was hung above the bed. He was buried in a spot chosen by himself in his lifetime, and, as it happened, not far from the resting-place of his promised bride. Doubts having been raised as to Raphael's grave, search was made, and his body was exhumed in 1833, and re-buried with great pomp. Raphael's life and that of Rubens form the ideal painter's life—bountiful, splendid, unclouded, and terminating ere it sees eclipse or decay—to all in whom the artistic temperament is united to a genial, sensuous, pleasure-loving nature.

Raphael was not above the middle height, and slightly made. He was sallow in colour, with brown eyes, and a full yet delicate mouth; but his beautiful face, like that of Shakspeare, is familiar to most of us. With regard to Raphael's face, the amount of womanliness in it is a striking characteristic. One hears sometimes that no man's character is complete without its share of womanliness: surely Raphael had a double share, for womanliness is the most distinctive quality in his face, along with that vague shade of pensiveness which we find not infrequently, but strangely enough, in those faces which have been associated with the happiest spirits and the brightest fortunes.

Of Raphael's Madonnas, we should like to speak of three. *The Madonna di San Sisto:* " It represents the Virgin standing in a majestic attitude; the infant Saviour enthroned in her arms; and around her head a glory of innumerable cherubs melting into light. Kneeling before her we see on one side St. Sixtus, on the other St.

Barbara, and beneath her feet two heavenly cherubs gaze up in adoration. In execution, as in design, this is probably the most perfect picture in the world. It is painted throughout by Raphael's own hand; and as no sketch or study of any part of it was ever known to exist, and as the execution must have been, from the thinness and delicacy of the colours, wonderfully rapid, it is supposed that he painted it at once on the canvas—a *creation* rather than a picture. In the beginning of the last century the Elector of Saxony, Augustus III., purchased this picture from the monks of the convent for the sum of sixty thousand florins ($30,000), and it now forms the chief boast and ornament of the Dresden Gallery.

The *Madonna del Cardellino* (our Lady of the Goldfinch): The Virgin is sitting on a rock, in a flowery meadow. Behind are the usual light and feathery trees, growing on the bank of a stream, which passes off to the left in a rocky bend, and is crossed by a bridge of a single arch. To the right, the opposite bank slopes upward in a gentle glade, across which is a village, backed by two distant mountain-peaks.

In front of the sitting matronly figure of the Virgin are the holy children, our Lord and the Baptist, one on either side of her right knee. She has been reading, and the approach of St. John has caused her to look off her book (which is open in her left hand) at the new comer, which she does with a look of holy love and gentleness, at the same time caressingly drawing him to her with her right hand, which touches his little body under the right arm. In both hands, which rest across the Virgin's knee, he holds a captive goldfinch, which he has brought, with childish glee, as an offering to the Holy Child. The infant Jesus, standing between his mother's knees, with one foot placed on her foot, and her hand, with the open book, close above his shoulder, regards the Baptist with an upward look of gentle solemnity, at the same time that he holds his bent hand over the head of the bird.

The third, *Madonna della Sedia*, or our Lady of the Chair. The Virgin, very young and simple-looking in her loveliness, is seated on a low chair, clasping the Divine Child, who is leaning in weariness on her breast, St. John with his cross is standing—a boy at the Virgin's knee. The meek adoring tenderness in the face of the mother, the holy ingenuousness in that of the child, are expressions to be long studied.

Whole clusters of anecdotes gather round the cartoons, which, as they have to do with the work and not the worker, we leave untouched, with regret. But we must forewarn our readers by mentioning some of the refuted criticisms which have been applied to the cartoons. Reading the criticisms and their answers ought to render us modest and wary in "picking holes" in great pictures, as forward and flippant critics, old and young, are tempted to pick them. With regard to the *Miraculous Draught of Fishes*, a great outcry was once set up that Raphael had made the boat too little to hold the figures he has placed in it. But Raphael made the boat little advisedly; if he had not done so, the picture would have been "all boat," a contingency scarcely to be desired; on the other hand, if Raphael had diminished the figures to suit the size of the boat, these figures would not have suited those of the other cartoons, and the cartoon would have lost greatly in dignity and effect.

In the cartoon of the "*Death of Ananias*," carping objectors were ready to suggest that Raphael had committed an error in time by introducing Sapphira in the background counting her ill-gotten gains, at the moment when her no less guilty husband has fallen down in the agonies of death. It was hours afterwards that Sapphira entered into the presence of the apostles. But we must know that time and space do not exist for painters, who have to tell their story at one stroke, as it were.

In the treating of the *Lame Man at the Beautiful Gate of the Temple*, some authorities have found fault with Raphael for breaking the composition into parts by the introduction of pillars, and, farther, that the shafts are not straight. Yet by this treatment Raphael has concentrated the principal action in a sort of frame, and thus has been enabled to give more freedom of action to the remaining figures in the other divisions of the picture.

TITIAN, or TIZIANO VECELLI, the greatest painter of the Venitian School, reckoned worthy to be named with Lionardo, Michael Angelo and Raphael, was born of good family at Capo del Cadore in the Venitian State, in 1477. There is a tradition that while other painters made their first essays in art with chalk or charcoal, the boy Titian, who lived to be a glorious colourist, made his earliest trials in painting with the juice of flowers. Titian studied in Venice under the Bellini, and had Giorgione, who was born in the same year, for his fellow-scholar, at first his friend, later his rival. When a young man Titian spent some time in Ferrara; there he painted his *Bacchus and Ariadne*, and a portrait of *Lucrezia Borgia*. In 1512, when Titian was thirty-five years of age, he was commissioned by the Venitians to continue the works in the great council-hall, which the advanced age of Gian Bellini kept him from finishing. Along with this commission Titian was appointed in 1516 to the office of la Sanseria, which gave him the duty and privilege of painting the portraits of the Doges as long as he held the office; coupled with the office was a salary of one hundred and twenty crowns a year. Titian lived to paint five Doges; two others, his age, equal to that of Gian Bellini, prevented him from painting.

In 1516, Titian painted his greatest sacred picture, the *Assumption of the Virgin*. In the same year he painted the poet *Ariosto*, who mentions the painter with high honour in his verse. In 1530, he was at Bologna, where there was a meeting between Charles V. and Pope Clement VII., when he was presented to both princes.

Charles V. and Philip II. became afterwards great patrons and admirers of Titian, and it is of Charles V. and Titian that a legend, to which we have already referred, is told. The Emperor, visiting the painter while he was at work, stooped down and picked up a pencil, which Titian had let fall, to the confusion and distress of the painter, when Charles paid the princely compliment, "Titian is worthy of being served by Cæsar." Titian painted many portraits of Charles V., and of the members of his house. As Maximilian had created Albrecht Dürer a noble of the Empire, Charles V. created Titian a Count Palatine, and a Knight of the Order of St. Iago, with a pension, which was continued by Philip II., of four hundred crowns a year. It is doubtful whether Titian ever visited the Spain of his patrons, but Madrid possesses forty-three of his pictures, among them some of his finest works.

Titian went to Rome in his later years, but declined to abandon for Rome the painter's native Venice, which had lavished her favours on her son. He lived in great splendour, paying annual summer visits to his birth-place of Cadore, and occa-

QUINTUS CURTIUS LEAPING INTO THE GULF.

sionally dwelling again for a time at Ferrara, Urbino, Bologna. In two instances he joined the Emperor at Augsburgh. When Henry III. of France landed at Venice, he was entertained *en grand seigneur* by Titian, then a very old man; and when the king asked the price of some pictures which pleased him, Titian at once presented them as a gift to his royal guest.

Titian married, as has been recently ascertained, and had three children,—two sons, the elder a worthless and scandalous priest; the second a good son and accomplished painter; and a daughter, the beautiful Lavinia,* so often painted by her father, and whose name will live with his. Titian survived his wife thirty-six years; and his daughter, who had married, and was the mother of several children, six years. His second son and fellow-painter died of the same plague which struck down Titian, in 1566, at the ripe age of eighty-nine years.

Towards the close of Titian's life, there was none who even approached the old Venitian painter in the art which he practiced freely to the last. Painting in Italy was everywhere losing its pre-eminence. It had become, even when it was not so nominally, thoroughly secularized;—and with reason, for the painters by their art-creed and by their lives were fitter to represent gods and goddesses, in whom no man believed, than to give earnest expression to a living faith. Even Titian, great as he was, proved a better painter of heathen mythology than of sacred subjects.

But within certain limits and in certain directions, Titian stands unequalled. He has a high place for composition and for drawing, and his colouring was, beyond comparison, grand and true. He was great as a landscape painter, and he was the best portrait painter whom the world ever saw. In his painting is seen, not, indeed, the life of the spirit, but the life of the senses " in its fullest power ;" and in Titian there was such large mastery of this life, that in his freedom there was no violence, but the calmness of supreme strength, the serenity of perfect satisfaction. His painting was the reflection of the old Greek idea of the life of humanity as a joyous existence, so long as the sun of youth, maturity, health, and good fortune shone, without even that strain of foreboding pain, and desperate closing with fate, which troubled the bliss of ancient poet or sculptor. A large proportion of Titian's principal pictures are at Venice and Madrid.

We have written, in connection with Lionardo's *Jaconde* and Raphael's *Fornarina*, of Titian's *Bella Donna*. He has various *Bellas*, but, as far as we know, this is *the Bella Donna*—" a splendid, serious beauty, in a red and blue silk dress," in the Sciarra Gallery, Rome.

We have read that critics were at one time puzzled by the singular yellow, almost straw colour, appearing profusely in the hair of the women of the Venitian painters of this time, and that it was only by consulting contemporary records that it was learnt that the Venitian women indulged in the weak and false vanity of dyeing their black hair a pale yellow—a process, in the course of which the women drew the hair through the crown of a broad-brimmed hat, and spreading it over the brim, submitted patiently to bleaching the hair in a southern sun.

* See Illustration.

CHAPTER VII.

GERMAN ART.—ALBRECHT DÜRER.

LBRECHT DÜRER carries us to a different country and a different race. And he who has been called the father of German painting is thoroughly German, not only in his Saxon honesty, sedateness, and strength, but in the curious mixture of simplicity, subtlety, homeliness, and fantasticalness, which are still found side by side in German genius.

Albrecht Dürer was born at that fittest birth-place for the great German painter, quaint old Nuremberg, in 1471. He was the son of a goldsmith, and one of a family of eighteen children; a home school in which he may have learnt early the noble, manly lessons of self-denial and endurance, which he practised long and well. He was trained to his father's trade until the lad's bent became so unmistakable that he was wisely transferred to the studio of a painter to serve his apprenticeship to art.

When the Nuremberg apprenticeship was completed, Albrecht followed the German custom, very valuable to him, of serving another and a "wandering apprenticeship," which carried him betimes through Germany, the Netherlands, and Italy, painting and studying as he went. He painted his own portrait about this time, showing himself a comely, pleasant, and pleased young fellow, in a curious holiday suit of plaited low-bodied shirt, jerkin, and mantle across the shoulder, with a profusion of long fair curls, of which he was said to have been vain, arranged elaborately on each side, the blue eyes looking with frank confidence out of the blonde face. He painted himself a little later with the brave kindly face grown mature, and the wisdom of the spirit shining in the eyes, and weighing on the brows.

On his return from his travels, Albrecht Dürer's father arranged his son's marriage with the daughter of a musician in Nuremberg. The inducement to the marriage seems to have been, on the father's part, the dowry, and on the son's the beauty of the bride. How unhappy the union proved, without any fault of Albrecht's, has been the theme of so many stories, that we are half inclined to think that some of us must be more familiar with Albrecht Dürer's wedded life than with any other part of his history. It seems to us, that there is considerable exaggeration in these stories, for granted that Agnes Dürer was a shrew and a miser, was Albrecht Dürer the man to be entirely, or greatly, at such a woman's mercy? Taking matters at their worst, dishonour and disgrace did not come near the great painter. He was esteemed, as he deserved to be; he had a true friend in his comrade Pirkheimer; he had his art; he had the peace of a good conscience; he had the highest of all consolations in his faith in Heaven. Certainly it is not from Albrecht himself that the tale of his domestic wretchedness has come. He was as manfully patient and silent as one might have expected in a man upright, firm, and self-reliant as he was tender. We do not think it is good for men, and especially for women, to indulge in egotistical sentimentality, and to believe that such a woman as Agnes Dürer could utterly thwart and wreck the life of a man like Albrecht. It is not true to life, in the first place; and it is dishonouring to the man, in the second; for although, doubtless, there are men who are driven to destruction or heart-broken by even the follies of women, these men have not the stout hearts, the loyal spirits, the manly mould of Albrecht Dürer.

In 1506 Albrecht Dürer re-visited Italy alone, making a stay of eight months in Venice, where he formed his friendship with the old Gian Bellini, and where Albrecht had the misfortune to show the proofs and plans of his engravings to the Italian engraver, Raimondi, who engraved Raphael's paintings, and who proved himself base enough to steal and make use of Albrecht Dürer's designs to the German's serious loss and inconvenience.

A little later Albrecht Dürer, accompanied by his wife, visited the Netherlands. The Emperor Maximilian treated the painter with great favour, and a legend survives of their relations:—Dürer was painting so large a subject that he required steps to reach it. The Emperor, who was present, required a nobleman of his suite to steady the steps for the painter, an employment which the nobleman declined as unworthy of his rank, when the Emperor himself stepped forward and supplied the necessary aid, remarking, "Sir, understand that I can make Albrecht a noble like and above you" (Maximilian had just raised Albrecht Dürer to the rank of noble of the empire), "but neither I nor any one else can make an artist like him." We may compare this story with a similar and later story of Holbein and Henry VIII., and with another earlier story, having a slight variation, of Titian and Charles V. The universality of the story shakes one's belief in its individual application, but at least the legend, with different names, remains as an indication of popular homage to genius.

Among Albrecht Dürer's greatest paintings are his *Adoration of the Trinity* at Vienna, his *Samson and the Lion* * at Florence, and that last picture of *The Apostles* presented by Albrecht Dürer to his native city, "in remembrance of his career as an artist, and at the same time as conveying to his fellow-citizens an earnest and lasting exhortation suited to that stormy period." The prominence given to the Bible in the picture, points to it as the last appeal in the great spiritual struggle. With regard to this noble masterly picture, Kugler has written, "Well might the artist now close his eyes. He had in this picture attained the summit of art; here he stands side by side with the greatest masters known in history."

* See Illustration.

CHAPTER VIII.

LATER ITALIAN ART.

GIORGIO BARBARELLI, known as "Giorgione,"—in Italian, "big," or, as it has been better translated, "strapping George"—was born at Castelfranco, in Treviso, about 1477, the same year in which Titian was born. Nothing is known of his youth before he came to Venice and studied in the school of Gian Bellini along with Titian.

The two men were friends in those days, but soon quarrelled, and Giorgione's early death completed their separation. Titian was impatient and arrogant; Giorgione seems to have been one of those proud, shy, sensitive men— possibly morbidly sensitive, with whom it is always difficult to deal; but it is recorded of him, as it is not recorded of his great compeer, that Giorgione was frank and friendly as an artist, however moody and fitful he might be as a man.

Giorgione soon became known. According to one account, he painted the façade of the house which he dwelt in, for an advertisement of his abilities as a painter, a device which was entirely successful in procuring him commissions; but unfortunately for posterity, these were frequently to paint other façades, sometimes in company with Titian; grand work, which has inevitably perished, if not by fire, by time and by the sea-damp of Venice, for to Venice Giorgione belonged, and there is no sign that he ever left it.

He had no school, and his love of music and society—the last taste found not seldom, an apparent anomaly, in silent, brooding natures—might tend to withdraw him from his art. He has left a trace of his love for music in his pictures of "Concerts" and of "Pastorals," in which musical performances are made prominent. In Giorgione, with his romantic, idealizing temperament, genre pictures took this form, while he is known to have painted from Ovid and from the Italian tales of his time. He was employed frequently to paint scenes on panels, for the richly ornamented Venitian furniture. Giorgione was not without a bent to realism in his very idealism, and is said to have been the first Italian painter who "imitated the real texture of stuffs and painted draperies from the actual material."

Giorgione died at the early age of thirty-three years, in 1511. One account represents him as dying of the plague, others attribute his death to a sadder cause. He is said to have had a friend and fellow-painter who betrayed their friendship, and carried off the girl whom Giorgione loved. Stung to the quick by the double falsehood, the tradition goes on to state that Giorgione fell into despair with life and all it held, and so died.

Giorgione's historic pictures are rare, his sacred pictures rarer still; among the last is a *Finding of Moses*, now in Milan.

In portraits Giorgione has only been exceeded by Titian. In the National Gallery, London, there is an unimportant *St. Peter the Martyr*, and a finer *Maestro di Capella giving a music lesson*, which Kugler assigns to Giorgione, though it has been given elsewhere to Titian. The "refined voluptuousness and impassioned sombreness" of Giorgione's painting have instituted a comparison between him and Lord Byron as a poet.

CORREGGIO's real name was ANTONIO ALLEGRI, and he has his popular name from his birth-place of Correggio, now called Reggio; although at one time there existed an impression that Correggio meant "correct," from the painter's exceedingly clever feats of fore-shortening. His father is believed to have been a well-to-do tradesman, and the lad is said to have had an uncle a painter, who probably influenced his nephew. But Correggio had a greater master, though but for a very short time, in Andrea Mantegna, who died when Correggio was still a young boy. Mantegna's son kept on his father's school, and from him Correggio might have received more regular instruction. He early attained excellence, and in the teeth of the legends which lingered in Parma for a full century, his genius received prompt notice and patronage. He married young, and from records which have come to light, he received a considerable portion with his wife.

The year after his marriage, when he was no more than six-and-twenty, Correggio was appointed to paint in fresco the cupola of the church of San Giovanni at Parma, and chose for his subject the *Ascension of Christ;* for this work and that of the *Coronation of the Virgin*, painted over the high altar, Correggio got five hundred gold crowns, equivalent to $7,500. He was invited to Mantua, where he painted from the mythology for the Duke of Mantua. Indeed, so far and wide had the preference for mythological subjects penetrated, that one of Correggio's earliest works was *Diana returning from the Chase;* painted for the decoration of the parlour of the Abbess of the convent of San Paulo, Parma.

Correggio was a second time called upon to paint a great religious work in Parma—this time in the cathedral, for which he selected *The Assumption of the Virgin*. A few of the cartoons for these frescoes were discovered thirty or forty years ago, rolled up and lying forgotten in a garret in Parma; they are now in the British Museum.

In 1533, Correggio, then residing in his native town, was one of the witnesses to the marriage of his sovereign, the Lord of Correggio. In the following year the painter had engaged to paint an altar-piece for an employer, who paid Correggio in advance twenty-five gold crowns, but the latter dying very soon afterwards, in the forty-first year of his age, 1534, his father, who was still alive, was in circumstances to repay the advance on the picture, which had not been painted.

Correggio is said to have been modest and retiring in disposition, and this, together with the fact that, like Giorgione, he did not have a school, has been suggested as the source of the traditions which prevailed so long in Italy. These traditions described the painter as a man born in indigent circumstances, living obscurely in spite of his genius (there is a picture of Correggio's in England, which was said to have been given in payment for his entertainment at an inn), and leading to the end a life of such ill-requited labour, that having been paid for his last picture in copper money, and being under the necessity of carrying it home in order to relieve the destitution of his family, he broke down under the burden, and overcome by heat and weariness, drank a rash draught of water, which caused fever and death.

The story, disproven as it is, is often alluded to still, and remains as a foil to those flattering and courtly anecdotes which we have been repeating of royal and imperial homage paid to Dürer, Titian, and Holbein. We fancy the last-mentioned stories may have grown from small beginnings, and circulated purely in the artist world; but that the former is an utterance of the ingrained persuasion of the great world without, that art as a means of livelihood is essentially non-remunerative in the sense of money-getting.

Modest as Correggio may have been, he was not without pride in his art. After looking for the first time on the St. Cecilia of Raphael, Correggio is reported to have exclaimed with exultation, "And I too am a painter."

He left behind him on his death a son and a daughter, the former living to be a painter of no great name. In the picture of Correggio in the attitude of painting, painted by himself, we see a handsome spare man with something of a romantic cavalier air, engaged in his chosen art.

In the National Gallery, London, there are fine specimens of Correggio. There is an *Ecce Homo:* Christ crowned with thorns, holding out his bound hands, with a Roman soldier softening into pity, Pilate hardening in indifference, and the Virgin fainting with sorrow. There is also *The Virgin with the Basket*, so named from the little basket in front of the picture; and *A Holy Family;* and there is a highly-esteemed picture from a mythological subject, *Mercury teaching Cupid to read in the presence of Venus.*

We must return to the Venice of Titian, and see how his successors, with much more of the true painter in them than the fast degenerating scholars of other Italian schools, were mere men, if great men, matched with Titian.

TINTORETTO is only Tintoretto or Tintoret because his father was a dyer, and "Il Tintoretto" is in Italian, "the little dyer." Tintoretto's real name was one more in keeping with his pretensions, Jacopo Robusti. He was born in Venice, in 1512, and early foreshadowed his future career by drawing all kinds of objects on the walls of his father's dye-house, an exercise which did not offend or dismay the elder Robusti, but, on the contrary, induced him to put the boy into the school of Titian, where Tintoretto only remained a short time. Titian did not choose to impart what could be imparted of his art to his scholars, and, in all probability, Tintoretto was no deferential and submissive scholar. There is a tradition that Titian expelled this scholar from his academy, saying of the dyer's son, that "he would never be anything but a dauber."

Tintoret was not to be daunted. He lived to be a bold-tempered, dashing man, and he must have been defiant, even in his boyhood, as he was swaggering in his youth, when he set up an academy of his own, and inscribed above the door, "The drawing of Michael Angelo and the colouring of Titian." He had studied and taught himself from casts and theories since he left the school of Titian, and then, with worldly wisdom equal to his daring, he commenced his artistic career by accepting every commission, good or bad, and taking what pay he could get for his work; but, unfortunately for him and for the world, he executed his work, as might have been expected, in the same headlong, indiscriminate spirit, acquiring the name of "Il Furioso" from the rapidity and recklessness of his manner of painting. Often he did not even give himself the trouble of making any sketch or design of his pictures beforehand, but composed as he painted.

Self-confident to presumption, he took for his inspirations the merest impulses, and grievously marred the effect of his unquestionably grand genius by gross haste and carelessness. He was a successful man in his day, as so energetic and unscrupulous a man was likely enough to be, and his fellow-citizens, who saw principally on the surface,* were charmed beyond measure by his tremendous capacity for invention, his dramatic vigour, his gorgeous, rampant richness and glare; or, by contrast, his dead dullness of ornament and colouring; and were not too greatly offended by his untruthfulness in drawing and colouring, and the notable inequality of his careless, slovenly, powerful achievements. Yet even Tintoret's fascinated contemporaries said of him, that he "used three pencils: one gold, one silver, one lead."

Naturally Tintoretto painted an immense number of pictures, to only three of which, however, he appended his name. These were, *The Crucifixion*, and *The Miracle of the Slave*, two of fifty-seven pictures which he painted for the school of St. Roch alone, in Venice; and the other was the *Marriage at Cana*, in the church of Santa Maria della Saluto, Venice.

There is an authentic story told of Tintoretto in his age, which is in touching contrast to what is otherwise known of the man. Besides a son, Dominico, who was a painter, Tintoret had a daughter, Marietta, very dear to him, who was also a painter—indeed, so gifted a portrait painter, as to have been repeatedly invited to foreign courts to practise her art, invitations which she declined, because she would not be parted from her father. To Tintoret's great grief, this daughter died as she was thirty years of age, and her father was in his seventy-eighth year. When her end was unmistakably near, the old man took brush and canvas and struggled desperately to preserve a last impression of the beloved child's face, over which death was casting its shadow.

* It is due to Tintoret to say, that there are modern critics, who look below the surface, and are at this date deeply enamoured of his pictures.

Tintoretto died four years later, in 1594. His portrait is that of a man who holds his head high and resolutely; he has, strange to say, a somewhat commonplace face, with its massive nose, full eye, short curly beard and hair. The forehead is not very broad, but the head is "long," as Scotch people say, and they count long-headedness not only an indication of self-esteem, but of practical shrewdness. Tintoret's power was native, and had received little training; it is a proof of the strength of that power that he could not quench it.

PAUL CAGLIARI of Verona is better known as Paul Veronese. He was born in Verona in 1530, and was the son of a sculptor. He was taught by his father to draw and model, but abandoned sculpture for the sister art of painting, which was more akin to his tastes, and which he followed in the studio of an uncle who was a fair painter.

Quitting Verona, Paul Veronese repaired to Venice, studying the works of Titian and Tintoret, and settling in their city, finding no want of patronage even in a field so fully appropriated before he came to take his place there. His first great work was the painting of the church of St. Sebastian, with scenes from the history of Esther. Whether he chose the subject or whether it was assigned to him, it belonged even more to him than to Tintoret, for Veronese was the most magnificent of the magnificent Venitian painters. From that date he was kept in constant employment by the wealthy and luxurious Venitians. He visited Rome in the suite of the Venitian ambassador in 1563, when he was in his thirty-fourth year, and he was invited to Spain to assist in the decoration of the Escurial by Philip II., but refused the invitation.

Veronese is said to have been a man of kindly spirit, generous and devout. In painting for churches and convents, he would consent to receive the smallest remuneration, sometimes not more than the price of his colours and canvas. For his fine picture now in the Louvre, the *Marriage of Cana*, he is believed not to have had more than $200 in our money. He died when he was but fifty-eight years of age, in 1588. He had married and left sons who were painters, and worked with their father. He had a brother, Benedotto, who was also a painter, and who is thought to have painted many of the architectural backgrounds to Veronese's pictures.

Veronese's portrait, which he has left us, gives the idea of a more earnest and impressionable man than Tintoret. A man in middle age, bald-headed, with a furrowed brow, cheeks a little hollowed, head slightly thrown back, and a somewhat anxious as well as intent expression of face; what of the dress is seen, being a plain doublet with turned-over collar, and a cloak arranged in a fold across the breast, and hanging over the right shoulder like a shepherd's "maud" or plaid. Looking at the painting, and hearing of Paul Veronese's amiability and piety, one has little difficulty in thinking of the magnificent painter, as a single-hearted, simple-minded man, neither vain nor boastful, nor masterful save by the gift of genius.

CHAPTER IX.

CARRACCI—GUIDO RENI—DOMENICHINO—SALVATOR ROSA.

IN the falling away of the schools of Italy, and especially of the followers of Michael Angelo and Raphael, into mannerism and exaggeration, fitly expressed in delineation of heathen gods and goddesses, there arose a cluster of painters in the North of Italy who had considerable influence on art.

THE CARRACCI included a group of painters, the founders of the later Bolognese School. Lodovico, the elder of the three, was born at Bologna, 1555. He was educated as a painter, and was so slow in his education, that he received from his fellow-scholars the nickname of "Il Bue" (the ox). But his perseverance surmounted every obstacle. He visited the different Italian towns, and studied the works of art which they contained, arriving at the conclusion that he might acquire and combine the excellences of each. This combination, which could only be a splendid patch-work without unity, was the great aim of his life, and was the origin of the term *eclectic* applied to his school. Its whole tendency was to technical excellence, and in this tendency, however it might achieve its end, painting showed a marked decline. As an example of the motives and objects supplied by the school, we must borrow some lines from a sonnet of the period written by Agostino Carracci:

> "Let him, who a good painter would be,
> Acquire the drawing of Rome,
> Venitian action, and Venitian shadow,
> And the dignified colouring of Lombardy;
> The terrible manner of Michael Angelo,
> Titian's truth and nature,
> The sovereign purity of Correggio's style,
> And the true symmetry of Raphael;
> . . . . . .
> And a little of Parmegiano's grace,
> But without so much study and toil,
> Let him only apply himself to imitate the works,
> Which our Nicolieno has left us here."

Lodovico opened a school of painting at Bologna, in which he was for a time largely assisted by his cousins. He died 1619.

AGOSTINO CARRACCI, cousin of Lodovico, was born at Bologna in 1559. His father was a tailor, and Agostino himself began life as a jeweller. He became a painter and an engraver in turn, devoting himself chiefly to engraving. Towards the beginning of the seventeenth century he was with his more famous brother, Annibale, at Rome, where he assisted in painting the Farnese Gallery, designing and executing the two frescoes of Galatea and Aurora with such success, according to his contemporaries, that it was popularly said that "the engraver had surpassed the painter in the Farnese." Jealousy arose between the brothers in consequence, and they separated, not before Annibale had perpetrated upon Agostino a small, but malicious, practical joke, which has been handed down to us. Agostino was fond of the society of people of rank, and Annibale, aware of his brother's weakness, took the opportunity, when Agostino was surrounded by some of his aristocratic friends, to present him with a caricature of the two brothers' father and mother, engaged in their tailoring work.

Agostino died at Parma when he was a little over forty, and was buried in the cathedral there, in 1602.

ANNIBALE, Agostino's younger brother, was born in 1560. It was intended by his parents that he should follow their trade and be a tailor, but he was persuaded by his cousin Lodovico to become a painter. After visiting Parma, Venice, and Bologna, he worked with his cousin and teacher for ten years. Annibale was invited to Rome by the Cardinal Odoardo Farnese, to decorate the great hall of his palace in the Piazza Farnese, with scenes from the heathen mythology, for which work he received a monthly salary of ten scudi, about $20, with maintenance for himself and two servants, and a farther gift of five hundred scudi. It was a parsimonious payment, and the parsimony is said to have preyed on the mind and affected the health of Annibale, and a visit to Naples, where he, in common with not a few artists, suffered from the jealous persecutions of the Neapolitan painters, completed the breaking up of his constitution. He painted, with the assistance of Albani, the frescoes in the chapel of San Diego in San Giacomo degli Spagnole, and pressed upon his assistant more than half of his pay. Annibale's health had already given way, and after a long illness he died, when forty-nine years of age, at Rome, 1609, and was buried near Raphael in the Pantheon.

The merit of the Carracci lay in their power of execution, and in a certain "bold naturalism, or rather animalism," which they added to their able imitations, for their pictures are not so much their own, as *After Titian, After Correggio*, &c. In this intent regard to style, and this perfecting of means to an end, thought and its expression were in a manner neglected. Yet to the Carracci, and their school, is owing a certain studied air of solemnity and sadness in *Ecce Homos*, and *Pietas*, which, in proportion to its art, has a powerful effect on many beholders, who prefer conventionality to freedom; or rather, who fail to distinguish conventionality in its traces. Annibale was the most original while the least learned of the Carracci; yet, even of Annibale, it could be said that he lacked enthusiasm in his subjects. His best productions are his mythological subjects in the Farnese Palace. A celebrated picture of his, that of the *Three Marys* (a dead Christ, the Madonna, and the two other Marys), has been exhibited at the Manchester Academy for Exhibition of Fine Art, where it attracted the greatest attention and admiration. We believe this was not only because Annibale Carracci in the *Three Marys* does attain to a most piteous mournfulness of sentiment, but because such work as that of the Carracci finds readiest acceptance from a general public, which delights in striking, superficial effects. The same reason, in conjunction with the decline of Italian art, may account for the great number of the Carracci school and followers.

Annibale Carracci was one of the first who practised landscape painting and genre pictures, such as *The Greedy Eater*, as separate branches of art. Two of Annibale's landscapes are in the National Gallery, London.

GUIDO RENI, commonly called "Guido," was born at Bologna, 1575. His father was a musician, and Guido was intended for the same calling, but finally became a painter and student in the school of the Carracci. He followed Annibale Carracci to Rome, and dwelt there for twenty years. He obtained great repute and favour, but taking offence at some supposed injustice, he left Rome, and settled at last in Bologna, where he established a large school. Though he made great sums of money, which might have enabled him to live in the splendour which he coveted, on account of his addiction to gambling and his grossly extravagant habits, he was constantly in debt, and driven to tax his genius to the utmost, and to sell its fruits for what they would bring, irrespective of what he owed to himself, his art, and to the giver of all good gifts. He died at Bologna, and was buried with much pomp in the church of San Dominico, 1642.

Of Guido we hear that he had three styles: the first, after the vigorous manner of Michael Angelo; the second, in the prevailing ornamental taste of the Rome of his day and the Carracci. This is considered Guido's best style, and is distinguished by its subtle management of light and shade. His third, which is called his "silvery style," from its greys, degenerated into insipidity, with little wonder, seeing that at this stage he sold his time at so much per hour to picture dealers, who stood over him, watch in hand, to see that he fulfilled his bargain, and carried away the saints he manufactured wet from the easel. Such manufactory took him only three hours, sometimes less. His charges had risen from $25 for a head, and $100 for a whole figure, to twenty times that amount. He painted few portraits, but many "fancy" heads of saints. Nearly three hundred pictures by Guido are believed to be in existence. Guido's individual distinction was his refined sense of beauty, but it was over-ruled by "cold calculation," and developed into a mere abstract conception of "empty grace" without heart or soul.

His finest work is the large painting of "Phœbus and Aurora" in the pavilion of the Rospigliosi Palace at Rome. In the English National Gallery there are nine specimens of Guido's works, including one of his best "Ecce Homos," which belonged to the collection of Samuel Rogers, the poet.

DOMENICO ZAMPIERI, commonly called Domenichino, was another Bolognese painter, and another eminent scholar of the Carracci. He was born in 1581, and, after studying under a Flemish painter, passed into the school of the Carracci. While yet a very young man, Domenichino was invited to Rome, where he soon earned a high reputation, competing successfully with his former fellow-scholar, Guido. Domenichino's "Flagellation of St. Andrew," and "Communion of St. Jerome," in payment of which he only received about $25; "Martyrdom of St. Sebastian," and his "Four Evangelists," which are among his masterpieces, were all painted in Rome, and remain in Rome.

Domenichino is said to have excited the extreme hostility of rival painters, and to have suffered especially from the malice of the Neapolitans, when he was invited to work among them. After a cruel struggle Domenichino died in Naples, not without a horrible suspicion of having been poisoned, at the age of sixty, in 1641. One of his enemies—a Roman on this occasion—destroyed what was left of Domenichino's work in Naples.

The painter's fate was a miserable one, and by a coincidence between his fortune and his taste in subjects, he has identified his name with terrible representations of martyrdoms. Kugler writes that martyrdom as a subject for painting, which had been sparingly used by Raphael and his scholars, had come into fashion in Domenichino's time, for "painters and poets sought for passionate emotion, and these subjects (martyrdoms) supplied them with plentiful food." Sensationalism is the florid hectic of art's decay, whether in painting or in literature.

Domenichino is accredited with more taste than fancy. He made free use of the compositions of even contemporary artists, while he individualized these compositions. His good and bad qualities are those of his school, already quoted, and perhaps it is in keeping with these qualities that the excellence of Domenichino's works lies in subordinate parts and subordinate characters.

Opposed to the Carracci school, whose triumphs and failures were essentially his own, SALVATOR ROSA, born in 1615 near Naples, was the son of an architect. In opposition to his father Salvator Rosa became a painter. Having succeeded in selling his sketches to a celebrated buyer, the bold young Neapolitan started for Rome at the age of twenty years; and Rome, "the Jerusalem of Painters," became thenceforth Salvator Rosa's headquarters, though the character of the man was such as to force him to change his quarters not once or twice only in his life, and thus he stayed some time, in turn, at Naples, Viterbo, Volterra, and Florence. At Volterra the aggressive nature of the painter broke forth in a series of written satires on a medley of subjects—music, poetry (both of which Salvator himself cultivated), painting, war, Babylon, and envy. These incongruous satires excited the violent indignation of the individuals against whom Salvator's wit was aimed, and their efforts at revenge, together with his own turbulent spirit, drove him from place to place.

Salvator Rosa was at Naples 1647, and took part in the riots, so famous in song and story, which made Masaniello, the young fisherman, for a time Captain-General and Master of Naples, when it was, according to law, a Spanish dependency governed by a viceroy. Salvator was in the Compagnia della Morte commanded by Falcone, a battle painter, during the troubles, a wild enough post to please the wild painter,

even had he not been in addition a personal adherent of the ruling spirit Masaniello, whom Salvator Rosa painted more than once. After so eventful a life, the painter died peaceably enough in his fifty-ninth year, of dropsy, at Rome, and left a considerable fortune to his only son.

Salvator Rosa was the incarnation of the arrogant, fickle, fierce Neapolitan spirit, and he carried it out sufficiently in an undisciplined, stormy life, without the addition of the popular legend that he had at one time joined a troop of banditti, and indulged in their excesses. The legend seems to have arisen from Salvator Rosa's familiarity with mountain passes, and his love of peopling them appropriately with banditti in action. Salvator Rosa was a dashing battle painter, a mediocre historical painter, and an excellent portrait painter as well as landscape painter. But it is chiefly by the savage grandeur of his mountain or forest landscapes, with their fitting *dramatis personæ*, that he has won his renown. Mr. Ruskin, while he allows Salvator's gift of imagination, denounces him for the reckless carelessness and untruthfulness to nature of his painting. Many of Salvator Rosa's pictures are in the Pitti Palace in Florence, in England and France, and a few have found a home in the States.

MICHEL ANGELO AMERIGHI or MERIGHI—commonly known as MICHELANGELO DA CARAVAGGIO, from his birthplace in the Milanese—was born in 1569. The son of a mason, he was employed, when quite a boy, in grinding the colours of several painters of Milan, and thus acquired an early taste for art. With no other teacher but nature, he laboured attentively at his new work, confining himself at first to painting portraits and flower-pieces. After five years of steady application in Milan, Caravaggio removed to Venice, where he studied the works of Giorgione. Thence he went to Rome, in which city, finding himself, through poverty, unable to gain a livelihood as an independent painter, he engaged himself to Cesare d'Arpino, who employed him to execute the floral and ornamental parts of his pictures. Caravaggio, however, was soon enabled to paint for himself, but after executing many important works, he was obliged to leave the city on account of the death of a friend, whom he had killed in a fit of anger; he repaired to Naples, whence he went to Malta, where he was patronized by the grand-master Vignacourt, whose portrait he twice painted. Once more, through his hot and fiery temper, Caravaggio was driven from the town of his choice. He quarrelled with a knight, who threw him into prison. Caravaggio, however, escaped from captivity and fled to Syracuse, whence he went to Naples by way of Messina and Palermo. Having obtained, through the influence of his friends, the Pope's pardon for the manslaughter of his companion—Caravaggio set sail from Naples for Rome, but he was taken prisoner on the way by some Spaniards, in mistake for another man. On being set at liberty, he had the misfortune to find that the boatmen had gone off with the felucca and his property. He continued his way as far as Porto Ercole, where partly from his loss and partly from the heat of the weather, he was taken ill shortly afterwards, and died in 1609.

In the Vatican at Rome is the *Descent from the Cross*, by Caravaggio, which is usually considered his masterpiece, and in which there is seen, if not the absence of his usual defects, at least a union of his most eminent qualities. The heads are all ignoble; never did he carry further the worship of the real and the repulsive. As to the men who are taking the body of our Lord down from the cross, their vulgar coarseness might have formed a contrast to the noble beauty of Jesus and Mary. But the Saviour himself and His Virgin Mother are no better treated; it might almost be said that Caravaggio was of the school of those Christian painters of the fourth century who followed the tradition of St. Cyril and some others among the early fathers, that our blessed Lord was the least beautiful among the sons of men.

The same may be said of one of his choicest works, now in the Louvre, the *Death of the Virgin*, which he painted for a church in Rome, was called Della Scala in Trastevere. We notice in it, at the first glance, the absence of all religious feeling, and even of worldly nobility; and still more the absence of traditional characters common to all sacred subjects. Who is it lying on that couch, breathing her last sigh? Is it the mother of Christ in the midst of His Apostles, or is it not rather an old gipsy among a number of the men of her tribe, dressed in ridiculous finery? It is the same with the *Judith* at Naples, which may yet be considered one of his most vigorous and energetic works. How can we recognize the timid and virtuous widow, who to save her people resolves to commit a double crime, in that infuriated Roman who is cutting the throat of Holofernes as a butcher slaughters a sheep?

Caravaggio, indeed, when he is on his own ground, is an eminent artist. He appears thus at the Louvre, in his *Fortune-teller*, and in the excellent *Portrait of Vignacourt*, Grand-master of Malta, in his armour; he is also seen to be a great artist at Rome in the picture of the *Gamesters*,* in which a young gentleman is seen robbed by two swindlers; and at Vienna in the Lichtenstein Gallery, in the *Portrait of a young girl* playing on the lute. This is an extraordinary work, for, laying aside his habitual exaggeration, his inclination to the ugly and strange, the master here shines in truth, grace, nobility, and beauty. The National Gallery has but one work by Caravaggio, a *Christ with the two disciples at Emmaus*, formerly in the Borghese Gallery at Rome; it was painted for Cardinal Scipione Borghese.

Caravaggio was a mason, who became a painter by seeing frescoes executed on the moist plaster he had laid on the walls; he was a painter who remained a mason, rough, unlettered, professing to despise antiquity, and scoffing at Raphael and Correggio; wishing for no other model than nature, he studied commonplace and low nature; yet in his fiery execution he attained a degree of energy, power, and truth, the only defects of which are probably their own excesses.

GIOVANNI FRANCESCO BARBIERI DI CENTO—surnamed GUERCINO or GUERCIO (the Squinter) because, while still in the cradle, a great fright caused a nervous convulsion which deranged the ball of one eye—was born at Cento, near Bologna, in 1592. As an artist, he was, in a great measure, self-taught. He was a disciple of the Carracci, not exactly from having received lessons from them, but from having learnt art, and made for himself a style by imitating their works. After studying at Venice and Bologna, Guercino went during the pontificate of Paul V. to Rome, where he stayed until 1623, when he returned to his native Cento, in which town he executed several works of importance. In 1642 he removed to Bologna, where he remained till his death in 1666. In the works of Guercino we can admire neither the sublimity of the

* See Illustration.

thought, nor the nobility of the forms: these qualities are not to be looked for in the son of a poor ox-driver; but we cannot but admire the exact and skilful imitation of nature which he attained at once by correctness in drawing, harmony in colour, and the wonderful use he made of chiaroscuro. It is to the latter quality that he owes his too ambitious surname of the "magician of painting." He has been charged with giving his shadows a degree of exaggerated force, as did Caravaggio and Ribera; but in those dark shades no one could have put more transparency and lightness than Guercino.

One of the greatest works of Guercino is in the gallery at Stafford House, London. This is the *Apotheosis* or canonization of a beatified pope, either St. Leo or St. Sixtus. Another, which is no less vast in composition and grand in its style, is the *St. Petronilla* in the Capitol at Rome; it does honour alike to the museum and to the artist. This work, which is of singular beauty, is divided, like so many other pictures, into two parts, heaven and earth. Quite at the bottom, grave-diggers are opening a sepulchre in order to take out the body of the daughter of the apostle Peter, who was thrown into it alive as a forsworn vestal. This exhumation takes place in the presence of several persons, amongst others, of the betrothed of Petronilla, a young man, dressed in the fashion of the sixteenth century, who does not seem very deeply affected at seeing the corpse of his beloved appear above the edge of the grave. As for the saint herself, free forever from the passions of the lower world, radiant with glory, and with her head encircled by a crown, she ascends on the clouds towards heaven, where the Eternal Father awaits her with outstretched arms.

CARLO DOLCI, sometimes called CARLINO, was born at Florence in 1616. He lost his father when but four years of age, and five years later was placed by his mother with one Jacopo Vignali, a pupil of Matteo Rosselli. He passed nearly all his life in his native town, where he was much patronized, and where he soon became famous. In 1670, he went to Innspruck to paint the portrait of Claudia, daughter of Ferdinand of Austria; but returning to Florence he died there in 1686. Dolci left one son and seven daughters, one of whom, Agnese, painted in the same style as her father, though not with equal success. Though Dolci's pictures are not uncommon in the European galleries, neither the Louvre nor the National Gallery possesses one. There are several, however, in private collections in England. A *Christ breaking bread* is in the possession of the Marquis of Exeter at Burleigh. The Earl of Ashburnham has a fine *St. Andrew*. Among Dolci's best pictures we may mention, a *Madonna and Child* and a *St. Andrew praying before the Cross*, both in the Pitti Palace; and a *St. Cecilia* in the Dresden Gallery. Dolci was a most prolific and at the same time a careful painter, but his renown has surpassed his merit. One might almost suppose that Vasari was thinking of him when he said of an earlier painter (Lorenzo da Credi), "His productions are so finished, that beside them those of other painters appear coarse sketches. . . . This excessive care is no more worthy of praise than is excessive negligence; in everything we should keep from extremes, which are equally vicious." This reflection serves to judge the works of Carlo Dolci on the material side. If we examine them from a moral point of view, we find their principal characteristic to be a feeble, insipid affectation of religious feeling. He does not attain to the mystic devotion of the art of Fra Angelico and Morales, but stops short at narrow devoteeism. The last of the Florentines in age, he was so also in style and taste. With him expired the great school which had been rendered celebrated by Giotto, Masaccio, Leonardo da Vinci, Michelangelo, Fra Bartolommeo, and Andrea del Sarto. If the painters of the periods of decay should never, any more than the poets, be chosen as models for study, they are yet of real use when placed near the works of classic masters, because they serve as examples of the most dangerous of all faults, those which are agreeable or fashionable, in contrast with severe, solid, and eternal beauties. The taste becomes formed by discriminating between these, and talent learns to shun the defects of the one whilst imitating the beauties of the other. Hence the works of Carlo Dolci have a use, even by the side of those of Michelangelo and Raphael.

THE WRECK OF THE MINOTAUR.
(From the original painting by J. M. W. Turner.)

CHAPTER X.

RUBENS—REMBRANDT—TENIERS, FATHER AND SON—WOUVVERMAN—CUYP—PAUL POTTER —CORNELIUS DE HEIM, &c.

LONG interval elapsed between the Van Eycks and Quintin Matsys, and Rubens; but if Flemish art was slow of growth and was only developed after long pauses, it made up for its slowness and delays by the burst of triumph into which Flemish and Dutch art broke forth in Rubens and his school, in Rembrandt and Cuyp and Ruysdael.

PETER PAUL RUBENS was born at Siegen in Westphalia, on the day of St. Peter and St. Paul, 1577. But though Rubens was born out of Antwerp, he was a citizen of Antwerp by descent as well as by so many later associations. His father, John Rubens, a lawyer, an imprudent, thriftless man in character and habits, had been compelled to leave Antwerp in consequence of religious disturbances which broke out there about the time that the northern provinces, more at one and more decided in their union than the southern provinces, established their independence. Rubens spent his early boyhood at Cologne, but on the death of his father when he was ten years of age, his mother, a good and "discreet" woman, to whom the painter owed much, and confessed his debt, returned with her family to Antwerp. His mother had destined him for his father's profession, but did not oppose her son's preference for art.

After studying under two different artists, and becoming a master in the guild of St. Luke, Rubens went to Italy in 1600, when he was a young man of three-and-twenty years of age. He was eight years absent, entering the service of the ducal sovereign of Mantua, being sent by him on a diplomatic mission to Madrid to Philip III. of Spain, visiting on his own account Rome, where he found the Carracci and Guido, at the height of their fame, Venice and Genoa, "leaving portraits where he went."

With Genoa, its architecture, and its situation, Rubens was specially charmed, but he quitted it in haste, being summoned home to attend the death-bed of his mother, from whom he had parted eight years before; and arriving too late to see her in life. A man of strong feelings in sorrow as in joy, he withdrew into retirement, and resided for his season of mourning in a religious house.

Loving Italy with a painter's enthusiasm, so that to the latest day of his life he generally wrote in Italian, and loved to sign his name "Pietro Paolo Rubens," he had intended to return and settle in Mantua, but having been named court painter to the Governess of the Netherlands, Clara Eugenia, and her husband Albert, Rubens had sufficient patriotism and sufficient worldly foresight to induce him to relinquish his idea, and establish himself in his native Antwerp. He was already a man of eminence in his profession, and a man of mark out of it. Go where he would he made friends, and he so recommended himself to his royal patrons by his natural suavity, tact, and sagacity, that he was not only in the utmost favour with them as a right courtly painter, but was employed by them, once and again, on delicate, difficult private embassies. But it was not only to his patrons that Rubens was endeared; he was emphatically what men call "a good fellow," alike to superiors, equals, and inferiors; a frank, honest, bountiful, and generous man. His love of courts and their splendour was the chivalrous homage which a man of his cast of mind paid to the dignity and picturesqueness of high estate.

He married a year after his mother's death, when he was in his thirty-third year. His first wife, Isabella Brant, was a connection of his own (and so was his second wife). He built and painted, in fresco, a fine house in Antwerp, and laid out a pleasant garden, which contained a rotunda, filled with his collection of pictures by the Italian masters, antique gems, &c., &c., already gathered abroad. He set himself to keep house in a liberal fashion, to dispense benefits, and to entertain friends—above all, to paint with might and main in company with his great school, the members of which, like those of Raphael's school where Raphael was concerned, were, for the most part, Rubens' devoted comrades. Counting his work not only as the great object, but the great zest of his life, never did painter receive such sweeping and accumulating commissions, and never, even by Tintoret, were commissions executed with such undaunted, unhesitating expedition.

Withal Rubens frequently left his studio and went abroad, either to act as an unofficial ambassador, or to paint at the special request of some foreign sovereign. Thus he was residing in Paris in 1620, planning for Marie de Medici the series of remarkable pictures which commemorated her marriage with Henry IV. When we were young, we went occasionally to a country house, the show place of the neighbourhood, where there were copies of this series of Rubens' pictures. (We can remember yet looking at them with utter bewilderment, caused by the dubious taste that impelled Rubens to indulge in the oddest mixture of royal personages, high church dignitaries, patron saints, and gods and goddesses.) In 1628 Rubens was in Spain on a mission from his sovereign to her kinsman, Philip IV.; in the following year he was in England, on a service of a similar description to Charles I., from whom, even as Rubens had already received it from King Philip, the painter had the honour of knighthood.

In the meantime Rubens' first wife died, after a union of seventeen years, in

1626; and four years later, in 1630, the painter, when he was a man of fifty years, remarried another connection of his own, Helena Fourment, a girl only in her sixteenth year. Both of his wives were handsome, fair, full-formed Flemish beauties. Elizabeth (in Spanish, Isabella) Brant's beauty was of a finer order than that of her successor, expressing larger capacity of affection and intellect. But on Helena Fourment Rubens doted, while to both women he seems to have been affectionately attached. He has painted them so often, that the face of no painter's wife is so familiar to the art world, and even to the greater world without, as are the faces of these two women, and above all, that of Helena Fourment. He had seven children, who frequently figure in their mothers' portraits. He has left notable portraits of his two sons by his first wife, of his eldest daughter, Clara Eugenia, when eight years of age, and of his daughter Elizabeth, a buxom baby, dressed in velvet and point lace, playing with toys.

After a life of unbroken success and the highest honours, the last distinction conferred on Rubens was, that he was chosen to arrange the gala, and to be the right-hand man who should conduct the Cardinal Infant, the successor of Clara Eugenia, on his first entrance into Antwerp. But the hand of premature disease and death, which not even he could resist, was already on the great painter; his constitution had been undermined by repeated attacks of gout, and he died at the age of sixty years, in 1640. He was the possessor of great wealth at the time of his death, and only a part of his collection, which was then sold, brought so large a sum in those days, as $100,000. Rubens' second wife, Helena Fourment, to whom he had been married ten years, survived him, a widow at twenty-six years of age, and married again.

Rubens' portrait is even better known than those of his wives, for, as we have said of Raphael in his popularity, Rubens in his life is the beau-ideal of a painter to the many. The portrait is worthy of the man, with something gallant in the manliness, and with thought tempering what might have been too much of bravado and too much of débonnaireté in the traits. His features are handsome in their Flemish fulness, and match well with hazel eyes, chestnut hair, and a ruddy complexion; his long moustache is turned up, and he wears the pointed beard which we see so often in the portraits by Rubens' scholar, Van Dyck. The great flapping hat, worn alike by men and women, slightly cocked to one side, is the perfection of picturesque head gear. Equally picturesque, and not in the slightest degree effeminate on a man like Rubens, is the falling collar of pointed mechlin, just seen above the cloak draped in large folds.

In his own day Rubens was without a rival as a painter. In a much later day Sir Joshua Reynolds pronounced Rubens "perhaps the greatest master in the mechanical part of the art, *the best workman with his tools* that ever exercised a pencil." His consummate excellence lay in his execution and colouring. It is brought as a reproach against his painting, that his noblest characters, even his sacred characters, were but big, brawny, red and white Flemings. His imagination only reached a certain height, and yet, if it were a very earthly Flemish imagination, it could be grandly, as it was always vigorously, earthly and Flemish. At the same time he could be deficient where proportion, and even where all the laws of art, are concerned.

Rubens' works are very many, nearly four thousand pictures and sketches being attributed to him and his scholars. Many are still at Antwerp, many at Madrid, but most are at Munich, where, in one great saloon and cabinet, there are ninety-five pictures by Rubens. In England, at Blenheim, there are fifteen pictures by Rubens, as the great Duchess of Marlborough would give any price for his works. We can only indicate a very few examples in the different branches of art which he made his own.

First, of his *Descent from the Cross*:* it is a single large group, distinguished by luminous colouring and correct drawing, and with regard to which the mass of white sheet against which the body of Christ is in relief in the picture, has been regarded as a bold artistic venture. An enthusiastic admirer has called it "a most wonderful monument of the daring genius of the painter. The grandest picture in the world for composition, drawing, and colouring." Its defects are held to be "the bustle of the incidents and the dreadfully true delineation of merely physical agony—too terrible, real, picturesque, but not sublime—an earthly tragedy, not a divine mystery."

> "Remit the anguish of that lighted stare;
> Close those wan lips! let that thorn-wounded brow
> Stream not with blood."

There is a tradition that an accident happened to the picture while Rubens was painting it, and that Van Dyck remedied the accident by re-painting the cheek and chin of the Virgin and the arm of the Magdalene.

A graphic story is related of two countrymen having on a holiday visited the picture gallery in which Rubens' *Descent* hung—and while one of the countrymen passed the great painting by with the common place inspection of the multitude—the other stood spell-bound before the picture—so long that at length his companion impatiently pulled him by the sleeve saying, "come along, are you going to stand there all day?"—to which the other replied—still absorbed in the picture, "HUSH! WAIT TILL THEY GET HIM DOWN." Perhaps the greatest compliment ever paid to a painter!

With regard to another picture of Rubens at Antwerp, *The Assumption of the Virgin*, it is said that he painted it in sixteen days, for sixteen hundred florins, his usual terms being a hundred florins a day.

The Virgin and Serpent (from the 12th chapter of Revelation) in the Munich gallery is very splendid. The Virgin with the new-born Saviour in her arms is mounting on the wings of an eagle, surrounded by a flood of light. The serpent, encircling the moon on which she stands, is writhing beneath her feet. God the Father is extending his protecting sceptre over her from above. The archangel, clothed in armour, is in fearful combat with the seven-headed dragon, which is endeavouring to devour the child. Although struck by lightning, the dragon is striving to twist his tail round the legs of the angel, and seizes the cloak of the Virgin with one of his hands. Other infernal monsters are writhing with impotent rage, and falling with the dragon into the abyss."

* See Illustration.

"Nothing was more characteristic of Rubens than his choice of subjects from the mythology of the Greeks and the works of the ancient poets; and in nothing did he display more freedom, originality, and poetry." Among his most famous mythological pictures is the *Battle of the Amazons*, now at Munich. "The women are driven back by the Greeks over the river Thermodon; two horses are in savage combat on the bridge; one Amazon is torn from her horse; a second is dragged along by a sable steed, and falling headlong into the river, where others are swimming and struggling. No other battle-piece, save that of the Amazons, can compare with Raphael's *Battle of Constantine*.

Another great picture is *The Carrying off of Proserpine*. "Pluto in his car is driven by fiery brown steeds, and is bearing away the goddess, resisting and struggling. The picture absolutely glows with genial fire. The forms in it are more slender than is general with Rubens. Among the companions of Proserpine the figure of Diana is conspicuous for grace and beauty. The victorious god of love hovers before the chariot, and the blue ocean, warmly tinted with the sunbeams, forms a splendid back-ground.

Rubens was famous for the loveliness and grace of his paintings of children. Perhaps the most beautiful is that of *The Infant Jesus and John playing with a Lamb*.

Rubens was a great animal painter. One of his celebrated animal pictures is *Daniel in the Lions' Den*, now at Hamilton Palace, in which each lion is a king of beasts checked in his fiercest wrath. It is said to have been painted by Rubens in a fit of pique at a false report which had been circulated that he could not paint animals, and that those in his pictures were supplied by the animal-painter, his friend and scholar, Schneyders.

Rubens' landscapes are not the least renowned of his pictures. He gave to his own rich but prosaic Flanders, all the breadth and breeziness and matchless aërial effects of a master of painting, and a true lover of nature under every aspect, who can indeed distinguish, under the most ordinary aspect, those hidden treasures which all but a lover and a man of genius would pass by. His *Prairie of Laacken*, " with the sun of Flanders piercing the dense yellow clouds with the force of fire," is of great repute.

Among his famous portraits we shall mention that called *The Four Philosophers* (Justus Lepsius, Hugo Grotius, Rubens, and his brother), with peaked beards and moustaches, in turned-over collars, ruffs and fur-trimmed robes, having books and pens, a dog, and a classic bust as accessories. The open pillared door is wreathed with a spray from without, and there is a landscape in the background. This portrait is full of power, freedom, and splendid painting.

Another portrait contains that sweetest of Rubens' not often sweet faces, called *the Lady in the Straw Hat*. Rubens himself did not name the picture otherwise in his catalogue. Tradition says the original was Mdlle Lundens, the beauty of the seventeen provinces, and that she died young and unmarried. Connoisseurs value the picture because of the triumph of skill by which Rubens has painted brilliantly a face so much in the shade ; to those who are not connoisseurs we imagine the picture must speak for itself, in its graceful, tender beauty. Forming part of the collection of the late Sir Robert Peel (we think he gave $15,000 for *the Lady in the Straw Hat*), which has been bought for England, this beautiful portrait is now in the National Gallery, London.

And now we must speak of the pictures of the Arundel Family. But first, a word about Thomas, Earl of Arundel. Thomas, Earl of Arundel, representing in his day the great house of Howard, had a love of art which approached to a mania; and without being so outrageously vain as Sir Kenelm Digby, there is no doubt that the Earl counted on his art collection as a source of personal distinction. James I., himself an art collector, so far humoured the Earl in his taste as to present him with Lord Somerset's forfeited collection, valued at $5,000. But Charles I. and the Earl became rival collectors, and little love was lost between them. The Earl of Arundel, impairing even his great revenues in the pursuit, employed agents and ambassadors—notably Petty and Evelyn—all over Europe, to obtain for him drawings, pictures, ancient marbles, gems, &c. &c. When the civil wars broke out, Lord Arundel conveyed his priceless collection for safety to Antwerp and Padua. Eventually it was divided among his sons and scattered far and wide. The only portion of it which fell to the nation, in the course of another generation, was the Greek Marbles, known as the Arundel Marbles, which were finally presented to the University of Oxford. But in Rubens' day all this grand collection was intact, and displayed in galleries at Arundel House, which the mob thought fit to nickname "Tart Hall;" and through these galleries Rubens was conducted by the Earl.

REMBRANDT VAN RHYN is said to have been born near Leyden about 1606 or 1608, for there is a doubt as to the exact date. His father was a miller or maltster, and there is a theory that Rembrandt acquired some of his effects of light and shade from the impressions made upon him during his life in the mill. He was a pupil at the Latin school of Leyden, and a scholar in studios both at Leyden and Amsterdam.

In 1630, when Rembrandt was a mere lad, he seems to have settled in Amsterdam, and married there in 1634, when he was six or eight-and-twenty years of age, a young Dutchwoman possessed of a considerable fortune, which, in case of her death and of Rembrandt's re-marriage, was to pass to her children, a provision that in the end wrought Rembrandt's ruin. The troubles of his country in the painter's time rendered his prices comparatively small and precarious, and Rembrandt, like Rubens, without Rubens' wealth, was eager in making an art collection and surrounding himself with those very forms of beauty in the great Italian masters' works, in the appreciation of which the Dutch master—judged by his own works—might have been reckoned deficient.

Rembrandt's wife died after eight years of marriage, and left him with one surviving son, Titus, and Rembrandt, having re-married, was called upon to give up the lad's inheritance. This call, together with the expenditure of the sums which Rembrandt had lavished on his collection, was too heavy upon funds never very ample, and the painter, after struggling with his difficulties, became a bankrupt in 1656. His son took possession of Rembrandt's house, and from the sale of the painter's art collection and other resources eventually recovered his mother's fortune, but Rembrandt himself never rose above the misery, degradation, and poverty of this period. He lived thirteen years longer, but it was in obscurity—out of which the only records which reach us, are stories of miserly habits acquired too late to serve their purpose, a desperate resort to low company dating from his first wife's death, and his gradual downfall.

Rubens and Rembrandt have been sometimes contrasted as the painters of light and of darkness; the contrast extended to their lives.

It will read like a humorous anti-climax after so sad a history, when we add that no other painter painted his own likeness so often as Rembrandt painted his. In the engraving before us the face is heavy and stolid-seeming enough to be that of a typical Dutchman. The eyebrows are slightly knit over the broad nose; the full lips are scantily shaded by a moustache; there is no hair on the well-fleshed cheeks and double chin. Rembrandt wears a flat cap and ear-rings. He has two rows of a chain across his doublet, and one hand thrust beneath the cloak hanging across his breast.

Rembrandt's great merits were his strong truthfulness, and his almost equally powerful sense of a peculiar kind of picturesqueness. It seems as if the German weirdness perceptible in Albrecht Dürer had in Rembrandt taken a homelier, but a more comprehensible and effective Dutch form. Kugler argues, that the long winter, with its short dark days, of Northern Europe produces in its inhabitants instinctive delight in hearth-warmth and light, and that the pleasure in looking at Rembrandt's pictures is traceable to this influence. It is in scenes by fire-light, camp-light, torch-light, that he triumphs, and his somewhat grim but very real romance owes its origin to the endless suggestions of the deep black shadows which belong to these artificial lights. There is this objection to be urged to the theory that Rembrandt was also a good painter of his own flat Dutch landscape, painting it, however, rather under the sombre dimness of clouds and tempests than in the brightness of sunshine. But whatever its source, there is a charm so widely felt in that wonderfully perfect surrounding of uncertainty, suspicion, and alarm, with which Rembrandt has encompassed so many of his otherwise prosaic, coarse, and sometimes vulgar Dutch men and women, that we have coined a new word to express the charm, and speak of groups and incidents being *Rembrandtesque*, as we speak of their being picturesque.

Rembrandt did not always leave the vague thrill of doubt, terror, or even horror, which he sought to produce, to imagination working in the mysterious depths of his shadows. A very famous picture of his is *Dr. Deeman* (an anatomist) *demonstrating from a dead subject*. In another picture a man stealing from the gloom is in the act of stabbing in the back the unconscious man in the foreground. Rembrandt's originality is as undoubted as his ability, and he was as great in etching as in painting. His defect as a painter was the frequent absence of any evidence in his work of a sense of refinement, grace, or beauty. One of his strongest pictures, which we engrave,* is the *defiance of Adolphe de Guildre to his father*—forcible and grand! The National Gallery, London, has a few examples, including two of Rembrandt's portraits.

* See Illustration.

Passing over Van Dyck, whom we reserve, as we have reserved Holbein, to class among the foreign painters resident in or closely connected with England, we come to the TENIERS—father and son. David the elder was born at Antwerp in 1582, and David the younger also at Antwerp, in 1610. David the younger is decidedly the more eminent painter, though the works of the father are often mistaken for those of the son. The two Teniers' class of subjects was the same, being ordinarily "fairs, markets, peasants' merry-makings, beer-houses, guard-rooms."

David the younger had great popularity, was court painter to the Archduke of Austria, and earned such an independence, that he bought for himself a château at the village of Perck, not very far from the Château de Stein of Rubens, with whom David Teniers was on terms of friendly intimacy. There Teniers, like his great associate, lived in the utmost state and bounty, entertaining the noblest of the land. David Teniers married twice, his first wife being the daughter of one of a family of Flemish painters, who were known, according to their respective proclivities in art, by the names of Peasant Breughel, Velvet Breughel, and Hell Breughel. Teniers had many children.

The elder Teniers died at Antwerp in 1649; the younger died at Brussels, and was buried at Perck, in 1694.

The distinction of the Teniers was the extreme fidelity and cleverness with which they copied (but did not explain) the life they knew—the homeliest, humblest aspect of life. They brought out with marvellous accuracy all its traits, except, indeed, the underlying strain of poetry, which, while it redeems plainness, sordidness, and even coarseness, is as true to life as is its veriest prose. With those who ask a literal copy of life, whether high or low, and ask no more, the Teniers and their school must always be in the highest favour; and to those who are wearied and sceptical of blunders and failures in seeking that underlying strain of life, the mere rugged genuineness of the Teniers' work recommends itself, and is not without its own pathos; while to very many superficial observers the simple homeliness of the life which the Teniers chose to represent, prevents the observers from missing what should be present in every life. Men and women are only conscious of the defect when the painters wander, now and then, into higher spheres and into sacred subjects, and there is the unavoidable recoil from gross blindness. We have taken the Teniers as the representatives of a numerous school of Flemish and Dutch artists, whose works abound in this country. David Teniers the younger appears at his best, several times, in Dulwich Gallery and the National Gallery.

PHILIP WOUVVERMAN was born at Haarlem in 1620. He was the son of a painter, able, but unrecognized in his own day. Philip Wouvverman found few patrons, disposed of his pictures by hard bargains to dealers, was tempted by his want of success to abjure his art, and even went so far, according to tradition, as to burn his studies and sketches, in order to prevent his son pursuing the career which had been to him a career of bitter disappointment. He died at Haarlem, 1668, when he was no more than forty-eight years of age. Yet some nine hundred paintings bear (many of them falsely) Wouvverman's name.

With all the truth and excellent execution of his contemporaries and country-

men, Philip Wouvverman, who had, as he thought, missed his mark, had something which those successful men lacked—he had not only a feeling for grace, but a touch of sentiment. His scenes are commonly "road-side inns, hunts, fights;" but along with an inclination to adopt a higher class of actors—knights and ladies, instead of peasants—there is a more refined treatment and a dash of tenderness and melancholy—the last possibly born of his own disastrous fortunes. In his love of horses and dogs, as adjuncts to his groups, he had as great a fondness for a special white horse, as Paul Potter had for black and white cattle.

ALBERT CUYP was born at Dort in 1605. He was a brewer by trade, and only painted as an amateur. In spite of this, he was a great landscape painter, and has given delight to thousands by his power of expressing his own love of nature. Little is known of Cuyp's life, and the date of his death is uncertain, farther than it was later than 1638.

In affected enthusiasm, Cuyp has been called the Dutch Claude, but in reality, Cuyp surpassed Claude in some respects. The distinction which Mr. Ruskin draws between them, is that, while Claude, in the sense of beauty, is the superior to Cuyp, in the sense of truth Claude is the inferior. Besides Cuyp's landscapes, he painted portraits, and what is called "still life" (dead game, fruit or flower pieces, &c.), but Cuyp's triumph was found in his skies, with their "clearness and coolness," and in "expressions of yellow sunlight." Mr. Ruskin admits, while he is proceeding to censure Cuyp, "parts might be chosen out of the good pictures of Cuyp which have never been equalled in art."

PAUL POTTER was born at Enkhuysen, in North Holland, in 1625, and was the son of a painter. Paul Potter settled, while still very young, at the Hague as an animal painter, and died in his thirtieth year, in 1654. His career, which was thus brief, had promised to be very successful, and he had established his fame, while no more than twenty-two years of age, by painting for Prince Maurice of Nassau that which continues his most renowned, though probably not his best picture, his *Young Bull*, for some time in the Louvre, now restored to the painter's native country, and place in the Museum at the Hague. This picture is considered nearly faultless as a vigorous, if somewhat coarse, representation of animal life in the main figure; but Paul Potter's later pictures, especially his smaller pictures of pastures with cattle feeding, having fine colouring and fine treatment of light, are now regarded as equally good in their essential excellences, and of wider scope. Paul Potter etched as well as painted.

JAN DAVID DE HEIM and his son Cornelius, the father born in 1600, the son in 1630, and Maria Von Oesterwyck, their contemporary, were eminent Flemish and Dutch flower and fruit painters. The gorgeous bloom and mellow ripeness in some of the flower and fruit pictures of Flemish and Dutch painters, like those we have mentioned, are beyond description. We would have you look at them for yourselves, where they are well represented, in the Dulwich Gallery; we would have you notice, also, how as travellers declare of the splendour of tropical flowers, that they are deficient in the tender sweetness and grace of the more sober-tinted and less lavishly-blossoming English flowers; so these Flemish and Dutch full-blown flower pieces have not a trace of the sentiment which modern flower painters cannot help seeking, with good or bad result, to introduce into every tuft of primroses or of violets, if not into every cluster of grapes and bunch of cherries.

From a fact which we have already mentioned, that so many Flemish and Dutch pictures, which we may often come across, are in England, we are sorry that our space will not suffer us to give more than a few special words to other famous painters of these schools or school, for they merge into one, to Snyders, Jan Steen, Gerard Douw, Ruysdael, Hobbema, Vandevelde, &c., &c.

METZU and TERBURG were painters of Dutch life in the higher classes. Terburg's *White Satin Gown* is famous for the marvellous fidelity with which the satin in the gown of one of the figures is rendered.

FRANS SNYDERS—who, among the Flemish animal painters of the time, was second only to Rubens—was born at Antwerp in 1579. He studed art under "Hell" Breughel, and also, it is said, under Hendrik van Balen, from whom he acquired the art of flower and fruit painting. Snyders subsequently changed his subject to wild animals, in the representation of which, in their untamed and savage natures, he especially excels. He is said to have studied for some time in Italy—chiefly at Rome. Snyders was invited to Brussels by the Archduke Albert, Governor of the Netherlands, for whom he executed numerous works. A *Stag-hunt*, which was sent by the Archduke to Philip III. of Spain, so much delighted that monarch, that he commissioned the artist to paint various works, which were, until recently, in the Bueno Retiro. Snyders died at Antwerp in 1657. He often worked in conjunction with Rubens and Jordaens. He painted animals and sometimes fruit, flowers, and vegetables, to suit Rubens' pictures, and that artist in return painted figures to suit those of Snyders. Pictures painted by all three artists—Rubens, Snyders, and Jordaens—are still in existence.

Terburg's greatest picture, *The Peace of Münster*, was sold about 40 years ago to the Marquis of Hertford for $36,000. We engrave his picture *Refreshment*,* which is in the Louvre. Terburg's pictures at the present day have advanced to such prices that they seldom change owners.

JACOB RUYSDAEL, the prince of Dutch landscape painters, was born at Haarlem about 1625. He was originally intended for the study of medicine, and received an education fitting the profession, which he is supposed to have practised for a short time. But his love of art prevailed, and he abandoned the pharmacopœia in favour of the brush. His first instructor in art was his elder brother, Solomon Ruysdael. Jacob is known to have lived in Amsterdam, and is supposed to have studied under Berchem, with whom he was on intimate terms of friendship. Little further is known of Ruysdael's life. He died in poverty at Haarlem in 1681.

Jacob Ruysdael is a striking proof of the saying of Bacon: *Ars est homo additus naturæ*. To the talents of his predecessors or contemporaries he added the dreamy and melancholy poetry of his own mind, which can only be well understood by cha-

* See Steel Engraving.

racters resembling his own. If we seek in Ruysdael merely the imitation, the portrait of nature, he is equalled, and, perhaps, even surpassed, in some technical points, by Hobbema, Decker, and a few others; but it is the inner sentiment, the poetry of solitude, of silence, of mystery, which place him in the front rank alone. Albrecht Dürer made a beautiful figure of Melancholy; without being personified, it is visible in all the works of Ruysdael.

We will seek throughout Europe for the choicest of his works. In the Louvre there are but a very small number—scarcely one-half of those which may be found at Munich, Dresden, or St. Petersburg—and these are not by any means the best of his works. There is, however, a charming landscape, of very fine execution, which is called the *Coup de Soleil;* then another landscape, still more simple, whose name of *The Bush* describes the whole subject. There is also a *Storm* on the coast and near the dykes of Holland, dark and strong, admirable in the rendering of the tumultuous waves and sinister aspect of the sky; Michelet calls it the "prodigy of the Louvre."

In Holland itself we find little more than the *Waterfall*, at the entrance to a wooded ravine, on the two steep banks of which stand old castles. This magnificent work is in the Museum of Amsterdam, with a *View of Bentheim Castle*, a small finely-painted landscape, lighted by brilliant sunshine. It was painted on one of his happiest days. Rotterdam also possesses another *View of Bentheim Castle*, which he painted so many times and under such different aspects; yet always with the greatest care and finish. But alas, in the foreground of this picture, some miserable painter has introduced, on the banks of the Moselle, the Gospel incident of the disciples going to Emmaus! So that the three figures are intended for our Lord and the disciples!

In England, Ruysdael is especially to be found in private collections, for instance, Mr. Baring's, the *Troubled River*, which equals the *Storm* in the Louvre. The National Gallery has no less than twelve *Landscapes* by him—six of which were acquired with the Wynn-Ellis bequest—all worthy examples of the great master.

In Russia, fifteen pictures represent him in the Hermitage. In the figures we often recognise the hand of Adriaan van Ostade and Adriaan van de Velde, which increase their value. Some of these *Landscapes* are especially noteworthy. One is very small and very simple: a sandy plain, a winding road, a peasant followed by his dog; nothing more: but over this is a veil of sadness which touches the heart as much as the most pathetic scene. Another is equally simple, though of much larger size: a pathway through a wood, and, on the banks of a sheet of stagnant water, a large beech-tree, half despoiled of its branches by time. A third seems to include the two preceding. This is also, in a deep forest, a fallen beech-tree, with a sheet of stagnant water almost hidden by the water-lilies; two or three water birds, standing on their webbed feet, and one passing in the distance, are all that animates this solitude; but the scene is full of silence, mystery, and soft melancholy, and Ruysdael has never spoken more eloquently to thoughtful and dreamy souls.

It is in Germany however, that his greatest works are to be found. At Munich there are nine *Landscapes*, all as beautiful as can be desired. In the largest there is a

Cascade foaming down over masses of rocks. This picture is valuable as well for its great perfection as from its unusual size. At Dresden there are thirteen of his paintings. Among these, several are justly celebrated. One of them is known by the name of *Ruysdael's Chase*. It is a forest of beech-trees, broken only by some sheets of water reflecting the clouds in the sky. Under these great trees, Adriaan van de Velde has painted a stag hunt, from which the name of the picture has been taken. This is one of the largest as well as most magnificent to be found in his entire works.

ADRIAAN VAN OSTADE was born at Haarlem in 1610. He studied under Frans Hals, and formed a friendship with Adriaan Brouwer. Like the latter, he chose his subjects from low life, but he was more laborious and less dissipated, and has accordingly left us more works. After a life of industry and success, Van Ostade died in 1685 at Haarlem, where he was buried. Some accounts say that he died at Amsterdam, and that his body was removed to Haarlem for interment.

Although Van Ostade's usual subjects are similar to those treated by Teniers, he yet differs from Teniers as Rembrandt differs from Rubens. Teniers treats light in the same manner as Rubens, lavishing it everywhere; Ostade concentrates it, in the style of Rembrandt. Except in Italy, Ostade may be found in every country where art is held in honour. At Madrid there is a *Rural Concert*, formed by some choristers, accompanied by the bagpipe, the handle of a broom, and the mewing of a cat, whose ears are being pulled to make him join. At St. Petersburg there are about twenty of his pictures, amongst which is the valuable series of the *Five Senses;* at Dresden, among others, two excellent works, a *Smoking Scene* and a *Painter's Studio* in a garret (his own, perhaps); at Munich, another superior work, a *Dutch Alehouse*, with peasants fighting, and their wives endeavouring to separate and pacify them; at Rotterdam, an *Old Man in his Study;* at Amsterdam, a *Village Assembly;* and lastly, at the Hague, two wonderful pendents, which may well be called the *ne plus ultra* of this master and his branch of art, the *Interior* and *Exterior* of a rustic house. The Louvre has also a good share of the works of Adriaan van Ostade. He has left there, in the ten small portraits composing *His Family* (which might do for any Dutch family), and especially in his *Schoolmaster*, the most complete and finished models of those small familiar scenes, comedies in private life, which the wonderful skill of the artist compels us to place amongst the finest paintings. The National Gallery in England has but one picture by him—an *Alchymist*—signed "A. v. Ostade, 1661." The Dulwich Gallery possesses four of his works.

GERARD DOU, or as he is commonly called Dow, and occasionally Douw, was born at Leyden in 1613. Though this painter ought really to be placed among the immediate scholars of Rembrandt, it seems more natural to place him with other great genre-painters of this time in Holland. His father, who was a glazier, educated his son with the intention of making him a painter on glass. But his merits were found to be too great to be allowed to be used on that branch of art. He was accordingly in 1628 apprenticed at Amsterdam to Rembrandt, with whom he remained three years. Dou was at first a portrait-painter, but afterwards, adopting the anecdotal style, began by treating small subjects with great breadth before he ascended, or descended, according to the taste of the critic, to extreme and minute delicacy.

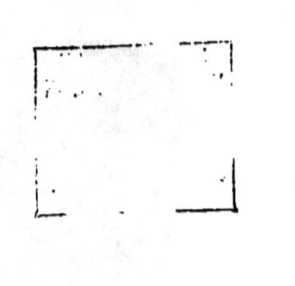

This patient and laborious artist, who made his own brushes, pounded his own colours, and prepared his own varnish, panels, or canvas, worked, in order to avoid dust, in a studio opening on to a wet ditch. Such was the popularity which Dou enjoyed at Leyden, that he received from an amateur, Spiering by name, no less than a thousand florins yearly for the refusal of his works. He died in Leyden in 1680.

JAN VAN HUYSUM was born at Amsterdam in 1682. His father, a scene painter, employed him together with his three brothers to assist him in his work. Young Jan shewed much aptitude for painting flowers, and accordingly selected that subject for his *genre*. He worked chiefly at Amsterdam, where he died in 1749.

Among the painters of flowers Van Huysum stands pre-eminent. He arranged flowers with so much taste and skill that flower-sellers might take lessons in their trade before his pictures, as well as painters in their art. The smiling *Vases of Flowers*, far preferable to the dark *Bouquets* of Baptiste Modnoyer—who was brought forward as a rival to Van Huysum in the time of Madame de Pompadour—are varied and improved by agreeable accessories, such as the vases themselves elaborately carved, the marble stands, the brilliant insects, the flowers of animal life. Two flower-pieces by Van Huysum are in the National Gallery. He is also well represented in the Dulwich Gallery, and in many private collections. His works abound on the Continent of Europe. Van Huysum occasionally painted landscapes, but with little success.

NICHOLAS CLAAS, called BERCHEM or BERGHEM, was born at Haarlem in 1624. The meaning of his nickname has been variously accounted for, but no rendering is of undisputed authority. He studied under numerous masters, his father, Pieter Claas, a painter of no note, Jan van Goyen, Jan Wils, and Weenix, but none of these left any lasting impression on Berchem. He completed in Italy the studies he had commenced in Holland, and introduced the new element of southern scenery into the subjects treated by his fellow-countrymen. Berchem died at Haarlem in 1683. A *Boaz and Ruth* is in the Museum of Amsterdam, which has other works by him, including a good *Ferry*; a *Cavalry Combat* is in the gallery of the Hague. The Louvre possesses a *View of Nice* and the *Port of Genoa*; and of his usual subjects, a *Ford* and *Cattle drinking*, *The Wayside Fountain*.* The works of Berchem are common in England, in the National Gallery, the Dulwich Gallery, and in most private collections.

* See Steel Engraving.

CHAPTER XI.

SPANISH ART—VELASQUEZ—MURILLO, &c.

PANISH art, from its dawn to the time of Velasquez, had been of a "severely devotional character," austere and formal; and although one man did not work a revolution by his independent example, he did something to humanize and widen art. In the rich city of Seville, in 1599, Diego Rodriquez de Silva y Velasquez,—and not, as he is incorrectly called, Diego Velasquez de Silva, was born, and, according to an Andalusian fashion, took his mother's name of Velasquez, while his father was of the Portuguese house de Silva. Velasquez was gently born, though his father was in no higher position than that of a lawyer in Seville.

The painter was well educated, though, according to his English biographer (Sir W. Stirling Maxwell), "he was still more diligent in drawing on his grammars and copy-books than in turning them to their legitimate use." The lad's evident bent induced his father to make him a painter. He studied in two different Spanish studios, and married the daughter of his second master, whom the talents, assiduity, and good qualities of Velasquez had already strongly attached to the young painter.

From the first, Velasquez struck out what was then a new line in Spanish art. He gave himself up to the materialistic studies, to which the Flemish and Dutch painters were prone, painting diligently "still life" in every form, taking his living subjects from the streets and way-sides, and keeping a peasant lad as an apprentice, "who served him for a study in different actions and postures (sometimes crying, sometimes laughing), till Velasquez had grappled with every variety of expression." The result of those studies was Velasquez's famous picture of the *Aguador*, or water-carrier of Seville, which was carried off by Joseph Buonaparte in his flight from Spain, taken in his carriage at Vittoria, and finally presented by Ferdinand VII. of Spain, as a grateful offering to the Duke of Wellington, in whose gallery at Apsley House the picture remains. "It is a composition of three figures," Sir W. Stirling Maxwell writes; "a sunburnt way-worn seller of water, dressed in a tattered brown jerkin, with his huge earthen jars, and two lads, one of whom receives a sparkling glass of the pure element, whilst his companion quenches his thirst from a pipkin.

The execution of the heads and all the details is perfect; and the ragged trader dispensing a few maravidi's worth of his simple stock, maintains, during the transaction, a grave dignity of deportment, highly Spanish and characteristic, and worthy of an emperor pledging a great vassal in Tokay."

Just such a group may still be seen, or was to be seen till very lately, in the quaint streets of Seville. We have read an anecdote of Velasquez and this picture, which is quite probable, though we cannot vouch for its accuracy. It is said that, while painting the water-carrier day after day, when he had been engaged with his work for several hours, Velasquez found himself vexed by perceiving, as it were, the effect of a shadow cast by some of the drapery. Small flaw as it might have been, it appeared to him to interfere with and spoil the picture. Again and again, in endeavouring to do away with this "shadow," Velasquez undid portions of his work, and had to repeat them next day, but always, towards the end of his task, the invidious shadow stole upon his vision. At last a friend, who was present and full of admiration for the picture, heard Velasquez exclaim, "That shadow again!" and saw him seize a brush and prepare to dash it across the canvas. The friend remonstrated, besought, and by main force held back the painter, and at last induced him to leave the picture untouched till next day, when Velasquez discovered, to his great relief, that the shadow had been in his own wearied young eyes, and not in his admirable representation of the *Water-carrier*.

Velasquez was in Madrid in 1623, when he was in his twenty-fifth year, and having been introduced by the Prime Minister, Olivares, to the King of Spain, Philip IV., a king who was only known to smile once or twice in his life time, whose government was careless and blundering, but who had the reputation of being a man of some intelligence and very considerable taste,—Velasquez was received into the king's service with a monthly salary of twenty ducats, and employed to paint the royal portrait.

From the time that he became court painter, Velasquez was largely occupied in painting portraits of members of the royal family, with special repetitions of the likeness of his most Catholic Majesty. With Velasquez's first portrait of Philip in armour, mounted on an Andalusian charger, the king was so pleased, that he permitted the picture to be publicly exhibited, amidst the plaudits of the spectators, in front of the church of San Felipe el Real in Madrid. Nor was the expedition a barren honour to the painter, for the king not only "talked of collecting and cancelling his existing portraits," but "resolved that in future Velasquez should have the monopoly of the royal countenance," he paid three hundred ducats for the picture.

About this time the Prince of Wales, afterwards Chas. I. went in his incognito of Charles Smith to Madrid on his romantic adventure of seeking to woo and win, personally, the Infanta of Spain, and Velasquez is said to have gained Charles's notice, and to have at least begun a portrait of him. If it were ever completed it has been lost, a misfortune which has caused spurious pictures, purporting to be the real work, to be offered to the public. Sir W. Stirling Maxwell holds, with great show of truth, that this visit of Charles to Madrid, when its altars were "glowing" with the pictures of Titian, confirmed the unhappy king's taste for art.

In 1628 Rubens came to Madrid as an envoy from the governess of the Netherlands, and the two painters, who had many points in common, and who had already corresponded, became fast friends. By the advice of Rubens, Velasquez was induced to put into execution his cherished desire of visiting Italy, the king granting his favourite painter leave of absence, the continuance of his salary, and a special sum for his expenses.

Velasquez went to Venice first, and afterwards to Rome, where he was offered, and declined, a suite of apartments in the Vatican, asking only free access to the papal galleries. There he copied many portions of Michael Angelo's *Last Judgment*—not a hundred years old, and "yet undimmed by the morning and evening incense of centuries," and portions of the frescoes of Raphael. At Rome Velasquez found there before him, Domenichino, Guido Reni, alternating ." between the excitements of the gaming table and the sweet creations of his smooth flowing pencil ;" "Nicolas Poussin, an adventurer fresh from his Norman village ; and Claude Gelée, a pastry-cook's runaway apprentice from Lorraine." Velasquez remained a year in Rome. Besides his studies he painted three original pictures, one of them, *Joseph's Coat*, well-known among the painter's comparatively rare religious works, and now in the Escurial. In this picture his biographer acknowledges, that "choosing rather to display his unrivalled skill in delineating vulgar forms than to risk his reputation in the pursuit of a more refined and idealized style," Velasquez's "Hebrew patriarchs are swineherds of Estramadura or shepherds of the Sierra Morena."

From Rome Velasquez proceeded to Naples, where he was enabled by his prudence and forbearance to face without injury the disgraceful "reign of terror" which the Neapolitan artists had established in the south of Italy. The Neapolitan artists more than any other Italian artists are believed to have influenced Velasquez's style.

In 1639 Velasquez painted his principal religious work, *The Crucifixion*, for the nunnery of San Placido in Madrid, a painting in which his power has triumphed successfully over his halting imagination.

With regard to the many court groups which Velasquez was constantly taking, we may quote Sir W. Stirling Maxwell's amusing paragraph about a curious variety of human beings in the Court Gallery. "The Alcazar of Madrid abounded with dwarfs in the days of Philip IV., who was very fond of having them about him, and collected curious specimens of the race, like other rarities. The Queen of Spain's gallery is, in consequence, rich in portraits of these little monsters, executed by Velasquez. They are, for the most part, very ugly, displaying, sometimes in an extreme degree, the deformities peculiar to their stunted growth. Maria Barbola, immortalized by a place in one of Velasquez's most celebrated pictures, was a little dame about three feet and a half in height, with the head and shoulders of a large woman, and a countenance much underjawed, and almost ferocious in expression. Her companion, Nicolasito Pertusano, although better proportioned than the lady, and of a more amicable aspect, was very inferior in elegance as a royal plaything to his contemporary, the valiant Sir Geoffrey Hudson; or his successor in the next reign, the pretty Luisillo of Queen Louisa of Orleans. Velasquez painted many portraits of these little creatures, generally seated on the ground; and there is a

HUNT THE SLIPPER.
(From the original painting by J. F. Chalon, A.R.A.)

large picture in the Louvre representing two of them leading by a cord a great spotted hound, to which they bear the same proportion that men of the usual size bear to a horse."

In 1648 Velasquez again visited Italy, sent by the king this time to collect works of art for the royal galleries and the academy about to be founded. Velasquez went by Genoa, Milan, Venice (buying there chiefly the works of Tintoret), and Parma, to Rome and Naples, returning to Rome. At Rome Velasquez painted his splendidly characteristic portrait of the Pope Innocent X., "a man of coarse features and surly expression, and perhaps the ugliest of all the successors of St. Peter."

Back at Madrid, Philip continued to load Velasquez and his family with favours, appointing the painter Quarter-Master-General of the king's household with a salary of three thousand ducats a year, and the right of carrying at his girdle a key which opened every lock in the palace.

Philip is said to have raised Velasquez to knighthood in a manner as gracious as the manner of Charles V. when he lifted up Titian's pencil. In painting one of his most renowned pictures, indeed his masterpiece, *The Maids of Honour*, Velasquez included himself at work on a large picture of the royal family. The painter represented himself with the key of his office at his girdle, and on his breast the red cross of the Order of Santiago. Philip, who came every day to see the progress of this picture, remarked in reference to the figure of the artist, that "one thing was yet wanting, and taking up the brush painted the knightly insignia with his own royal fingers, thus conferring the accolade with a weapon not recognized in chivalry."

As it is believed, Velasquez's court office, with all its prestige and influence, helped in causing his death. King Philip went in June, 1660, to the Isle of Pheasants in the river Bidassa, where, on ground which was neither Spanish nor French, the Spanish and French courts were to meet and celebrate with the greatest magnificence the marriage of the Grand Monarque and the Infanta Maria Teresa. One of Velasquez's official duties was to prepare lodgings for the king on his journeys, and in this instance the lodging included not only the decoration of the castle of Fuenterrabia, but the erection of a sumptuous pavilion in which the interviews of the assembled kings and queens and their revelries were to be held. Velasquez did his part of the preparations, and doubtless shared in the royal festivities, but returned to Madrid so worn out by his undertaking, and by constant attendance on his master, that he was seized with tertian fever, of which he died a few days later, while but in his sixty-first year, to the great grief of his countrymen, and above all of his king. Velasquez's wife, Doña Juana, died eight days after her husband, and was buried in his grave. The couple left one surviving child, a daughter, married to a painter.

In one picture, now at Vienna, Velasquez gives a glimpse of his family life at a time when it would seem that he had four sons and two daughters, so that the fortunate painter's home had not been free from one shadow—that of death, which must have robbed him of five of his children. In this pleasant picture, "his wife dressed in a brown tunic over a red petticoat, sits in the foreground of a large room, with a pretty little girl leaning on her knees, and the rest of her children grouped around her; behind are the men in deep shadow, one of them, perhaps, being Mazo, the lover or the husband of the eldest daughter, and a nurse with a child; and in an alcove Velasquez himself appears, standing before his easel, at work on a portrait of Philip IV. This is one of the most important works of the master out of the Peninsula; the faces of the family sparkle on the sober background like gems. As a piece of easy actual life, the composition has never been surpassed, and perhaps it excels even *The Meninas*, inasmuch as the hoops and dwarfs of the palace have not intruded upon the domestic privacy of the painter's home, in the northern gallery."

Velasquez seems to have been a man of honour and amiability. He filled a difficult office at the most jealous court in Europe with credit. He was true to his friends, and helpful to his brother artists. His biographer writes of Velasquez as handsome in person, and describes his costume when he appeared for the last time with his king in the galas at Pheasants' Isle:—"over a dress richly laced with silver he wore the usual Castilian ruff, and a short cloak embroidered with the red cross of Santiago; the badge of the order, sparkling with brilliants, was suspended from his neck by a gold chain; and the scabbard and hilt of his sword were of silver, exquisitely chased, and of Italian workmanship." In the likeness of Velasquez, which is the frontispiece of Sir W. Stirling Maxwell's "Life," the painter appears as a man of swarthy complexion, with a long compressed upper lip, unconcealed by his long, elaborately trimmed moustache; his hair, or wig, is arranged in two large frizzed bunches on each side of a face which is inclined to be lantern-jawed. He wears a dark doublet with a "standing white collar."

Velasquez's excellence as a painter was to be found, like that of Rembrandt, in his truth to nature; but the field of truth presented to the stately Spaniard, while it had its own ample share of humour, was a widely different field from that which offered itself to the Dutch burgher. Together with absolute truth, Velasquez had the ease and facility in expressing truth which are only acquired by a great master. Like Rubens, Velasquez made essays in many branches of painting. In sacred art, if we except his *Crucifixion*, he did not attain a high place. With regard to his landscapes, Sir David Wilkie bore witness:—"Titian seems his model, but he has also the breadth and picturesque effect for which Claude and Salvator Rosa are remarkable;" and Sir David added of those landscapes, "they have the very same sun we see, and the air we breathe, the very soul and spirit of nature."

Velasquez's *genre* pictures, of which he painted many, are excellent, but the fate was kind which confined him largely to portrait painting. It was brought as a reproach against Velasquez in his life time, that he could paint a head and nothing else, to which he replied with mingled spirit, sense, and good nature, that his detractors flattered him, "for he knew nobody of whom it could be said that he painted a head thoroughly well."

BARTOLOME ESTEVAN MURILLO was born at Seville in 1618, and was therefore nearly twenty years younger than his great countryman Velasquez. Murillo seems to have been of obscure origin, and to have begun his life in humble circumstances. There are traditions of his being self-taught, of his studying ragged boys, himself little more than a boy, in the gipsy quarter of Triana in Seville; of his painting in the market-place, where he probably found the originals of the heads of saints and Madonnas (by which he made a little money in selling them for South America) in the peasants who came to Seville with their fruit and vegetables. In 1642, Murillo, then twenty-four years of age, visited Madrid, and was kindly received, and aided in his art by his senior and fellow artist, the court painter, Velasquez. It had been Murillo's intention to proceed to England to study under Van Dyck, but the death of the latter put a stop to the project. Murillo was prevented from making the painter's pilgrimage to Italy by want of means, but the loss of culture was so far supplied by the instructions given to him by Velasquez.

In 1645, when Murillo was twenty-seven years of age, he returned to Seville, and settled there, becoming as successful as he deserved; and being acknowledged as the head of the school of Seville, where he established the Academy of Art, and was its first president. Murillo married, in 1648, a lady of some fortune, and was accustomed to entertain at his house the most exclusive society of Seville.

In 1682, Murillo was at Cadiz painting a picture of the marriage of St. Catherine in the church of the Capuchins there, when, in consequence of the accidental fall of the scaffolding, he received so severe an injury, that he was forced to leave his work incomplete, and to return to Seville, where he died within a few weeks, aged sixty-four years. He had two sons, and an only daughter, who was a nun, having taken the veil eight years before her father's death.

Murillo appears to have been in character a gentle, enthusiastic man, not without a touch of fun and frolic. He would remain for hours in the sacristy of the cathedral of Seville before the solemn awful picture of the *Deposition from the Cross*, by Pedro de Campana. When Murillo was asked by the sacristan why he stood thus gazing there, the painter answered, "I am waiting till these holy men have finished their work." By his own desire, Murillo was buried before this picture. Before another "too truthful picture of *Las dos Cadaveres*" in the small church of the hospital of the Caridad, Murillo used to hold his nose. One of Murillo's pictures has the odd name of *La Virgen Sarvilleta*, or the Virgin of the Napkin. Murillo was working at the Convento de la Merced, which is almost filled with his works, when the cook of the convent begged a memorial of him, offering as the canvas a napkin, on which Murillo at once painted a "brilliant glowing Madonna," with a child, "which seems quite to bound forward out of the picture."

Murillo's portrait by himself represents him in a dark doublet having wide sleeves and a square collar closed in front. His thumb is in his pallet, and the other hand, with fingers taper and delicate as those of a hand by Van Dyck, holds one of his brushes. The smooth face, with regular features, is pale and thoughtful, and with the womanliness of the aspect increased from the dark hair, which is divided slightly to one side, being allowed to fall down in long wavy curls on the shoulders.

In spite of the naturalistic studies of his early youth, and even of the naturalistic treatment which he gave to his first religious work, Murillo was possessed of greater and higher imagination than Velasquez could claim, and the longer Murillo lived and worked, the more refined and exalted his ideas became. Unlike Velasquez, Murillo was a great religious painter, and during the last years of his life he painted sacred subjects almost exclusively. But, like Velasquez, Murillo was eminently a Spanish painter—his virgins are dark-eyed, olive-complexioned maidens, and even his *Holy Child* is a Spanish babe.

Without the elevation and the training of the best Italian painters, Murillo has left abundant proofs of great original genius. The painter's works are widely circulated, but the chief are still in Seville. Six are in the church of the Caridad, and these six include his famous *Moses Striking the Rock*, and his *Miracle of the Loaves and Fishes;* seven *Murillos* are in the Convento de la Merced, among them Murillo's own favourite picture, which he called *Mi Cieadro* of *St. Thomas of Villanueva*. "St. Thomas was the favourite preacher of Charles V., and was created Archbishop of Valencia, where he seemed to spend the whole of his revenues in charity, yet never contracted any debt, so that his people used to believe that angels must minister to his temporal wants. He is represented at his cathedral door, distributing alms, robed in black, with a white mitre. A poor cripple kneels at his feet, and other mendicants are grouped around."

In the cathedral, Seville, is Murillo's *Angel de la Guarda*, "in which a glorious seraph, with spreading wings, leads a little trustful child by the hand, and directs him to look beyond earth into the heavenly light;" and his *St. Antonio*. "The saint is represented kneeling in a cell, of which all the poor details are faithfully given, while the long arcade of the cloister can be seen through the half-open door. Above, in a transparent light, which grows from himself, the Child Jesus appears, and descends, floating through wreaths of angels, drawn down by the power of prayer.

Another of Murillo's renowned pictures is that of the patron saints of Seville, *Santa Rufina and Santa Justina*, who were stoned to death for refusing to bow down to the image of Venus.

With regard to Murillo's pictures of flower-girls and beggar-boys, we think our readers are sure to have seen an engraving of one of the former, *The Flower-Girl*, as it is called, with a face as fresh and radiant as her flowers. In the National Gallery there is a large Holy Family of Murillo's, and in Dulwich Gallery there is a laughing boy, an irresistible specimen of brown-cheeked, white-teethed drollery.

FRANCISCO DE RIBALTA has left the greater number of works, because he lived seventy-seven years, and his son only thirty-one. Francisco was born at Castellon de la Plana in 1551. He learned his art first at Valencia, but subsequently perfected his style by studying the great masterpieces in Italy, especially Raphael and the Carracci. On his return to Spain, Ribalta was much honoured and patronized, and his works have since been highly praised. His pictures are chiefly to be seen in Valencia, and rarely to be met with out of Spain. Sir W. Stirling says, "His best pictures are remarkable for grandeur and freedom of drawing, and for the good taste in composition, and the knowledge of anatomy which they display." A picture of *Christ bearing the Cross* in Magdalene College, Oxford, formerly attributed to Morales, is said to be by one of the Ribaltas. The artist died at Valencia in 1628.

JUAN DE RIBALTA, the son of the preceding artist, was born at Valencia in 1597. He painted, at the early age of eighteen, a most praiseworthy composition representing the *Crucifixion*, which is now in the Museum of Valencia. There is no doubt but

that if Juan de Ribalta had lived to maturity he would have been an excellent artist. He died soon after his father in 1628, only thirty-one years old. In the Museum at Madrid may be found the *Four Evangelists*, a *Dead Christ*, sustained by angels, and a *St. Francis of Assisi*, whom an angel is consoling and filling with holy ecstasy by playing on his celestial lute; but it is not specified to which of the two Ribaltas these compositions belong.

JOSEF DE RIBERA was born at Xativa in 1589. When quite young, he was the pupil of Francisco Ribalta and a fellow-student with Juan.

It is said that in the beginning of the seventeenth century a cardinal, passing through the streets of Rome in his carriage, perceived a young man, scarcely beyond childhood, who though clothed in rags, and having by his side a few crusts of bread given him out of charity, was yet with profound attention drawing the frescoes on the façade of a palace. Struck with pity at the sight, the cardinal called the boy, took him to his own house, clothed him decently, and admitted him as a sort of dependent of the family. He learnt that his young *protégé* was named Giuseppe de Ribera; that he was born at Xativa (now San Felipe), near Valencia; that his parents had early sent him to that provincial capital to study at the university, but that his irresistible inclination had led him to prefer the studio of Francisco Ribalta to his classes; that he had made such rapid progress that he had soon been chosen to assist his master; but that then a passion had arisen in him to study art at its fountain head; and, no longer thinking of anything but Rome and its marvels, he had abandoned family, friends, and country, and had at last arrived in that capital of the artistic as well as of the religious world. There, without any means of support, making the street his studio, and a milestone his easel, copying the statues, the frescoes, and the passers-by, he lived on the charity of his comrades, who called him, for want of another name, "Lo Spagnoletto." But Ribera could not be condemned to the idleness of the antechamber of a prince of the church. One day throwing off his livery and resuming his rags, he fled from the cardinal's house to recommence joyously his life of poverty and independence.

Of all the great works that surrounded him, those that Ribera admired with the greatest enthusiasm, because they best answered the instincts of his own genius, were the paintings of the proud and fiery Caravaggio. There, in the violent effects of chiaroscuro, the young Spaniard beheld the greatest prodigies of art; he obtained admission to the studio of this master, but he could not have received his lessons long, as Caravaggio died in 1609, when Ribera was only twenty. He then left Rome, and went to Parma, where he was attracted by the great renown of Correggio. Before his works a fresh enthusiasm seized Ribera. He began to study them with a sort of frenzy, and, laying aside his former touch, which was strong and violent, he threw himself into the opposite extreme, endeavouring to make his style as soft, tender, and delicate as that of his new master.

Soon afterwards Ribera settled at Naples, and married the daughter of a rich picture-dealer: there he had only to work hard, finding in the profession of his father-in-law an easy means of making his name and his paintings known. A singular circumstance helped to found his reputation suddenly. The house he occupied with his wife's family was situated in the same square as the palace of the Viceroy. One day, according to the Italian custom, his father-in-law had placed on the balcony, for public exhibition, a *Martyrdom of St. Bartholomew*, which Ribera had just completed. A crowd, attracted by the sight of this magnificent work, soon covered the square, making the air resound with cries of enthusiasm. The noise became such, that it was believed there was a popular outbreak, and that a Masaniello was haranguing the people. The Viceroy, Don Pedro Giron, Duke of Ossuna, came out armed, saw the cause of the disorder, admired the picture, and ordered the artist to appear before him. His joy was so great to find in him a fellow-countryman, that he made him painter to the Court, with a monthly salary of fifty doubloons, and gave him apartments in his own palace.

The ragged student of the streets of Rome had thenceforth attained the summit of fortune; he possessed both riches and authority. He became soon the most opulent and luxurious of artists, the equal of nobles and princes, and at Naples he continued to live until he died "full of wealth and honour" in 1656.

Although he painted all his pictures in Italy, Ribera is thoroughly Spanish; he never forgot his birth, and, indeed, showed himself so proud of it, that in signing his best pictures he never failed to add to the words "Giuseppe de Ribera" *Español*.

The paintings of Ribera, like those of the Italian artists, are scattered throughout the whole of Europe: but Naples has retained some of his principal works. It was for the Carthusian Convent, called San Martino, that Ribera painted his great work, the *Communion of the Apostles;* twelve *Prophets* on the windows of the different chapels; and, lastly, the *Descent from the Cross*, which is almost unanimously said to be his masterpiece. Here we may find, beside the qualities enumerated above, much pathos and expression, and a power of feeling which is not usually to be met with in his works; so that this picture seems to unite to the fiery energy of Caravaggio not only the grace of Correggio, but the religious fervour of Fra Angelico.

In the museum "degli Studj" two of Ribera's works have been placed in the room of the "Capi d'Opera:" *St. Jerome in the desert*, listening to the trumpet of the angel, and the large picture of *Silenus*, in which the foster-father of Bacchus is lying on the ground, receiving drink from the satyrs who surround him. At the bottom of this picture may be read the following inscription: "Josephus a Ribera, Hispanus Valentinus et coacademicus Romanus, faciebat Parthenope, 1626." This long inscription is traced on a scroll, which a serpent seems to bite and tear. How could Ribera complain of envy, or represent himself as its victim, when he was rich, honoured and powerful, and when he himself carried his jealousy even to ferocity? It was, indeed, in his own house that the "fazzioni de' pittori," those coteries of painters, were formed, which deserve the name of factions, because they made war on rival schools, even with the dagger. The faction of Naples, which had Ribera at its head, numbered among its members "bravi," such as Correnzio and Caracciolo, who maintained the superiority of their master at the sword's point, and permitted the entry of the city to no painter who did not belong to his school.

Annibale Carracci and Guido were obliged to fly, in order to escape the blows of this brotherhood of a new order; and when Domenichino died before he was able to reach Rome, rumours of poisoning prevailed. Such outrages cannot be too severely condemned.

In the Louvre there is only one of Ribera's works—an *Adoration of the Shepherds*—and, although it is very beautiful, it is insufficient to make him known, because it is not in his usual style, and he shows himself in it less as the continuer of Caravaggio than as the imitator of Correggio.

The Museo del Rey, at Madrid, is more fortunate in having a great number of his works, and in all his styles. If we wish to see him employing the calm, soft style of Correggio, we have only to look at *Jacob's Ladder*, an excellent specimen of the second phase of his life. Of his latter style, when he returned to the natural bent of his genius, we find the *Twelve Apostles*—a valuable series of expressive heads, in which may be seen every age, from the youthful St. John, the beloved disciple, to the old St. James the Great; a striking *Mary the Egyptian;* a *St. James and St. Roch*, magnificent pendants brought from the Escurial; and lastly, a *Martyrdom of St. Bartholomew*, the most celebrated of his paintings of this terrible subject. Here he has shown as much talent in composition and power of expression, in the union of grief and beatitude, as incomparable force in the execution.

The Academy of Fine Arts at Madrid has several other works by Ribera, among which are two very singular full-length portraits in one frame which deserve great attention. The National Gallery possesses two—a *Piety* and a *Shepherd with a lamb*.

FRANCISCO ZURBARAN was born of parents who were simple labourers in the town of Fuente de Cantos in Estremadura in 1598. He belongs to the Andalusian school, because he studied under Roélas at Seville, and passed his whole life there. He only once, when very old, went to Madrid, and then returned to his native province to paint eight large pictures, representing the *History of St. Jerome*, for the church in the little town of Guadalupe, between Toledo and Caceres. In 1625 he painted for the Marquis of Malazon some scenes from the *Life of St. Peter*, for the chapel dedicated to that Saint in the Seville Cathedral. About the same time, too, he painted his famous *St. Thomas Aquinas*.

In 1630 Zurbaran was invited to Madrid, and was soon afterwards appointed painter to Philip IV.; he signs himself thus as early as 1633. In 1650, the monarch employed him to paint the *Labours of Hercules* in the palace of Buen Retiro. It is said that the king one day, on visiting the artist at work, was so much pleased with the picture on which he was engaged, that he addressed him as "painter of the king, and king of painters." Zurbaran continued to paint for Philip IV. until his death in 1662.

It is universally acknowledged that the best of Zurbaran's compositions, that in which all his good points are united, and where there is greatest display of talent, is the *St. Thomas Aquinas*, which he painted for the church of the College of that saint at Seville, placed under the patronage of the celebrated author of the "Summa Theologiæ." This picture is now in the Museum of Seville, which gallery possesses the best collection of his works. Christ and the Virgin are above in glory with St. Paul and St. Dominic; in the centre is St. Thomas standing, surrounded by the four doctors of the Latin Church seated on the clouds; lower down in an attitude of devotion and admiration, on one side Charles V., clothed in the imperial mantle, with a *cortège* of knights; on the other, the Archbishop Deza, the founder of the college, with a suite of monks and attendants. Several of his works have been recently scattered throughout Europe; some were at Paris in the little Spanish museum formed by Louis Philippe, and were dispersed after his death. (There were as many as ninety-two attributed to him in the catalogues.) In the collection of the Pardo at Madrid there are fourteen pictures attributed to Zurbaran. In England, the National Gallery, in which the artists of Spain are so poorly represented, has but one picture by this artist. It is a portrait of a *Franciscan Monk*, and was formerly in the Spanish collection of Louis Philippe, where it was much admired by Kolloff and other writers. In the Duke of Sutherland's collection at Stafford House, there is a fine specimen of Zurbaran, a *Madonna and Child with the Infant St. John*.

Zurbaran has been called the "Spanish Caravaggio," but if he deserved this name, it was not by the fire of his pencil, or by an exaggerated seeking after effect; for he is colder and more reserved, though, at the same time, nobler and more correct, than Caravaggio. If Zurbaran resemble Caravaggio, it is through his frequent use of bluish tints, which sometimes predominate so much in his pictures as to make them appear as if seen through a veil slightly tinged with blue; and also from his deep knowledge of his art, and happy use of light and shade. This is the real point of resemblance between the two masters. As for the nature of the subjects—except a small number of large compositions which were ordered of him—Zurbaran preferred simple ones, easy of comprehension, and requiring only a small number of personages, whom he always placed in perfectly natural attitudes. Yet he never painted comic or popular scenes, as Velasquez and Murillo sometimes did; nor strange and grotesque ones, like Ribera. He painted some female saints, and has given them attractions and grace; but severe religious feeling always predominates with him. No one, indeed, has expressed better than Zurbaran the rigours of an ascetic life, and the austerity of the cloister; no one has shown better than he, under the girdle of rope and the thick hood, the attenuated forms and pale heads of the cenobites, devoted to mortification and prayer, who in the words of Buffon, when their last hour arrives, "do not cease to live, but succeed in dying."

Among his scholars were BERNADE DE AYALA and the two brothers POLANCO.

ALONSO CANO, who was born at Granada in 1601, has been termed the "Spanish Michelangelo." This is merely because he practised the three arts which are especially called "fine." He was a painter, sculptor, and architect. Like Michelangelo, he was a better sculptor than painter, but his only works in architecture were those heavy church decorations called "retablos" (church screens), which he not only designed, but for which he himself made all the ornaments, either statues or pictures. Alonso Cano lived for some time at Seville, afterwards at Madrid, and towards the close of his life at Granada, his birthplace, and, provided with a rich benefice, tranquilly passed the last years of a life which had been agitated by travels, passions, and adventures. He died in 1667 "in a manner highly exemplary and edifying to those about him." Cano left seven of his works to the Museum of Madrid. Amongst

INTERIOR OF THE GREEK CHURCH, CONSTANTINOPLE.
From the original painting by David Roberts, R.A.

these are a *St. John writing the Apocalypse;* the *Dead Christ mourned by an Angel,* and a fine *Portrait.* As a painter, he has been—not unjustly—called the "Spanish Albani," for, contrary to what might have been expected from his passionate temper, the principal characteristics of his works are softness and suavity. By a skilful arrangement of draperies he makes the outline of the form they cover sufficiently marked. He also took so much care in the execution of hands and feet—always a great difficulty—that on this account alone his works might be distinguished from any other painter of his country. Less fiery and powerful than Ribera, less profound and less brilliant than Murillo, he takes a middle place between these two masters, being correct, elegant, and full of grace. The works of Cano are to be found in most Spanish towns.

LUIS DE MORALES—called EL DIVINO—was born at Badajoz in 1509. Of his life very little is known. About 1564 he was summoned to Madrid by Philip II., who, it is said, was displeased with him for appearing in too rich a dress; the poor artist explained that he had spent all his spare money in order to buy a costume befitting—as he thought—the occasion, and on hearing this the king was pacified. Morales, however, soon returned to Badajoz. When Philip II. visited that city in 1581, and found the artist in poverty, he gave him a yearly pension of three hundred ducats. Morales lived at his native Badajoz until his death, which took place in 1586.

There is one painter whom universal admiration has saluted by the title "divine." This is Raphael. In Spain, one painter also has received this magnificent surname. But with him, it was not a universal cry of admiration which thus proclaimed his merit and superiority; it was, simply, his too great fastidiousness in the choice of his subjects, which always bore the imprint of an ardent piety. This name has, in some respects, been a misfortune to him; all the pictures of his time which have the slightest analogy with his style are attributed to him. When anyone meets with an *Ecce Homo,* dry, lean, and livid; a *Mater dolorosa* with hollow cheeks, pale lips, red eyelids; even though it be a horrible caricature, he exclaims at once, "There is a divine Morales!" Those who have examined his fine works attentively are not so prodigal of their author's name. His pictures, frequently painted on copper or wood, are as a rule very small and simple; the most complicated are those representing the *Madonna supporting a Dead Christ.* There are some works, however, of Morales in which there are whole-length figures, such as the six large paintings of the *Passion,* which decorate the church of a small town in Estremadura, Higuera de Fregenal. Madrid has only succeeded in collecting five works by his hand, which proves that they are rare, when authentic. The *Circumcision* is the largest, and seems to be the best of the five. If Morales has the defects common to his period; if he is minute in the execution of the beard and hair; if he may be accused of too much hardness in the outlines and too little relief in the model; we must, at all events acknowledge that he drew with care and correctness, that he understood the anatomy of the nude, and rendered faithfully the fine gradations of demi-tints. He excelled also in the expression of religious grief, and no one has succeeded better than he in painting the agonies of Our Lord when crowned with thorns, or of a Virgin pierced with the seven swords of grief. Genuine works by Morales are rarely to be seen out of Spain.

ALONSO SANCHEZ COELLO, a Portuguese by birth, was born about the year 1515. He removed when young to Spain, where he afterwards chiefly resided.

Alonso Sanchez Coello was not only the *pintor de camera* to the son of Charles V., but also one of his intimate courtiers (*el privado del rey*). Pacheco says, that "the king gave him for his lodging an immense house near the palace, and as he had a key to it . . . he often entered at inopportune moments into the painter's apartments; sometimes the monarch came in when he was at dinner with his family . . . ; at others, he surprised him when painting, and approaching him from behind laid his hand upon his shoulder. . . . Sanchez Coello several times painted the *Portrait of the King*, armed, on foot, on horseback, in travelling garments, in a cloak and with a cap. He also painted seventeen royal persons, queens, princes, and infantas, who honoured him so much as to enter his house familiarly to hold intercourse with his wife and children. . . . His house was frequented by the greatest persons of the time, Cardinal Granvelle, the archbishop of Toledo, the archbishop of Seville, and, what was a still greater honour, Don John of Austria, Don Carlos, and such numbers of nobles and ambassadors that many times, horses, litters, coaches, and chairs, filled the two large courts of his house." Sanchez Coello painted several pictures on sacred history for different altars in the Escurial; and also the portrait of the celebrated founder of the Jesuits, *Ignatius Loyola*. This portrait, which is said to have been much like him, was painted after his death from a cast of the face taken in wax. Coello died, honoured and regretted, in 1590. He excelled especially in portrait painting.

JUAN FERNANDEZ NAVARRETE—called on account of his being deaf and dumb, EL MUDO—was born at Logrono in 1526. He is one of the most striking proofs of the power of natural taste, and of its constant superiority to what can be produced by education. If the Roman rhetorician was right in asserting that a poet must be born a poet, El Mudo has shown that a painter must be one from his birth. Deprived of the usual means of communicating with other men, and kept back by the circumstances surrounding him, he yet succeeded in accomplishing his destiny, merely by following the natural bent of his nature. When about three years old, a severe illness deprived him of his hearing, and, like those who are deaf from their birth, he was unable to learn to speak.

At this time, the Spanish monk, Fray Pedro de Ponce, who preceded by so long a time the Abbé de l'Epée, had not yet essayed the education of deaf-mutes. (It was about the year 1570 that Fray Pedro de Ponce, a Benedictine monk of the convent of Ono, found means to instruct the two brothers and the sister of the Constable of Castile, all three born deaf.) Nothing was taught to Juan during his infancy; but he soon revealed his true vocation, for he was constantly occupied in drawing on the walls with charcoal every object that he saw around him. His natural talent was shown so clearly in these rough sketches, that his father took him to the convent of La Estrella, at a short distance from Logrono, where one of the monks, Fray Vicente de Santo Domingo, understood painting. This monk became much attached to the young mute; he taught him the first elements of art, and, soon finding his pupil making such progress that he could no longer instruct him, he persuaded his parents to send the youth to Italy.

El Mudo, whose family was very well off, soon started for the land of the arts. He visited Rome, Naples, Florence, and Venice, and settled down near Titian, whose disciple he became. His residence in Italy was long—twenty years at the least. When in 1568 his reputation, already great, and doubtless increased by the fact of his infirmity, reached Spain, Philip II., who was beginning the decorations of the Escurial, sent for him to return to Spain. It was at the Escurial that El Mudo completed his principal work, a series of eight large pictures, some of which have since perished in a fire. Amongst those which were preserved may be mentioned, a *Nativity*, in which El Mudo undertook to vanquish a formidable difficulty; he introduced three different lights into his picture; one which proceeds from the Holy Child, another which descends from the Glory and extends over the whole picture, and a third from a torch held by St. Joseph. The group of shepherds is the best part of the composition. It is said that the Florentine painter, Pelligrino Tibaldi, never wearied of admiring them, and was continually calling out in his enthusiasm: *Oh! gli belli pastori!* This exclamation has become the title of the picture, which is called the *Beautiful Shepherds*. El Mudo died at Toledo in 1579. The works of this artist are scarcely known at all, for those which still exist are buried in the royal solitude of the Escurial, and are now almost inaccessible. We must, then, be satisfied with hearing that he was unanimously called the "Spanish Titian."

FRANCESCA GOYA Y LUCIENTES was born at Fuente de Todos in 1746. He was his own master, and took lessons only of the old masters. From this singular education his talent took a peculiar bent—inaccurate, wild, and without method or style, but full of nerve, boldness, and originality. Goya is the last heir, in a very distant degree, of the great Velasquez. His is the same manner, but looser and more fiery. Being under no delusion as to the extent of his own talent, Goya did not lose himself in too high-flown ideas; he confined himself to village processions, choristers, and scenes of bull-races—in short, to all sorts of painted caricatures. In this genre he is full of wit, and his execution is always superior to the subjects. But, like Velasquez, Goya founds his best title to celebrity on his portraits. His equestrian portraits of *Charles IV.* and *Maria Louisa* have been placed in the vestibule of the Museo del Rey. These works are, doubtless, very imperfect, being full of glaring faults, especially in the forms of the horses. But the heads and busts have singular beauty; and on the whole, though very defective when analyzed, there is so much effect, such truth in the colouring, and boldness in the touch, that one cannot fail to admire these high qualities, although regretting the essential defects which they cannot entirely redeem.

CHAPTER XII.

FRENCH ART—NICOLAS POUSSIN—CLAUDE LORRAINE—CHARLES LE BRUN— WATTEAU—GREUZE.

NICOLAS POUSSIN was born at Andely in Normandy in 1594. Of his parentage little seems to have been ascertained, but it is believed that he was well educated, and his classical learning in after life was reckoned great. He was regularly trained to be a painter under a master in his native town, and afterwards in Paris.

Dissatisfied with the patronage which he received in Paris, Poussin went to Rome when he was about thirty years of age. In Rome he is said to have lived on familiar terms with a sculptor whose devotion to antique art influenced his taste, and lent it the strong classical bent which it retained. Poussin studied regularly in the school of Domenichino. After some delay in attracting public notice, *The Death of Germanicus*, and *The Capture of Jerusalem*, which Poussin painted for Cardinal Barberini, won general approval. In 1629, when Nicolas Poussin was in his thirty-fifth year, he married the sister of his pupil, Gaspar Dughet, who took Poussin's name, and is known as a painter, inferior to his master, by the name of Gaspar Poussin.

Nicolas Poussin returned to Paris when he was a middle-aged man, was presented to the king, Louis XIII., by Cardinal Richelieu, and offered apartments in the Tuileries, with the title of painter in ordinary, and a salary of a hundred and twenty pounds a year. Poussin agreed to settle in Paris, but on his going back to Rome to fetch his wife, and on the King of France's dying, the attractions of the Eternal City proved too great for the painter, and in place of removing his household and studio to his native country, he lived for the rest of his years in Rome, and died there in 1665, when he was seventy-one years of age.

Except what can be judged of him from his work, we do not know that much has been gathered of the private character and life of Nicolas Poussin, notwithstanding that there was a biography written of him fifty years ago by Lady Calcott, and that his letters have been published in Paris. In the absence of conclusive testimony one

may conclude with some probability that he was "quiet," like his best paintings; a man who minded his own business, and did not trouble the world by astonishing actions, good or bad.

In painting his own picture, from which an engraving has been taken, Poussin's classical preferences seem to have passed into the likeness, for in the dress of the seventeenth century, the cloak (not unlike a toga), the massive hand with the heavy signet-ring resting on what looks like a closed portfolio, the painter has something of the severe air and haughty expression of an old Roman; still more, perhaps, of the French-Romans, if we may call them so, of whom revolutionary times nearly two centuries later, afforded so many examples. This is a handsome, dignified face, with austerity in its pride. The slightly curled hair is thrown back with a certain consciousness from the knit brow, and from the shoulders. There is only the faintest shadow of a moustache over the cleanly cut, firmly closed mouth.

Poussin painted largely, and his pictures have been often engraved. With harmonious composition, good drawing and colouring, his pictures alike profited and suffered from the classical atmosphere in which they had their being. They gained in that correctness which in its highest form becomes noble truthfulness, but they lost in freedom. The figures in the pictures had frequently the statuesqueness which in sculpture suits the material, but in painting is stiffness.

Nicolas Poussin had an exceptional reputation for a historical painter in his day. As a landscape painter, Mr. Ruskin, while waging war with Nicolas Poussin's brother-in-law and assumed namesake, Gaspar, notably excepts Nicolas from his severest strictures, and treats his efforts in landscape painting with marked respect. At the same time, however, the critic censures the painter for a want of thorough acquaintance with nature, and the laws of nature, ignorance not uncommon in any day, and nearly universal in Nicolas Poussin's day. "The great master of elevated ideal landscape," Mr. Ruskin calls Nicolas Poussin, and illustrates his excellence in one respect, after contrasting it with the slovenliness of Sir Joshua Reynolds, by describing the vine in Poussin's *Nursing of Jupiter*, in the Dulwich Gallery, thus:—

"Every vine-leaf, drawn with consummate skill and untiring diligence, produces not only a true group of the most perfect grace and beauty, but one which in its pure and simple truth belongs to every age of nature, and adapts itself to the history of all time." "One of the finest landscapes that ancient art has produced, the work of a really great mind," Mr. Ruskin distinguishes the *Phocian* of Nicolas Poussin in the National Gallery, before proceeding to point out its faults.

Again, Mr. Ruskin, writing of the street in the centre of another landscape by Nicolas Poussin, indicates it with emphasis:—"the street in the centre of the really great landscape of Poussin (great in feeling, at least) marked 260 in the Dulwich Gallery." The criticism with which Mr. Ruskin follows up this praise is so perfect a bit of word-painting, that we cannot refrain from writing it down here. "The houses are dead square masses, with a light side and a dark side, and black touches for windows. There is no suggestion of anything in any of the spaces, the light wall is dead grey, the dark wall dead grey, and the windows dead black. How differently would nature have treated us. She would have let us see the Indian corn hanging on the walls, and the image of the Virgin at the angles; and the sharp, broken, broad shadows of the tiled eaves, and the deep ribbed tiles with the doves upon them, and the carved Roman capital built into the wall, and the white and blue stripes of the mattresses stuffed out of the windows, and the flapping corners of the neat blinds. All would have been here; not as such, not like the corn, nor blinds, nor tiles, not to be comprehended nor understood, but a confusion of yellow and black spots and strokes, carried far too fine for the eye to follow; microscopic in its minuteness, and filling every atom and space with mystery, out of which would have arranged itself the general impression of truth and life." Once more, Mr. Ruskin freely admits that "all the landscape of Nicolas Poussin is imagination."

Mr. Ruskin's first definition of ideal landscape is in this manner. Every different tree and leaf, every bud, has a perfect form, which, were it not for disease or accident, it would have attained; just as every individual human face has an ideal form, which but for sin and suffering it would present: and the ideal landscape-painter has realized the perfect form, and offers it to the world, and that in a sense quite distinct from the fallacy of improving nature.

But we wish to take our readers further into imaginative landscape, and to show it to them, if possible, under additional lights. We despair of succeeding if we cannot do it by one or two simple examples. In passing through a gallery we may stop before a picture to be struck, almost startled, by the exact copy which it presents of some scene in nature; how like the clouds in the sky, the leaves on the trees, the very plumage of the birds! But pass on to another picture which may or may not have the same exact likeness, and we are possessed with quite another feeling; instead of being merely surprised by the cleverness of the imitation, we feel a thrill of delight at a reproduction of nature. In this picture there are not only the clouds we remember, but we can almost feel the shadows which they cast, and the air which stirs them. These tree-leaves are not only green, or yellow, or russet, they are tender, or crisp living leaves. One half expects to see the birds' throats swell, and hear the sweetness or the shrillness of their songs.

The first picture, with all its correctness, brightness, richness, or delicacy it may be, remains bare, hard, and barren, compared to the second. We cannot explain to our readers the cause of the difference, we can only show it to them as they may see it for themselves, and say that we suppose it proceeds from this—that the second painter has seen farther into the heart of nature than the first, and has been able by subtler touches to make us see with his eyes.

Again, landscape often tells a story, and tells it inimitably. Our readers have heard of the ballad of the "Twa Corbies," which the writer of the ballad has made to meet and tell gruesomely where and on what carrion their feast has been. Suppose the writer of the ballad had been a painter, he might have painted the story as intelligibly by the lone hill-side, the bleaching bones of the faithful hound and gallant grey, the two loathly blue-black birds satiated with their prey. There is a significant old Scotch song with a ballad ring, by Lady Nairne, two verses of which form each a complete picture not only of different seasons, but of different phases of feeling— happiness and misery.

"Bonnie ran the burnie down,
    Wandering and winding;
Sweetly sang the birds aboon,
    Care never minding.
"But now the burn comes down apace,
    Roaring and reaming,
And for the wee birdies' sang
    Wild howlets screaming."

Imagine these two verses painted, and the painter, from a lack of comprehension, introducing the "wild howlets screaming" beside the burnie, "wandering and winding," and the "wee birdies" foolishly and inconsequently singing with their feeble song drowned in the rush of the burn (no longer a burnie), "roaring and reaming," when the "spate" is spreading desolation on every side. Don't we see how the picture would be spoilt, and the story of complete contrast left untold? We have taken advisedly an extreme and therefore an unlikely case of halting imagination. But in imaginative landscape every "white flower with its purple stain," every crushed butterfly, is made to play its part in the whole, and at the same time due proportion is never lost sight of, and the less is always kept subordinate to the greater.

We have already had occasion to mention examples of Nicolas Poussin in the National Gallery and in Dulwich Gallery.

CLAUDE GELÉE, better known as Claude Lorraine, was a native of Lorraine, and was born at Chateau de Chamagne in the Vosges, in 1600. His parents were in humble life, and apprenticed Claude to a baker and pastry-cook. According to some biographers the cooks of Lorraine were in such request that they occasionally repaired to Rome with their apprentices in their train to serve the successor of St. Peter, and Claude was thus carried, in the way of trade, to the city which might well have been the goal of his ambition. According to other writers of art histories, Claude abandoned the kneading-trough and the oven; and it was as a runaway apprentice that by some occult means he reached Rome. And when he had arrived he entered into the service of a landscape painter of good repute, to whom he was colour-boy as well as cook. The last is the account, so far, which Claude gave of himself to a friend, and it is hardly likely either that he misrepresented his history, or that his friend invented such details, though lately French authorities have questioned the authenticity of the narrative. Claude remained for nearly the entire remainder of a long life in Rome. He only once re-visited France, while he was yet a young man, under thirty years of age, in 1625 or 1627. He is supposed to have painted his earliest pictures and executed his etchings about this time, 1630, and to have painted his best pictures fifteen years later, when he was in the maturity of his life and powers. He was counted successful during his life-time, as a landscape painter, but did not amass a larger fortune than about $10,000. He was a slow and careful painter (working a fortnight at a picture with little apparent progress); his painstaking work, and his custom of keeping a book, in which he verified his pictures, are about the most that we can tell of the habits of one of the foreign painters, who has been more fully represented in England, than anywhere else. Claude Lorraine died at Rome in the eighty-third year of his age, in 1682.

Claude Lorraine's name has become a very vexed name with art critics. There was a time when he had an unsurpassed reputation as a landscape painter. The possession of a Claude was enough to confer art glory on a country-house, and possibly for this reason England, in public and private collections, has more "Claudes" than are held by any other country. But Claude's admirers, among whom Sir George Beaumont, the great art critic of his generation, took the lead, have had their day, and, if they have not by any means passed away, are on the wane.

The wrathful indignation of the English landscape painter, Turner, at the praise which was so glibly lavished on Claude—an indignation that caused Turner to bequeath two of his own landscape paintings to the trustees of the National Gallery, on the caustic condition that they should always be placed between the two celebrated "Claudes," known as *The Marriage of Isaac and Rebecca* and *The Embarkation of the Queen of Sheba*—helped to shake the English art world's faith in its former idol. Mr Ruskin's adoption and proclamation of Turner's opinion shook the old faith still further. This reversal of a verdict with regard to Claude is peculiar; it is by no means uncommon for the decision of contemporaries to be set aside, and we shall hear of an instance presently, in the case of the painter Le Brun. In fact, it is often ominous with regard to a man's future fame, when he is "cried up to the skies" in his own day. The probability may be that his easy success has been won by something superficial and fleeting. But Claude's great popularity has been in another generation, and with another nation. English taste may have been in fault; or another explanation seems preferable—that Claude's sense of beauty was great, with all its faults of expression, and he gave such glimpses of a beautiful world as the gazers on his pictures were capable of receiving, which to them proved irresistible.

While Claude adopted an original style as a landscape painter, so far as his contemporaries were concerned, he was to such a degree self-taught, and only partially taught, that it is said he never learnt to paint figures—those in his pictures were painted by other painters, and that Claude even painted animals badly.

Mr. Ruskin has been hard on Claude, whether justly or unjustly, we cannot pretend to say.

The critic denies the painter not only a sense of truth in art, but all imagination as a landscape painter.

Claude was fond of painting scenes on the Tiber and in the Roman Campagna, but while he tried to reproduce the hills and woodlands of Italy, he did not seek to paint the mountain landscapes of the Apennines.

Besides Claude's numerous works in England and scattered through other countries, some of his finest paintings are in the Doria and Sciarra palaces in Rome. He rarely put his name to his works; when he did so he signed it frequently "Claudio," sometimes "Claudius." We have spoken of his book of sketches, in which he had been wont to note on the back of the sketch the date of the completed picture, and to whom sold. This book he called the "Libro di Verita," or, Book of

SUNSHINE.
(From the original painting by John Lewell.)

Truth, and its apparent use was to check the sale of spurious paintings in Claude's name, even during his life-time. The "Book of Truth" is in possession of the Duke of Devonshire, and has been employed in recent years with reference to the end for which it seemed designed, so woe to that country-house which has long prided itself on possessing a "Claude," if that "Claude" does not happen to have a place in the "Book of Truth," though we do not know that it is at all certain that Claude took the precaution of inscribing *every* painting which he painted after a certain date in the "Book of Truth."

JACQUES CALLOT, the son of a noble family, was born at Nancy in Lorraine in 1592. He was an enemy to all discipline, and, in order to give free course to his fancy, fled from his father's house in the train of a troop of mountebanks. Entirely occupied with etching according to processes of his own invention—his *Beggars, Gipsies, Nobles, Devils,* and scenes descriptive of the *Miseries of War,* Callot finished but a very small number of paintings. Thus, while he has left fifteen or sixteen hundred engravings, both large and small, we have not met with more than two pictures bearing his name, the *Military Execution,* at Dresden, and the *Village Fair,* at Vienna; both are on copper, with very small figures, and such pale colouring that at the first glance one is not favourably impressed. Callot's talent has remained so thoroughly *sui generis* that he has had no descendants. He was a great artist, who has no place in the history of the fine arts, even of his own country. He died at Nancy in 1635.

CHARLES LE BRUN was born in Paris, in 1619. He was trained to be a painter, and went young to Rome, studying there for six years under the guidance of Nicolas Poussin. Le Brun returned to Paris, and, through the patronage of the Chancellor Segnier, was introduced to the court, and got the most favourable opportunities of practising his profession with worldly success. He speedily acquired a great name, and was appointed painter to the King, Louis XIV. Le Brun had enough influence with his royal master, and with the great minister Colbert, to succeed in establishing, while the painter was yet a young man, the Royal Academy of Art, of which he was the first member, and virtually the head, holding, in his own person, the directorship of the Gobelin tapestry works, which was to be the privilege of a member of the Academy. Le Brun continued in the utmost favour with the King, who, not content with employing the painter largely at Fontainebleau and in Versailles, invested him with the order of St. Michael, bestowed on him letters of nobility, and visited him frequently at his work, occasions when there were not wanting adroit courtiers to liken the Grand Monarque to the Emperor Charles V., and Le Brun to Titian.

Le Brun seems to have been a man of energy, confidence, and industry, neither mentally before nor after his time, and by no means too retiring, meditative, or original, to fail to profit by his outward good fortune. He wrote, as well as painted, artistic treatises, which were received as oracular utterances, and entirely deferred to in the schools of his day. He died at Paris in 1690, when he was in his seventieth year.

Le Brun's real merits as a painter were limited to respectable abilities and acquirements, together with florid quickness and ease, and such an eye to what was splendid and scenic as suited admirably a decorator of palaces in an age which prized sumptuousness, and an exaggeration of dramatic effect, over every other quality. Nicolas Poussin's quiet refinement of style became in Le Brun what is called academic (conventionally learned), pompous, and grandiose, and men decidedly preferred the degeneration. But later critics, who have not the natural partiality of the French to the old master, return to their first loves, and condemn Le Brun's swelling violence, both in the tints and poses of his figures. Among his most famous works, which have been magnificently engraved, are his "Battles of Alexander."

ANTOINE WATTEAU was born at Valenciennes in 1684. A very different painter from Le Brun, he was yet as characteristic of French art in the reign of Louis XIV. We don't know if his birth-place at Valenciennes, with its chief product of dainty lace, had anything to do with it, but the other items of poor Watteau's history are considerably removed from the very artificial grace which one connects with his name. He was the son of a carpenter, and struggled up, by the hard instrumentality of third-rate masters and of picture-dealers, to the rank which he attained among artists, taking his stand from the first, however, as the painter of well-bred, well-apparelled people—the frequenters of *bals masqués*, and *fêtes champêtres*, who were only playing at shepherds and shepherdesses.

Watteau was elected an Academician in 1717, when he was thirty-three years of age, and he afterwards came to England, but did not remain there. He died of consumption at Nogent-sur-Marne in 1721, when he was thirty-six years of age. Watteau's gifts were his grace and brilliance on a small scale. He did not draw well; as to design, his composition may be said to be suited to such a work as the collection of "fashionable figures," which he engraved and left behind him. Yet, if we were to see at this moment some of his exquisite groups of ladies in sacques and Watteau hats, and cavaliers in flowing wigs and lace cravats, we have no doubt that the most of us would admire them much, for they are exceedingly pretty, and exceeding prettiness is attractive, particularly to women. But we would have our readers remember that this art is a finical and soulless art, after all. We would fain have them take this as their maxim, "That the art is greatest which conveys to the mind of the spectator, by any means whatsoever, the greatest number of the greatest ideas."

JEAN BAPTISTE GREUZE was born at Tournus in Burgundy in 1726. He studied painting from his youth in the studios of artists at Lyons, Paris, and Rome, and his studies resulted in his being a celebrated genre painter. He only painted one historical picture, but, with the touchy vanity which seemed natural to the man, he ranked his genre pictures as high art; and when he was placed in the ordinary list of genre painters on his election as a member of the French Academy of Painting, Greuze resented the imputation, and withdrew from the Academy. He died in 1805, aged seventy-nine years. Greuze was a showy, clever, but neither earnest nor truthful painter of domestic subjects and family pictures. His pictures of women and heads of girls are among his best known works, and by these he is represented in the National Gallery, London.

CHAPTER XIII.

THE FOREIGN SCHOOL OF ENGLAND.—HOLBEIN, VAN DYCK, LELY, CANALETTO, KNELLER.

ANS HOLBEIN, sometimes entitled Hans the Younger, was born at Augsburg about 1494 or 1495. He was the son of a painter, and belonged to a family of painters, one or more of whom had preceded Hans Holbein in leaving Augsburg, and taking up his residence at Basle. There Holbein was under the patronage of and on terms of friendly intercourse with, the great scholar Erasmus. One bad result proceeded from this friendly familiarity, that of establishing or originating the charge that Holbein, as a young man, at least, was coarse and dissipated in his habits. The evidence is sufficiently curious. There is still in existence the copy of a Latin book, called the "Praise of Folly," written by Erasmus, which Holbein, not being a scholar, could not have read for himself, but which, according to tradition, Erasmus himself, or some other friend, read to him, while Holbein was so delighted with the satire, that he covered the margin of the book with illustrative sketches. (The sketches remain, and are unmistakably Holbein's.) Opposite a passage, recording the want of common sense and energy in many learned men, Holbein had drawn the figure of a student, and written below, "*Erasmus*." The book coming again into the hands of Erasmus, he was offended with the liberty taken by the painter, and sought to retaliate in kind by writing below the sketch of a rude boor drinking, "*Holbein.*" In spite of the rough jesting, the friendship between scholar and painter was not interrupted.

In these early days Holbein sometimes practised painting on glass, after the example of some of his kinsmen. At Basle, Holbein painted what is considered his finest work, the *Meier Madonna*, now at Darmstadt, with a copy in the Dresden Gallery, and there he executed the designs for his series of wood-cuts of the *Dance of Death*.

At Basle Holbein married, while still a young man. The presumption that the painter's marriage, like that of his countryman, Albert Dürer, was unhappy, has rested on the foundation that he left his wife and her children behind when he repaired to England, and that although he re-visited Basle, and saw his wife and family, they did not return with him to England. A fancied confirmation to the unhappiness of the marriage is found in the expression of the wife in a portrait which Holbein painted of her and his children when he was at Basle. "Cross-looking and red-eyed," one critic calls the unlucky woman; another describes her as "a plain, coarse-looking, middle-aged woman," with an expression "certainly mysterious and unpleasant." Holbein's latest biographer has proved that the forsaken wife, Elssbeth Schmid, was a widow with one son when Holbein married her, and has conjectured that she was probably not only older than Holbein, but in circumstances which rendered her independent of her husband. So far the critic has done something to clear Hans Holbein from the miserable accusation often brought against him, that he abandoned his wife and children to starve at Basle, while he sunned himself in such court favour as could be found in England. But, indeed, while Hans Holbein may have been honest and humane enough to have been above such base suspicions, there is no trace of him which survives that goes to disprove the probability that he was a self-willed, not over-scrupulous man, if he was also a vigorous and thorough worker.

Holbein went to England about 1526 or 1527, when he must have been thirty-one or thirty-two years of age, and repaired to Chelsea to the house of Sir Thomas More, to whom the painter brought a letter of introduction, and still better credentials in the present, from Erasmus to More, of the portrait of Erasmus, painted by Hans Holbein. There are so many portraits and copies of portraits of Erasmus, not only by Holbein, but by other painters—for Erasmus was painted by Albert Dürer and Quintin Matsys—that this special portrait, like the true Holbein family portrait of the More family, remains very much a subject of speculation. Most of us must be well acquainted with the delightful account which Erasmus gave of Sir Thomas More's country-house at Chelsea, and the life of its occupants. It has been cited hundreds of times as an example of what an English family has been, and what it may be in dutiful discipline, simple industry, and high cultivation, when Sir Thomas's young daughters repeated psalms in Latin to beguile the time in the drudging process of churning the butter. During Holbein's residence in or visits to the Mores' house at Chelsea, he sketched or painted the original of the More family picture.

Holbein was introduced to Henry VIII. by Sir Thomas More, and was immediately taken into favour by the king, and received into his service, with a lodging in the palace, a general salary of thirty pounds a year, and separate payment for his paintings. According to Horace Walpole, Holbein's palace lodging was probably "the little study called the new library" of square glazed bricks of different colours, designed by the painter at Whitehall. (This gateway, with the porch at Wilton, were the painter's chief architectural achievements). By another statement, Holbein's house was on London Bridge, where it was destroyed in the great fire.

We have already alluded to the anecdote of the value which Henry VIII. put on Holbein. It was to this effect: that when an aggrieved courtier complained to the king that the painter had taken precedence of him—a nobleman, the king replied, "I have many noblemen, but I have only one Hans Holbein." In fact, Holbein received

nothing save kindness from Henry VIII.; and for that matter, there seemed to be something in common between bluff King Hal and the equally bluff German Hans. But on one occasion Hans Holbein was said to have run the risk of forfeiting his imperious master's favour by the too favourable miniature which the painter was accused of painting of Anne of Cleves.

At Henry's court Holbein painted many a member of the royal family, noble and knight, and English gentleman and lady. His fortune had made him a portrait painter, but he was fully equal to other branches of art, as shown by his *Meier Madonna*, and still more by the designs which have been preserved of his famous allegory of *the Triumphs of Riches and Poverty*, painted for the hall of the Easterling Steelyard, the quarters of the merchants of Allemagne, then traders in London. In addition to painting portraits Holbein designed dagger hilts, clasps, cups, as some say after a study of the goldsmith's work of Cellini.

For a long time it was believed that Hans Holbein died after Mary Tudor succeeded to the English throne; indeed, some said that his death had been occasioned or hastened by that change in the affairs of men, which compelled him to quit his lodgings in the palace to make room for "the new painter," Sir Antony More, who came in the suite of Mary's well-beloved husband, Philip of Spain. There was even a theory, creditable to Hans Holbein, drawn from this conclusion, that he might have adopted the Protestant views of his late gracious master, and have stood by them stoutly, and so far forfeited all recognition from the bitter Catholic Mary. But, unfortunately for the tradition and theory, and for the later pictures attributed to Hans Holbein, his will has been discovered, and that quite recently, proving, from the date of its administration, his death of the plague (so far only the tradition had been right), when yet only in his forty-eighth year, as early as 1543, four years before the death of Henry VIII. In spite of court patronage Holbein did not die a rich man, and there is an impression that he was recklessly improvident in his habits.

Holbein had revisited Basle several times, and the council had settled on him a pension of fifty florins a year, provided he would return and reside in Basle within two years, while his wife was to receive a pension of forty florins a year during Holbein's two years' absence. Holbein did not comply with the terms of the settlement. About the time of his death his son Philip, then a lad of eighteen, was a goldsmith in Paris. Of Hans Holbein's portraits we have two to draw from; one, painted in his youth at Basle, shows the painter in an open doublet, and curious stomacher-like shirt, and having on his head a great flapping hat. His face is broad and smooth-skinned, with little hair seen, and the features, the eyes especially, rather small for such an expanse of cheek and chin. The other picture of Holbein to which we have referred belongs certainly to a considerably later period of his life, and represents him with short but bushy hair, and short bushy beard and moustache, a man having a broad stout person with a mixture of dauntlessness and *bonhommie* in his massive face.

Mr. Ruskin says of Holbein, as a painter, that he was complete in intellect; what he saw he saw with his whole soul, and what he painted he painted with his whole might.

In deep and reverential feeling Holbein was far behind his countryman Albert Dürer, but Holbein was far more fully furnished than Dürer (unless indeed as Albrecht Dürer showed himself in that last picture of *the Apostles*) in the means of his art; he was a better draughtsman in the maturity of his powers, and a far better colourist. For Hans Holbein was not more famous for the living truthfulness of his likenesses ("a man very excellent in making physiognomies"), than for the "inimitable bloom" that he imparted to his pictures, which "he touched till not a touch became discernible." Yet beneath this bloom, along with his truthfulness, there was a dryness and hardness in Holbein's treatment of his subjects, and he is far below Titian, Rubens, and even Rembrandt as a portrait painter.

Holbein was in the habit of painting his larger portraits on a peculiar green, and his miniatures on a blue background. He drew his portrait sketches with black and red chalk on a paper tinted flesh-colour. It is said, that with the exception of Philip Wouvvermann, no painter has been so unfortunate in having the works of other painters attributed to him as Hans Holbein has been, and "that three out of every four pictures ascribed to him are misnamed."

The *Meier, or Meyer Madonna,* is otherwise called *the Meier Family adoring the infant Christ in the arms of the Virgin.* The subject is understood to prove that it must have been painted in Holbein's youth, before Protestantism was triumphant at Basle. The figures are the Burgomaster Meier and his wife, whom Holbein painted twice; their son, with a little boy *nude* beside him; another woman, elderly, conjectured to be a grandmother of the family, and beside her the young daughter of the house. In the centre on a turkey carpet stands the Madonna, holding in her arms an infant stretching out its left hand to the group of worshippers. In course of time, and in its transfer from hand to hand, a doubt has arisen with regard to the subject of this picture. Some critics have regarded it as a votive picture dedicated in a private chapel to commemorate the recovery from sickness or the death of a child. This conjecture seems to rest mainly on the fact, that the child in the Dresden copy (it is said to be otherwise in the Darmstadt picture) is of an aspect so sickly, as to have given rise to the impression that it represented an ailing, or even a dead child, and no glorious child Christ. Critics have gone still farther, and imagined that the child is a figure of the soul of a dead child (souls were sometimes painted by the old painters as new-born children), or of the soul of the elder and somewhat muffled-up woman who might have been recently dead. Mr. Ruskin regards the picture as an offering for the recovery of a sick child.

The idea of the *Dance of Death* did not originate with Holbein, neither is he supposed to have done more than touch, if he did touch, the paintings called the *Dance of Death,* on the wall of the Dominican burial-ground, Basle, painted long before Holbein's day, by the order of the council after the plague visited Basle, and considered to have for its meaning simply a warning of the universality of death. But Holbein certainly availed himself of the older painting, to draw from it the grim satire of his wood-cuts. Of these there are thirty-seven designs, the first, *The Creation;* the second, *Adam and Eve in Paradise;* the third, *The Expulsion from Paradise;* the fourth, *Adam Tilling the Earth;* the fifth, *The Bones of all People;* till the dance really begins in the sixth. Death, a skeleton, as seen through the rest of the designs, sometimes playing on a guitar or lute, sometimes carrying a drum, bagpipes, a dulcimer, or a fiddle, now appearing with mitre on head and crozier in hand to summon the Abbot; then marching before the parson with bell, book, and candle; again crowned with ivy, when he seizes the Duke, claims his partners, beginning with the Pope, going down impartially through Emperor, King (the face is supposed to be that of Francis I.), nobleman, advocate, physician, ploughman, countess, old woman, little child, &c. &c., and leading each unwilling or willing victim in turn to the terrible dance. One woman meets her doom by Death in the character of a robber in a wood. Another, the Duchess, sits up in bed fully dressed, roused from her sleep by two skeletons, one of them playing a fiddle.

Granting the grotesqueness, freedom, variety, and wonderful precision of these woodcuts, we beg our readers to contrast their spirit with that of Albrecht Dürer's *The Knight, Death, and the Devil*, or Orcagna's *Triumph of Death*. In Holbein's designs there is no noble consoling faith; there is but a fierce defiance and wild mockery of inevitable fate, such as goes beyond the levity with which the Venitians in the time of the plague retired to their country-houses and danced, sung, and told tales, till the pestilence was upon them. It has a closer resemblance to the piteous madness with which the condemned prisoners during the French Reign of Terror rehearsed the falling of the guillotine, or the terrible pageant with which the same French, as represented by their Parisian brethren, professed to hail the arrival of the cholera.

The miniature of Anne of Cleves, if it ever existed, is lost; it is probable that what was really referred to was the portrait of Anne by Holbein in the Louvre, where she appears "as a kindly and comely woman in spite of her broad nose and swarthy complexion, but by no means such a painted Venus as might have deceived King Hal."

A well-known portrait by Holbein is that of a *Cornish Gentleman*, with reddish hair and beard. We saw this portrait not long ago, as it was exhibited among the works of the Old Masters, and so much did it look as though the figure would step from the frame, that it was hard to believe that more than three hundred years had passed since the original walked the earth.

Doubtless the last of Holbein's portrait pieces, which it is reported he left uncompleted when he died, is that of the *Barber Surgeons*, painted on the occasion of the united company receiving their charter from the king, and including the king's portrait. This picture still hangs in the old company's hall.

ANTONY VAN DYCK was born at Antwerp, in 1599. His father was a merchant; his mother was famous for painting flowers in small, and for needlework in silk. The fashion of painting "in small" had prevailed for some time. Horace Walpole mentions that the mother of Lucas de Heere, a Flemish painter, born in 1534, could paint with such "diminutive neatness" that she had executed "a landscape with a windmill, miller, a cart and horse, and passengers," which half a grain of corn could cover. At ten years of age, Van Dyck began to study as a painter, and he soon became a pupil, and afterwards a favourite pupil, of Rubens. In 1618, when Van

Dyck was but a lad of seventeen years, he was admitted as a master into the painters' guild of St. Luke. Two years later, he was still working with Rubens, who, seeing his tameness of invention, counselled him to abide by portrait painting, and to visit Italy. A year later, in 1621, when Van Dyck was twenty years of age, he went to London, already becoming a resort of Flemish painters, and lodging with a countryman of his own, worked for a short time in the service of James I.

On Van Dyck's return to Flanders, and on the death of his father, he was able to take Rubens' advice, and in 1623, when Van Dyck was still only twenty-two years of age, he set out for Venice, the Rome of the Flemish painters. Before quitting Antwerp, Van Dyck, in proof of the friendship which existed between the painters, presented Rubens with several of the former's pictures, among them his famous portrait of *Rubens' wife*. As a pendant to this generosity, when Van Dyck came back to Antwerp, and complained to Rubens that he—Van Dyck—could not live on the profits of his painting, Rubens went next day and bought every picture of Van Dyck's which was for sale.

Van Dyck spent five years in Italy, visiting Venice, Florence, Rome, and Palermo, but residing principally at Genoa. In Italy, he began to indulge in his love of splendid extravagance, and in the fastidious fickleness which belonged to the evil side of his character. At Rome he was called "the cavalier painter," yet his first complaint on his return to Antwerp was, that he could not live on the profits of his painting! He avoided the society of his homelier countrymen.

At Palermo, Van Dyck knew, and according to some accounts, painted the portrait of Sophonisba Anguisciola, who claimed to be the most eminent portrait painter among women. She was then about ninety years of age, and blind, but she still delighted in having in her house a kind of academy of painting, to which all the painters visiting Palermo resorted. Van Dyck asserted that he owed more to her conversation than to the teaching of all the schools. A book of his sketches, which was recovered, showed many drawings "after Sophonisba Anguisciola." She is said to have been born at Cremona, was invited at the age of twenty-six by Philip II. to Spain, and was presented by him with a Spanish don for a husband, and a pension of a thousand crowns a year from the customs of Palermo.

The plague drove Van Dyck from Italy back to Flanders, where he painted for a time, and presented his picture of the *Crucifixion* to the Dominicans as a memorial gift in honour of his father, but in Flanders Rubens' fame overshadowed that of every other painter, and Van Dyck, recalling an invitation which he had received from the Countess of Arundel while still in Italy, went a second time to England, in 1630, when he was about thirty years of age, and lodged again with a fellow-countryman and painter named Gildorp. But his sensitive vanity was wounded by his not at once receiving an introduction to the king, or the countenance which the painter considered his due, and the restlessness, which was a prominent feature in his character, being re-awakened, he withdrew once more from England, and returned to the Low Countries in 1631. At last, a year later, in 1632, Van Dyck's pride was propitiated by receiving a formal invitation from Charles I., through Sir Kenelm Digby, to visit England, and this time the painter had no cause to complain of an unworthy

THE RACE UP THE HILL.
(From the original painting by Birket Foster.)

reception. He was lodged by the king among his artists at Blackfriars, having no intercourse with the city, save by water. He had the king, with his wife and children, to sit to him, and was granted a pension of two hundred a year, with the distinction of being named painter to his Majesty.

A year later Van Dyck was knighted. Royal and noble commissions flowed upon him, and the king, who had a hereditary love of art, visited the painter continually, and spent some of the happiest and most innocent hours of his brief and clouded life in Van Dyck's company. Thus began Van Dyck's success in England, and it rested with himself whether that success was to be real or only apparent, enduring or temporary.

To give you an example of how often, and in how many different manners, Van Dyck painted the king and royal family, we shall quote from a list of his pictures—

"King Charles in coronation robes."

"King Charles in armour" (twice).

"King Charles in white satin, with his hat on, just descended from his horse; in the distance, view of the Isle of Wight."

"King Charles in armour, on a white horse; Monsieur de St. Antoine, his equerry, holding the king's helmet."

"The King and Queen sitting; Prince Charles, very young, standing at the King's side; the Duke of York, an infant, on the Queen's knee."

"The King and Queen holding a crown of laurel between them."

"The Queen in white."

"Prince Charles in armour (two or three times)."

"King, Queen, Prince Charles, and Princess Mary."

"Queen with her five children."

"Queen with dwarf, Sir Geoffrey Hudson having a monkey on his shoulder."

Van Dyck had several great patrons, after the king. For the Earl of Arundel, in addition to portraits of the Earl and Countess, the painter designed a second Arundel family picture, which was painted by Fruitiers. For George, Duke of Buckingham, Van Dyck painted one of his finest double portraits of the Duke's two sons, when children. For the Northumberland family Van Dyck painted, besides portraits of Henry and Algernon, Earls of Northumberland, another famous picture, that of the two beautiful sisters, Lady Dorothy Percy, afterwards Countess of Leicester, and her sister, Lady Lucy Percy, afterwards Countess of Carlisle, whose charms figure frequently in the memoirs of her time. William and Philip, Earls of Pembroke, were also among his patrons, and for the second he painted his great family picture, *The Wilton Family*. Sir Kenelm Digby, too, whose wife Venitia was more frequently painted than any woman of her day, and was not more distinguished for her beauty than for her lack of nobler qualities. Van Dyck alone painted her several times, the last after her sudden death, for her vain and eccentric, if gallant, husband, who in the end was no friend to Van Dyck.

But these high names by no means exhaust the list of patrons of a painter who, among various contradictory qualities, was indefatigably industrious. His work is widely distributed among the Scotch as well as the English descendants of the nobility whom he painted, so that the possession of at least one ancestral "Van Dyck" accompanies very many patents of nobility, and is equivalent to a warrant of gentle birth.

The Earl of Clarendon, in the next reign, had a great partiality for Van Dyck's pictures, and was said to be courted by gifts of them until his apartments at Cornbury were furnished with full-length "Van Dycks." A third of his collection went to Kitty Hyde, Duchess of Queensberry, one of the Earl's three co-heiresses. Through the Rich family many of these "Van Dycks" passed to Taymouth Castle, where by a coincidence they were lodged in the company of numerous works of George Jamieson of Aberdeen, who is said to have been for a short time a fellow-pupil of Van Dyck's under Rubens, who has been called "the Scotch Van Dyck," and who is certainly the first native painter who deserves honourable mention. Since the death of the last Marquis of Breadalbane these travelled "Van Dycks" have gone back to the English representative of the Rich family.

Van Dyck had $200 for a half, and $300 for a whole-length picture;— for a large piece of the King, Queen, and their children, he had $500. For the Wilton family picture he had $25.00. But Van Dyck soon impaired his fortune. He was not content with having a country-house at Eltham in Kent, where he spent a portion of each summer; he would emulate in his expenditure the most spendthrift noble of that reign. "He always went magnificently dressed, and had a numerous and gallant equipage, and kept so good a table in his apartment that few princes were more visited and better served." His marriage was not calculated to teach him moderation. In his thirty-ninth year the King gave him the hand of Marie Ruthven, who was nearly related to the unhappy Earl of Gowrie. She was his niece, her father having been the scarcely less unhappy younger brother Patrick, a physician, who, apprehended when a young man on the charge of being concerned in the treason of his elder brothers, spent his manhood in the Tower. He was kept a prisoner there from 1584 to 1619, nearly forty years, and was only released in his age and infirmity when his mind was giving way. Patrick Ruthven's infant daughter had been adopted, either through charity or perversity, by Anne of Denmark, and brought up first at the court of Anne, and afterwards at that of Henrietta Maria. The assertion that Marie Ruthven was a very beautiful woman has been contradicted. It was said that she was bestowed in marriage on Sir Antony Van Dyck as much to humble further the already humbled and still detested family of Ruthven, as to honour the painter; but this does not seem consistent with King Charles's known favour for Van Dyck. Yet such a view might have been entertained by Marie Ruthven herself, who, according to tradition, held herself degraded by the marriage, and never forgave the degradation. She was not a loving wife to a man who could hardly have been a very loving or loyal husband. And certainly the marriage did not unite the painter closer to the king.

With his professional industry, Van Dyck combined an equally unquenchable love of pleasure, which, with his luxurious and sedentary habits, induced paroxysms of gout, from which Rubens also suffered severely. This must have ultimately disqualified him for good work, and when his debts accumulated in greater proportion even than his receipts, in place of having recourse, like Rubens, to his painting-room, Van Dyck tried a shorter road to get rich, by following the idle example of Sir Kenelm Digby in his pursuit of alchemy and the philosopher's stone.

In the year of his marriage, Van Dyck re-visited Flanders, in company with his wife, and then repaired to France, it is understood with the intention of settling there. He was instigated to the step by his wife, and his own ambition of rivalling Rubens' triumphs at the Luxembourg; but the preference which the French gave to the works of their countryman, Nicolas Poussin, roused his latent jealousy, and so mortified him as to induce him to renounce his intention. He determined to return to England, and was, to his credit, confirmed in his resolution by the threatening civil war which was to shake his royal master's throne to the foundation, rather than deterred from it.

Again in England, Van Dyck employed Sir Kenelm Digby to make an offer on the painter's part that for eight hundred pounds he would paint the history, and a procession of the Knights of the Garter on the walls of the Knights' banqueting-room at Whitehall—that palace which was to have surpassed the Louvre, the Tuileries, and the Escurial, and from one of the windows of which Charles stepped out on his scaffold. But the proposal was rejected, and immediately afterwards the civil war broke out, and was speedily followed by the death of Van Dyck, about a year after his marriage, when he was a little over forty years old, at Blackfriars, in 1641. He was buried in old St. Paul's, near the tomb of John of Gaunt. His daughter, Justiniana, was born a short time—some say only eight days—before her father died, and was baptized on the day of his death. Van Dyck left effects and sums due to him to the amount of $100,000; but the greater part of the debts were found beyond recovery at the close of the civil war. His daughter grew up, and married a Mr. Stepney, "who rode in King Charles's life guards." His widow re-married; her second husband was a Welsh knight.

Van Dyck's character was one of those that are made of very contradictory elements. He was actuated by opposite motives which are hard to analyze, and which in their instability have within themselves, whatever their outward advantages, the doom of failure in the highest excellence. He was a proud man, dissatisfied both with himself and his calling, resenting, with less reason than Hans Holbein showed, that he should be condemned to portrait painting, yet by no means undervaluing or slurring over his work. He "would detain the persons who sat to him to dinner for an opportunity of studying their countenances and re-touching their pictures," "would have a sitter, sitting to him seven entire days, mornings and evenings, and would not once let the man see the picture till it pleased the painter." Van Dyck appears to have been a man with the possibilities in him of greater things than he attained, possibilities which were baffled by his weakness and self-indulgence, leaving him with such a sense of this as spoiled his greatest successes.

We have the varying indications of two pictures of Van Dyck from which to get an impression of his personal appearance. The first picture is that of a youthful face, soft, smiling, with dark eyes, finely-formed nose, a slightly open mouth, having a full cleft under lip, the hair profuse and slightly curled, but short, and no beard or moustache. The dress is an open doublet, without a collar, a lace cravat, and one arm half bare. The second is the picture of Van Dyck in the Louvre, which is judged the best likeness of the painter. In this his person is slender, his complexion fair, his eyes grey, his hair chestnut brown, his beard and whiskers red. He wears a vest of green velvet, with a plain collar.

In his art, Van Dyck, with something of the glow of Rubens, and with a delicacy peculiarly his own, was decidedly inferior to his great master, both in power and in fertility of genius. In the superficial refinement which was so essential a part of Van Dyck, he had the capacity of conferring on his sitters a reflection of his own outward stateliness and grace. When he painted at his best his portraits were solid, true, and masterly, but he has been reproached with sacrificing truth to the refining process which he practised. Even in the case of Charles I., whose portraits are our most familiar examples of Van Dyck, and who thus lives in the imagination of most people as the very personification of a noble and handsome cavalier, there have not been wanting critics who have maintained that Charles,—the son of a plain uncouth father, and of a mother rather floridly buxom than delicately handsome, and who was in his childhood a sickly rickety child,—was by no means so well endowed in the matter of manly beauty as we have supposed. These students of old gossip and close investigation, have alleged that Charles was long and lanky, after he had ceased to be Baby Charles; that his nose was too large, and, alas! apt to redden; that his eyes were vacillating; and his mouth, the loosely hung mouth of a man who begins by being irresolute, and ends by being obstinate. Again, in the hands of a sitter, which Van Dyck was supposed to paint with special care and elegance, it has been argued that he copied always the same hand, probably his own, in ignorance, or in defiance of the fact that hands have nearly as much and as varying character as a painter can discover in faces. Though Van Dyck painted many beautiful women, he did not excel in rendering them beautiful on canvas, so that succeeding generations, in gazing on Van Dyck's versions of Venitia, Lady Digby, and Dorothy Sydney—Waller's Sacharissa,—have wondered how Sir Kenelm, Waller, and their contemporaries, could find these ladies so beautiful.

Van Dyck certainly owed something of the charm of his pictures to the dress of the period, with regard to which he received this credit that "Van Dyck was the first painter whoe'er put ladies' dress into a careless romance." But in reality never was costume better suited for a painter like Van Dyck. The hair in the men was allowed to flow to the shoulders or gathered in a love knot, while the whiskers and beard formed a point. In the women the hair was crisped in curls round the face. The ruff in men and women had yielded to the broad, rich, falling collar, with deep scallops of point lace. Vest and cloak were of the richest velvet or satin, or else, on the breaking out of the civil war, men appeared in armour. The man's hat was broad and flapping, usually turned up at one side, and having an ostrich feather in the band; his long wide boots were of Spanish leather, and he wore gauntlet gloves, and rich ruffles at his wrists. The women wore hoods and mantles, short bodices, ample trains, and wide sleeves terminating in loose ruffles at the elbow, which left half of the arm bare. Pearl necklaces and bracelets, round feather fans, and "knots of flowers," were the almost universal ornaments of women. Another ornament of both men and

women, which belonged to the day, and was very common in the quarters we have been referring to, was a miniature enclosed in a small case of ivory or ebony, carved like a rose, and worn on the left side in token of betrothal. Van Dyck had few pupils: one, an Englishman named Dobson, earned an honourable reputation as a painter.

From Sir Antony More's time down to that of Lely and Kneller, the rage for portraits was continually increasing, and took largely the form of miniatures, which were painted chiefly by foreigners; notably by Hilliard and two Olivers or Olivier, as father and son of French extraction, and by a Swiss named Petitot. A collection of miniatures by the Oliviers, including no less than six of Venitia, Lady Digby, had a similar fate to that of Holbein's drawings. The miniatures had been packed in a wainscot box and conveyed to the country-house in Wales of Mr. Watkin Williams, who was a descendant of the Digby family. In course of time the box with its contents, doubtless forgotten, had been transferred to a garret, where it had lain undiscovered for, it has been supposed, fully a hundred years. It was two hundred years after the date of the painting of the miniatures, that on some turning over of the lumber in the garret, the exquisite miniatures, fresh as on the day when they were painted, were accidentally brought to light.

Sir PETER LELY was born in Westphalia in 1618. His real name was Vander Faes, and his father was a "Captain of Foot," who, having chanced to be born in rooms over a perfumer's shop which bore the sign of a lily, took fantastically enough the name of Du Lys, or Lely, which he transmitted to his son. Sir Peter Lely, after studying in a studio at Haarlem, went to England when he was twenty-three years of age, in 1641, and set himself to copy the pictures of Van Dyck, who died in the year of Lely's arrival in England, and whom he succeeded as court painter. Lely was knighted by Charles II., married an English woman, and had a son and a daughter, who died young. He made a large fortune, dying at last of apoplexy, with which he was seized as he was painting the Duchess of Somerset, when he was sixty-two years of age, in 1680.

With regard to Lely's character, we may safely judge from his works that he was such a man as Samuel Pepys, "of easy virtue," a man holding a low enough standard by which to measure himself and others. Mr. Palgrave quotes from Mr. Leslie the following characteristic anecdote of Lely, which seems to prove that he was aware of, and coolly accepted, the decline of art in his generation and person. A nobleman said to Lely, "How is it that you have so great a reputation, when you know, as well as I do, that you are no painter?" "True, but I am the best you have," was the answer. Lely's punishment followed him into his art, for beginning by copying Van Dyck, it is said of Lely that he degenerated in his work till it bore the very "stamp of the depravity of the age." Lely's sitters were mostly women. Among them was one who deserved a fitter painter, Mistress Anne Killigrew, Dryden's—

"Youngest virgin daughter of the skies."

In Lely's portrait of her, she is a neat, slightly prim, delicate beauty, with very fine features, and such sleepy eyes, as were probably the gift of Lely, since he has bestowed them generally on the women whom he painted.

Lely painted both Charles I. and Cromwell, who desired his painters to omit "no pimple or wart," but to paint his face as they saw it.

At Hampton Court also there are several of the eleven portraits of Admirals whom Lely painted for James II. when Duke of York.

ANTONIO CANAL, called CANALETTO, incorrectly Canaletti, was born at Venice in 1697. He was the son of a scene painter at the theatre. In his youth he worked under his father; a little later he went to Rome, and studied for some time there. Then he came to England, where he remained only for two years. We have hesitated about placing his name among those of the foreign painters resident in England, but so many of his works are in that country that he seems to belong to it in an additional sense. He is said to have "made many pictures and much money." He died at Venice when he was seventy years of age, in 1768.

The great wood-carver GRINLING GIBBONS deserves mention among the artists of this date. He was a native of Rotterdam, where he was born in 1648. He went to London with other carvers the year after the great fire of London, and was introduced by Evelyn to Charles II., who took him into his employment. "Gibbons was appointed master carver in wood to George I., with a salary of eighteen-pence a day." He died in his house at Bow Street in the sixty-third year of his age, in 1721. It is said that no man before Gibbons "gave to wood the lightness of flowers." For the great houses of Burghley, Petworth, and Chatsworth, Gibbons carved exquisite work, in festoons for screens, and chimney-pieces, and panels for pictures, of fruit, flowers, shells, and birds.

SIR GODFREY KNELLER was born at Lübeck in 1646, and was the son of an architect. He is said to have studied under Rembrandt; but if this be true, it must have been in Kneller's early youth. It is more certain that he travelled in Italy and returned to settle in Hamburg, but changing his plans, he went to England, when he was about thirty years of age, in 1675. London became his home. There he painted portraits with great success. Charles II. sat at the same time to Kneller and to Lely. Not Titian himself painted more crowned heads than it fell to the lot of Kneller to paint—not less than six reigning kings and queens of England, and, in addition, Louis XIV. of France, Charles VI. of Spain, and the Czar Peter of Russia.

Kneller was highly praised by Dryden, Addison, Prior, and Steele. Apropos of these writers, among the most famous works of Kneller are the forty-three portraits, painted originally for Tonson, the bookseller, of the members of the Kit Cat club, the social and literary club of the day, which got its name from the chance of its holding its meetings in a house the owner of which bore the unique name of Christopher Cat. Another series of portraits by Kneller are what ought to be, in their designation, the Hampton Court Beauties. These are still, like the other "Beauties," at Hampton. The second series was proposed by William's Queen Mary, and included herself, Sarah Jennings, Duchess of Marlborough, and Mary Bentinck. To Sarah Jennings men did award the palm of beauty, but poor Queen Mary, who had a modest, simple, comely, English face as a princess, had lost her fresh youthful charm by the time she became Queen of England, and was still further disfigured by the swelling of the face to which she was liable.

THE TABLE BOOK OF ART.

SECOND PART.

THE PEDDLER.
From the original painting by John Burr.

MODERN PAINTERS AND THEIR PAINTINGS.

CHAPTER I.

ENGLISH ART—THORNHILL—HOGARTH—REYNOLDS— GAINSBOROUGH—BARRY—BLAKE, &c.

RT in England was declining day by day when the first English painter who won popularity appeared in the person of Sir James Thornhill. But when we use the term popularity, we must remind our readers that popular art-ignorance was great, and that all which it had gained from the partiality of the public for foreign painters and their works, when foreign painters were no better than Le Brun and Verrio, was an artificial and affected passion for allegories which had little thought or sentiment. Even that little was most frequently not comprehended, for the allegories were simply looked at and admired for what was considered their grand effect. We do not say that there was nothing that was imposing in the result, but for the most part it was a piece of huge, hollow pomposity. It was on ceilings and staircases that these allegories were flourished or sprawled, and Sir James Thornhill was the most successful English painter of such allegories "after the style of Verrio."

Sir JAMES THORNHILL was born at Weymouth, in 1676. He came of a good Dorsetshire family, whose lands had passed from them. It was by the help of an uncle, an eminent physician, that young Thornhill was enabled to study art in London. Among his first important works was the painting of the cupola of St. Paul's, with eight large pictures from the life of the apostle. For these he was paid at the rate of ten dollars the square yard; and when one hears of painting being paid by the yard, one has reason to tremble for the production of endless yards costing still less to the painter than to his employers. Yet Thornhill's painting in the cupola of St. Paul's was valued in his own day, and not only procured for him his appointment of historical painter to Queen Anne, but numberless commissions to decorate palaces, great mansions, and churches in a similar manner. Although Sir James was no artist, he seems to have been an honest hard-working Englishman, with regard to whom one is glad to hear that he was enabled to buy back the family estate, and was knighted by George I. He also sat as member of parliament for his native town, Weymouth, and he had a real feeling for the art for which he could do little in his own person, and promoted its interests manfully and liberally.

He formed a small collection of works of the Old Masters and threw it open to young students. He urged on the government the foundation of an Art Academy, and failing in his laudable efforts, he opened at his own expense a free academy for the purpose which he had in view. Although it was not with Sir James Thornhill's will that he became, as our readers may have heard or presently will hear, closely linked with a great English painter, one recognizes poetic justice in the fact.

Sir James Thornhill died at his own seat of Thornhill in his fifty-ninth year, 1734. He had a son, sergeant painter to the navy, but otherwise undistinguished. Sir James's daughter Jane had become the wife of William Hogarth.

WILLIAM HOGARTH was born in London in 1697. His father had been a Westmoreland schoolmaster, but had come up to London and established himself there as a printer's reader. Young Hogarth, like so many of his great foreign brethren in art who were goldsmiths, began life as an apprentice to a silversmith, Ellis Gamble, in Cranbourn Alley, Leicester Square, and from his master Hogarth learned the craft of engraving on metal. When he was twenty-one years of age he renounced silver engraving for copper engraving, and began to work for the booksellers. His first known illustrations of a book were twelve small plates for Hudibras, executed when he was twenty-nine years of age. Finding copper engraving unremunerative, Hogarth, who had studied in Sir James Thornhill's academy, became a portrait painter, and made rapid progress as an artist.

In 1730, when Hogarth was thirty-three years of age, he eloped with and married Jane Thornhill, Sir James disapproving of the marriage because of the inferior birth and uncertain prospects of his proposed son-in-law. That was the generation of elopements, when they were provoked alike by the harshness of parents and the rashness of children. But very few elopements were so far justified by an honourable subsequent career, a happy and suitable union, and eventual satisfaction to parents and children alike, as happened in the case of William Hogarth and Jane Thornhill.

In a very few years Hogarth was at the head of his profession, and within the ten years between his thirty-eighth and forty-eighth years he produced his different series of moral and satirical pictures; but, though a successful painter, Hogarth was not without the mortification of seeing that his contemporaries could only partially appreciate his great genius. His series of six scenes known as *Marriage à la Mode** were sold by auction in 1750, when the painter was at the height of his power, in his forty-seventh year, but only one bidder appeared, and the whole series were knocked down to him at $575, while the frames alone had cost the painter $125.

On one occasion Hogarth paid a very short visit to France, and commemorated it and his strong English prejudices by his picture of the Calais Gate.

* See illustration for second picture of the series.

HOGARTH.

When Hogarth was fifty-six years of age he wrote a contribution to works on art under the name of "the Analysis of Beauty;" here are his own lines on his book:

> "What! a book, and by Hogarth! then twenty to ten
> All he's gained by the pencil he'll lose by the pen.
> Perhaps it may be so—howe'er—miss or hit,
> He will publish—here goes—it's double or quit."

Four years later he had the dignity of sergeant painter to the king conferred on him, and seven years later still, in 1764, when he was in his sixty-eighth year, William Hogarth died at his house in Leicester Square, but was buried in the churchyard of Chiswick near his summer villa there. His wife long survived him, and was remembered by a third generation as a lively, somewhat irascible old lady, particularly when the superiority of her William Hogarth was impugned. It is said that she was in poor circumstances before her death. We are happy to think that the statement is doubtful, though she was not in a position to refuse the Academy's pension of $200 a year, for such circumstances would have been a great contrast to those of the days when she tripped to church with her black boy walking behind his mistress, carrying her prayer-book. William and Jane Hogarth had no children.

William Hogarth was honest and frank, blunt yet benevolent. Certainly we know his portrait, or engravings from it, in which everything is English, down to his dog Trump, whose likeness is taken along with his master's. We have heard it said that the picture was characteristic in more ways than one, for that there was much of the pug and bull-dog in William Hogarth's disposition, but whether Trump were a bull-dog or no, it was rather the English mastiff which was typical of Hogarth. In his picture he sits in his plain English coat, vest, and cravat, and furred cap. It is the most unsophisticated painting costume in the world, and it suits perfectly a man whose broad face with its clumsy features, unshaded by a particle of hair, is not in the least handsome or graceful, but is wholesome and pleasant in its perfect manliness and openness, and in the abundant evidence of brains in the prominent forehead. Mr Redgrave, in his "Century of Painters," mentions a deep scar on Hogarth's forehead, faithfully rendered, as Oliver Cromwell desired his warts to be re-produced. There is no ostentation of simplicity in ignoring his position and profession, for his palette with the "curved line of beauty," which he afterwards explained and insisted upon, drawn on it and several books, volumes of Swift, Hogarth's favourite author, keep Trump in countenance in bearing Hogarth company.

As a moralist and satirist of work-a-day humanity among painters, Hogarth has never been surpassed or even equalled. His power of observation was immense, and his faculty of rendering what he observed was equal to the power. His satire is more direct than subtle, and perhaps for that very reason he comes down as with the blow of a sledge-hammer on vice and folly. He never flinched, or faltered, or screened guilt in high places; he was even careless of giving offence or forfeiting favour. Never blame Hogarth, because the vice and the folly of his day were very gross and shameful vice and folly. He saw what there was to be seen, and it was his part to scourge it, which he did so effectually that the best men of that and of succeeding generations, have thanked William Hogarth for the service that he did to truth and righteousness.

It has been objected to Hogarth, that with all his marvellous gifts of perception and execution, he was deficient in a correct idea of colour, and even in a true sense of beauty; and that with regard to the last, there is not a beautiful face to be seen in all the crowded dramatic scenes which he painted. We believe that if his colouring is not always just, he has shown instances of an excellent judgment in colour, and that while it was not his calling to illustrate beauty as such, he has here and there, as in the face and figure of the miserable wife when she is informed of the tragical death of her husband in *Marriage à la Mode*, and in the person of the innocent wife of the *Distressed Poet*, afforded ample proof that he was not without a fine feeling for beauty.

What a living and breathing gallery of old English life we have in Hogarth's series of the *Idle and Industrious Apprentices*, and how perfect it is, so far as it goes. It is complete and self-consistent—from the first picture, where the ill-conditioned, ill-looking lad sits dozing, neglecting his work, with the evil ballad of " Moll Flanders" hung up on his loom; while the pleasant, comely-faced youth is sedulously minding his business, with the volume of the "Apprentice's Guide" lying open near him,—through each intervening stage of the rise and fall (notably perfect for tender and grim humour are the industrious apprentice singing off the same book with his master's daughter in church, two reverent, obedient figures full of purity and bloom ; and the idle apprentice with his hang-dog associates gambling on the tomb-stone),—on to the noble pathos of the last meeting of the early companions, when the justice on the bench hides his face after pronouncing condemnation on the felon at the bar. What a quaint, gone-by spectacle does the *Country Inn Yard* present, from the sign of *The Old Angle* to the back of the fat woman, who is being slowly hoisted into the coach. Equally gone by is the abandonment to no discipline of *The March of the Guards to Finchley;* a ludicrous burlesque of martial pomp, which cost Hogarth the good will of George II. What riotous saturnalias are the *Election Scenes*. What overflowing fun there is in the *Enraged Musician*, distracted by street music and noises, or in the comical revelations and pretensions of the *Dancing Academy*. What terrible condemnation there is in *Gin Lane*, on which you must hear Charles Lamb. He says :—

"Here is plenty of poverty and low stuff to disgust upon a superficial view ; and, accordingly, a cold spectator feels himself immediately disgusted and repelled. I have seen many turn away from it, not being able to bear it. The same persons would perhaps have looked with great complacency upon Poussin's celebrated picture of the *Plague at Athens*. Disease and death, and bewildering terror, in Athenian garments, are endurable, and come, as the delicate critics express it, ' within the limits of pleasurable sensation.' But the scenes of their own St. Giles', delineated by their own countryman, are too shocking to think of. Yet if we could abstract our minds from the fascinating colours of the picture, and forget the coarse execution (in some respects) of the print, intended as it was to be a cheap plate, accessible to the poorer sort of people, for whose instruction it was done, I think we could have no hesitation in conferring the palm of superior genius upon Hogarth, comparing

this work of his with Poussin's picture. There is more of imagination in it—that power which draws all things to one, which makes things, animate and inanimate beings, attributes and their subjects, with their accessories, take one colour, and serve one effect. Everything in the print, to use a vulgar expression, tells. Every part is full of 'strange images of death.' It is perfectly amazing and astounding to look at. Not only the two prominent figures, the woman and the half-dead man, which are as terrible as anything which Michael Angelo ever drew, but everything else in the print contributes to bewilder and stupefy;—the very houses, as I heard a friend of mine express it, tumbling all about in various directions, seem drunk—seem absolutely reeling from the effect of that diabolical spirit of phrensy which goes forth over the whole composition. To show the poetical and almost prophetical conception of the artist, one little circumstance may serve. Not content with the dying and dead figures which he has strewed in profusion over the proper scene of the action, he shows you what (of a kindred nature) is passing beyond it. Close by the shell in which by the direction of the parish beadle, a man is depositing his wife, is an old wall, which, partaking of the universal decay around it, is tumbling to pieces. Through a gap in this wall are seen three figures ; which appear to make a part in some funeral procession which is passing by on the other side of the wall, out of the sphere of the composition. This extending of the interest beyond the bounds of the subject could only have been conceived by a great genius."

The National Gallery of England possesses Hogarth's series of *Marriage à la Mode** and his portrait of himself. The Foundling Hospital has Hogarth's fine portrait of its founder, Captain Coram,—Hogarth being one of eighteen painters of repute who presented works to the Foundling Hospital, where, in the dearth of exhibitions, the paintings had a chance of being publicly seen.

A new decade in English art begins with Sir JOSHUA REYNOLDS, who was born, in 1723, at Plympton in Devonshire, his father having been master of the Plympton Grammar School. The reading of the "Treatise on Painting" by the portrait painter, Jonathan Richardson, is said to have first given young Reynolds the eager wish to be a painter; and his earliest master was Richardson's son-in-law, Hudson, established in London, where Reynolds went to study at the age of nineteen years. Quarrelling with Hudson, Reynolds returned to Devonshire and began to practise portrait painting as a profession at Plymouth Dock, remaining and working there till his twenty-fifth year, (1746,) when his father died, and Reynolds resolved on settling in London. But three years later there occurred an important crisis in his career, when another Devonshire man, Commodore Keppel, a kind patron to the young painter, carried him off in his ship, the Centurion, to the Mediterranean, landing him in Minorca. From the Balearic Isles Reynolds made his way to Leghorn, thence to Rome, and, finally, to the cities of the north of Italy, and to Paris, from which he came back to London, after a profitable tour that lasted fully three years. From a cold caught whilst he was abroad Sir Joshua dated his deafness, and from a fall which occurred about the same time he received the wound and scar that caused the slight indentation in his under lip.

In Leicester Fields Sir Joshua's house was kept by his homely, kindly sister, Frances Reynolds, who was not without talent of her own, which she exercised in

* See Illustration.

miniature painting, and in writing a theory of beauty and taste. (She once painted Dr. Johnson, but so little to his satisfaction, that he stigmatized the likeness as "the grimly ghost of Johnson.") Sir Joshua's house was further enlivened by the presence of his young nieces, one of whom became, after the death of his sister, his heiress; and the other was the "Offie," or Theophila Palmer, who sat to her uncle for a charming portrait. The brother and sister's house became the chosen resort of all the wisdom and wit, and, following with a hankering in their train, of a good deal of the rank and fashion of London. Very inexpensive entertainments were these "evenings," modelled on the royal invitations to tea sent out by George III. and Queen Charlotte, but very matchless, when the guests included Johnson and Garrick, Goldsmith and Burke, and Dr. Burney, and with him his young daughter Fanny, who was so pleasantly cherished by these great men till her gift as a novelist came to light, when each cried out in triumph over it, as he had never cried out over his own gift. We need hardly spend more time in dwelling on that historical literary circle, where Sir Joshua made nearly as fine a figure as in his own strictly artistic walk. We can read its records in the lives of Johnson and Goldsmith, or as given by the pens of Madame D'Arblay and Mrs. Piozzi.

Besides his house in Leicester Fields, Sir Joshua had a villa at Richmond, to which he repaired for a holiday on a summer afternoon, but where he never spent a night. Indeed so unremitting was his devotion to his art, that in an interval of many years, he boasted that he had never "lost a day, or missed a line." His friend, Dr. Johnson, remonstrated solemnly, and not unsuccessfully, with Sir Joshua, on a service which had in it something of slavery and idolatry to the material and temporal, and was apt to involve the neglect of the unseen and eternal.

It was on the occasion of Reynolds being elected president of the Academy, to which George III. had consented to give the royal patronage, that the King conferred on the painter the distinction of knighthood.

When over sixty years of age a partial loss of sight compelled Sir Joshua to renounce his well-loved art, and he obeyed the compulsion with simple dignity and resignation. The end was not far off; he died in his seventieth year, in 1792. His body lay in state at the Royal Academy. At the funeral the pall was borne by "dukes, marquises, and earls." He was buried beside Wren, in the crypt of St. Paul's. A good example of Sir Joshua's smaller style is *The Coquet*,* now in the Royal collection at Windsor, and those of the *Count Ugolino and his sons*, the *Hercules Strangling the Serpents*, not to say those pictures which have more or less of fancy in them, such as *Mrs. Siddons as the Tragic Muse*, *Garrick between Tragedy and Comedy*, have enjoyed a great reputation. For his *Count Ugolino* Reynolds had $2000, for his *Hercules Strangling the Serpents*, $7,500 for his *Death of Cardinal Beaufort*, now in the Dulwich Gallery, he had $2500, and for *Mrs. Siddons as the Tragic Muse*, in the same gallery, he had $3500. These prices are given as examples of the popularity—not of the excellence of his work, for prices are no test of excellence. In the National Gallery there are excellent specimens of Sir Joshua's powers, among them his portrait of Lord Heathfield.

* See Steel Engraving.

THOMAS GAINSBOROUGH was born at Sudbury, in Suffolk, in 1727. His father was a manufacturer of says and crapes, and his uncle was master of the grammar school where Gainsborough was educated. Sudbury was then rich in picturesque old houses, and the town was set in the pleasant Suffolk scenery, for which Gainsborough had a marked preference throughout his life. Not the least picturesque house was that which the Gainsboroughs inhabited, that had once been an inn known as the Black Horse.

Gainsborough gave early signs of the bent of his genius. An anecdote is told of the robbery of a pear-tree in the Gainsboroughs' garden, when the painter was a mere boy, and of the clever sketch by which the lad was enabled to "show up" the robber. In his sixteenth year, Gainsborough went to London to pursue his studies as a painter, under artists comparatively obscure, but the best which his family could find, and in the academy in St. Martin's Lane.

When he was eighteen years of age, Gainsborough set up for himself in London as a portrait and landscape painter, but not succeeding in the bold attempt, as it was hardly possible so young a lad could succeed, he returned to Sudbury, and committed the still more daring deed of marrying at nineteen years of age. Notwithstanding the apparent audacity of the step, this marriage, which had the full approval of his friends, seems to have been the great safeguard of Gainsborough. He was just such an impulsive man, so heedless of self-interest, as, in spite of his strong will, strong common-sense, and great genius, most needed a safeguard. Marriages were made betimes more than a century ago, so that nineteen was not held so juvenile an age for a bridegroom in Gainsborough's day as it would be in ours. Besides, Margaret Burr, the bride, held an annuity of $1000, which was regarded as a comfortable little independence in those simpler times, and which, prudently managed at any time, would have placed the couple above the reach of want, and enabled the young painter, in place of painting for bread and dear life, to take time, look about him, and cultivate his talents to the highest pitch they could reach. Some men, indeed, require the spur of necessity, but it is questionable whether these are the painters of nature's creation. But of far more moment than Margaret Burr's little fortune was the fact that she was a loving wife to Gainsborough, and that, in spite of his defects of temper and of such faults as she might own, the two were an affectionate and united couple till death. It is to Mrs. Gainsborough's fond care of every scrap of her husband's work that we owe the preservation of many of the great careless painter's drawings. A pleasant story, in which her small fortune played no part, is told of the first meeting of Gainsborough and his wife. It is said that he was sketching a landscape near Sudbury, having begun to turn his attention to landscape painting, when he was interrupted in his work by a lady, who was unconscious of his occupation, and who crossed the field in front of him. The painter was forced to stop, naturally looked at the intruder, and was love-smitten on the spot.

Soon after Gainsborough's marriage he took a house in Ipswich, where he resided and painted for more than twelve years. There, while he was still a young man, he learned something in art from a friendship with Mr. Kirby, a well-reputed writer on perspective, and there he indulged in his inclination to social, and especially musical entertainments, by cultivating the acquaintance of the greatest glee singers in the town.

Gainsborough was only thirty-three years of age when he removed to Bath in 1760. He remained in Bath about the same length of time that he had dwelt in Ipswich, fourteen years, and when he was forty-seven years of age, in 1774, he came back to London as the acknowledged rival alike of Sir Joshua Reynolds in portrait painting, and of Richard Wilson in landscape painting, able to take part in the old house of the Duke of Schomberg, in Pall Mall, and to claim a high career. So well established was his reputation, that the king and queen sat to him, as they had sat to Sir Joshua Reynolds.

An interregnum occurring in Gainsborough's strife with Sir Joshua, Gainsborough exhibited seven pictures in 1777, and as many as sixteen in 1780, showing a marked preference for landscape painting in his works, and receiving in this new direction another and still stronger tribute of praise from Horace Walpole, who said with truth of a picture shown by Gainsborough in 1777, that it was "by far the finest landscape ever exhibited in England."

Gainsborough's continual wrangling with Sir Joshua Reynolds gave rise to the well-known picture called the *Blue Boy*. Reynolds had laid down the law that blue ought not to be employed in masses in a picture, when, more from a spice of malice which led Gainsborough to show that such a law was not without an exception, than with the intention of expressing his grave dissent from the view, Gainsborough painted the son of Mr. Buttall in an entire suit of blue. The result was the triumph of Gainsborough's art in the treatment of a difficult subject, so as to produce an agreeable effect under disadvantages, rather than an upsetting of Sir Joshua's theory.

In 1783 Gainsborough gratified his passion for nature, and his still growing inclination to landscape rather than portrait painting, by a sojourn among the English Lakes; but although he painted some of his finest pictures after this time, he ceased altogether to send them to the Academy's exhibitions, his other feuds having culminated in an irreconcileable quarrel with the Academy's committee on the occasion of the hanging of a particular picture, *The Village Beau*.*

Joining the great world in its rush to attend the trial of Warren Hastings, Gainsborough caught a cold which was the beginning of his last illness. A short time before his death he sent for Sir Joshua Reynolds, expressed his reconciliation with his moved rival, and murmured the memorable speech—"We are all going to heaven, and Van Dyck is of the company."

Gainsborough was in his sixty-first year at the date of his death, in 1787. He was buried at Kew. His family, who were left in moderate affluence, consisted only of his widow and two daughters, one of whom had married, we think, without her father's knowledge, and, as it proved, unhappily, the musician Fischer, with whom Gainsborough's delight in music had brought himself and his household in continual contact.

A portrait by Gainsborough startled the art world, after an interval of years, like a revelation. It was that of Mrs. Graham, of Lynedoch, and has a pathetic history attached to it. The portrait of the much-loved wife was taken shortly before her

* See Steel Engraving.

THE DEATH OF SOCRATES
(From the original painting by J. L. David)

death, which occurred previous to the completed pictures' being sent home. The bereaved husband could not bear to look on the semblance of what he had lost in this world, and did not even have the picture removed from its case. In the extremity of his grief, as an effort against the melancholy, which was darkening down upon him, he joined the army, engaged in the Peninsular war, and as a volunteer distinguished himself in his first battle. Obtaining a commission, he rose step by step, attaining one martial honour after another, till, first hailed as the gallant Sir Thomas Graham, the hero of Vittoria and Barossa, he had conferred on him the title of Lord Lynedoch. Waterloo and the long peace came, and the sorrowing widower merged into the veteran soldier, lived on till white-haired and blind, and more than ninety years of age, and still the picture of his dead wife remained in its case, in the care of a London merchant, and by the art world forgotten or unknown as a gem of art. It was not till Lord Lynedoch died, and was laid beside his wife of more than half-a-century before, in Methven Kirk-yard, that his heir came into the possession of the picture in its case, sent it to the Manchester Art Exhibition in 1856, where it flashed in its fresh glory on the art world, and generously presented it to the National Gallery, Edinburgh. Mrs. Graham was a beautiful woman, stately and blooming, in a full-dress hat, turned up at one side, and with the gown looped up, and showing the petticoat and the shoes and buckles. She holds in one hand an ostrich feather.

RICHARD WILSON was born, in 1715, at Pinegas, in Montgomeryshire; his father was a Welsh clergyman. A Welsh patron brought young Wilson up to London when a boy, and placed him in the studio of an obscure portrait painter. When Wilson had completed his art-training, such as it was, he attempted to start in life as a portrait painter, but though he had some good patrons, he did not succeed; indeed he did not establish, in that branch of his art, any claim to success. In 1749, when he was thirty-six years of age, he was able to visit Italy, and there, by the disinterested advice of the Italian and French artists, Zuccherelli and Vernet, renounced portrait for landscape painting. (Wilson had been waiting for Zuccherelli, and, in order to pass the time, had sketched the landscape from his open window. Zuccherelli looked at the sketch and inquired, with surprise, if Wilson had ever studied landscape painting. "No," answered Wilson. "Then I advise you to try, for you are sure of a great success," said Zuccherelli, and he was.

Wilson died in 1782, in his sixty-ninth year, at Llanferras, in Denbighshire.

HENRY FUSELI, or HEINRICH FUESSLY, as his name stood in the original Swiss, was born at Zurich in 1741. By descent, he inherited both his literary and artistic tastes, for his father and grandfather were alike miniature painters and compilers of memoirs of artists. Henry Fuseli was educated for the Church, but having left Zurich for Berlin, and being advised to repair to England, he established himself in London as a literary man. His talents and tastes attracted the notice of Sir Joshua Reynolds, who suggested to Fuseli his becoming a painter, and he again made an overturn of his arrangements, and started to study in Italy when he was nearly thirty years of age. He did not return to England for eight years, and it was three years later, when Fuseli was fully forty years of age, that he made the first decided impression as an artist, in exhibiting his picture of *Nightmare*. This wild and fantastic picture is said to have had its origin in experience, an experience eagerly coveted by Fuseli, and gained after many vain endeavours to produce the desired result, by his consenting to sup on raw pork; no doubt the story has its rise in the oddness of the subject of the picture, and in Fuseli's warm pursuit of whatever end he had in view. After working for Boydell's Shakespearian Gallery, Fuseli produced his principal works, which he termed his "Milton Gallery," in forty-seven large pictures from the "Paradise Lost," at which he painted for the space of nine years—brief enough space for so ambitious an attempt. It was not a success in a money-making point of view; and the artist, when he was a man of fifty years, in 1780, just ten years after his return to London, in closing his exhibition of what had constituted a gallery of his works, observed bitterly, "I am fed with honour and suffered to starve, if they could starve me." Eight years later Fuseli was elected an associate member of the Royal Academy, and married an English woman, and native of Bath, in the same year. In the following year he was elected an Academician, and about ten years later, when he was in his sixtieth year, he was appointed to an office very congenial to his literary as well as artistic tastes—that of the Academy's professor of painting. Except during his temporary resignation, for an interval of five years, he continued professor of painting till his death, at the age of eighty-four years, in 1835.

GEORGE ROMNEY was born at Dalton, in Lancashire, in 1734. His father was a cabinet-maker, and George worked with his father for a time, but, on account of his liking for drawing, was placed, at the age of nineteen, with a portrait painter in Kendal, when having learnt what his master could teach him, George Romney himself began to paint portraits. He remained for five years at Kendal, making a provincial success, and marrying in his twenty-third year a north-country girl, named Mary Abbot, who had nursed him through an illness.

In 1762, six years after his marriage, when he was the father of two children, Romney became so discontented with his whole surroundings, that he started to push his fortune in London, leaving his wife and children behind him, under the impression that they were to join him as soon as it was convenient to remove the whole family. But a homely wife and two children did not appear to the aspiring and heartless painter as desirable appendages in a rising career. He preferred to keep his household in the dark, far away in the primitive Westmoreland dales, where they continued to dwell in obscurity and frugality, while the husband and father rose rapidly into eminence and affluence. Romney's conduct was an unnatural exaggeration of selfishness and personal ambition, and our readers may think that it did not meet its deserts; but while we must be prepared for the truth of the French saying, that "a cold heart and a good digestion" form a highway to worldly success, we may be sure that, in the loss of all that makes a man worthiest and most honourable, retribution encountered the offender.

In a few years Romney took his rank with Reynolds and Gainsborough as portrait painters. He was also in repute as a genre painter. Starting in his charges with $10 a head at Kendal, he ended with $175, the same charge as Sir Joshua made, beginning even to supersede the courtly and courteous president, who had no love for the rough-hewn, over-bearing "man of Cavendish Square." Romney was never an exhibitor or member of the Academy, but he exhibited his paintings occasionally in the rooms of the rival Society of British Artists, which had an earlier date than the Academy.

Romney visited at different times Paris and Italy, remaining abroad on the second visit for two years.

In 1799, when Romney was in his sixty-sixth year, feeling his health failing, he suddenly, with characteristic cool selfishness, and callous shamelessness, returned to Westmoreland to the wife whom he had only gone to see twice in the course of thirty-seven years, an interval during which his daughter had died, and his son had grown to manhood, and entered the Church. The wife, who had been incapable of asserting her rights and retaining the respect of her husband, was equally incapable of resenting her wrongs, and so became again the dutiful nurse to the painter, who fell into a state of imbecility, and died thus, three years later, when he was in his seventieth year, in 1802.

ALLAN RAMSAY, the son of Allan Ramsay the poet, and author of the *Gentle Shepherd*, was born in Edinburgh in 1713. In accordance with his tastes he was trained a painter, and sent early, by considerable self-sacrifice on his father's part, to Italy, where he remained for years. On returning and establishing himself in London, he was appointed painter to the king. Though Allan the painter hardly equalled Allan the poet in his art, he was a good and careful portrait painter. At one time Walpole gave Ramsay the preference over Reynolds in painting women. Ramsay's excellent portraits of King George and Queen Charlotte are still at Kensington. Allan Ramsay the painter was, like his father, Allan the poet, a good and honourable man. He had inherited the taste for literature, and was remarkable for his great information and accomplishments. He died at Dover in his seventy-second year, in 1784.

JOHN OPIE, or Oppy, was born near Truro, Cornwall, in 1761. His father was, not even in the position of a small tradesman, as Romney's father was, but was a poor carpenter, so that Opie came of peasant descent, and worked at any craft which came to his hands in his youth. He became foot-boy (Mr. Redgrave doubts this fact) to Dr. Wolcott, a physician in Truro, but better known when he removed to London, as the smart unscrupulous satirist who signed himself *Peter Pindar*. Opie's master having been attracted to his protégé, in the first place, by his cleverness in taking likenesses, encouraged him in the practice both in Truro and in London, finding him sitters in the Cornish town at the modest rate of $200 a head.

By the injudicious instrumentality of his bullying patron, who quarrelled violently with Opie the moment he attempted to escape from the intolerable tyranny, the young painter, having been made to change the spelling of his name to suit what were considered the requirements of refined taste (Mr. Redgrave contradicts the change of name), was established as a portrait painter, and "puffed immoderately as an untaught genius." The puffing, as often happens, was successful for a time; "strings" of carriages full of enthusiastic sitters literally impeded the traffic in the neighbourhood of the studio of the *Cornish Wonder*.

Opie was married in 1798 to Amelia Alderson, daughter of Dr. Alderson of

Norwich, when the bridegroom was in his thirty-ninth and the bride in her thirty-first year.

Opie is said to have been uncouth, and sometimes petulant (not without reason), when made a lion of in London society. A bit of repartee is preserved by which he silenced the condescending cross-questioning of a would-be patron. With what did he mix his colours? the tormentor had blandly asked, probably primed with suggestions of amendment in the medium. "With brains, sir!" answered Opie shortly. He continued a reserved, sensitive man. He did not live long to cultivate his powers. In 1807, nine years after his marriage, and not long after he had been elected professor of painting to the Academy, Opie died, after a short illness, at the age of forty-seven. His wife, who survived him many years, edited his four lectures and wrote his biography.

GEORGE MORLAND was born in 1763. His father was a tolerable painter, famous for his crayon drawings. The elder Morland apprenticed his son to himself, withdrawing him from the Academy, which he had just entered as a student, and so far stopped his art education. Two explanations are given of this unfortunate step. The first is, that finding that the boy's clever and spirited sketches easily procured buyers, his father was so selfishly and foolishly grasping, as to cause the lad to spend the time which ought to have been given to self-improvement, on crude, faulty work. The second explanation is, that the father was a man of a strict and severe religious moral standard, and fearing for his son the corruptions of the Academy and the world, kept him under the paternal roof; and that it was in revolt from the stern discipline of his father that George Morland broke out into utter license. Probably there is a portion of truth in both statements.

The close of his apprenticeship freed Morland from the yoke which his father had made too hard for him, but he soon showed that he had received irremediable injury both morally and intellectually. He worked as little as he could help, avoided all study, and gave himself up to folly and debauchery. He could paint such paintings as would sell with the greatest facility, and purchasers never failed him, which was all that he cared for.

In 1786, when George Morland was twenty-three years of age, but wretchedly old in vice, he married a sister of Ward, the engraver's, who, in his turn, married a sister of Morland's. It is said that there was a real, and even a lasting attachment between the first couple, but it must have only served for their mutual misery, as it certainly had not the slightest effect in reclaiming Morland.

At this time, Morland's pictures were often sold, like Guido's, with the paint wet upon them, having been executed on the spur of the moment, while the buyer sat over the painter.

After a life of gross and shameless dissipation, George Morland died while lying under an arrest for debt in Eyre Street, Cold Bath Fields, in 1804, when he was forty-one years of age. His wife fell into convulsion fits upon hearing the news of his death, and died within four days, in her thirty-seventh year, husband and wife being buried together. While living, Morland had dictated his own epitaph—"Here lies a drunken dog."

JAMES BARRY was born at Cork in 1741. If Morland figured as "the prodigal" among painters of the last century, Barry was "the Wild Irishman," and as immeasurably self-conceited and arrogant in his dash of nobility as such wild heroes are apt to be. His father was a coasting trader, who kept a small public-house. When a poor, unknown lad, young Barry painted a picture, the design of which was full of poetry and feeling, representing the barbarian king of Cashel, baptized by St. Patrick. In the course of the ceremony, the saint unintentionally thrusts his spiked crozier through the bare foot of the king, who, believing the wound to be part of the initiation into the Christian life, bears it in heroic silence. This picture appeared at an exhibition in Dublin, and attracted great notice, and, what should have been of service to Barry, won him the friendship of a generous benefactor in his great countryman, Edmund Burke, who sent Barry, at his expense, to travel and study in Italy. But to such a self-willed, intolerant temper as Barry's, it is hard to say whether early success, or early disappointment, is most disastrous.

When Barry returned to England, he made what was "the pity" of his undisciplined violent nature the greater, that he showed in his works a stuttering, stammering grandeur of design and theory, all but fatally marred by the absence of qualities which he despised, but which in great painters form part of their inspiration—loving, patient truthfulness, whether displayed easily, or with sore pains in execution and colouring.

Yet, for six years he worked indomitably at a series of imaginative paintings, which he called his Elysium, and which he subsequently presented to the Society of Arts (a sad enough trophy—warning as well as trophy—of undoubted genius).

Barry's Elysium—his pictures for the Adelphi were six in number—four, 15 feet 2 inches long; and two, 42 feet long; all 11 feet 10 inches high. He proposed to illustrate the truth "that the attainment of happiness, individual as well as public, depends on the development, proper cultivation, and perfection of the human faculties, physical and moral." His first picture was Orpheus by music and song elevating a savage group. His second was a Grecian harvest-home, or thanksgiving to Ceres and Bacchus. His third was the victors of Olympia in the Greek games. His fourth was Navigation, or the Triumph of the Thames, in which a male figure borne in a car represents the river, while round the car float Drake, Raleigh, Cabot, Cooke, and in full costume, and, in oddest juxta-position, as typifying music, Dr. Burney in coat and wig of the time, while naiads and nereids are sporting round them in the waves. His fifth was *the Distribution of the Society's Rewards*, a painting of the day, and without allegory, unless in its strange anti-climax to Barry's last picture, which was *Elysium and Tartarus*, or the state of Final Retribution—a dark hill with Justice weighing the vices and virtues of mankind, and a bright Elysian field filled with groups of all who were great in learning, art, and theology. Homer, Milton, Shakespeare, Raphael and Titian, popes and cardinals, with Bishop Butler, for whose "Analogy" Barry had a special partiality, figure in the last to the number of eighty figures.

The attempt was bold and ambitious, but Barry's powers, and especially their cultivation, were not equal to his ambition. His images, though sometimes grand, were often confused, and occasionally a burlesque on his central idea. His drawing and colouring had many faults. When he began this work "he had only $4," and he had to depend for his subsistence in the long interval between beginning and ending on the uncertain profits of such night work as he could get, while all the time he held portrait painting in such high disdain, that when sitters occasionally straggled in to him he turned them off contemptuously to "the fellow in Leicester Square," Sir Joshua Reynolds, who was his pet aversion among his enemies. One cannot tell whether to cry out at the devotion, or the impractical folly of the man. Even Burke was alienated from Barry, until, though Barry could boast that he had never in his life borrowed a sixpence from any private individual, his straits in his miserable garret became so terrible that he was humbled to solicit from the Academy he had outraged, aid, which was at first refused, but afterwards granted twice in sums of $250. When his Elysium was completed Barry exhibited the pictures, and gained by the exhibition $5,000, less acceptable to his proud spirit than the recognition of his ability which was afforded by the crowds that came to see and marvel at his work. The sale of etchings of the Elysium formed his principal income afterwards. But Barry was still an art Ishmaelite, poor, and his hand against every man.

Mr. Redgrave gives this melancholy account of the wild painter's last days. "From his unceiled room which had been a carpenter's shop, not even impervious to the weather, uncleaned, unfurnished, with scarcely a bed, he had been, in the early spring of 1806, to the house where he usually dined. When about to return he was seized with a pleuritic fever; after some cordial had been administered to him, he was taken in a coach to the door of his lonely home. Alas! he either had neighbouring enemies, or some mischievous boys had stuffed the key-hole with dirt and stones; the door could not be opened, and the poor painter, shivering with cold and disease, was obliged to resort to the temporary shelter which a companion found for him, and then left him sick and alone. He unfortunately remained two days without medical aid; delirium and severe inflammation ensued, and although he rallied so much as unadvisedly to go forth to seek his friend, he lingered but a few days, and died on the 22d of February, 1806 (when he was sixty-five years of age). His body lay in state in the rooms of the Adelphi in the presence of his great work, and was buried in St. Paul's. There he rests side by side with the great ones of his profession. Posterity has reversed the position of West and his competitor: the first is last, and the last first."

WILLIAM BLAKE was born in Carnaby Market, in 1757. He was as tender, though his tenderness was not without passionate impatience and unassailable persistence, as Barry was fierce, and withal William Blake was fully the more impractical of the two men. His father was a respectable hosier, who wished to rear the son to the father's trade; but at the earnest suggestion of the wife and mother, aided by the silent appeal of the boy's drawings and poems on the back of shop bills, he consented to William's being a painter. At his own request he was apprenticed not to a painter but to an engraver, under whom he worked hard, studying also under Fuseli and Flaxman, while he still found odd moments to "make drawings illustrated by verses," to hang in his mother's room. He was not less happy as an apprentice than he was all through his life of struggles and privations, down to his poverty-stricken death-bed. Blake's history is one of the most signal instances of triumph of spirit over matter, and of the possibility of a man's holding within himself—within his reverent spirit, and the exercise of its gifts under God's permission,—the capabilities of the highest happiness in the most adverse circumstances. William Blake was always happy, and always at work from youth to age, while he was as indifferent to money-getting as to the so-called pleasures of idleness. He was a little crazy, it is true, but his craze was a very gracious craze.

When six-and-twenty years of age William Blake married a poor girl called Katherine Burtcher, conducting his courtship in his own odd, gentle, indomitable fashion. He had been telling the girl some of his troubles, when she said, "I pity you." "Do you pity me?" responded Blake, "then I love you for it;" and "so they were married;" and never had a poor genius a wife more absorbed in him and his genius, more sympathetic and uncomplaining. She never doubted the wisdom of his wildest exploits in art, saying, even when her loving eyes, under his teaching, failed to see any disentanglement from the dire, glorious puzzle, "that she was sure it had a meaning, and a fine one."

Blake began business as a print-seller with a friend for a partner, and a favourite brother for an apprentice, but the brother died, and the friend quarrelled with him. The shop was soon given up, and Blake worked thenceforth in his poor home surrounded by his family. He wrote poetry, designed, engraved, composed music to his heart's content. The closest proximity to domestic bustle did not jar upon him, for such bustle had no sordid care for him; he continued wonderfully indifferent to, and independent of, the appreciation of the world, even when he was reduced to such poverty that "he could only buy copperplates about four inches by three." But it is questionable whether this withdrawing from the outer world did not foster the vivid realization of his own visions which tended to craziness, and in Blake became absolute craziness. He began quickly to believe that the spirit of his dead brother visited him, and revealed to him secrets of tinting and engraving which he imparted to his wife, who was to be his proud and happy assistant in his art, and to none besides.

In these early days he composed his first important, and his most lasting work—the volume called "Songs of Innocence and Experience," including sixty-eight lyrics. These songs, which might have been written by an inspired child, are unapproached, save by Wordsworth—and that at a later period, for exquisite tenderness and pure fervour. The lines on the Tiger, the Chimney Sweep, and another song which dwells on the ineffable grace of God, are beyond praise. The whole have now a high reputation, but the book did not sell in Blake's day.

He proceeded as dauntless in his own very different way, as Barry was in his, as convinced of his own high calling, and at the same time an infinitely happier man, to design and engrave his *Gates of Paradise* with sixteen illustrations, his *Urizen* (the very name unintelligible) with twenty-seven illustrations, and his *Jerusalem* with one hundred tinted engravings, on which he put the moderate price of twenty-five guineas, but failed in finding a purchaser. The failure did not cost him a moment's self-distrust in the middle of his dreams, or—and the exemption was more singular—the least grudge at the heedless world. He believed that he knew himself to be so great and favoured a man that he could smile placidly at the world's blindness, and set himself to touch and re-touch his *Jerusalem* to the last.

The world indeed, so far as he crossed its path, was completely mystified by Blake. Sober-minded, matter-of-fact Englishmen, who went and looked at what they were told was "the spiritual form of Nelson guiding Leviathan," or "the spiritual form of Pitt guiding Behemoth," in an exhibition of Blake's works at the house of his brother, came away shaking their heads.

The shock which his fellow-countrymen's common sense had received, was not lessened if one of them was bold enough to visit the strange painter at work, and found himself authoritatively waved back from the chair on which the visitor was proceeding to seat himself. "Don't you see that chair is already occupied?" exclaimed the indignant painter. "By whom?" asked the open-mouthed stranger, blinking and staring at the empty chair. "Why, Lot is sitting there," says the painter quietly and decisively; and he goes on unmoved with the delineations of "enormous fishes preying on dead bodies, the great sea serpents, angels pouring out spotted plagues and furies in the sun."

Blake's small amount of remunerative work consisted in his illustrations of books, such as "Young's Night Thoughts." Perhaps the happiest period of Blake's happy life was when summoned down to Sussex by Hayley, to illustrate for him his Life of Cowper, and spent three years in the country. During that sojourn Blake used to "wander at evening by the sea, believing that he met Moses and Dante," "gray, luminous, majestic, colossal shadows," as he called them; or in the garden, "seeing fairies' funerals, and drawing the demon of a flea." And the most vexed season was on account of a misunderstanding between Cromek the publisher, and Blake and Stothard the two painters, with regard to a commission to paint a *Canterbury Pilgrimage*, when Cromek said disrespectfully of Blake's account of his having received the commission, that the statement was "one of Blake's dreams."

But the dreamer soon shook off the momentary disturbance to his impregnable peace. Getting always poorer, and it seemed happier, with "but one room for study, kitchen, and bed-room," and earnings of eighteen shillings a week for income, the poet painter was growing old, with his spirit unabated, and his gladness in life and work undimmed; constantly devising and executing fresh prophetical fancies, always more fantastic and incomprehensible. His last home was in Fountain Court, Strand, where the kindness of friends in buying his poems placed him at least above the reach of want. He began to illustrate Dante, and he still tinted his *Jerusalem* sitting bolstered up in bed at last, in order to put the final touches before he said "It is done, I cannot mend it." As he had rejoiced in life, he rejoiced in death, telling his wife—"I glory in dying, I have no grief but in leaving you, Kate;" and he asked again for pencils and brushes in order to try and paint a last likeness of his best and life-long friend. "He lay singing extemporaneous songs," and "died without his wife, who watched him, knowing the moment of his death." He died in his seventy-second year, in 1828.

In personal appearance William Blake was a little man, with a high forehead and large dark eyes.

THE TEMPTATION ON THE MOUNT.
(From the original painting by Ary Scheffer.)

An attempt was made to induce his widow to disclose the process by which he attained his brilliant, sometimes gorgeous, tints, but regarding her fidelity to her husband's memory as involved in the preservation of his secret, she constantly refused to tell it, and so it perished with her. Besides his strange designs, Blake left not less than a hundred MS. volumes of verse, which had grown for the most part as extravagant and incoherent as his drawings. A large part of Blake's MSS. are in the possession of Mr. Rossetti the painter.

JOHN FLAXMAN was a sculptor rather than a painter. He was born in 1755 at York, but was brought up in London, where his father kept a plaster-cast shop in the Strand, in which Flaxman had his first lessons in art. His delicate constitution only rendered him a more diligent scholar, and, when a lad, he was not disheartened by a painter's seeing some eyes which young Flaxman had painted, and asking him if he meant them for flounders. Flaxman early distinguished himself as an art student, and, having been counselled to direct his attention to form in classical subjects, became a modeller. In this light he was employed by Wedgwood, and was chiefly instrumental in producing the artistic excellence of the finest of the Wedgwood pottery. In 1782, when Flaxman was twenty-seven years of age, he married happily a young English woman, named Anne Denman. Meeting Sir Joshua Reynolds soon after his marriage, and being told with considerable severity, if the speech were not made in jest by the veteran bachelor artist, "So, Mr. Flaxman, I hear that you are married; if so, you are ruined as an artist," Flaxman took the remark so much to heart, that he was spurred on by it to go with his wife to Italy, and there try to reach the height of his profession.

It was while in Rome that Flaxman executed the work on which his reputation mainly rests,—no marble or plaster group, though he did good work as a sculptor, but his series of graceful, life-like, and yet scholarly designs from Homer, Æschylus, and Dante for Mrs. Hare, the Countess of Spenser, and Mr. Hope. These designs, of which there are many copies, are regarded as so thoroughly artistic, and in the spirit of the masters, as to be unrivalled.

Flaxman's position was established when he returned to London, and he was elected, first an associate, then a member of the Academy, and latterly its first professor of sculpture. He died in 1826, when he was in his seventy-second year, having survived his wife six years. He was a mild, unassuming, devout man, somewhat tinged by Swedenborgian opinions, and was greatly liked by his friends and contemporaries.

THOMAS STOTHARD was born in London in 1755. His father was landlord of the Black Horse in Long Acre, London. Thomas Stothard was a delicate little child, and was boarded, for his health, in the country, up in Yorkshire, his father's native county, with the widowed mistress of the village school of Acomb. Already he amused himself by drawing. From Acomb he was removed to a better school, and at the age of thirteen returned to London, where he still pursued his education. His father died when he was fifteen years of age, leaving the lad six thousand dollars. He was apprenticed to a silk pattern designer, and occupied his spare time in drawings from the poets. The publisher of the *Novelist's Magazine* engaged Stothard in these illustrations for books, in which the artist won name and fame, and for which he renounced pattern drawing. He was paid five dollars for each of his designs for the *Novelist's Magazine*, and his work meeting at once with appreciation, employment was freely offered him. He designed illustrations for the *Poetical Magazine*, the *Town and Country Magazine*, the *Ladies' Magazine* (where the vagaries of fashion must have tried him sorely), for *Bell's British Poets*, *Ossian*, &c., &c. Among his drawings for goldsmith's work, that of the Wellington Shield is well known.

Thomas Stothard died at his house in Newman Street, London, when he was seventy-eight years of age, in 1834.

ANGELICA KAUFMANN was, as her name implies, of German origin, and was born at Schwarzenberg in the Vorarlberg, in 1742. Her father was a portrait painter, as, we think, we shall find all the women who were artists, received their artistic bent by descent. Joseph Kaufmann cultivated his daughter's talents, carrying her for that purpose to Milan, to Rome, and Venice. An English woman of rank brought Angelica Kaufmann to England, in 1765, when she was in her twenty-fourth year. Her gifts and accomplishments were regarded with much respect by a generation in which English women were struggling to free themselves from the illiteracy that had become their portion at the Restoration.

Three years after she came to England, while she was still under thirty years of age, Angelica Kaufmann—or Mrs. Kaufmann, as people named her with old-fashioned courtesy, when gallant artists did not term her the "fair Angelica"—was elected a member of the Royal Academy, being treated with marked distinction by the president, Sir Joshua himself. In return for this consideration and her gratitude, the artistic world chose to couple the two painters' names together, and make game of the connection, saying now that the fair Angelica had a "tenderness" for Sir Joshua, now that she coquetted with him. The painter who seemed really to have been smitten by the accomplished lady, and who followed her abroad, was Nathaniel Dance.

In reality, Angelica Kaufmann was rather an accomplished woman, a good linguist, and a fine musician, than an artist of any value; her painting was simply mediocre. Unhappily for her she became, during her stay of seventeen years in England, the victim of one of those sorry tragedies, the elements of which are credulous vanity on the one side, and heartless fraud on the other. At the same time that Angelica Kaufmann appeared and was made much of in English society, a Swedish nobleman, called Count Horn, presented his credentials and got an equal welcome from the great world. Not unnaturally, as it might seem, the Swedish nobleman was attracted by the much-admired and sought-after German artist, showed himself more and more won by her, and ended by tendering her an offer of marriage, an offer which was accepted, and the marriage was celebrated immediately and quietly, to satisfy the impatience and the sensitive modesty of the bridegroom. Within a few weeks another Swedish nobleman arrived in England, announcing and proving himself to be the true Count Horn, while he denounced the roguery of his valet who had stolen his master's letters of introduction, and used them to personate the Count, trusting to put the deception to profit before he could be overtaken and exposed. The story reads like a scene in Molière, but it was no sparkling comedy to the miserable and unfortunate woman who had been deluded and betrayed by the base misrepresentation. So far it was unsuccessful, for Angelica Kaufmann had the courage and honesty to accept her release from a marriage which had been concluded under false pretences, and to leave the pretender to such punishment as could find him. After his death, and thirteen years later, in 1781, Angelica Kaufmann was married again more fitly to Antonio Zucchi, a Venitian painter, and an associate of the Academy. But this marriage proved also an unhappy one. The husband and wife went together to Rome the year after their marriage, and twenty-five years later she ended in Rome a varied and troubled career. Her death occurred in 1807, when she was sixty-five years of age. "Her funeral was conducted with great pomp. Above one hundred ecclesiastics in the habit of their different orders, the members of the literary societies in Rome, and many of the nobility, walked in the procession. The pall was borne by young women dressed in white. Two of Angelica Kaufmann's best pictures were carried immediately after the corpse."

Sir THOMAS LAWRENCE was born at Bristol in 1769. His father was a well-born inn-keeper in the town of Devizes, and young Lawrence, a beautiful child, early showed signs of his future calling by taking the likenesses of his father's customers. The boy was so praised and pushed on, that "he set up as a portrait painter in crayons at Oxford, where his brother was a clergyman, when he was no more than ten years of age, and a short time afterwards took a house at Bath," and actually "at once established a good business," but this early ripeness was a doubtful omen.

In a few years, Lawrence relinquished crayons, and adopted oil painting as his medium in art. He came up to London in his nineteenth year, and had the discretion to become a student in the Academy. He was then as remarkable for his personal attractions and winning manner, as for his precocious talent. He was a very handsome lad, with "chesnut locks flowing on his shoulders," and his fellow-students thought that another "young Raphael" had come amongst them. His success and popularity were still against him, for after being elected an associate of the Academy, and appointed Sir Joshua Reynolds' successor as painter to the king, while he was yet no more than twenty-two years of age, it would have required the great mental calibre of the old painters to have enabled the young man to go on seeing his faults and correcting them. It is said triumphantly that Lawrence was "at the head of his profession at an age in which other painters have generally been labouring in the toils of studentship." But premature pre-eminence is the ruin of many a clever man, who may not indeed be a genius, because genius will surmount the subtlest as well as the severest assaults, but who, had he been lucky enough to have been kept a journeyman, might have been at least the best that the range of his faculties would have permitted him to be. Lawrence neither went abroad (until he was in middle age) to study the great works of the foreign masters, nor did he ever try experiments or alter his method, though, as he advanced in fame and in life, he grew much slower in his practice, and took great pains with his work.

Lawrence possessed a dangerous charm to fascinate his contemporaries, and even Reynolds is reported as having fallen under its influence. The painter enjoyed the utmost prosperity, having an accumulation of work upon his hands, which prevented him latterly from painting much more than the heads of his sitters, leaving the rest of the figures and their accessories to his assistants. His prices, after 1820, were $1,050 for a head, $2,100 for a half-length, and $3,150 for a full-length. For *Lady Gower and Child* he received $7,500.

Lawrence was sent to Aix-la-Chapelle by the Regent to paint the allied sovereigns as the nucleus of the Waterloo Gallery at Windsor, and from Aix-la-Chapelle the painter went to Vienna, a great journey in those days, and then to Rome, where he painted the portraits (two of the best) of the Pope and Cardinal Gonsalvi. The terms of the commission to go to Aix-la-Chapelle were not more than $5,000 for travelling expenses and loss of time, with the usual price for each picture. The painter travelled in his own carriage, and was treated with every mark of distinction, and in the end reaped such a harvest of royal and noble commissions from the expedition, that the year which it occupied brought to him the sum of at least $100,000.

When at work at Aix-la-Chapelle with the Emperor of Russia for a sitter, the emperor put the pegs into Lawrence's easel, and helped him to lift the portrait on them, after the fashion of Charles V.'s condescension to Titian. Jewelled snuff-boxes and diamond rings proved more substantial tokens of the allied sovereigns' favour for the painter. The true Waterloo heroes who sat to Lawrence in England had their ranks fitly headed by the Duke of Wellington in the dress which he wore and the horse which he rode on the field of Waterloo.

Lawrence was elected a full member, and was afterwards President of the Academy; he was made a member of the Academy of St. Luke at Rome; he was knighted by the Prince Regent, and he was created a Chevalier of the Legion of Honour.

While Lawrence was in the receipt of a large income, he was constantly in pecuniary difficulties. His passion for art collection was the cause.

Sir Thomas Lawrence died at his house in Russell Square, in 1830, when he had reached the age of sixty-one years.

CHAPTER II.

TURNER—WILKIE—HAYDON—ETTY—CONSTABLE —NASMYTH—COX—PROUT, &c., &c.

HE great landscape painter, JOSEPH WILLIAM MALLORD TURNER, was born in 1775, in Maiden Lane, Covent Garden, London. His father was a hairdresser, in humble circumstances. His mother was a woman of violent temper, which ended in insanity. Young Turner practised his art betimes, exhibiting his drawings, it is said, in the windows of his father's shop. A drawing of the old church at Margate is believed to have been executed in his ninth year. It is Mr. Redgrave's opinion that, though Turner's early home was in a labyrinth of lanes, in the heart of a great city, it was not without its advantages, which he laid hold of in his future career. The quaint old city buildings fostered, perhaps originated, his taste for architecture, and the broad Thames developed his predilection for river scenery, under every aspect; while visits to uncles at Brentford and Bristol brought him in contact with fresh landscapes.

Turner became a student of the Royal Academy when fourteen years of age. Unlike Lawrence in every respect, it is probable that the gruff, uncouth man of later years was as gruff and uncouth a boy. But whatever Turner wanted in amiability, he was from the first the most industrious and independent of lads. From an early date, he coloured prints for the engravers, thus beginning the connection with booksellers, which he maintained so largely throughout his life. He also washed in backgrounds for architects, and gave lessons in drawing.

In 1790, when fifteen years of age, Turner exhibited his sketch of *A View of the Archbishop's Palace at Lambeth*. Of thirty-two drawings shown between the same year, 1790, and 1796, twenty-three were views of the great cathedrals and abbey churches of the kingdom. He had already started on those sketching tours, which he prosecuted indefatigably, and which he turned to marvellous account. He seemed to make his arrangements from the first, with the jealous secrecy which was so marked a feature in the man, and to conduct himself with characteristic eccentricity.

When sketching in a street in Oxford, being annoyed by the curiosity of the passers-by, he hired an old post-chaise, brought it on the scene of action, entered the chaise, and from its window finished his sketch.

Turner confined himself at first to water-colour painting, which might be said to be still in its infancy. A trait of his genius, on which most of his critics agree, was his tendency to commence, by imitating successfully the masters, in any field in which he desired to excel. Mr. Redgrave's theory is that Turner, with full consciousness of his own powers, desired to match himself with successful painters, and having done so (with what grim satisfaction to himself, who can say?), his originality carried him far beyond his models. In his youth, landscape painting was but an exercise of topography; that is, a literal rendering, bit by bit, of a landscape, without special selection in grouping, special phase, or the employment of the ideal faculty. Turner soon began to draw from the precious store which his devotion to nature from boyhood, and his equally devoted practice of his art in his perpetual sketches, taken at all times and in all places—from the top of a coach, from the deck of a boat—had enabled him to accumulate, in order to break this dead level of water-colour art. These sketches, many of them in the possession of the nation, show the passion of art which possessed the man, and impelled him to never-ending attempts to seize, arrest, and preserve not only every form of animal and vegetable life, but, what was yet dearer to him, every shifting, changing light, every glorious effect of atmosphere, every blended and contrasted hue—silvery and pearly, ashen grey and purple black, fiery red and golden yellow—which the sky, with its reflection on the earth, could assume. His studies of sky alone "are reckoned by thousands." Such an unhalting, unabated pursuit of art, takes away one's breath.

Turner exhibited his first picture in oils—*View of the Thames at Millbank by Moonlight*—in 1797, when he was twenty-two years of age, and just as he had begun his efforts by following closely his predecessors in water-colour painting, he now followed in oil the Dutch school, and Wilson and Claude, all in their turn to be left behind, while Turner pursued his own solitary and often transcendant way. His growing disposition to deal with his subjects as " sun-lighted, or shrouded in mist or storm," is illustrated by such quotations from the catalogue of his works at this time, as *Fishermen previous to a Storm, Kilgarran Castle, hazy sunrise, Warkworth Castle, Thunderstorm, approaching sunset, Abergavenny, clearing up after a Shower, The wreck of the Minotaur.** He was elected an associate of the Academy in 1799, a member in 1800, when he was in his twenty-fifth and in his twenty-eighth year. He had early removed from his father's house to rooms in Hand Court. In 1800, he established himself in Harley Street, and the following year in Norton Street, Portland Place.

In 1801 and 1802, Turner extended his sketching tours to France and Switzerland. In 1807, when he was thirty-two years of age, he was appointed professor of perspective in the Academy, filling the office for thirty years. In 1808, he began his famous series of prints in brown ink, called *Liber Studiorum*, a sort of version of Claude's *Liber Veritatis*. Turner continued the series for eleven years, till it extended

---

* See Illustration.

to seventy-one plates, which he sold in 1820 for $73.50, a sum that one of the plates would bring now. Turner was constantly engaged by the booksellers in such works as *Southern Coast Scenery*, *England and Wales*, *Rivers of England*, *Rivers of France*, *Rogers' Italy*. His exhibited pictures, between 1787 and 1850, are 275—a rare amount of work (and such work!) in modern days. In 1819, Turner visited Italy, and from that visit dates one of the changes in, and new developments of, his genius. He visited Italy twice again, in 1829 and about 1840. Close upon the year of Turner's last visit to Italy dates the final and, as many hold, disastrous transition in his style.

In 1812, Turner had built for himself a house and gallery in Queen Anne Street, and he had also a country-house at Twickenham, which he sold in 1827. He was amassing a large fortune, and at the same time establishing and spreading his fame, while his habits were becoming always more cynical and repulsive. A reserved and morose man from his youth, at the same time he was not without a certain bearish geniality, where his brethren in art were concerned. He seems to have been regarded with mingled admiration, wonder, and awe, and doubtless with some asperity and disgust, by his comrades and his pupils. Mr. Redgrave, who appears to have received from Turner marks of favour, and who, in addition to his gratitude, appreciated the giant in art's saturnine humour, gives a very amusing, while a kindly description of Turner's manner as a critic and lecturer. His growls, his mumbled words, his pokes in the side, his use of his broad thumb, or snatches at porte crayon and brush to point out an error, with the half of his lecture delivered over his shoulder, in the midst of directions to the attendant who was arranging the sketches and diagrams. In appearance, Turner was a short, stout man, with a very red and somewhat blotched face, in which the eyes were bright and restless, and the nose aquiline. His hands were fat, and were kept not over-clean. He was slovenly in his dress, wearing a black dress-coat in want of brushing, and in the warmest as well as the coldest days, he wore round his throat a wrapper, which he would unloose and let the ends dangle down in front, and dip into the colours on his ample palette. He worked hat on head, or else with a large wrapper over his head. Mr. Redgrave compares Turner's appearance to that of a coach driver of the old school. Mr. Leslie likens the great master's personality to that of a ship-captain.

Latterly, Turner did not live in his house in Queen Anne Street, but kept his pictures there, suffering not merely the house but the pictures to fall into the greatest dilapidation. Nothing was more curious in that strange nature of Turner's than his behaviour with regard to his pictures. He was exacting in his money transactions, and sordid in his way of living, and he was bent well-nigh with fierceness on asserting his claims to the highest fame, yet in the later years of his life he not only refused to sell many of his pictures—appearing to take a malicious pleasure in the refusal,—but bought back several pictures which he had sold, and suffered the whole collection to be irreparably injured by the damp and decay of utter neglect, before he bequeathed it, like the gift of a prince, to the nation.

As a landscape painter, Turner fills now the first place. Other landscape painters may have equalled or even surpassed him in some respects, but none " has yet appeared with such versatility of talent." This is the testimony of so impartial a judge as Dr. Waagner, though—after referring with enthusiasm to Turner's power over earth and air and sea, and to his deep sympathy with the most varied moods of nature, in its grandeur, melancholy, and cheerfulness,—he qualifies it by the clause, "I should not hesitate to recognize Turner as the greatest landscape painter of all times, but for his deficiency in an indisputable element in every work of art, viz., a sound technical basis." Turner died in 1851.

SIR DAVID WILKIE was born in the manse at Cults, Fifeshire, in 1785. His father was a minister of the Kirk of Scotland, and parish minister of Cults, one of the smallest parishes in the Kirk; nevertheless the minister on his slender income married three times, and the painter was a son of the third wife's.

Wilkie went as a boy to the village school of Pitlessie, and electrified school-fellows, dominie, and all, by chalking a head on the floor.

Wilkie left the Edinburgh Academy and returned to Cults in 1804, when he was in his nineteenth year. In his first attempt at painting on his own account, and at home, he hit, by a happy prevision, on the very vein which he was to work to such profit. Wilkie chose for his first picture the great yearly event of the parish, no doubt the great gala of his childhood, Pitlessie Fair, with its innumerable rustic interests and homely fun. In the very choice there was the individuality of genius, since the lad had been kept in his Academy studying the antique, with allegorical and historical art, or portrait painting, held up as the sole aim of his ambition. Of a species of genre painting Hogarth had, indeed, already afforded the best English example; but not only was Wilkie removed from much association with Hogarth's works, which it was not the fashion of the day to turn to, but the young Scotsman early instituted a school of genre, distinct from Hogarth's, far less dramatic, deficient in the terror, if not in the pity, aiming at no vigorous moral, but cultivating "the beauty of innocence instead of the hideousness of crime."

The *Village Politicians* was followed in due time by the *Blind Fiddler*,* *Alfred in the Neat-herd's Cottage* (a mistaken turning aside into historical painting), *The Rent Day*, the *Jews Harp*, &c., &c., until the *Village Festival* was attained. This fine picture was sold to Mr. Angerstein for four thousand dollars, and is now in the National Gallery. Between *Pitlessie Fair* and the *Village Festival* there was an interval of five years in time, but the advance in art Mr. Redgrave declares "is almost that of a life-time." Wilkie in his twenty-fifth year was assured of the fame which he had coveted, and already a year earlier, in 1809, he had been elected an associate of the Academy.

In 1811, when Wilkie was twenty-six years of age, he was elected a member of the Academy. The following year his father died, and his mother and sister came up to London to find a home with the son and brother at No. 24, Lower Phillimore Place, Kensington. The affectionate companionship of the women of his family was a great boon to a delicate man of domestic habits, who had shown no inclination to marry.

Wilkie had just before tried a private exhibition of his works, which as a money speculation proved a failure.

---

* See Frontispiece, Steel Engraving.

PRAYER IN AN ARABIAN MOSQUE.
From the original painting by Mariano Fortuny

In 1814 Wilkie visited Paris along with his brother artist, Haydon, remaining five or six weeks in France; and in 1816 he visited Holland and Belgium, without showing himself on either occasion impressed as he was by his next foreign tour. In 1820, when Wilkie was thirty-five years of age, he painted his *Reading of the Will*, for which he had a commission from the art-loving King of Bavaria. It formed then an almost isolated instance of a British painter being asked to paint for a foreign gallery.

In 1816 Wilkie received from the Duke of Wellington a commission to paint a picture, which resulted in the famous *Chelsea Pensioners Reading the Gazette of the Battle of Waterloo*. Wilkie's health failed in the course of painting the picture, and delayed its completion, but he was enabled to exhibit it in 1822, when it was acknowledged to be, what it continues to be held, one of his best works. So great was the enthusiasm of the public, which had but a few years before hung breathless on the war news, that "the visitors to the exhibition had to be railed off from it, waiting *en queue* their turn to pass in front.

Wilkie's *Penny Wedding* and *Blind Man's Buff* had found their way to the English Royal Collection, and in 1822 the painter received a commission from George IV. to paint a companion picture, which Wilkie desired to make *John Knox Preaching before the Lords of the Congregation*, but, to meet the king's preference for a humorous subject, Wilkie substituted his *Parish Beadle*.

In the autumn of 1840, when Wilkie was fifty-five years of age, while his hands were full of commissions, and he had recovered his earlier prosperity, if not his popularity, he suddenly started on a voyage to the East. His explanation of this step was, that, while he had been strongly affected by the religious art of Italy, he had been struck by the fact that none of the great Italian painters had possessed the advantage of visiting and becoming personally acquainted with the scenes of sacred history. He was convinced that a new and deeply interesting field awaited the painter in the Holy Land; and he hoped, by his example, to incite his younger countrymen to repair at once to the localities of Scriptural events, when the great work was to be essayed of representing Scripture history. After a prosperous journey to Constantinople, where he was delayed by a war in Syria, and where he improved the delay by painting the Sultan, Wilkie, by way of Smyrna and Beyrout, reached Jerusalem, and resided there five weeks, taking sketches and notes, finding himself much impressed with what he saw of the theatre of that awful drama with which he had been familiar from his earliest childhood in the Scotch manse. On his return to Alexandria he began a portrait of the Pasha of Egypt, but longed for home. He sailed from Alexandria, still enjoying the better health which had latterly been his portion; but at Malta, in consequence of eating fruits and ices, he was seized with illness, which was only partially subdued, and recurred with greater violence during the night before the ship left the island. Wilkie sank under the attack, and died within an hour of clearing the harbour, on the 1st of June, 1841, in the fifty-sixth year of his age. The vessel put back, but the authorities would not permit the body to be landed, and it was buried at sea the same evening.

BENJAMIN ROBERT HAYDON was born at Plymouth in 1786. He was the son of a bookseller, who claimed descent from an old Devonshire family. He was educated at the Plymouth grammar school (where he had a congenial companion in the future water-colour painter Prout), and apprenticed to his father; but having a passion for art, he resolved, against the wishes of his parents, on being a painter, and came up to London in 1804, when he was eighteen years of age, with one hundred dollars in his pocket. He was, we are told, self-willed and self-reliant. In addition, his inordinate self-conceit was already developed. He aimed at revolutionizing and reforming art, by introducing a higher standard. He was another Barry without Barry's independence and consistency, and Haydon's fate was still more tragic than Barry's, for the gleams of success and good fortune which occurred in Haydon's case, and of which he might have availed himself, served but to present a broader contrast to his ultimate failure and destruction.

When Haydon came up to London he brought a letter of introduction to his townsman, Northcote, who, hearing his arrogant as well as confident aspirations, tried in vain to warn him. "Historical painter! Why, ye'll starve with a bundle of straw under your head." But Haydon, with constancy worthy a more modest and wiser man, would not be deterred from his course. He entered the Academy as a student, and had Wilkie for a fellow-pupil, and the following year Haydon set himself to paint a great picture. Which is greater—the pathos, or the juvenile audacity of the statements of the lad of twenty on the occasion! "On the first of October, 1806, setting my palette, and taking brush in hand, I knelt down and prayed God to bless my career, to grant me energy to create a new era in art, and to rouse the people and patrons to a just estimate of the moral value of historical painting." Having painted this picture, the subject of which was *the Flight into Egypt*, Haydon, whose talents and theories were not likely to pass into obscurity from any want of assurance and pertinacity on his part in pressing their claims, dunned the authorities till the picture was hung. Content for the moment, and satisfied of the certain success of a work whose immense superiority for a first picture, he did not hesitate to write many years later, he returned to Plymouth for a time, and practised portrait painting.

He had no want of sitters, nor of fair prices, at the rate of $100 a head, for the very vanity and self-assertions of the man were imposing, while his genuine enthusiasm for art was infectious. One is struck in reading Haydon's life, not so much with his reverses as with the fascination which he exerted, at different times, over many people, and at the fitful bursts of prosperity which that fascination, quite as much as any exhibition of his abilities, procured for him. Haydon's opinion of the portraits executed by him did not at all equal his conviction of his power as a historical painter. He calls them plainly "execrable," and only hugs himself on the desire to encourage him manifested by his sitters. Later in this matter of portraits, he is guilty of the outrage on honour and feeling of protesting that he had "an exquisite gratification in painting portraits wretchedly;" he loved "to see the sitters look as if they thought, Can this be Haydon's painting?" He chuckled. He was "rascal enough to take their money and chuckle more." But possibly Haydon, in his mad pride, made himself out worse than he really was, and this base malice was but a creation of his monstrous egotism.

On coming to London a second time, he got from Lord Mulgrave a commission to paint the "*Murder of Dentatus*, at the moment when the old Roman tribune makes his last effort against his own soldiers, who attacked and murdered him in a narrow pass." For the painting of this picture, which occupied him some time, Haydon studied closely the Elgin marbles, giving a very characteristic account of the origin of his study. Having gone to visit the marbles in company with Wilkie (no two men could have been more unlike than Haydon and Wilkie, yet a considerable intimacy seems to have existed between them), he saw at once that here were the principles which he had been struggling for in his first picture; "here were the principles which the great Greeks, in their finest time, established;" and here was he, the most prominent historical student, perfectly qualified to appreciate these principles. He would draw from the marbles, according to his own account, "for ten, fourteen, fifteen hours at a time, holding a candle and my board in one hand, and drawing with the other," and so he should have stayed till morning if the porter had not put him out at twelve o'clock, when he went home benumbed and damp, his clothes steaming up as he dried them. He would spread his drawings on the ground, would drink his tea at one o'clock in the morning, look at his picture, dwell on his drawings, ponder the changes of empire, and pray to God to enlighten his mind to discover the principles of Divine things, and then he had "inward assurances of future glory." Alas, alas! for all this enthusiasm in which there was no moderation, and this reverence in which there was no humility. Lord Mulgrave invited the painter to his house, and Haydon was not above being dazzled with a vision of rank and fashion, and despised from that time the society of the middle classes. His own statement is that the upper ten thousand flattered and caressed him, which might well appear the fact to a man so inflated with his own importance.

When *Dentatus* was finished, and sent to be hung, it need hardly be said that Haydon was furious at the picture's only getting a fairly good place in the estimation of his brother artists. Another check, which almost any other man would have felt more keenly, was that, though Lord Mulgrave paid Haydon two hundred guineas for the picture, the noble patron was cold in his praises, and even Haydon's friend Wilkie could not say much in the picture's behalf. But if the whole world had stood cold and silent, Haydon would only have concluded that the whole world had conspired against him, who was more especially a victim of the jealousy and tyranny of the Academy, against which he now entered, like Barry, on a life-long feud, in which there were few truces. His ravings at the injustice dealt to him, and the persecutions inflicted on him, were like the ravings of a mad-man. His friends remonstrated and reasoned with him in vain, and in the end he consoled himself for the breach with the lofty assertion that otherwise he should never have won his "grand and isolated reputation."

The baffled man was at last reduced to painting for bread, chiefly repetitions of *Napoleon at St. Helena*, *Napoleon in Egypt*, *Napoleon in his bedroom*, of which he records in 1844, "I have painted nineteen Napoleons, thirteen of them at 'St. Helena;' by heavens! how many more?" At least ten or twelve more followed, when, despairing of getting work from the Royal Commission, he resolved, in self-justification, to complete his designs for the House of Lords. He struggled on and finished two, *The Banishment of Aristides—the injustice of Democracy*, and *Nero playing on his Lyre while Rome was burning*, and *Quintus Curtius*. Haydon also attempted a private exhibition of these pictures, but, unlike his former exhibitions, it proved a failure, and he lost five hundred and fifty-five dollars, with the poor consolation that his successful rival who was exhibiting in the same building, was General Tom Thumb. Haydon made this mocking, bitter entry, one of the last, in his diary, "Tom Thumb had 12,000 people last week, B. R. Haydon 133½ (the half a little girl). Exquisite taste of the English people."

The wretched painter was, in addition to the heavy difficulties with which he had been for many years struggling, wounded to the quick. "Young men were selected for the work which he had made the ambition of his life, and he was contemptuously passed by." The public refused to redress or even listen to his wrongs. He began his third design for the work he had lost, *Alfred and the Jury*, and sat staring at his picture like an idiot."

On the 22nd of June, 1846, he made this ghastly grotesque entry into his diary: "God forgive me! Amen. Finis, B. R. Haydon. 'Stretch me no longer on the rack of this rough world,' *Lear*," and shot himself. It is a comfort to add that the doctors who were engaged in the post-mortem examination declared that Haydon's brain was diseased.

WILLIAM ETTY was born in 1787 in York. His father was, "like the fathers of Rembrandt and Constable," a miller. He was also a baker of ginger-bread, which his wife sold. The industrious couple were Methodists, and brought up their family not only respectably but piously.

"My first panels on which I drew were the boards of my father's shop floor, and my first crayons a farthing's worth of white chalk," wrote Etty long afterwards.

Etty began his independent efforts in his profession with marked and protracted want of success, and he is a lively illustration of the gain of perseverance. His trials for the Royal Academy's gold and silver medals unfortunately failed. Work after work of Etty's was refused admission to the Academy and to the British Institution, till 1811, when he was twenty-four years of age.

In 1820, when Etty was thirty-three years of age, his *Coral Finders* at last made an impression on the public. The year after, the splendid colour of his *Cleopatra sailing down the Cydnus* was a still more decided hit, and, according to Leslie, " one morning he—Etty—woke famous, after the opening of the Exhibition." He had also found a worthy patron in Sir Francis Freeling.

In the following year, 1822, Etty went abroad—he was still but thirty-four years old—and remained for eighteen months, this time visiting Rome and Naples, as well as Florence, but making his longest stay, as was natural for him who was to be the great English colourist, in Venice, which he apostrophized as " Venice the birth-place and cradle of colour, the hope and idol of my professional life."

In 1826 he tried a much larger canvas in *The Combat—woman Pleading for the Vanquished*, which was bought by his fellow-worker Martin (the painter of high art in ideal landscapes, and such historical scenes as *Belshazzar's Feast;* a man of genius,

* See Illustration.

but crippled in the expression of his imagination, so that its effects were turgid and exaggerated). Etty's next great work was his *Judith and Holofernes*, forming a series in three acts after the manner of a triptych, the principal subject being in the centre, the two secondary subjects in wings. The series was bought by the Royal Scottish Academy, which has also his *Combat*, and his culminating work, *Benaiah—he slew two lion-like men of Judah*.

William Etty died in 1849, at York, in the sixty-third year of his age. He received a public funeral, when they laid him in " a quiet corner of the churchyard of St. Olave," almost within the shadow of the old cathedral familiar to his boyish days.

JOHN CONSTABLE was born in 1776 at East Bergholt in Suffolk. His father was that rural dignitary, a miller, so favoured in being associated with painters. But the elder Constable was in a different position from Etty's father, being a man of substance and wealth in his way. He had destined his son for the Church, and when young Constable's vocation for art proved insurmountable, he was able to send him to London, and enter him as a student at the Academy. This was not however till 1799, when young Constable was twenty-three years of age. Three years afterwards he exhibited his first picture, and after trying historical painting, and wasting much time on portrait painting, for which he had no genius, but which was "the only art which he found paid," he discovered his true walk in landscape painting.

Constable never went abroad, nor did he derive a single picture from foreign sources, though he would admire the foreign masters of landscape, and would dwell on the beauties of Ruysdael, and on the nobleness of Titian's landscapes; if he showed himself limited in his sphere, it was, at least, thoroughly English, a quality which, in addition to his great merit, did not fail, at last, to recommend him irresistibly to his countrymen.

He dwelt for many years at Hampstead, but died suddenly in London, in a house in Charlotte Street, Fitzroy Square, in 1837, when he was sixty-one years of age.

As a man, Constable was independent and estimable, apart from his minor defects of temper and stinging speech. He found a warm friend and sympathetic biographer in his fellow-artist, Leslie.

While far inferior to Turner in variety and power, and in some respects decidedly behind Gainsborough, who with Wilson was the only predecessor that Constable had cared to follow, he was possessed of great merits, great in any day, and peculiarly great in his generation. He was a faithful as well as a fond student of nature, capable not merely of seeing the earth at his feet, but of entering into atmospheric effects, and of giving them as he saw them.

PATRICK NASMYTH was born in 1786 in Edinburgh. His father, a pupil of Allan Ramsay's, was a good landscape painter.

The young Nasmyth early played truant from school to stroll and sketch in the fields. What education he consented to receive was had in his father's studio. From an accident received in boyhood to his right hand, he painted with his left hand. Another youthful misfortune was an illness which resulted in deafness. Thus disabled and thrown in upon himself, with a tendency to take refuge from his isolation in excess and low company, Nasmyth came to London when he was in his twentieth year, and immediately attracted notice by his works. The first which he exhibited at the Royal Academy was a romantic Scotch subject, *Loch Katrine*, but it was by English subjects of the homeliest and most familiar rustic life that he won his name as a painter. These lanes and hedgerows, bits of commons, and village streets, with the dwarf oak in its " contorted limbs and scrubby foliage, in preference to other trees," were the subjects which he painted with felicitous Dutch relish, as well as accuracy, which procured for him the somewhat cockney sobriquet of the " English Hobbema." Not unlike Morland in his tastes, Nasmyth was not unlike the English painter in a corrupted nature and miserable fate. He was reduced to paint merely to supply his necessities, painting to the last attack of influenza, of which he died in the middle of a thunder-storm, that he was raised up in bed at his own request to watch. His death occurred in 1831, when Nasmyth was but in his forty-sixth year.

DAVID COX, the water-colour painter, was born in 1783, in Birmingham. He was the son of a blacksmith, and having broken his leg when a delicate little lad, was presented with a box of colours and a supply of paper, in which he took such delight, that on his recovery his father sent him to a drawing school. He was afterwards apprenticed to a locket painter, but losing his master, he undertook to grind colours for the scene painters at the Birmingham Theatre. In time he rose to be a scene painter himself; then a teacher of drawing and painting in water colours, diligently studying nature and those old masters whose works he could command. Eventually he painted in oil as well as in water colours.

SAMUEL PROUT was born in 1783 at Plymouth, and as a child gathering nuts and blackberries was sun-struck, a misfortune which affected his health throughout his life.

After lodging, with Britton for the purpose of studying during two years in London, *St. Keynes Well, Cornwall*, was Prout's first work exhibited in the Royal Academy, in 1804, when he was twenty-one years of age. From this time he maintained himself largely by teaching as well as painting in water colours, writing several manuals on the acquisition of his art.

Prout became a member of the Water-colour Society in 1815, when he was thirty-one years of age, and when his reputation was fast rising. The popular use of lithography greatly facilitated his career, and enabled him to publish his views in France, Switzerland, and Italy, &c. &c. The subjects for which Prout was celebrated as a painter were, after he went abroad in 1818, in search of health, Norman Cathedrals, and busy market-places, with their quaintly-dressed peasants and their glowing, vivid piles of fruit and vegetables; subsequently he added Venice and the other old Italian towns, with those of Germany and Bohemia, to his stores of subjects. He rarely introduced trees into his scenes. The marked exception to his usual class of paintings was his *Indiaman Ashore*, exhibited in 1819, and supposed to be a reminiscence of the *Dalton*, wrecked in Prout's boyhood on the rocks off Plymouth, and sketched at the time both by Prout and Haydon.

After suffering from prolonged bad health Prout died at Camberwell in 1858, at the age of sixty-eight.

PAUL SANDBY, "the father of water-colour art," was born at Nottingham in 1725. After some years' service as surveyor to the army, he settled in 1752 at Windsor, near which town he took the subjects of many of his landscapes. He subsequently painted many views in Wales for Sir Joseph Banks and Sir Watkin Wynne. Sandby was instructor in drawing to the children of George III., and was in 1768 elected one of the original members of the Royal Academy, and in the same year was appointed drawing-master to the Military Schools at Woolwich. He died at London in 1809. Besides his views in water-colour and body-colour, Sandby executed numerous engravings in aquatint, a medium then scarcely known in England. Examples of his art may be seen in the South Kensington Museum.

ROBERT SMIRKE, who was born at Carlisle in 1752, was apprenticed in London to a herald-painter; he was also a member of the Incorporated Society of Painters. The first works which he exhibited in the Royal Academy were *Narcissus and Sabrina;* they appeared in 1786. In 1791 he was made an Associate, and two years later he became a full member. In 1804 Smirke was elected to the office of Keeper of the Royal Academy, but owing to his revolutionary politics, the royal sanction was denied. Smirke died in London in 1845, at the advanced age of ninety-three. He was one of the painters who illustrated Boydell's *Shakspeare Gallery.* Smirke also executed numerous works in illustration of authors both English and foreign.

JAMES NORTHCOTE was born at Plymouth in 1746. By his father, who was a watchmaker, he was made to serve seven years' apprenticeship to that trade. On quitting his home in 1771, young Northcote obtained an introduction to Sir Joshua Reynolds, who received him into his studio as a pupil, and into his house as a friend. At the same time Northcote studied in the Academy schools, but as he began to learn art so late in life, he never fully acquired its technicalities, and, like Fuseli, his method of execution always remained slovenly. In 1777, he went to Italy, where he studied the works of the old masters, more especially those of Titian. On his return to England in 1780, Northcote, after a short time spent in his native county, settled in London, where, as before, he maintained himself by portrait painting. His first great work did not appear until 1786. It was one of the nine pictures which he painted for Boydell's "Shakespeare Gallery," and the subject was the *Murder of the young Princes in the Tower,* afterwards followed in quick succession, *The Meeting of the young Princes; Romeo and Juliet; The Death of Mortimer; King Edward IV. and his Queen; Prince Arthur and Hubert,* and lastly, *King Richard II. and Bolingbroke.*

One of his best works is the *Death of Wat Tyler,* painted for the Corporation of London. It now hangs in the Guildhall. Of other works by him we may notice the series of the *Diligent Servant and the Dissipated, Idle and Industrious Apprentice.* He died in London in 1831.

CHAPTER III.

FRENCH ART.—VIEN—DAVID—ISABEY—INGRES— GERICAULT—VERNET—DELAROCHE— ARY SCHEFFER—TROYON, &c., &c.

AT Montpellier, in 1710, was born JOSEPH MARIE VIEN. He studied first in Paris, and it was he who in historical painting, gave the signal for reform when, in 1771 to 1781, he directed the French school at Rome. In studying the works of the earlier ages, he learned to understand the greatness of the art which had almost perished. He endeavoured to return to the style of the great masters. To Vien, then, belongs the honour of having clearly seen the evil and its remedy, and of having been the first to attempt the part of a reformer, which was accomplished by his pupil Louis David. This honourable attempt may be seen, in his fine composition, *St. Germain of Auxerre and St. Vincent of Saragossa* receiving martyrs' crowns from an angel; and for chastened and powerful execution, in the *Hermit asleep.* It is said of this last picture that one day, in his studio at Rome, the hermit who served him for a model went asleep whilst playing on the violin. The artist took his portrait in this attitude, and with much success.

Vien said, "I have only half opened the door; it is M. David who will throw it wide open." Vien, the regenerator of painting in France, died at Paris in 1809.

LOUIS DAVID was born in Paris, in 1748. He was reared under the guardianship of an uncle who was an architect, and who destined the lad for the same profession, but in the meantime he attracted the notice of the court painter of the day, and was, at his request, placed in his studio, and thence transferred to the studio of a more regular teacher of painting. Louis David was eccentric always, and his mind seemed to share in a degree the distortion of his person, for the painter was mis-shapen in body. Because he had tried repeatedly and failed, in a great measure because of his own scorn for rules, to get the highest honours from the Academy, David, in a frenzy, threatened to starve himself to death. After his mad and bad project had been frustrated, and he had gained the prize he had coveted, he started with his master for

THE ARAB SCRIBE.
(From the original painting by J. F. Lewis, I.R.A.)

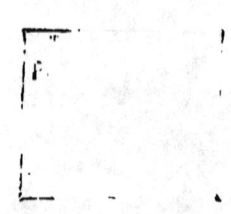

Rome, and remained ardently studying the antique in Italy, during five years, in the course of which he painted the *Plague of St. Roch*. On his return to France his style presented an entire change, from that which had been marked by the flimsy prettiness of Watteau and his followers. Not only so, the severe and spasmodic classicism which David re-introduced has always held, whether in painting, literature, or politics, for the impressible French nation, a peculiar charm, with which other styles and tones of thought, romantic and realistic, have constantly to renew their rivalry. David, on his return to the stern simplicity of ancient art, was welcomed with open arms; he was made a member of the Academy, and lodged in the Louvre, and when he went to Italy a second time, after his marriage, and returned with his picture of *the Horatii*, in what proved the popular enthusiasm, Louis XVI., by a subtle coincidence, ordered from the young painter a companion-picture which should be that of *Brutus*. At this same time he painted *The Death of Socrates*.*

Immediately afterwards the revolution broke out, and David, plunged into the political excitement of the moment, was elected a member of the Convention, and was an active party in the condemnation of his former royal patron. Over such a morbid nature as David's, indeed, the awful intoxication of the period must have exercised triple power. He was in the Reign of Terror with Robespierre, and was its willing painter. Twice David was himself thrown into prison, and on one occasion, at least, he owed his release to the homage which the wildest of the "bonnets rouges" paid to art in David's person.

Under the First Consul and Emperor, David returned to his studio, and became as fervent a follower of Napoleon as he had been a fierce republican. He was rewarded by being the painter of the Empire, as he had been that of the Republic, the artistic master of its splendours, and, along with Vernet—the battle-painter, the enthusiastic delineator of Napoleon's victories, and of *Le petit Caporal* in every attitude of triumph. And to Napoleon personally David showed a dogged fidelity—remaining shut up in his studio when the allies entered Paris, submitting, because he could not help himself, to the Duke of Wellington's visit to the studio, but refusing haughtily to paint the conqueror of his imperial master.

With the final restoration of the Bourbons David was banished from France, and his name erased from the roll of the Institute. He took up his residence at Brussels, and spent there a long exile, during which he employed himself in painting. His friends in France had a medal struck in the painter's honour, before he died in 1825, in his seventy-eighth year, exclaiming in his last moments with reference to his painting of *the Thermophyles* with characteristic arrogance, "no other but myself could have conceived such a Leonidas." Nearly ten years afterwards his sons solicited of Louis Philippe permission to bring back the exile's body and give it a French grave. They were met by a refusal. The circumstance was the occasion of one of Béranger's lyrics. David's aim was the restoration of the Greco-Roman school with its classical severity and exaltation of form.

A very different painter from Louis David, but one who was equally associated with Napoleon, was Isabey, the accomplished miniature and water-colour painter.

* See Illustration.

JEAN BAPTISTE ISABEY was born at Nancy in 1767. He went to Paris in 1786, and painted lids of snuff-boxes and coat buttons. Towards the close of the reign of Louis XVI., he was presented at Versailles, and had a commission to paint a medallion portrait of Marie Antoinette. After the revolution he was introduced to the Buonaparte family, and painted a portrait of *General Buonaparte at Malmaison*, which was much admired. Eventually Isabey was appointed *peintre de cabinet* to the Emperor, and director of the Imperial fêtes and assemblies. In the former capacity he painted upwards of two hundred miniatures of Napoleon to be given away, as presents, yearly, receiving five hundred francs for each miniature. In 1814 he painted miniatures of the strangers of distinction in Paris, not being withheld from the work by any sympathy with David's scrupulous fidelity to his master. Isabey was even sent by Talleyrand to paint the portraits of the members of the congress of Vienna, of whom he made a large-group picture. He was *peintre de cabinet* to Charles X., and honorary conservator of the public museums under Louis Philippe. At different times Isabey painted most of the contemporary sovereigns of Europe. Isabey died a veteran artist in his eighty-ninth year, in 1855. His miniatures, full of taste and talent, are still much prized, and when exposed to sale continue to fetch considerable sums of money. Isabey's son is a clever French marine and landscape painter.

JEAN DOMINIQUE AUGUSTE INGRES was born at Montauban in 1781. He was the son of a painter who was at the same time a musician. Young Ingres studied the violin to such purpose, that at the age of thirteen years he took part in a concert in the theatre of Toulouse at a festival held in honour of the King's execution. At sixteen years Ingres entered the school of David, and no longer thought of music as a profession, though he remained a violin player, for his own delectation, to the end of his days. Ingres very soon became David's best pupil. He and the old painter Greuze were both commissioned to paint the First Consul, who declined to sit for his portrait, so that the only opportunity for obtaining a particular likeness of him afforded to the painters, was the chance of observing him as he passed through a gallery at St. Cloud. But the great man also observed the painters, and said to one of his officers—"Are these the painters who are to paint my portrait? H'm! as to this one" (staring at Ingres), "I consider him too young; as to that one" (staring at Greuze), "he's too old."

Ingres went to Rome in 1806, when he was twenty-five years of age, and remained there fourteen years, till 1820 when he was in his fortieth year. For the next four years he lived in Florence, and in 1824 he returned to Paris, and opened an atelier for pupils.

During his long residence abroad Ingres produced many historical and religious pictures from Greek, Roman, and French history, and from the lives of the saints, among which was his *Vow of Louis XIII*. His countrymen received him back with acclamation; he was made member of the Institute, appointed professor in the school of the Fine Arts, and had the Cross of the Legion of Honour bestowed on him. In 1827 Ingres painted his "long circular composition," the *Apotheosis of Homer*, for the ceiling of the Louvre, which his admirers have regarded as one of his master-pieces.

In 1829, when Ingres was in his forty-ninth year, he went again to Rome to fill the post of director to the French Academy there, and continued in the congenial city of the Cæsars and of the triumphs of Michael Angelo, till 1841, when the painter again returned to his native country, a man of sixty years of age, but still not near the end of his long and illustrious career.

Ingres married twice, and Mr. Hamerton tells us how much the first Madame Ingres did secure to her husband the uninterrupted tranquillity which was so helpful to his success in art; how she transacted all the business part of the sale of the portraits in pencil, by which, while he was still a poor and unknown man, he had to maintain himself and his household; how she stood between her husband and his employers, taking upon herself the worry of such details, and guarded his privacy and his precious moments of time.

That Ingres was very successful even in a worldly point of view, is proved by the fact of his long list of honours—as "senator; great officer of the Legion of Honour; knight of the order of civil merit, Prussia; commander of the order of St. Josephe of Tuscany; knight Grand Cross of the order of Guadaloupe; member of the Institute of France, of the academies of Florence, Amsterdam, Antwerp, Berlin, Vienna;" and that he lived to see a picture of his sold for $18,000. Ingres died in 1867, in the eighty-seventh year of his age. Among Ingres' great paintings are his *Œdipus, Stratonice, Vow of Louis XIII., Andromache*, and *the Slave and her Slave*.*

JEAN LOUIS GÉRICAULT and EUGÈNE DELACROIX led the French re-action against classical painting, and formed the romantic school which is said to have had its origin in the poetry of Goethe, Scott, and Byron. Jean Louis Géricault was born at Rouen, in 1790, and was the pupil, first of one of the Vernets, and afterwards of Guérin, who was a distinguished pupil of David's, and of the extreme classical school. Géricault, however, rebelled against classicism, and entered his best protest against it in his great picture of a shipwreck, *The Raft of the Medusa*, which is now in the Louvre. He painted this in assertion of his own instincts, and in defiance of the fiat of his master, who had pronounced Géricault incapable of painting. "A state of isolation" his position is justly defined, and it might have also been called a state of mutiny till he eacomplished his protest, and enlisted a crowd of followers on the side of simple, and natural, if too physical power. His picture has come to be regarded as "one of the principal attractions" of the French portion of the gallery. The results of the terrible shipwreck with its living and dead victims are only too signally effective, and seem made to shake, if not to overthrow, traditional art. They are like the rough expression of the living present, beside the most scholarly fruit of the dead past. Géricault was not thirty when he painted *The Raft of the Medusa;* he died five years after its exhibition, when he was only thirty-four years of age.

HORACE VERNET, or Emile Jean Horace Vernet, was born in Paris, in 1789. He was the son of a race of painters, like the old families of the Caracci, the Bassani, or the Hoibeins. He may be said to have been born a painter, and to have taken to it as other children take to play. When he was but eleven years he drew a tulip, for which he was given twenty-four sous; and when a lad of thirteen, the famous battle-

---

* See Steel Engraving.

painter of future days was able to earn his livelihood by painting. At twenty, by his father's advice, in order to deter him from a military career, young Vernet married, and took upon himself the cares of a family, and he contrived to make, in his own way, progress, and to prosper through great political changes, and a long life. As early as 1814, when he was a young man of five-and-twenty, he received from Napoleon I. the Cross of the Legion of Honour; before he was forty he was elected a member of the Institute. Two years later, in 1828, he was appointed Director of the French Academy at Rome, in which he resided for nine years, and then returned to France. In 1844, when he was yet in the prime of life, his daughter was married worthily to another great French painter, Paul Delaroche, but her death in the year after her marriage threw the first heavy cloud over the genial temper of her father.

At the Paris Exhibition of 1855 Vernet was awarded a Grand Medal of honour. He had exhibited on the occasion twenty-two pictures, including several of his most famous battle-pieces.

Vernet was a typical Frenchman, brave, frank, kindly, good-humoured, and innocently vain, with immense powers of work, and a wonderful memory, to which he trusted, in place of subjecting himself to the restraint and delay involved in the use of a model. Horace Vernet died at Paris in 1863, in his seventy-fifth year.

PAUL DELAROCHE was born at Paris in 1797. His baptismal name was Hippolyte, but he was called by his family Paul, and from the year 1827 his signature to his pictures was Paul Delaroche—a signature now become world renowned. His father was an official valuator of the works of art offered to the Monte-de-Piété, while his uncle was curator of the engravings in the Paris library, so that the lad breathed early an atmosphere of art. The effects of such an atmosphere were shared by an elder brother, who, along with Paul, sought to be a painter, and with regard to this brother's right of choice, Paul decided to confine himself to landscape painting, but the early abandonment by Jules Delaroche of the profession of art, enabled the true painter, Paul, to widen his field indefinitely. Finally he fixed on historic art as his career, and entered the atelier of Gros, a well-known leader of the classic school.

While still a pupil of Gros's, Delaroche received a commission from the Duchess of Orleans, the future Queen Amalie, to paint for her a *Descent from the Cross*, which was to be placed in the chapel of the Palais Royal. Contrary to the etiquette of the ateliers, Delaroche accepted the commission, and worked at it without the knowledge of Gros. On its completion the young painter had the courage and frankness to ask his master to come and look at his work. The master refused to visit a pupil's atelier, but forgave the offence so far, as to bid the pupil bring the work to the master's atelier, when he might have his opinion. To the credit of both master and pupil, when Delaroche complied with the stipulation, Gros praised generously all that was praiseworthy in the picture. But Delaroche of all painters was least likely to be held fast by the classic school, and while endeavouring to found a school of his own, which should be distinct from the dramatic school of Géricault and Delacroix, he retained no more of the classic school's austerity than what was necessary for his careful and correct rendering of a simple purpose, in which expression of human feeling was always the most powerful element.

Delaroche's first picture which drew attention was *Joas rescued by Josabeth*, exhibited in 1822, when the painter was twenty-five years of age. Two years later he executed his picture of *Jean d'Arc examined in prison by the Cardinal of Winchester*, which is as well known by engravings in England as in France. Indeed Delaroche, by the bent of his genius, quite as much as by his fondness for English subjects, shares with Ary Scheffer a wide English popularity. In 1827, when the painter was thirty years of age, he obtained the Cross of the Legion of Honour.

Four years later Delaroche produced his *Children of Edward the IV. in the Tower*,* which induced a French poet to write a tragedy on the pathetic old story, that is said to be also the origin of the ancient ballad—long sacred to nursery literature, of *The Babes in the Wood*. The following year, 1832, Delaroche, in his thirty-sixth year, became a member of the Institute, and exhibited what judges hold a still finer work than that of *The Princes in the Tower*, his *Cromwell looking on Charles I. in his coffin*. In 1833 the painter suffered a great disappointment. He had received a commission to decorate the church of the Madeleine, and had made preparatory studies for the work during a year and a half, when he was prevented from going on with his task. It was small compensation to the enthusiastic painter that he was appointed professor to the School of Fine Arts.

An instance of Paul Delaroche's inaccessibility to the temptations of avarice is given by Ottley in connection with this *Hémicycle*. The original order given for the work by the Minister of the Interior was that it should consist of twenty-four figures, of which Delaroche submitted a sketch, to be finished in a year, and for which he was to receive a payment of $15,000. The twenty-four figures grew under Delaroche's hand to seventy-five in number, and the time to be spent in the work extended to four years. A proposal to make a corresponding increase of the remuneration was intimated to the painter. But he answered—perhaps with a recollection of the speech of Ghirlandajo, in his day, and if with something of the perennially youthful, grand air, nearly inseparable from the Frenchman in the circumstances, still, certainly, with much dignified moderation and singleness of heart—"No, of my own will I did what I have done, and I shall receive nothing beyond the stipulated sum." He added, "and I shall be amply paid for my labour, inasmuch as I have learned more from the execution of this work than by all my studies that preceded it."

In 1855, when Paul Delaroche was in his fifty-ninth year, by an accidental fire his Hémicycle, in the School of the Fine Arts, was almost completely destroyed, without disturbing the equanimity of the painter; he was only eager to have a fresh opportunity to correct the faults which he was constantly seeing in his work, and to do it all over again in order that he might do it better than he had done it before.

But another hand was to restore the Hémicycle of Delaroche; a disease which had been neglected in its earlier approaches, wasted his strength in the short space of three weeks. "Stay, don't go to-night," he begged of a favourite pupil on the last night of his life, and towards morning, when the faithful watcher left the room for a moment, he returned to find his master dead. Paul Delaroche died, in 1856, in the fifty-ninth year of his age.

* See Steel Engraving.

In token of Delaroche's inclination to take English subjects for his work, we may name, in addition to the examples given, his *Death of Queen Elizabeth*, his *Execution of Lady Jane Grey*, and his *Strafford on his way to the Scaffold*, the two last shown in this year's Exhibition of the Works of Old Masters. His famous French subjects, *Cardinal Richelieu on the Rhine*, *Cardinal Mazarin Dying*, *The Death of the Duke of Guise*, *Marie Antoinette after hearing her Sentence*, *Napoleon I. at Fontainebleau*, and *General Bonaparte Passing the Alps*, were not rendered with more feeling. Three other pictures of Delaroche's are widely known by engravings, *St. Cecilia playing on the Organ, supported by Angels*, *Moses saved from the Nile*, and a girl martyr floating on the Tiber, with an aureole above her head. Celebrated pictures of his, still more distinctly sacred, are *The Virgin while Jesus is led to Execution*, and *The Virgin contemplating the Crown of Thorns*; he was engaged on a picture of *The Death of the Virgin* when he was seized with his last illness.

We shall describe, as far as we can, from our engraving, the *Princes in the Tower*. The two unhappy little lads sit together on the bed where they are to be murdered. The elder, just proclaimed Edward V., in his mourning black velvet mantle, with his fair hair cut short across the brow, and hanging down in wavy locks on his shoulders, in a fashion that the renewal of an old mode has made familiar to us, has been beguiling the weary time, while he tries to play the man, by reading in a great book which he holds open, but he glances from it jealously to the door, attracted there by a slight noise. The same noise causes a dog, an old playfellow, and the last faithful follower of the king's sons, to rise and prick one ear, while it stretches forward to gaze suspiciously in the same direction. The poor young Duke of York, in his crimsoned hose and pointed shoon, jerkin and velvet bonnet, makes no pretence of being man or prince, but is only a wan and weary little boy, so crushed by misfortune, that terror itself is extinguished in him, and only his desperate weariness and his want of his mother is perceptible, where he sits with his hands clasped, and resting for support on his elder brother's shoulder, his heavily-drooping head leaning also on that of his youthful protector. Nothing can exceed the air of innocent helplessness, even in the sad watchful expression of the elder brother, and the useless warning given by the roused dog, with the haunting presage of a great and most cruel crime, which pervades the whole group.

ARY SCHEFFER was born in 1795 at Dort. His father was a German and a painter; his mother, who was the good genius of her son's life, was a Dutch lady. Ary Scheffer showed his love of art when a child in dabbling with paint and brushes in his father's studio. His father died when Ary Scheffer was about fifteen years of age, and his mother, desirous to give him and his two brothers the best education in her power, after sending Ary, her eldest son, to a school at Lille, removed to Paris and settled there, enduring courageously many privations, in order to promote the welfare of her sons, and finding her chief happiness in them.

Ary Scheffer received an introduction to Lafayette, and went in 1818, when the painter was twenty-three years of age, to the Chateau de la Grange to paint its master—

* See Steel Engraving.

at the time when Lady Morgan visited La Grange, and made her sketches of its household, for the benefit of the English world. An important effect of Ary Scheffer's connection with Lafayette may be traced in the influence by which the impulsive painter became an Orleanist—to the extent of joining with his two brothers, at the risk of their liberties, if not of their lives, in the plots which preceded the revolution of 1830. Another result was the heroic element beginning to appear and gradually to predominate over the domestic in Ary Scheffer's pictures. Thus, in 1819, he exhibited *The Devotion of the Burghers of Calais;* in 1822, *St. Louis attacked by the Plague visiting the Sick;* in 1824, *Gaston de Foix found dead at Ravenna;* in 1827, *The Death of Jean D'Arc;* in 1828, *An Episode of the Retreat from Russia* (with which we think our readers must be familiar by engravings). Ary Scheffer showed also at this time an inclination to English, or rather Scotch subjects, which has not been rare in French artists, but which it is rather curious to find in a man who, half in jest, half in earnest, disliked England and the English. Ary Scheffer confessed with regard to England to an English woman—" I do not like England—that is, the English. They are such proud, insolent, scornful, conceited people! looking upon themselves as superior to all the rest of the world!" and in the seizure from his last illness, which overtook him in London, he kept continually crying out—" I shall die of this heavy London air." Yet among the early pictures by Ary Scheffer we find one from a scene in the *Antiquary;* a second, from a scene in *The Heart of Midlothian;* and a third, from *Macbeth;* a fourth, a famous picture after the artist had begun to know and exercise his power, is from an English source—Byron's *Giaour*. But before he painted the last, Ary Scheffer had vindicated his German origin by beginning the series of pictures from Faust, which the painter continued at intervals to the end of his life, that proved how Goethe's great poem had enthralled and absorbed his countryman.

The return of the painter Ingres from Italy to Paris had produced a great effect on Scheffer as an artist, and after adding to the names of the poets whose works he had illustrated, that of Dante, Scheffer's genius began to take a higher flight still. The death of his much-cherished mother in 1839 probably gave a bent to this flight, for about 1841 he painted his *Annunciation to the Shepherds;* in 1842, his *Suffer Little Children to come unto Me;* in 1844 appeared his *Magi;* and in 1847 his *Holy Women*.

In 1854 Scheffer painted, what are among his finest works, *The Ruth and Naomi, The Magdalene in ecstacy, The Groanings,* and *The Temptation.**

Ary Scheffer died in his own house on the 15th of June, 1858. He was in the sixty-fourth year of his age.

To those who judge of French landscape painters by the bits of strangely, however artfully, manipulated landscape which appear in the background of the painters of the classic school, and to whom even the great popularity of ROSA BONHEUR has not come as a revelation, Constantine Troyon and his merits ought to be specially mentioned.

CONSTANTINE TROYON was born at Sèvres in 1813, and spent much of his youth as a porcelain painter. Later he studied in the atelier of Riocreux, and the know-

---

* See Engraving.

ledge which he acquired there, together with the loving study which he had already given to nature, induced him to become a landscape painter. In 1833, while he was still but twenty years of age, he exhibited his first pictures, among them *A Nook in the Park of St. Cloud;* and for a number of years he produced *landscapes* taken from the neighbourhood of Paris, which have long been held in high estimation, and have passed into various private art collections in France. His *Oxen Ploughing* was bought by government. His *Valley of the Touque* was exhibited with several other pictures by Troyon at the great Paris Exhibition of 1855. He had already been elected a member of the Academy of Amsterdam, and had received the decoration of the Legion of Honour. Constantine Troyon died in his fifty-third year, in 1865.

LEOPOLD ROBERT was born in Switzerland, in 1794. At first an engraver, then a pupil of David and Gerard at Paris, whilst Géricault was studying under Pierre Guérin, he went very late to Italy to become an original painter, and almost immediately after gave up art by a voluntary and premature death. In Italy he returned to the tradition of historical landscape—scenes of history mixed with the scenes of nature. His subjects varied, are chosen intelligently, and carefully studied even in their slightest detail, and are full of poetry. We always feel in them his love of the beautiful as well as of the true; and the country round Rome, as he represents it, becomes as noble as ancient Arcadia. Three of his most important works were presented to the Louvre by King Louis-Philippe—the *Italian Improvisatore*, the *Feast of the Madonna di Pie-di-grotta*, and the *Harvest Feast* in the Roman Campagna.

FERDINAND VICTOR EUGENE DELACROIX was born at Chareton Saint-Maurice, near Paris, in 1799. When eighteen years of age he was apprenticed to Guérin; but, being dissatisfied with that master's art, he struck out a new path for himself and became the leader of the so-called "Romantic School." In 1830 Delacroix visited Spain, Algiers and Morocco, and on his return was much patronized by M. Thiers, who procured for him the commission to paint numerous works in the Palais Bourbon; the Hotel de Ville; the Luxembourg; the Louvre; and other public buildings, as well as churches in Paris. He died in 1863.

Eugene Delacroix is well represented by the four works in the Louvre, which bear his name: *Dante and Virgil* painted in 1822, the *Massacre of Scio* in 1823, the *Algerian Women* in 1834, and the *Jewish Marriage in Morocco*, in which we are able to follow the several phases of his talent. These works were succeeded by the *Bridge of Taillebourg*, a *Medea*, the *Shipwrecked Mariners*, the *Entrance of Baldwin into Constantinople*, and many others.

JEAN BAPTISTE CAMILLE COROT, one of the best of modern French landscape painters, was born at Paris in 1796. He was apprenticed to a draper, but young Corot was determined to be a painter, and, in spite of all that his parents did to dissuade him, entered in 1822, the studio of Michallon. When that artist died, Corot studied for a time under Victor Bertin, but quitting that master, he went to Italy, where, during a stay of several years, he applied himself diligently to study landscape painting from nature. In 1827 appeared Corot's first works, a *View of Narni*, and the *Campagna of Rome;* in the Paris Exhibition of 1855, he exhibited *Morning Effect* and *Evening*, and in the same year received a first-class medal; in the London

Exhibition of 1862, he was one of the artists who represented the French school, and again in 1871, in which year he exhibited no less than twenty-one pictures. He was also a frequent exhibitor in the French Gallery, Pall Mall. He died in 1875. "Corot was a poet, and his canvasses are the expression of refined ideas.

JOSEPH LOUIS HIPPOLYTE BELLANGÉ was born in Paris in 1800, and took his earnest lessons in art from Gros, acquiring some reputation for his lithographic drawings of military figures when scarcely more than a boy. In 1824 Bellangé won a second-class medal for an historical picture; in 1834, he was made a member of the Legion of Honour; in 1835, he obtained one of the prizes of the French International Exhibition; his best known picture is *A Square of Republican Infantry repulsing Austrian Dragoons*. His most important pictures, however, are to be seen in the Collections at Versailles and the Luxembourg, and include his *Battle of the Alma*, *Painful Adieux*, the *Departure from the Cantonment*, the *Cuirassiers at Waterloo*, the *Battle of Fleurus*, the *Return from Elba*, the *Morning after the Battle of Gemappes*, and *The Image Seller*.* This popular painter of battle-scenes died in May, 1865.

ALEXANDER GABRIEL DECAMPS, who was born at Paris in 1803, is chiefly celebrated for the pictures of Eastern subjects which he introduced to the Parisian public. The gallery of Sir Richard Wallace contains more than thirty paintings by this artist—many of which are Scriptural subjects. His *Turkish School*, the *History of Samson*, and the *Defeat of the Cimbri*, are among his most celebrated works. Decamps died at Fontainebleau in 1860.

JEAN HIPPOLYTE FLANDRIN was born at Lyons in 1809, and accompanied by his brother Jean Paul, went to Paris to enter the school of Les Beaux-Arts in 1829, carrying off during his studentship there the first grand prize for his picture of *Theseus recognizing his Father at a Banquet*, besides several minor honours. In 1832 he went to Rome and became a student in the French school of art in that city, then presided over by Horace Vernet. In 1835 Vernet was replaced by Ingres, who conceived a warm affection for young Flandrin, and did much to forward his career. The chief works produced by the young artist at this time were a scene from the *Inferno*; *Euripides writing his Tragedies in a Cavern near Salamis*; and *St. Clair first Bishop of Nantes healing the Blind*, which last (now in the cathedral at Nantes) took the Roman gold medal of the first class. About 1839 Flandrin returned to Paris and the next few years of his life were devoted to the decoration of the chapel of St. John in the church of St. Séverin. That task satisfactorily accomplished, and rewarded with the order of the Legion of Honour, Flandrin painted, first, a picture of *St. Louis dictating the Laws of the Constitution*, for the present senate-house, and then a series of twenty subjects from the Old and New Testament in the church of St. Germain des Prés. He also contributed a frieze, containing over two hundred figures, to the decorations of the church of St. Paul at Nantes. In 1853 Flandrin became an officer of the Legion of Honour, and a member of the French Academy. In 1857 he was elected professor of painting at that institution, and held the appointment until his death, which took place in March, 1864.

* See Steel Engraving.

JEAN FRANÇOIS MILLET was born at Greville, near Cherbourg, in 1815. As his parents were but peasants, and unable to afford to give their son an art education—which his early-displayed talent showed would not be thrown away upon him—the authorities of Greville furnished him with the means of going to Paris, and entering the studio of Paul Delaroche. But young Millet showed neither taste nor aptitude for historic painting, and accordingly, after a short sojourn with Delaroche, he left that master and sought instruction from nature alone. He married, and settled at Barbizon, near the Forest of Fontainebleau, and there from the fields and woods, and from the peasants he took the subjects of his works. His first exhibited picture, the *Milkwoman*, appeared at the Paris Salon in 1844; to the Paris Exhibition of 1855 he sent his *Peasant grafting a Tree*; in the London Exhibition of 1862 appeared a *Rustic Scene*; and in the Paris Exhibition of 1867, no less than nine pictures of rustic life. The *Flax Crushers*, one of his best pictures, was exhibited in the French Gallery, Pall Mall, in 1874. Millet died at Barbizon on the 20th of January, 1875.

JEAN LOUIS HAMON was born at Ploaha, Côtes-du-Nord, in 1821, and was educated for the priesthood. His love of art, however, led him to renounce the sacred profession; and having obtained a grant of five hundred francs from his native place, he made his way to Paris, and began the study of painting under Paul Delaroche and M. Gleyre. In 1848 appeared his first pictures, one a genre subject called *Le Dessus de Porte*, and the other a sacred work, *Christ's Tomb*, succeeded a little later by a *Roman Placard*, the *Scraglio*, and other similar productions which scarcely met with the recognition they deserved. Compelled to earn his daily bread, Hamon now for a time gave up easel painting, and accepted employment in the Sèvres manufactory, where he succeeded so well, that in 1852 he was able to resume oil-painting—producing in the same year his *Comédie Humaine* which made his reputation. The most noteworthy of his later works are *Ma sœur n'y est pas; Ce n'est pas moi; Les Orphelins; L'amour de son Troupeau*. In 1856 Hamon went to the East, and most of the pictures subsequently painted are on Oriental subjects. He resided some years at Capri, but returned to France shortly before his death, which took place at St. Raphael, in the department of the Var, in 1874.

ALEXANDRE GEORGES HENRI REGNAULT was born at Paris in 1847, and was the pupil of MM. Lamothe and Cabanel. In 1866 Regnault won the prize of Rome, and in 1869 a gold medal. In the succeeding years he attracted much notice by his *Still Life*, his portrait of *General Prim*, and *An Execution at the Alhambra*, all exhibited at the Gallery of the Society of French Artists in New Bond Street, and *Salomé la danseuse*, exhibited in the Paris Salon of 1870, in which the first art critics of the day recognized an originality of design, and force of execution, likely to entitle the possessor to the highest rank amongst contemporary painters; but the terrible war of 1870-71, which frustrated so many hopes, and cut short so many careers, broke out just as Regnault was attaining celebrity. The news of the declaration of hostilities reached him when he was studying at Tangier, and leaving his unfinished work upon his easel, he returned to France, took service as a national guard, and was killed in a sortie from Paris. He was only twenty-four years old.

CHAPTER IV.

MODERN GERMAN ART.—OVERBECK—CORNELIUS —KAULBACH—BENDEMANN, &c.

WITH the remarkable men of whose lives and works we are going to write, a new era of art began in Germany. The movement arose in Rome early in the nineteenth century. At that time there was a colony of young German artists established in the Eternal City, men single-hearted, united by common gifts and a common enthusiasm. They were not without its extravagance, however, since one mode of the expression of the artists' principles was their adopting a primitive costume, and wearing their hair flowing over their shoulders, by which practice they provoked from their neighbours the nickname of *Nazarites*. But the young Germans did much more than be guilty of this boyish mummery, they laboured from morning till night at developing their art and vindicating their theories. Their chief theory was the earliest manifestation of what we have learned, without much consideration of the meaning of the word, to call præ-Raphaelitism.

These Germans held that "Christian art had died out with the decline of religious faith in the successors of Giotto, Orcagna, Fra Angelico, and their scholars; since Michael Angelo, Raphael, and their contemporaries had combined in the revival or re-assertion of classical, that is to say, Pagan art. The Germans proposed to recover this lost religious art, by setting themselves sedulously and sympathetically to cultivate the "asceticism, symbolism, pale colour, and calm symmetrical arrangement" of the early masters, even to a modified imitation of the "attenuated forms and quaint drawing" which characterized these Christian fathers of art. In acknowledgment also of the fact, that their examples had drawn and painted under the promptings of devout lives, and under the discipline of Church authority, several of these German students, as a necessary introduction to their work, solemnly joined the Roman Catholic Church.

At the head of these young Germans in Rome, who cast their challenge without fear or doubt at the art dogmas of the last three centuries, was Friederich Overbeck, who was born at Lübeck in 1789. He studied art in Venice, and proceeded to Rome in 1810, when he was twenty-one years of age; having already adopted the opinions of Friedrich Schlegel. He lodged at that time in an old convent in the company of his countryman, Peter Von Cornelius, who was then his chosen friend and constant associate. At the end of every week the two young painters showed each other the product, in both cases, of the week's zealous labour, with a tacit understanding that each should "pronounce in sincerity" on the attainment of the other.

The work which stamped Overbeck as a genuine reformer, and as thoroughly imbued with the profound reverence and the lofty aspirations of his guides, was the large painting of *Christ entering Jerusalem*, painted for the Marienkirche at Lubeck in 1816, when he was twenty-six years of age. Another celebrated performance of the painter's was his great representation of the *Influence of Christianity on the Arts*, which was painted for the Stadelische Institute, at Frankfort-on-Main.

Overbeck devoted himself entirely to religious art, executing many large paintings both in oil and fresco, with the subjects taken from sacred history, or purely symbolical and allegorical. In addition, he accomplished innumerable drawings and designs—all having the same inspiration.

Overbeck was elected president of the Academy of St. Luke, and foreign member of the French Institute, besides being member of all the German Academies. He never left Rome; and however his followers might swerve, Overbeck adhered strictly, to the last, to the new art-faith, which he and they had first promulgated, and not only professed but practiced it in an unworldly life. Overbeck died in 1869, aged eighty years.

The judgment now pronounced on Overbeck's works is the frank acknowledgment by those most opposed to him and his school, of the awe and beauty of holiness of which these paintings are full; neither does any one deny, that as a man of unquestionable genius, he showed great ability and learning in his art. The objection made to his designs in their fulfilment, is their chillness, mysticism, and growing conventionality, in which nature, as if it were unredeemed, had little part. The school of Overbeck, which, after all, was but a strong re-action, is said to be passing away, especially in Germany.

In England admiration of Overbeck—to the extent of a full consent to his theories—has been naturally held very largely by, and in a certain degree has become identified with, that party in the Church of England which is defined by the denomination High Church.

PETER VON CORNELIUS, Overbeck's early friend, was born at Düsseldorf in 1784, and though his father was inspector of the Düsseldorf Gallery, the family was so poor that on the father's death the mother was urged to stop the career of Cornelius, who had already displayed a great love of drawing, as an artist, in order to apprentice him to the more practical and remunerative work of a goldsmith. But the mother had faith in her son's genius as a painter, and young Cornelius justified the faith, by causing the loss of his father and the poverty of the family to serve only as stimulants to urge him on in the progress which was to end, not merely in independence, but in honour and renown.

In 1811, a year later than Overbeck, Cornelius, who was five years Overbeck's senior, went also to Rome, and soon joined the brotherhood of German artists, then

passing to a marked extent under the influence of his younger countryman. But the very susceptibility which rendered Cornelius so open to the strange teaching of his comrade, was part of a wider and more catholic nature than that of Overbeck, a nature which in Cornelius's case was capable of receiving different impressions, and tending in various directions, throughout his long life and art-career. Even while in Rome, and under the very shadow of Overbeck, Cornelius diverged from severe religious art to his illustrations of the great German mediæval poem and collection of ballads, answering in some respects to the "Mort d'Arthur," and known as the "Niebelungenlied."

From Rome Cornelius returned to Düsseldorf, and thence proceeded to Munich, where King Ludwig, at that time Crown Prince of Bavaria, was inaugurating his patronage of art, by his schemes for the frescoes in the art-temple of the Glyptothek. Cornelius became the ruling spirit in the new and vigorous art-life of Munich. He had by that time lapsed so far from Overbeck's principles as to include profane history in his field, nay, to have recourse to the old mythology with all the instinctive ineradicable partiality of a man who, after the study of the Bible, delighted in the heroes of Homer and of the German troubadours, and next to them, in what had charmed his youth, in the "Faust" of Goethe, and in the "Inferno" of Dante. But it might have been an adaptation of Overbeck's views which induced Cornelius and some of his followers to accord a strong preference to work which should belong to the public and political life of their country.

At Munich, amidst an amount of work which beside that of other modern painters appears vast, the painter was indefatigably industrious, and abounded in ever fresh and gigantic designs. Cornelius decorated in the Glyptothek two large halls, called respectively the Hall of the Heroes and the Hall of the Gods, with frescoes founded on the antique. In the Pinacothek he painted the *History of Painting*. For the church of St. Louis he executed the large frescoes of *God the Father*, *The Nativity*, *The Crucifixion*, and the *Last Judgment*, which measures alone sixty-two feet in height and thirty-two feet in width.

For the royal mausoleum of the kings of Prussia Cornelius designed what are among his masterpieces, *The Four Riders of the Apocalypse;* and at the same time the painter executed a very different commission for the same royal employer, the silver shield which was King William's gift to his god-child, the Prince of Wales.

Along with every distinction with which his country could invest him, Cornelius was elected a foreign member of the Institute of France. He died in 1867, aged 83 years.

WILHELM VON KAULBACH is the greatest of Cornelius' scholars. He was born, in 1805 at a small town in Westphalia, and was the son of an engraver. With considerable difficulty in the circumstances of the family, Kaulbach was sent to the Art Academy at Düsseldorf, while Cornelius was still acting as its director, and soon attracted the attention and won the approbation of the gifted painter. When Cornelius proceeded to Munich and was appointed director of the Academy there, many of his Düsseldorf scholars, and among them Kaulbach, followed their teacher.

At Munich the young Westphalian, like so many German painters, found an eager patron in the king. King Ludwig was then presiding over the erection of the Odéon, a hall for musical and social purposes. He commissioned from Kaulbach frescoes of Apollo and the Muses in colossal proportions for the ceiling of the Odéon, and appointed him a share in the decoration of the palace garden arcades, for which Kaulbach painted "the four principal rivers of the kingdom, and a *Bavaria*, in colossal allegorical figures in fresco," besides designing cartoons on the various virtues of a sovereign. When the king's new palace was built, the architect engaged Kaulbach to paint the queen's throne-hall with twelve representations from Klopstock's Battle of Hermann, a commission followed by another to paint a second room in the palace, with "a series of subjects from Goethe's poems, partly in fresco, partly in wax colour, the whole being disposed in various compartments on the walls, the ceiling, and the lunette below the latter." At the same time he painted a series of frescoes with *Cupid and Psyche* for the subject, in the Palace of Prince Maximilian.

For the King of Bavaria Kaulbach painted in oils his splendid *Destruction of Jerusalem*, in which he displayed, along with noble composition, correctly studied colouring.

Kaulbach might have continued to this day the genius which nature made him, and which he showed himself in such works as *The Madhouse;* he died 1875.

EDWARD BENDEMANN was born in 1811 at Berlin. He went, when he was sixteen years of age, to Düsseldorf to pursue his art studies, and in the following year, 1828, painted a portrait of his grandmother, which attracted attention, and won some celebrity for the young lad. In 1830, when he was still under twenty years of age, he went to Italy, and remained there for a year. On his return to Düsseldorf, at the age of twenty years, Bendemann began his well-known picture of *The Sorrowing Jews in Exile*, in illustration of the verse:—

"By the rivers of Babylon there we sat down, yea, we wept."

This picture was exhibited in the following year at the Berlin Exhibition, and from its own great merits of pathetic sentiment, fine individual figures, and good painting, and from the circumstance that its painter was a native of Berlin, and a young man of twenty-one years of age, created a great sensation. This picture, which has been engraved, is now at Cologne. In addition to small pictures Bendemann painted in 1836 his *Jeremiah amidst the Ruins of Jerusalem*, which is the property of the King of Prussia.

But in the new era of art in Germany, Bendemann was not satisfied with confining his efforts to easel pictures, and he was soon summoned by the King of Saxony, and commissioned to execute frescoes for three rooms in the Royal Castle at Dresden. For the Throne Room he designed a frieze painted on a gold ground running round the room, and intended to show in one continuous design, with a Christian moral, human life from birth to death. Over the throne he designed an emblematic figure of *Saxonia*, attended by eight figures of law-givers and kings living before the Christian era, and eight similar figures belonging to later periods.

The easel picture of Bendemann's more mature years, entitled the *Shepherd and Shepherdess*, is famous. Like his fellows, he also has contributed to illustrate the dear treasure of German romance contained in the *Niebelungenlied*. Bendemann is said to be deficient in strong delineations of fierce passion, but to excel in the expression of simple beauty and nobility.

Bendemann has been elected member of various German academies; appointed professor of painting at the Academy, Dresden, created Knight of the royal Saxon order of Civil Merit, of the Prussian order of the Red Eagle, and of the Belgian order of Leopold.

RETHEL AND STEINLE were students of Overbeck, and later of Cornelius. Rethel's pair of pictorial *moralities* have received high commendation. Another German painter, Hildebrandt, has given a good German version of *The Murder of the Princes in the Tower*.

HILDEBRANDT showed great talent as a landscape painter in a series of pictures entitled *Tour du Mond*—pictures all round the world, including New York, Salt Lake City, and Sacramento—he was a brilliant and daring colourist. He only recently died.

CHARLES TSCHAGGENY, born at Brussels in 1815, was one of the best of the later Belgian animal painters which boasts such masters as Verbeckhoven. He was eminent as a landscape painter, and his men and women have a quaint force of character bespeaking the versatility of a master We engrave his well-known picture, *The Cow Doctor*.*

* See Steel Engraving.

CHAPTER V.

MULREADY—DYCE—MACLISE—PHILLIP—LANDSEER— STANFIELD—ROBERTS—HUNT—LANCE, &c.

ILLIAM MULREADY was born at Ennis in 1786. His father was a leather breeches maker, who removed to Dublin, and then went to London, before the future painter was six years of age. As a boy he showed his love of art by drawing a hare, which did not require a written commentary, at the age of three years. He was educated at various Roman Catholic schools, and is said to have obtained his first introduction to a studio by sitting as a model for the young Solomon in a design of *David and Solomon* executed for Macklin's Bible. By the aid of Banks the sculptor, he procured admission to the Academy at the age of fourteen years. His first independent efforts, which must have begun betimes, (since, like the French painter, Vernet, Mulready is said to have kept himself from his fifteenth year), were designs for children's books, such as the *Butterfly's Ball*, and the *Cat's Concert*.

Mulready as a mere lad was attracted to the studio of Varley the water-colour painter, then a resort of promising young painters. The doubtful consequence of Mulready's intimacy with Varley was the former's marriage before he was eighteen years of age to Varley's sister. Before he was nineteen Mulready was a father; by the time he was twenty-four years of age his family numbered four sons. In addition to the great strain to provide for a household which was thus thrown upon him in his undeveloped powers, Mulready's marriage proved as unhappy as it was imprudent. The boy and girl who were husband and wife seem to have separated by agreement before they were well man and woman, and to this separation there came no reunion. No wonder that the early manhood of the painter was one of extreme drudgery and wearing care.

The first work of Mulready's which attracted notice was his *Punch*, painted in 1812, when he was twenty-six years of age, and from that date he continued to rise in general estimation, but, above all, in the estimation of his brother artists; for, although his subjects were drawn from popular sources, the evidence of painstaking and culture in his style, was addressed to a higher than a popular audience. In 1815, three years after the painting of *Punch*, when Mulready was in his thirtieth year, he

BEGGING MONK AT THE DOOR OF

was elected an associate, and three months later a member of the Academy, a rare instance of rapid promotion by the voice of his fellows.

After his *Idle Boys*, which was the apparent cause of Mulready's election as an associate of the Academy, and his *Fight interrupted*, he painted in succession, with higher and higher degrees of excellence of its kind, in a transition from the Dutch school to a school of his own, his *Dog of Two Minds*, *Wolf and Lamb*, *Careless Messenger*, and *Travelling Druggist*, and his *Interior of an English Cottage*, which has more poetry and simple pathos than Mulready's pictures usually possess.

In 1827, a little over his fortieth year, Mulready moved from his other house at Kensington to No. 1, Linden Grove, Bayswater, which had been newly built, and where the architect had erected a studio for the painter according to his wishes. This house continued his home for thirty-six years, down, indeed, to his death.

In 1837, when Mulready was over fifty years of age, he painted his illustrations of Shakespeare in *The Seven Ages*, and of original poetry in *First Love*, and *The Sonnet*. Three years later he fell on what was to him a yet happier vein. He executed a series of twenty drawings on wood, taken from the "Vicar of Wakefield." These drawings, when engraved, were so much admired, that they not only procured Mulready commissions, but proved the originals of some of his best pictures.

In 1848, there was an exhibition of Mulready's works in the rooms of the Society of Arts, and in 1864, the year following his death, there was a second exhibition of his pictures at Kensington which had been associated with some of his earliest successes in landscape—*Keston*, *The Cottage*, and *Gravel Pits*.

William Mulready lived to attain a high place in his profession, but the evil effects of his marriage—the one fatal mistake of his history—continued to be felt throughout his life. His desolate home, no doubt, helped to render him the reserved, isolated man he was, and probably his abiding by what he called "the old faith," in days when political opinion ran high against it, contributed to the same result. His children, whom he had left to themselves, did not grow up so as to add to their father's credit and happiness, though one son lived with Mulready, and was with his father when he died, somewhat suddenly, in his seventy-eighth year, in 1863.

As an artist Mulready has been classed with Leslie, to whom we turn in the American School, for what seems, on the whole, a just definition.

AUGUSTUS WALL CALLCOTT was born at Kensington Gravel-Pits—then a country hamlet—on February 20th, 1779. He studied under Hoppner, and began life as a portrait painter. His first exhibited picture was a *Portrait of Miss Roberts*, which appeared in 1799. In 1802 he discovered that his natural taste lay in another direction, and abandoned portraiture for landscape painting. In February, 1827, Callcott married, and shortly afterwards started on a tour through Italy. On his return, he took a house in the "Mall," and became a fashionable artist. His wife, who was an accomplished woman, assisted him by her literary labours on art subjects. On the accession of her Majesty the Queen, Callcott, who was then one of the favourite artists of the day, received the honor of knighthood.

Sir Augustus Callcott died in 1844, regretted by those who knew him, for he was a liberal patron of young artists and kind and courteous to all.

His works are mostly views of English scenery, though he sometimes varied them by producing figure subjects in conjunction with landscape. Some of his best known paintings are—the *Old Pier at Littlehampton; Calm in the Medway, Rochester; Entrance to the Pool of London, Dutch Peasants returning from Market*, and *Crossing the Stream*.* There are nine of his paintings in the National Gallery.

WILLIAM DYCE was born in 1806 in Aberdeen, where his father was a physician. Young Dyce graduated, and took the degree of Master of Arts at Mareschal College, Aberdeen, when he was but sixteen years of age. He went to Edinburgh, and in his seventeenth year became a student of the Royal Scottish Academy, but shortly afterwards went up to London and entered as a probationer the school of the Royal Academy. Still dissatisfied with the instruction which he was receiving, and having the command of means to serve his purpose, Dyce went in his nineteenth year to Italy, and the future extent of his art learning, together with the large measure in which he was imbued with the highest Italian art, is attributed to his having come thus early, with his faculties fresh as well as capable, in contact with the chefs-d'œuvres of the best old masters. In addition, Dyce became intimately acquainted with, and deeply enamoured of, mural or wall art, in itself—with its decorative aspect, and the value of the arabesques, which form a subordinate but necessary part of the whole. His first stay in Rome did not last longer than a year, but on his return home he showed the distinct bent which his mind had taken by preparing a set of arabesque designs, and transferring them to a room in his father's house in Aberdeen.

In the following year, 1827, when he was twenty-one years of age, he exhibited his first work—classical without fail—*Bacchus nursed by the Nymphs of Nyssa*, in the Royal Academy's Exhibition, and shortly afterwards went back to Rome, remaining there on this occasion three years, and devoting himself to the study of frescoes and wall decorations. When Dyce went back to Edinburgh he was the most scholarly of the British painters of his generation, and one on whom the purity and dignity of high art, even in the quiet elegance of its simplest accessories, had made an ineffaceable impression.

In 1844, when he was thirty-eight years of age, he exhibited his very scholarly, and in many respects fine, picture of *King Joash shooting the Arrow of Deliverance*, and had its merits acknowledged by his immediate election as an associate of the Royal Academy; four years later he was elected a full member.

ALFRED EDWARD CHALON, the younger brother of John Chalon, was born at Geneva in 1781. He adopted painting as a profession in opposition to the wishes of his parents, who had intended him to be a merchant. In 1796, he entered the Royal Academy schools, and soon afterwards became popular as a portrait painter in water-colours. He was elected an Associate of the Academy in 1812, and a full member four years afterwards. Soon after the accession of her Majesty the Queen, Chalon painted her likeness, and was also appointed portrait painter in water-colours to her Majesty. In 1855, his own works, with those of his recently deceased brother, were exhibited in the rooms of the Society of Arts at the Adelphi. Alfred Edward Chalon

* See Steel Engraving.

died at Kensington in 1860, and was buried by the side of his brother in Highgate Cemetery. The most popular, perhaps, of his historic works, is *John Knox reproving the Ladies of Queen Mary's Court*, and among his genre subjects, *Hunt the Slipper*.

DANIEL MACLISE was born in 1811, at Cork. His father was a Scotchman who had borne the name of Macleish, and been an Ensign in the Elgin Fencibles, but who had thrown up his ensigncy and entered into trade in Cork, where he married and settled. Young Maclise, in spite of a preference for art, was placed in a bank, which he left at the age of sixteen to follow his natural calling, trusting to his pencil for a livelihood. He was a student in the Cork School of Art while maintaining himself by the sale of his drawings. (We think it is of Maclise as a lad in a bookseller's shop during Sir Walter Scott's visit to Ireland that the story is told of Sir Walter's entering the shop, and having his likeness so cleverly caught by the unsuspected artist, that it was for sale on the following day in the same shop, to the great amusement of the kindly literary king.)

Maclise went to London in 1828, when he was no more than seventeen years of age, and entered the Royal Academy as a student, carrying off in succession all its medals. In 1830 Maclise made his way to Paris, and studied in the art galleries there. His first oil pictures were *Mokanna Unveiling*, and *All Hallow Eve*, exhibited at the British Institution and the Royal Academy; the former in 1833, when Maclise was twenty-two years of age, and both regarded as works of promise. In the mean time the young painter was earning his bread by drawing for the booksellers, and painting portraits. In 1834 and 1835 he exhibited his *Captain Rock* and *Vow of the Ladies and the Peacock*, showing marked improvement, and forming in the latter case so decided a success, that Maclise was elected an associate of the Academy at the age of twenty-four years; five years later, immediately after the exhibition of his *Merry Christmas in the Baron's Hall*, he was elected a full member. To a certain extent, and with a wider range, Maclise followed Mulready and Leslie in genre painting, in his popular subjects from the Vicar of Wakefield and Gil Blas, Shakespeare and Scott. Along with David Roberts Maclise illustrated Bulwer's " Pilgrims of the Rhine." But gradually he gave himself more and more to historical painting on large canvases crowded with figures, in which his success was more doubtful.

He next painted *The Meeting between Wellington and Blücher after Waterloo*, of which his *Death of Nelson at Trafalgar* was the companion picture in another compartment in the Royal Gallery.

Maclise devoted the later years of his life to these immense works. He died in 1870, aged fifty-nine years. Like many another artist, he had strayed into the neighbouring region of poetry and written a few sonnets.

Maclise was a man of undoubted original genius and of an earnest and laborious life. He never married, but had his house presided over by his sisters, once famous for their beauty, with the children of one of the sisters completing the family circle. His intimacy with the great novelist, Charles Dickens, and the social meetings and gay

* See Illustration.

excursions into which the intimacy led, have been but lately brought prominently before us.

JOHN BURNET, who was born near Edinburgh, probably at Musselburgh, on the 20th of March, 1784, was apprenticed to Robert Scott, an engraver of Edinburgh, and also studied in the Trustees' Academy in that city. While engaged in this way, he made the acquaintance of Wilkie, who remained his friend for life. In 1806 Burnet went to London, where, though chiefly known as an engraver, he attained fame by his painting.

Of his pictures the best known and most worthy of merit is the *Greenwich Hospital and Naval Heroes*, which he painted for the Duke of Wellington, and which was exhibited at the British Institution in 1837. He was capable also of humourous illustration in a very happy degree as may be seen in *The Dancing Dolls** in the National Gallery, London. As a writer on art he will be long remembered by treatises on the principles and practice of different branches of art. He died at Stoke Newington, on the 29th of April, 1868, aged eighty-four.

JOHN PHILLIP was born in 1817, in Aberdeen, and by the time he was fifteen years of age was practising drawing with the desire of being a painter. Apparently his relations thwarted his wishes, for in 1834, when he was seventeen years of age, he left home without leave asked or obtained, and worked for his passage on board a coasting vessel from Aberdeen to London, for the purpose of visiting the Royal Academy's exhibition.

In 1851, when Phillip was thirty-four years of age, he was driven by a severe illness to take the step which proved to him a short road to prosperity. He went to Spain and remained there for one year. Since Wilkie's day more than one young English artist had sought inspiration at the source which he had proclaimed to be so rich and fertilizing, but on none did Spain produce the effect which it wrought on John Phillip. His natural vigour was thenceforth displayed with an entire change of spirit and colour, which, as the change partook largely of the fervid sunshine and ripe luxuriance of the south, acted like a charm on an English public to whom such qualities have all the wistful fascination of the unknown. Phillip's rise to fame and fortune when he had not begun his art career by taking them by storm, was thenceforth rapid beyond precedent.

In 1852 Phillip returned from Spain, and in the following year he exhibited his *Visit to the Gipsy Quarters*, striking the first blow with a new and potent weapon. In 1854 he painted his *Andalusian Letter-writer* for the Queen. In 1856 he went again to Spain, and painted his *Prayer of Faith shall Save the Sick*, a still more striking picture, and one appealing to deeper feeling. The year after his second return, in 1857, when Phillip was forty years of age, he was elected an associate of the Royal Academy, and two years later he became a full member. In 1860 he paid his last visit to Spain, and the same year he exhibited the picture which had been a royal commission, it is said reluctantly accepted by him, so triumphant was his success with his Spanish subjects, *The Marriage of the Princess Royal*.

* See Steel Engraving.

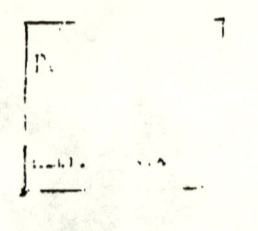

For ten years Phillip continued to use the stores of his Spanish sketch-book, selling his pictures as rapidly as he painted them, at prices till then, with, perhaps, one exception, among modern painters unheard of. M. Rossetti quotes the rumour that for "some dozen" of Spanish pictures Phillip received from two dealers, the sum of $100,000. It was vain for critics to protest that the pictures—the colours of which were so glowing, that they caused the colours of all other pictures to look tame and dull in comparison—were deficient in the very highest excellence, and that even their great merits were linked to faults—their gorgeousness was allied to vulgarity, and their dramatic strength to bravura. The tide of popularity—generally so one-sided, was too strong to be turned. There came no abatement to the flood of praise and patronage, until the premature death of the painter—whose hearth had been overshadowed by a domestic affliction—in 1867, at fifty years of age.

SIR EDWIN LANDSEER ranks with the past as well as the present generation. He was born, in 1802, in London. His father was a well-known engraver, whose sons, inheriting his artistic tastes, became in turn either engravers or painters. When he was sixteen, he painted his *Dogs Fighting*, which was exhibited, and bought by Sir George Beaumont, and engraved by the elder Landseer.

But the success of this juvenile work was far surpassed by that of *The Dogs of St. Gothard Discovering a Traveler in the Snow*, which was exhibited in 1820, when Landseer was eighteen years of age, and having been engraved by his father became one of the most popular prints of the day. In Landseer's case precocious talent was not so fatal as it is apt to prove, but his circumstances were peculiar, ensuring him constant instruction from his infancy, instruction which he supplemented by becoming the pupil of Haydon, when Landseer applied himself with great energy and industry to profit by his master's lessons, one of which was, aptly enough, that of dissecting a dead lion, and enthusiastically mastering its anatomy. Neither is it beyond contradiction, that the great animal painter, with all his power and ability, may not have been injured, rather than lastingly benefited, by success too early won.

In 1826, as soon as he had attained the prescribed age of twenty-four years, Landseer was elected an associate of the Royal Academy; four years later he became an Academician. From the date of a visit to the Highlands in 1826 he is said to have thrown aside his carefully and minutely finished work for the bold and free style in which he has continued to win laurels for fully forty years. With his early visit to the Highlands also may be connected his preference for deer as the subjects of his pencil, evinced not only in his famous *Children of the Mist, Seeking Sanctuary, Night, and Morning*, but in innumerable examples of mountain scenery, peopled by the denizens of the old forests. Along with deer Landseer has "possessed" horses and dogs to the fullest extent. In a lower, though still in a high degree, he has established his mastery over the other forms of animal life, witness his picture *Caught*.*

Landseer has, in addition, an established reputation as a figure painter, three of his most popular works being *A Dialogue at Waterloo* (the Duke of Wellington pointing out the scene of the incidents of the battle to the Marchioness of Douro), *Bolton Abbey in the Olden Time*, and the *Return from Hunting*.

* See Steel Engraving.

Landseer, who received much favour from the Queen, painted in fresco *Comus*, for the Queen's summer-house. His 'life-size chalk drawings are well known. In conjunction with Baron Marochetti, he originated the lions in Trafalgar Square.

Landseer received the honour of knighthood from the Queen in 1850. At the French Exhibition of 1855 he was awarded the only large gold medal given to an English painter. He died in 1875.

CLARKSON STANFIELD was born in 1798 at Sunderland. He was brought up to a sea-faring life, and on board ship met Douglas Jerrold, who got up plays for the sailors after the fashion of his father, the manager of the theatre at Deptford. For the young sailor Jerrold's plays, the other young sailor, Stanfield, painted the scenes. Years after, the amateur play-writer and scene-painter met as eminent professional dramatist and scene-painter at Drury Lane.

Eventually Stanfield left scene-painting, which he brought to great perfection, to become a landscape and marine painter of no mean merit. His first large picture, *Wreckers off Fort Rouge*, was exhibited at the British Institution in 1827, the same year that he exhibited *A Calm* at the Royal Academy. Stanfield was then in his thirtieth year. He was elected an associate of the Academy five years later, in 1832, and three years later, in 1835, he became a full member.

Stanfield visited the continent frequently, and showed that he could not only paint land as well as water, but land so varied as that presented by the low banks of Dutch canals in their monotony—still gloriously picturesque, by the shores of the Mediterranean, and by the sunny champagne country of France. The painter was commissioned in 1830 to paint a series of large pictures for the Marquis of Lansdowne's banqueting-room at Bowood, and in 1834 he had an order from the Duchess of Sutherland to paint a series of views in Venice to be hung at Trentham. A series of forty views in the British Channel and on the coast of France, called *Stanfield's Coast-scenery*, was engraved.

Stanfield, as well as Maclise and the great actor Macready, formed a trio that Foster's Life of Dickens has shown to the world as intimately associated with the novelist in his happiest years. Stanfield died in 1867, at the age of sixty-nine years.

Among Stanfield's most famous pictures are the *Abandoned*, the *Battle of Trafalgar*, painted for the United Service Club; the *Castle of Ischia*, one of the three pictures sent by him to the French Exhibition of 1855; and the *Victory towed into Gibraltar after the Battle of Trafalgar*, painted for Sir S. Morton Peto.

As an example of the price given for Stanfield's pictures, Ottley quotes that his *Beilstein on the Moselle* was sold, in 1863, for $7,500, and his *Castle of Ischia*, in 1865, for $6,250. The National Gallery, London, has four *Stanfields*, partly marine pictures, partly landscapes.

DAVID ROBERTS was born in 1796, at Stockbridge, Edinburgh. Roberts, whose family were in humble circumstances, had the fair education of a Scotch lad, and was then apprenticed to a decorator and house painter for seven years. He completed his apprenticeship, showing marked ability, and immediately joined a company of strolling players, having arranged with them to be scene painter. Beyond what he had learnt in house-painting, he had not received a regular lesson in art since he had left the Trustees' Academy. One unfortunate consequence of Roberts' connection with the strolling players was his marriage with one of the troop, which proved an unsuitable, unhappy connection.

In 1820, when Roberts was twenty-four years of age, he had risen so far in his profession as to be engaged in scene-painting for the Glasgow and Edinburgh theatres. A little later he found employment at Drury Lane, of which, in 1822, he was appointed scene-painter. He exhibited for the first time in the Royal Academy in 1826, when he was in his thirty-first year, *A View of Rouen Cathedral*.

Roberts' love for architecture never wavered, and in order to gratify it and perfect himself in the art in which he was fast rising, he travelled and drew in France, Belgium, Germany, Spain, Morocco, and Holland.

In 1838, when Roberts was forty-two years of age, he was elected an associate of the Academy. The same year, unencumbered as he was with family ties, save in the person of one daughter, and having, but for her, a solitary hearth, since he had early separated from his wife, Roberts set out on more distant expeditions to Egypt and Syria. On his way through Constantinople he painted the *Church of St. Sophia*,* a fine interior. His diligence and devotion in making a large number of fine sketches requiring the utmost care and pains, under every disadvantage of climate and circumstance, deserved and obtained great praise. In 1841 he was elected an Academician. He died in 1864.

WILLIAM HENRY HUNT was born in 1790 at Belton Street, Long Acre, London, in a labyrinth of wretched alleys not far from the birth-place of Turner. His father was a tin-plate worker, and it was only the son's sickliness which induced the father to consent to young Hunt, at sixteen, renouncing the learning of a profitable trade, for art, by becoming an apprentice for a term of seven years to Varley the watercolour painter.

At Varley's Hunt met Mulready, who advised the lad to become a student of the Royal Academy, where he had a fellow-pupil and friend in Linnel, the well-known landscape painter. While Hunt was in his apprenticeship he was introduced to Dr. Munro, one of the king's physicians, and an enthusiastic lover and patron of art, at whose country house, at Bushy, Hunt met Turner, Eridge, Hearne, and the doctor's son, a young artist (the three last of whom are buried side by side in Bushy churchyard). Hunt visited Dr. Munro at his town house in the Adelphi, and would stay for a month at a time at Bushy, contributing to Dr. Munro's portfolio at the rate of $1.87 a day. While in the neighborhood of Bushy sketching, Hunt encountered the Earl of Essex, and was commissioned to take views in the park and grounds of Cashiobury.

Hunt's first picture exhibited at the Royal Academy was *A Scene near Hounslow*, in 1807, when he was seventeen years of age. He continued to exhibit at the Royal Academy's Exhibition, his progress in life being marked by the successive changes of his address from his master Varley's, back to his father's house, then to Brownlow Street, Drury Lane, and Marchmont Street, Brunswick Square, till he settled, on

* See Illustration.

account of his health, at Hastings. He was connected with the "Society of Painters in Water-colours" from its establishment, and was elected one of its associate members in 1824, when he was thirty-four years of age, becoming a full member three years later.

It is said of Hunt, that " from the beginning he painted with all his might, sketching loyally what he saw, making portraits of everything he selected as worth painting, and selecting wisely." Hunt was fond of rustic life and common familiar things, but treated the homeliest object with a delicate perception of its merits which removed it from vulgarity. Among his subjects are *The Attack*, a country boy about to feast on a huge pie, *The Defeat*, the same lad overcome with sleep when the feast is ended, and *The Brown Study*, a mulatto boy struggling to overcome a sum in addition. Hunt's fruit and flowers were wonders of loving fidelity and exquisite colour. Of his *Study of Hyacinths*, " he boasted that each of its leaves was a portrait," yet nothing of the kind can be less formal or more idealized into perfection than those flowers. His *Plums* formed another triumph. Still finer were his *Study of Gold*—a smoked Pilchard; his *Study of Rose-grey*—a mushroom, and his *Dead Humming-Bird*, of which it is said that " it glows with turquoise, blue, green, and gold, and even from the farthest side of the room sparkles marvellously."

When eleven of the painter's works were shown in the Great Paris Exhibition of 1855, the French painters hailed them with delighted acclamation. He died in 1864.

ERSKINE NICOL, was born at Leith in 1825, received his art-education at the Trustees' Academy, Edinburgh, under the direction of Sir William Allan and Mr. T. Duncan. In 1846 he went to Ireland, where he resided three or four years, returned to Edinburgh, and after exhibiting for some time in that city, was elected a member of the Royal Scottish Academy. In 1862 he settled in London. Among his most popular pictures (all relating to Irish subjects) may be mentioned. *Did it Pout with its Betsy? Renewal of the Lease Refused*, exhibited in 1863; *Among the Old Masters*, and *Waiting for the Train*, in 1864; and *A Deputation* in 1865. At the Winter Exhibition of the Institute of Painters in Water-colours, Mr. Nicol has exhibited *Caught, Rent-Paying, Kept in,* Both Puzzled, Missed It*, etc. Mr. Nicol was elected A.R.A. in June, 1866. He has since then painted *Steady Johnny*, the landing of a fine salmon, "Johnny" handling the landing net.

GEORGE LANCE was born in 1802 at the old manor-house of Little Easton, in Essex. His father had been an officer in a regiment of light horse, and was afterwards an adjutant in the Essex Yeomanry, and an inspector of the horse patrol, which rid the great roads of their footpads.

George Lance was sent to Leeds to be a manufacturer, but on his own urgent entreaty, was allowed to give up the attempt, and going to London he became a pupil of Haydon's. Mr. Redgrave tells the story that Lance had visited the British Museum, and, seeing a lad drawing from the Elgin marbles, with the words written on his copy " Pupil of Haydon," inquired eagerly whether Haydon would take other pupils. He was conducted by the lad, a brother of Sir Edwin Landseer's, to the

* See Steel Engraving.

ELAINE.

(From the original painting by T. E. Rosenthal.)

painter. On the new comer's making a modest statement of his wish, with a hesitating inquiry as to terms, Haydon, with the impulsiveness—half generosity, half bluster, which was so much a part of him, exclaimed—"Terms, my little fellow! when I take pupils I never look at the fathers' purses. Bring me some of your work, and if I think they promise success I will take you for nothing."

Haydon did become the master of Lance, and in Haydon's studio, and as a student of the Royal Academy, he learnt what could be learnt of art. But the high art which Haydon taught was not congenial to his young pupil, and by a happy accident he found a more suitable field for his gift. Having been sent to paint some still life to improve his skill, the work was admired and bought by Sir George Beaumont, and commissions for the same description of work followed from the Earl of Shaftesbury and the Duke of Bedford. (For the Duke of Bedford Lance painted afterwards a great fruit piece to adorn a summer-house at Woburn, on the occasion of the visit of William IV.)

Lance became a painter of still life, and as such he was famous, not merely for his fruit and flowers, but for the adjuncts of glass, plate, and draperies, while his dead game were even more valued. Mr. Redgrave mentions two pictures by Lance, out of his usual course, which gave indication of a capacity for higher walks of art—*Melancthon's first misgivings of Rome*, and the *Seneschal*. George Lance died in the neighbourhood of Birkenhead in 1864, at the age of sixty-two years. He has left a daughter who paints in her father's style.

WILLIAM COLLINS, the charming interpreter of English rural and seaside life, was born in London of Irish parents on the 18th of September, 1787. He learned the first principles of art in the studio of George Morland—one of the earliest English painters who chose his subjects from the home life of the lower classes of his native land—whose influence is very distinctly noticeable in the works of his pupil.

In 1807, young Collins entered the Royal Academy schools, and exhibited two fine landscapes; but compelled to earn his living by portrait painting, he did not follow them up with anything of a similar character until 1810, when, having saved money, he was able to choose his own subjects. He then produced a series of scenes of outdoor life, such as *Children Bird's-Nesting*, or *Swinging on the Gate*,* *Prawn Fisheries*, *Shrimpers*, *Fishermen on the look-out*, treated in a simple, life-like and effective manner which elicited high praise from the art critics of the day.

In 1820, Collins was elected a Royal Academician, and until 1836 was a continual exhibitor of subjects similar to those which he had made his reputation. Unfortunately for his art, he then went to Italy with a view of improving his style, and enlarging his experience. After two years of travel he returned home full of enthusiasm for the beauties of Italian scenery, and Italian peasantry; and discontented with what now seemed the "humdrum" simplicity of every-day English life, he tried a higher style, and produced Italian landscapes, such as the *Cave of Ulysses*, and the *Bay of Naples*, following them up with the yet more ambitious subjects, *Christ in the Temple with the Doctors*, and the *Two Disciples at Emmaus;* these subjects were not very

* See Steel Engraving.

successful, and with true wisdom the ambitious artist returned to his first style, and remained faithful to it until his death, which took place in Devonport Street, Hyde Park Gardens, on the 18th of February, 1747.

WILLIAM HOLMAN HUNT was born, in 1827, in London. He was a student of the Royal Academy. His first exhibited picture was in the Royal Academy's Exhibition of 1846, when he was nineteen years of age. Three or four years later, about 1850, he took his stand as a Præraphaelite in his *Converted British Family sheltering a Christian Missionary from the persecution of the Druids*. His most famous pictures since have been, in 1854, his *Light of the World* (a noble allegory, in which the Saviour stands, lantern in hand, at a closed door, under a star-lit sky); in 1856, after the painter's visit to the East, *The Scape-Goat*, another pathetic allegory as read by the light of the Old Testament law; and in 1860, when the painter was in his thirty-fourth year, after four years' study and labour, *Christ discovered in the Temple*, which thousands flocked to see, not only in London but in every town where it was exhibited, for the public's verdict on it was, that whatever its imperfections, it was the one modern English picture which thrilled the spectators as with a glimpse of the divine.

Among Holman Hunt's pictures of lower import are his *Hireling Shepherd, Awakened Conscience*, and *Isabella and the Pot of Basil*. After the Prince of Wales's marriage the painter exhibited *London Bridge as illuminated and decorated on the occasion of the entry of the Princess Alexandra of Denmark on March 7, 1863*.

Holman Hunt has recently completed a sacred picture of Christ in the carpenter's shop, *The Shadow of Death* (sold for $50,000.)

JOHN EVERETT MILLAIS was born in 1829 at Southampton. His early youth was spent in France and the Channel Islands. His love of art showed itself betimes, and at nine years of age he won a medal for drawing from the Society of Arts. In 1840, when he was only eleven years of age, he entered the Royal Academy as a student, and distinguished himself in the schools—getting the silver medal in each.

In 1846, the same year that Holman Hunt exhibited his first picture at the Royal Academy's Exhibition, Millais, then in his eighteenth year, exhibited at the same place, his *Pizarro seizing the Men of Peru*. In 1847 he obtained the gold medal awarded for historical painting, and his picture—*The Tribe of Benjamin seizing the Daughters of Shiloh*, was exhibited at the British Institution in the following year.

This painter's first really popular picture was his *Huguenot on St. Bartholomew's Day refusing to shelter himself from danger by wearing the Roman Catholic badge*, exhibited two years later, in 1852. In 1853, at the earliest prescribed age, twenty-four years, the painter was elected an associate of the Academy. With various degrees of success and favour Millais painted afterwards, among other pictures, his *Ophelia, Order of Release*, and *Rescue*, (a fireman bearing children out of a burning house, and restoring them to the arms of their mother), a picture on which severe strictures were pronounced, because of the crimson tint supposed to be given by the fire, and because of the drawing of the figures, but which is a fine picture.

In 1856, when Millais was twenty-seven years of age, he struck a new chord with his *Autumn Leaves*, a group of children gathering and burning fallen leaves, in which his critics acknowledged much grace and poetry, and in which there were strong indications of the excellence in landscape painting which he has since attained. Several pictures of more doubtful or less valued merit followed, until again, in 1860, the painter, in his thirty-first year, renewed the impression made by his *Huguenot*, in a picture somewhat similar in character, that of the *Black Brunswicker*. This picture was followed by a succession of pictures of children in groups or singly, with an occasional picture of graver, but not very great interest, except it might be in technical merits.

In 1864, four years after being elected an associate, Millais became a full member of the Academy. In 1865 he painted another picture of some importance, *The Romans leaving Britain*. In 1871 he electrified once more the art-loving public by the unsurpassable truth of his *Chill October*, a landscape picture—the exquisitely subdued tone of which is one great element of its strength. In 1872 Millais had another triumph—this time technical, since the picture called *Hearts are Trumps*, with all its splendid handling and colouring, especially in the flesh tints, is but the representation of three fair English women (Misses Armstrong) playing whist with a dummy.

GEORGE FREDERICK WATTS was born in 1818 in London, and he first exhibited in 1837, when he was in his twentieth year. He began his career in art as a historical painter. During the sitting of the commission for the decoration of the new Houses of Parliament, Watts, in 1843, when he was twenty-five years of age, sent in cartoon of *Caractacus* to the competition proposed by the commissioners, and got a $1,500 prize. In the subsequent competition he gained one of the first-class prizes of $2,500 for his cartoon of *Alfred inciting the Saxons to Maritime Enterprise;* and he was commissioned to paint *St. George and the Dragon* for the Houses of Parliament. He painted also a large fresco "illustrative of the History of Justice," in the New Hall of Lincoln's Inn.

But it is by his mythological and ideal subjects, and above all by his portraits, that the painter has won a great name among his brother artists and in the outer world. His *Daphne* has been pronounced "perfectly admirable;" his *Diana and Endymion* worthy of his *Daphne;* his *Study with the Peacock's feathers* of "extraordinary merit and beauty."

Watts' portraits include those of Mr. Tennyson, Sir John Lawrence, the Hon. W. E. Gladstone, but whether of distinguished men, or of men and women utterly unknown to the world, these portraits stand out in "strong relief" from the portraits by the painter's contemporaries, redeeming portrait painting from the charge of decline in our days. "Classic," "thoughtful," "powerful," "rich," "luminous," full of "character and expression," "very tender and beautiful" in the painting, are terms exhausting the vocabulary of art, applied by critics to the qualities in Watts' portraits.

FREDERICK TAYLER, born in London, 1804, has been famous as a successful water-colour painter for nearly half a century.

In the English section of the Fine Art Gallery at Philadelphia, in 1876, he exhibited a beautiful high-class painting, *Crossing the Ferry*, which won universal admiration. We have illustrated one of his oil paintings, which appeared first forty years since, *The Young Chief's First Ride.**

FREDERICK LEIGHTON was born in 1830 at Scarborough. He was taken abroad in his childhood, and was brought to Rome, where he received lessons in drawing from an Italian painter, in his thirteenth and fourteenth years. In his fifteenth year he became a student of the Royal Academy, Berlin, studying in the following years at Florence, Frankfort-on-the Main, Brussels, and Paris, and again at Frankfort, where he worked under Steinle, a pupil of Overbeck's. Finally he resided several seasons in Rome, where he painted his picture *Cimabue's Madonna carried through Florence*, described in the catalogue thus:—"Cimabue's celebrated Madonna is carried in procession through the streets of Florence. In front of the Madonna, and crowned with laurels, walks Cimabue himself with his pupil Giotto; behind it Arnofo di Lappo, Gaddo Gaddi, Andrea Tafi, Nicolo Pisano, Buffalmacco, and Simone Memmi; in the corner, Dante." This picture was exhibited at the Royal Academy's Exhibition, London, in 1855, when Leighton was twenty-five years of age. The effect of such a picture, painted by a young man of twenty-five, whom Mr. Rossetti calls "a born artist," and who was full of the learning of the foreign schools, while he was unknown in England, was naturally great. The picture was at once bought by the Queen.

Leighton returned to Paris, and remained there for four years, profiting by the counsels of Ary Scheffer and Robert-Fleury. Eventually Leighton settled in London, where he had exhibited in 1856 his *Triumph of Music*—Orpheus playing his viol in the gloomy regions of Pluto, for the purpose of winning back Eurydice to earth. Other pictures of Leighton are, a *Reminiscence of Algiers*, *Paris on his wedding morning finds Juliet apparently lifeless*, *The Star of Bethlehem*, (one of the Magi from the terrace of his house stands looking at the star in the East; the lower part of the picture indicates a revel which he may be supposed to have just left); *Michael Angelo nursing his dying servant*, *Helen of Troy* and *Dante in Exile*.

WILLIAM POWELL FRITH is as unlike Leighton, as one artist can be unlike another. Frith was born in 1819, near Ripon, Yorkshire. He learned drawing in the art school at Bloomsbury, presided over by Mr. Sass, several of whose pupils have become eminent painters. Frith was a student of the Royal Academy, in 1837, when he was eighteen years of age. Two years later he first exhibited a picture, that of the head of one of Mr. Sass's children, at the British Institution. In 1840, when the painter was twenty-one years of age, he exhibited at the Royal Academy his picture of *Malvolio before the Countess Olivia*, which attracted much notice.

In 1845, when Frith was twenty-six years of age, his *Village Pastor*, from The Deserted Village, was still more admired, and gained the painter his election as an associate member of the Academy. At this time he seemed to be walking in the footsteps of Leslie, and painted in succession such pictures as *The Parting Interview of Leicester and the Countess Amy*, *Measuring Heights*, from the Vicar of Wakefield, *An English Merry-making a hundred years ago*, *The Coming of Age*, *Pope making love to*

---

* See Steel Engraving.

Lady Mary Wortley Montagu, and *The Beau's Stratagem*.* In 1853, when he was thirty-four years of age, Frith was elected a Royal Academician.

In the following year Frith struck on the vein of the familiar humours of a great English crowd, in which he may be said to walk alone, for Hogarth's election crowds had strict unity among dramatic episodes, in stories—the morals of which were one of their strongest points. Frith's *Life at the Sea-side, Ramsgate*, was but a lively version of a huge cockney, rather than motley, gathering, of which he made, with the greatest skill, all that could be made. The picture of the good citizens of London taking their annual holiday was warmly welcomed, and was bought by the Queen. Frith's *Derby Day*, belonging to 1858, was a vivid realization of a great popular spectacle, executed with wonderful fidelity and niceness of finish. It became at once very popular, and was the picture of the year, "in the same sense," Mr. Rossetti observes, "as the Derby Day is the event of the year to sight-seers and people in search of amusement."

The painter, with occasional deviations, followed up his advantage by a large picture, which involved two years' labour, and was completed in 1862, *The Railway Station*. It was commissioned for the joint purpose of exhibition and engraving by a well-known picture-dealer, who, according to a report quoted by Mr. Rossetti, gave the painter as the price of his work, $46,000, and we find in Ottley that the dealer was no loser by the transaction, since he re-sold the picture with his list of subscribers for the engraving, for $80,000.

Another large painting of Frith's, and on this occasion with, perhaps, more of Hogarthian motive in its throng of figures, was his *Homburg*.

The painter had from her Majesty a commission to paint the Marriage of the Prince of Wales, receiving for the picture $15,000, and for the sale of the copyright to a dealer $25,000.

ALMA TADEMA, a native of Friesland, while still giving the address, Rue de Palais, Brussels, exhibited in the Royal Academy's Exhibition, 1870, three small pictures: *Un Intérieur romain*, *Un Amateur romain* (empire), and *Un Jongleur*, which immediately drew the attention of the artists to the unknown foreign painter by magnificent points in the painting of the pictures. At the Academy's Exhibition of 1872, the painter, already settled in London, exhibited two pictures: *A Roman Emperor* and *Grand Chamberlain to his Majesty Sesostris the Great*. The first of these was sufficient to establish a reputation. The *Roman Emperor* was Claudius hidden behind the curtain, and found by the Prætorian guards, when, having murdered Caligula and his family, the soldiers rush back the next day, to discover if any member of the Imperial family survive, in order to drag him away and proclaim him emperor. The ghastliness of the situation, with the grandeur and sumptuousness of the surroundings (surely the painter had learnt a lesson in the school of the French painter Gérôme), the thrill of power conveyed by the whole picture, the depth and richness of the colouring, with the careful learned finish of details, could not fail to make a deep impression.

* See Steel Engraving.

THOMAS FAED was born in 1826, at Burley Mill, Kircudbrightshire, Scotland. His father was an engineer and mill-wright. Thomas Faed's elder brother, John, was a painter of fair repute in Edinburgh, able to offer a home to his younger brother while he studied in the School of Design under Sir W. Allan. In 1849, when he was twenty-three years of age, Faed had become an associate of the Royal Scottish Academy, and exhibited the picture of *Scott and his Friends at Abbotsford*, which was afterwards engraved. At the same time he painted for Sir Walter Scott *Jeanie Deans and the Duke of Argyle*,* illustrative of "The Heart of Mid-Lothian." Three years later he settled in London.

In 1855 Faed exhibited his *Mitherless Bairn*, the first of his rustic scenes which attracted much attention. The picture was condemned by Mr. Ruskin as "commonplace Wilkieism," yet made its mark in the line which the painter has since followed somewhat monotonously, but with the decided encouragement of the public, since his *Sunday in the Back Woods* was bought by the late Mr. Holdsworth for $4,500, and re-sold for $6,600. Faed was elected an associate of the Royal Academy in 1861, when he was thirty-five years of age.

One of Faed's best pictures is *From Dawn to Sunset*, the death-bed of an aged peasant, whose gaunt hand is stretched out on the counterpane; by the bed sits the son, a middle-aged care-worn labouring man; around him are another generation of children of various ages, from the unconscious infant in its mother's arms, to the eager half-awed "haflins" arriving from school, and bringing with them the medicine, which comes too late. The picture, which is honestly and harmoniously painted, is full of homely pathos and solemn simple feeling.

Sir J. NOEL PATON was born in 1823 at Dunfermline, Fifeshire, Scotland. His father was a pattern designer, and was his son's early teacher. The painter was afterwards a student, first of the Royal Scottish Academy, and afterwards of the Royal Academy, London. At the Westminster Hall competition of cartoons so often alluded to, Noel Paton's cartoon, *The Spirit of Religion*, gained a $1,000 prize in 1845, when he was twenty-two years of age; and two years later his oil painting of the *Reconciliation of Oberon and Titania*—in which, besides the king and queen, a multitude of tiny figures float in air, dive into flower-cups, nestle

"Under the blossom which hangs from the bough"—

won one of the $1,500 prizes.

The painter lingered in fairy-land not only in his companion picture of the *Quarrel of Oberon and Titania*, painted in 1849, and bought (and put in the Scottish National Gallery, Edinburgh) by the Scottish Academy for $3,500, but in his *Thomas the Rhymer and the Queen of Fairyland*, his *Nicker the Soulless*, &c., &c.

Noel Paton's most approved pictures have, probably, been *In Memoriam*, an episode of the Indian war, where a group of fugitives taking refuge in a cellar, by a desperate impulse gather round one brave woman at the crisis when either their foes or their deliverers are heard approaching; and his *Home from the Crimea*, where a

* See Illustration.

weary wounded soldier has returned from the wars, and is welcomed by his young wife and aged mother. The picture, of which the engraving must be familiar to many, was bought by the Queen.

Noel Paton was knighted in 1867. Like not a few of his artist brethren, the painter has sought to be a poet also, and has published poems. Sir Noel Paton's brother is a landscape painter of some reputation, while his sister, Mrs. D. O. Hill, has mastered great difficulties in becoming a sculptor in established practice.

Sir GEORGE HARVEY was born in 1806, at St. Ninian's, Stirlingshire. He was apprenticed to a bookseller, when he spent all his spare time in drawing. He entered the Trustees' Academy, Edinburgh, as a student, when he was eighteen years of age, in 1824, and made rapid progress in art. He became an associate of the Scottish Academy at its foundation two years later, in 1826, and a full member in 1829, when he was twenty-three years of age. He was President of the Scottish Academy until his death, which occurred a year or two ago.

Harvey's paintings were from the first popular in Scotland, while their extreme sobriety gave them a cold effect in English eyes, delaying and limiting his popularity in England. His subjects, too, have been more akin to Scottish than to English taste, having been largely taken from the histories of the Covenanters and the Puritans. But through every obstacle, those who look for the qualities, see in the painter's pictures manly earnestness and thoughtfulness, and true poetic feeling well if gravely expressed. His *Covenanters Preaching, Bunyan with his blind daughter selling laces at the door of Bedford Gaol, Battle of Drumclog, First reading of the Bible in the Crypt of St. Paul's,* and *Highland Funeral,* are among his best pictures.

JAMES CLARKE HOOK was born in 1819, in London. His father was a judge at Sierra Leone, and his mother a daughter of Dr. Clarke, the Bible Commentator. Hook entered the Royal Academy in 1836, when he was seventeen years of age, and gained medals in the schools. Having won the gold medal by his picture of *The Finding of the Body of Harold,* Hook tried historical painting.

In 1846, when Hook was twenty-seven years of age, he got the Academy's three years' travelling pension, and started for Italy, but he did not remain the allotted term abroad. He returned to England, resigning half the pension. Hook was elected an associate of the Academy, in 1850, when he was thirty years of age; ten years later he became an Academician.

From 1850 Hook has practised painting scenes from country, and especially from coast life, in Cornwall, the latter in his hands inexpressibly fresh and life-like, as well as skilful. His *Coast-Boy Gathering Eggs,* his *Luff-Boy,* which Mr. Ruskin pronounced "a glorious picture, most glorious," and which created a wonderful sensation; and since them his *Jolly as a Sand Boy,* his *Oyster "severals" of Hampshire,* and his *Between Tides,* are enough to remind us that the British are islanders by birth, and that the sea being part of their inheritance, they awake to claim it, when they are presented with such a reminder of its restless waves and breezy skies as Hook can offer.

JOHN LINNEL, whose landscape of *Sunshine** we engrave, is the veteran head of

---

* See Illustration.

a family of painters. He was born in 1792, in London. He was a pupil of Benjamin West's, and of Varley's, and a fellow-pupil of William Hunt's. He began in his profession by being a portrait and miniature painter, and by practising engraving, but gradually devoted his attention to landscape painting, in which he has won so honourable a name. He first exhibited a picture in the Royal Academy in 1807, when he was but fifteen years of age. The following year he gained the Royal Academy's premium of $250 in a competition with Chalon.

John Linnel's sons, J. T. Linnel, T. G. Linnel, and W. Linnel, have inherited largely their father's gifts, and the name of Linnel, in connection with landscape painting, is not likely to die out in England. The merits of the Linnels are said to be breadth of treatment, along with faithful study of nature, power over atmospheric effects, and great feeling for colouring. The fault found with the artists is too uniform a preference for "warm glowing atmospheres," with an occasional tendency to exaggeration in colouring. But the results of these labours in English landscape are very delightful—above all to English eyes, in such pictures as the famous *Barley Harvest, The Timber Waggon, Under the Hawthorn, At Work in the Wood, Haying and Playing.*

One is glad to think that the appreciation of such art is general, and that the painters meet their reward—not only in its higher, but in its lower form, of ample prices.

JOHN FREDERICK LEWIS was born in 1805, in London. His father was a line-engraver, and gave his son lessons in painting. At fifteen, Lewis exhibited at the British Institution his first picture, which found a purchaser. Two years afterwards, in 1822, the painter exhibited a large picture of *Deer Shooting at Bellus, Essex,* and the following year he was commissioned by George IV. to paint scenes in Windsor Forest, which he exhibited together with portraits of the King's keepers.

About this time Lewis forsook painting in oils for painting in water-colours, and in 1828, when he was twenty-three years of age, he was elected a member of the Water-colour Society.

In the course of the next four or five years, Lewis travelled in Germany, Northern Italy, Spain, and the Mediterranean. In his foreign travel he developed the elaborately fine finish which he has given to his art. From 1834 to 1837, when he was about thirty years of age, he exhibited Spanish subjects, some of which—including the Alhambra series, he published in lithography. Returning to Italy, and proceeding to Rome, Lewis made the sketch which resulted in a "gorgeously executed" picture of *Easter Day at Rome, the Pope Blessing the People,* exhibited in 1841.

In the meantime Lewis had gone to Turkey, Egypt, and Asia Minor, not returning to England till ten years later, in 1851. He then exhibited his *Harem,* one of his most famous pictures, followed in succeeding years by similar pictures: *An Arab Scribe,** *The Halt in the Desert, A Frank in the Desert of Mount Sinai.* The last picture was exhibited in 1856, when Lewis was fifty-one years of age.

In 1855, Lewis was elected President of the Society of Painters in Water-colours,

* See Illustration.

THE EVE OF ST. JOHN'S DAY.
(From the original painting by Jules Breton.)

an office which he resigned in anticipation of his election, as an associate of the Royal Academy, in 1859, when he was in his fifty-fifth year.

BURTON AND FRIPP, and other painters—whether of figures or landscapes—in water-colours, have established reputations, though scarcely equal to those of their predecessors, David Cox and W. Hunt.

HENRIETTA WARD is the wife of E. M. Ward, R.A., the genre and historical painter; the daughter of George Raphael Ward, the engraver; and the grand-daughter of James Ward, R.A., the cattle painter. Indeed, her extensive art-connections do not end there, for her uncle was Jackson the painter, her grand-uncle was William Ward, the engraver, and her grand-aunts were respectively George Morland the painter's sister and his wife. After all, the old artist families have not ceased to exist.

GEORGE CRUIKSHANK was born in 1792, in Bloomsbury, London. He was the son of a caricaturist, a contemporary of the famous caricaturist Gilroy. After relinquishing an early desire for a sea-faring life, and after being disappointed in an endeavour to enter the Royal Academy as a student, George Cruikshank, on the death of his father, took his unfinished blocks and manfully resolved to do his best to support his mother, by becoming in turn a designer and engraver.

George Cruikshank's first caricatures were almost all political satire, and it is said that to inspect them—in order, as they have been exhibited, is to walk through a curious gallery of ancient political squibs. *Lampoons on the Fashions*, always exaggerated and often offensive, formed the next division of the old art of caricature. George Cruikshank's best work is said by Rossetti to have been done in the twenty years between 1825 and 1845—when he was in the prime of life, and to include particularly the etchings for *Grimm's Goblins, Boz Sketches, Oliver Twist, Jack Shepherd*, and *The Tower of London*.

The miserable fate of an early friend is believed to have first roused in George Cruikshank the extreme antagonism towards every form of drunkenness, which ended in his becoming a convert to the Total Abstinence movement, and to his lending to the movement the energetic support of his power as an artist. About 1842, Cruikshank, then a man of fifty years of age, probably with Hogarth's example in his mind, published a series of eight prints called *The Bottle*, which, with the addition of *Sunday in London, The Gin Trap*, and the *Gin Juggernaut*, were meant to show the terrible effects of strong drink.

After he was well advanced in life George Cruikshank began to paint in oil, exhibiting both at the Royal Academy and the British Institution genre pictures, among them *Tam O'Shanter, Titania and Bottom the Weaver, Cinderella, Grimaldi Shaving, Disturbing the Congregation*,—the last was bought by the late Prince Consort. Finally, Cruikshank labored for three years at a huge picture, thirteen feet four, by seven feet eight, and containing within its bounds eight hundred figures, called *The Worship of Bacchus*, and intended to be an embodiment of his fervently held dogma of Total Abstinence. The picture was painted, indeed, for the Temperance League, to serve as a text for their discourses. Its moral is that the British drink, always and everywhere, and that none can foresee what may be the end of the habit—

even of moderate drinking. Rossetti writes, with justice in the name of those who differ in view from George Cruikshank, that "the man who in his old age occupies himself for nearly three years in painting this homily upon canvas, to the most negative of results in point of art, deserves respect."

Cruikshank's deficient education in art, unremedied by his efforts when far in life, renders his pictures very defective. Particular faults attributed to him even as a designer, are "want of drawing of the human figure, which he is apt to treat with the caricaturist's free-and-easy license, limp limbs and vapid old-fashioned faces," and the tendency to exaggeration and burlesque, that constitutes him a caricaturist rather than a humourist. But as a caricaturist he has many and great merits—a wide knowledge of human nature, and a lively feeling alike for the terrible and the grotesque, with an inexhaustible fertility of invention. Over the tools employed in etching, George Cruikshank is said to have possessed great skill. He died in 1878.

JOHN LEECH was born in 1817. His father kept for many years the London Coffee House, in Ludgate Hill. Young Leech was educated at the Charter House, and became a student in the Royal Academy. He exhibited several genre pictures, which did not attract attention. Some sketches of character in "Bell's Life in London," were the first of Leech's work which gave promise of genius. His sketches in "Punch," on which his fame rests, were begun in 1847, when Leech was in his thirty-first year, and were continued for eighteen years. In these sketches Leech proved himself a great humourist, who never passed the boundary between humour and caricature. If his satire were less triumphant than Cruikshank's, it was far broader, while it was more refined. Nothing was more characteristic of Leech, and nothing was more enjoyable in his work, than the evident genial sympathy with which he entered into every phase of the many-sided English life of the hunting-field, the sea-side, the ball-room, the drawing-room, the nursery; while he faithfully represented —not without a touch of idealism, for he had, what may well belong to a humourist, but what scarcely finds place in a caricaturist, a fine feeling for beauty—the grace as well as the fresh charm of high-bred English girls, who were never better given than by Leech, so that in the immense circulation of "Punch," Leech must have raised the standard of Englishwomen's beauty in the minds of foreigners. John Leech had also a fine appreciation of English scenery,—and in those bits of it which he introduced into his sketches, he did it full justice, while he elevated, by their artistic completeness, the character of the sketches.

THOMAS ALLOM. Among the architectural and landscape painters Thomas Allom ranks very high. Born in London in 1804, he was educated at Oxford, and after studying as an architect he came before the notice of the public in 1836, in the Academy Exhibition, with a series of water-colour landscapes which earned great praise. He sold his sketches readily to the publishers, who at that time employed talent like his very liberally. He was of the same school as Prout, Bartlett, Turner, Stanfield, Creswick, Roberts, and Brockden—a school which seems to have nearly passed away. We illustrate one of his best pictures, *Constantinople from the Golden Horn*.*

* See Steel Engraving.

FREDERICK WALKER, one of the best of modern English subject painters, was born in London on the 24th of May, 1840. On leaving school he passed a short time in the office of an architect and surveyor, and then, feeling that art was his true vocation, entered as a student at Leigh's night-classes in Newman Street. Walker also occasionally studied in the Royal Academy schools. He first appeared as a book illustrator, for the "Cornhill Magazine," executing the pictures for Mr. Thackeray's "Philip and his Adventures on his way through the World," which received much praise. When but twenty-four years of age Walker was elected a member of the Old Water-colour Society, and subsequently became an Associate of the Royal Academy. He was a constant exhibitor at both institutions for a few years. To the great regret of the art world, this promising young artist died suddenly at St. Fildan's, Perthshire, in June 1875, before he had reached either the prime of his life or the summit of his art. He was buried in Cookham churchyard.

BIRKET FOSTER, born at Manchester, 1825, ranks very high as an English painter both in oil and water-colour. He has been before the public prominently for the last fifteen years, and is well known in America from chromos of his water-colour works, notably *The Primrose Bank, English Labourer's Cottage, The Convalescent*, and *The Race up the Hill*.* There is a freshness and reality in his execution which attract the eye and heart at once. Foster is of Quaker descent, and is a great favourite among the "Friends."

WILLIAM JOHN MÜLLER, the son of a German father, was born at Bristol in 1812. He studied landscape painting under J. B. Payne and more especially from nature. In 1833 he started on a journey through Germany, Switzerland, and Italy, and returning to Bath in the following year, established himself there as a landscape painter, but met with little success. In 1838 he went to Greece and Egypt, and returning to England in the following year, after a short sojourn in his native place, settled in London. In 1851, Müller again started on his travels when he accompanied Sir Charles Fellowes to Lycia. From the sketches he made on this journey, Müller painted several of his best works: the *Burial-ground, Smyrna*, exhibited in the Academy in 1844; *Landscape with two Lycian Peasants*—engraved by Cousins, and now in the National Gallery—and others, exhibited at the Royal Academy and British Institution. Müller died in 1845 at Bristol, whither he had retired on perceiving signs of declining health.

FRANK STONE, who was born at Manchester in 1800, was his own instructor in art. When thirty-one years of age he came to London, and at first painted in water-colour, but he finally abandoned that method in favour of oil. His pictures are sometimes portraits, sometimes scenes of domestic life, and occasionally historical pieces. In 1840 appeared the *Legend of Montrose*, then came the *Last Appeal*, painted in 1843, and *The Course of True Love never did run smooth*, in the following year. Some time after he exhibited his homely and humourous *Impending Mate and Mated*—all well known by engravings. In 1851, Stone was elected an Associate of the Royal Academy, but he died in 1859, before he was elected to the honour of full membership.

* See Illustration.

THOMAS CRESWICK—one of the most distinguished members of the modern English school of landscape painting, whose works rival, in knowledge of aerial perspective and mastery of colour, those of Turner himself—was born at Sheffield in 1811. At the age of seventeen he went to London to seek his fortune, and his paintings being readily accepted both by the Society of British Artists and by the Royal Academy, he made the capital his home, and enriched the exhibitions with scenes from Wales and Ireland. About the year 1840, he turned his attention to the beauties of the North of England, and produced some of his finest works—the quiet beauty of England inland scenery with its broad rivers, shady glens, and romantic dells, living again on his canvas.

In 1842 Creswick was elected an Associate of the Royal Academy, and received a premium of $250 for the general excellence of his productions. 1851 he became a full member of the Academy, and somewhat later painted several works in conjunction with his colleagues Frith and Ansdell, who gave life and animation to his pictures by the introduction of figures and cattle. Creswick died in December, 1869, at Linden Grove, Bayswater, after a long career of unceasing activity, and was buried in Kensal Green Cemetery.

JOHN BURR, born in Scotland in 1831, has been famous for some ten years by his humourous Wilkie-like treatment of home subjects. In 1866 appeared his *Domestic Troubles*, which at once secured him substantial notice; and two years later he exhibited *The Peddler*,* which was immediately purchased at a high price. Since then he has worked steadily, and his paintings are readily purchased.

* See Illustration.

CHAPTER VI.

THE AMERICAN SCHOOL.—WEST—COPLEY—STUART— ALLSTON—CHURCH—HUNTINGDON, &c., &c.

HE last School of Painting which claims our attention, both from its high merit and its promise of future excellence, is that which, during the last hundred years, has sprung up in America. Beginning, as in England, with portrait painting, this school has progressed until it now numbers in its ranks many very excellent figure and landscape painters. Their works are constantly taken to Europe to be exhibited, and are received with the greatest admiration. Year after year we hear of new men coming to the front, and there can be no doubt but that the late Centennial Exhibition has done much to forward the true interests of Art throughout the land.

We give a brief history of those painters who have, hitherto, been most distinguished; regretting that the plan of our book does not permit us to include, at length, sketches of a great many living artists.

BENJAMIN WEST was born at Springfield, in Pennsylvania, United States, in 1738. His family were descended from English settlers and farmers, and were Quakers by persuasion. Reared in a sect which abjured painting as a worldly and sensual art, the lad's promptings to the practice of painting had no outer aid, and were pursued in spite of the remonstrances and admonitions of the Friends, though it does not seem that his father and mother opposed his exercise of the gift which he had received. It is said that some Indians, who had imparted to him the secrets of the mixture of their war paint, were his first teachers; to their red and yellow his mother added indigo, and his brush he made from hairs cut from the cat's back. A council of neighbouring Quakers, called together to decide on the question of young West's infringement of the rules of the sect, agreed wisely and reverently that God would not bestow faculties and forbid their employment, and gave West permission to follow his calling. Mr. Redgrave writes that "the women rose and kissed him, the men one by one laid their hands on his head, a solemn dedication which he never forgot."

Having studied under a painter named Williams, West tried portrait painting, first in Philadelphia, and afterwards in New York. He was then but twenty years of age, and in his twenty-second year, 1760, his ambition and discretion led him to travel to Italy, where he studied for three years. His intention was to return to America, and merely to visit England on his way home, but on his arrival in London he found his prospects there so promising, that he sent for the young American girl to whom he was engaged, married, and settled with her in the old country, in his twenty-seventh year, 1765.

The Archbishop of York presented West to the king, George III., who took a violent fancy to a young man, quiet, steady, and domestic, as the good king himself. George's not very intellectual or artistic taste imagined that he had discovered—with all the glory of the discovery—a great genius. The American war did not shake the king's fidelity to his protégé. George III.'s almost entire patronage was thenceforth given to Benjamin West. The royal regard, thus exclusive, was viewed with lively indignation by many other painters, with claims to notice, but struggling for bread, while West was receiving from royal commissions, for a period of thirty years, sums at the rate of $5,000 a year—then considered a large income to be derived from art. Neither was the king's exclusive patronage beneficial to Benjamin West himself as an artist, though as a man he remained the simple, unpretending, kindly man he had come to England. He had soon renounced portrait painting for historical and religious painting, and the constant demands made on his imagination, together with the absence of any stimulating competition or anxiety with regard to worldly success, and perhaps—unassuming man though he was—in consequence also of the constant sops administered by royal favour, to his self-satisfaction, West's invention became wearisomely dull and tame.

One of West's most striking pictures had been the *Death of General Wolfe*, a subject for which his nationality had qualified him particularly, and in which, among other accessory figures, he had introduced his old friends, the Red Indians, strange, picturesque beings to English eyes. He had also the enterprise and courage to break through all English artistic precedents prevailing till then, and, against the advice of Sir Joshua Reynolds himself, to paint his English and French soldiers, not in Roman togas, which had been thought the only garments equal to the dignity of historic occasion, but in their respective ordinary uniforms, thus adding largely to the truth and therefore to the pathos of the incidents. But West made no great advance in his art from the *Departure of Regulus*, his first commission from the king, and from the *Fall of Wolfe*; rather he retrograded through the endless list of his historical and classical pictures, forced, formal, and stiff, which he painted to the perfect contentment of King George.

After the king's illness, when West was left more to his own inspiration and resources, he seemed to take a new start in his art, and his *Christ Healing the Sick** and *Death on the Pale Horse* are still valued for far more than respectable drawing and colouring. West was one of the first thirty-six members of the Royal Academy, and succeeded Sir Joshua Reynolds as president, retaining the office till his death, at the age of eighty-two years, in 1820.

* See Steel Engraving.

Another American had arrived in London to dispute the palm of victory with the English painters. JOHN SINGLETON COPLEY was born at Boston, in 1737. He went to England in 1774, and after visiting Rome, settled in England in 1775. Like West, he had been a portrait painter, and, like him also, Copley adopted historical painting as his chosen branch of art. Like West still, and very unlike Barry, or the later British historical and imaginative painters, Copley had a prosperous history. He was fortunate in taking for his first historical work a contemporary scene, which had made a deep impression on the English nation—*The Death* (or rather the death-blow) *of Chatham in the House of Lords*. Popular as this picture became through engravings, it was inferior to a later work of Copley's—*The Death of Major Pierson* (in the rescue of the island of Jersey from the French)—which is regarded as superior to West's *Death of Wolfe*. Copley introduced successfully portraits into his historical pictures.

In character, Copley was industrious, painstaking, and unobtrusive. He died full of years, and having attained an honourable independence, in his seventy-ninth year, in 1815, and left a more distinguished son—the great barrister and chancellor, Lord Lyndhurst, who continued for many years to reside in his father's old house in George Street, Hanover Square, where many of the painter's works were retained and cherished. As a historical painter, Copley, while a far less cultivated artist, is said to have been fresher and more original than West.

GILBERT CHARLES STUART, the portrait-painter, was born at Narragansett, in Rhode Island, in 1756. He received his instruction in art from Cosmo Alexander, who took him to Scotland with him, but Stuart returned to America soon afterwards. In 1771, he went again to Great Britain, and established himself as a portrait-painter in London, where he enjoyed the friendship and society of some of the famous men of the day. In 1793 he returned to America, and after residing in New York, Washington, and Philadelphia, he re-established himself finally, in 1806, at Boston, where he continued to paint with uninterrupted success until his death, which occurred in 1828.

Of the works of Stuart we may notice—in the Boston Athenæum, the original *Portrait of Washington*, whom the artist painted from life but three times; the first portrait was destroyed by Stuart because it did not meet with his approval; the second was painted for the Marquis of Lansdowne, and the third is the one above-mentioned. The artist frequently repeated these pictures. The Boston Athenæum has a *Portrait of Mrs. Washington*, and other works by Stuart. His works are commonly seen both in the public and private galleries in America.

JOHN TRUMBULL, the historical painter, who was born at Lebanon, Connecticut, in 1756, is one of the best of the early American artists. He combined the professions of a soldier and a painter, and thus had the means of being an eye-witness of scenes which suggested the subjects of many of the works which have made his name famous. He graduated at Harvard, entered the army, was made aide-de-camp to Washington, and became a colonel. In 1780, Trumbull went through France, to London, where he studied under his fellow-countryman, West. Arrested as a spy, he was obliged to leave the country; he returned to America, but on the cessation of hostilities, he went again to England, and resumed his studies under West. In 1789,

Trumbull returned once more to America, and employed himself in painting the portraits of the celebrated soldiers of the late war. After a visit to London of nineteen years (1796 to 1815) seven of which were spent in diplomatic service—he lived constantly in America. He died in New York in 1843, at the advanced age of eighty-seven, and was buried in Yale College, in a tomb built by himself under a gallery which formerly contained his original sketches for the four great works executed in the rotunda of the Capitol at Washington—the *Declaration of Independence;** the *Surrender of Burgoyne;* the *Surrender of Cornwallis;* and the *Resignation of Washington at Annapolis.* They have since been moved to the Art Gallery in Yale College. Of the first-mentioned of these works, Henry Greenough says, "I admire in this composition the skill with which Trumbull has collected so many portraits in formal session, without theatrical effort, in order to enliven it, and without falling into insipidity by adherence to trivial fact. These men are earnest, yet full of dignity; they are firm, yet cheerful; they are gentlemen; and you can see at a glance that they meant something very serious in pledging their lives, their fortunes, and their sacred honours."

Of other works by Trumbull we may notice—in the City Hall, New York, portraits of Governors *Lewis* and *Clinton,* and one of *Washington*—an oft-repeated subject; at New Haven, the *Death of General Montgomery,* "one of the most spirited battle-pieces ever painted," the *Battle of Bunker Hill,* a full-length *Portrait of Washington,* in addition to the original sketches for the rotunda pictures, and numerous historic works.

CHARLES WILSON PEALE, who was born at Chesterton, Maryland, in 1747, was not only a painter, but a worker in wood, metal, and leather. Besides his oil-paintings, he executed numerous miniatures, for which he "sawed his own ivory, moulded the glasses, and made the shagreen cases." He studied under various masters—in Philadelphia under a German, in Boston with Copley, and in London with West.

Peale was the most popular portrait-painter of his time, and was especially remarkable from the fact that he painted, in 1772, the first authentic likeness of *Washington.* He subsequently made thirteen other portaits of that President. Peale died in 1826. Philadelphia is rich in his works—more especially in the Independence Hall, where there is a complete gallery of his pictures.

JOHN VANDERLYN, who was born in 1776 at Kingston, New York, like Quintin Matsys began life as a blacksmith. His talents were noticed by Colonel Burr, who gave him a start in life at New York. In 1803, Vanderlyn went to Europe, and was in Paris and Rome the friend and companion of Allston. In Rome he painted, in 1807, his famous *Marius sitting on the Ruins of Carthage,* to which Napoleon personally awarded the prize medal in the *Salon* of 1808, and which the emperor tried to buy; but Vanderlyn wished to take it to America, and it was subsequently purchased by Bishop Kip, in whose possession it still remains at San Francisco. This work is especially noteworthy for the care which the artist has taken to represent, as nearly as possible, the architecture and the costumes of the time. Vanderlyn's life was a series of successes and failures, of riches and poverty, though unfortunately the latter

* See Steel Engraving.

preponderated, and he died in great want at his native town, Kingston, in 1852. He was buried in the Wiltwyck Cemetery, hard by. Besides the *Marius*, abovementioned, this artist executed but one other work worthy to be compared to it. This is the *Sleeping Ariadne*, which the Boston Athenæum refused to purchase for five hundred dollars, and for which Mr. Harrison of Philadelphia gave ten times that amount. Of his remaining works, most of which are portraits, we need not speak.

WASHINGTON ALLSTON, the chief painter of the American School, was born at Waccamaw in South Carolina, in 1779. After the completion of his university career at Harvard, he took up his abode at Charlestown, where, however, desiring to go to Europe for the improvement of his art, he did not long remain. He arrived in London in 1801, and at once entered the Royal Academy schools, where he became acquainted with his fellow-countryman West, who was then president. In 1804, Allston went with his friend Vanderlyn to Paris and thence to Rome, where in the following year he painted his *Joseph's Dream*. At Rome, Allston commenced with Washington Irving a friendship which lasted for life. He also became acquainted with Coleridge, and the Danish sculptor, Thorwaldsen. In 1809, Allston returned to America, married a sister of Dr. Channing, and then went to London, where he produced his *Dead Man revived by the bones of Elisha*, which gained a prize of $1,000 from the British Institution. It is now in the Pennsylvania Academy of Fine Arts at Philadelphia. Then followed the *Liberation of St. Peter by the Angel*, now in the church of Ashby-de-la-Zouch; *Uriel in the Sun*, in the possession of the Duke of Sutherland; and *Jacob's Dream*, in the Petworth Gallery. In 1818, Allston returned to America, and settled at Boston, with his health weakened by sorrow for his wife, lately deceased, and by over-work. In the same year he was elected an Associate of the Royal Academy. Of the works which he executed in the following years, we may notice, the *Prophet Jeremiah*, now in Yale College; *Saul and the Witch of Endor; Miriam's Song* and *Dante's Beatrice*. In 1830, Allston married again. His second choice was the daughter of Chief Justice Dana, of Cambridge, Massachusetts, where he settled. At Cambridge, Allston spent the rest of his life in secluded industry, occasionally interrupted by illness. He then produced one of his best known works, *Spalatro's Vision of the Bloody Hand*, from "The Italian," by Mrs. Radcliffe—especially remarkable for the effects of light and shade, and for the expression of fright ,and a guilty conscience on the face of Spalatro, and the firm determination visible on the countenance of the monk. This work, which was painted for Mr. Ball, of South Carolina, was in the Taylor Johnston Collection in New York; it has been engraved by W. J. Linton. His *Rosalie*, executed late in life, is also worthy of mention.

Allston died at Cambridge in 1843, leaving unfinished a large work, on which he had been engaged at various times for about forty years. It represents *Belshazzar's Feast*; and is now in the Boston Athenæum, where there is also a *Portrait of Benjamin West*, which, with that of *Coleridge*, by the same artist, in the National Portrait Gallery, proves that Allston excelled in portraiture as well as in historic painting.

The works of Allston, the pride of his country, the "American Titian," are especially remarkable for the beauty and power of colouring. In his subjects, he was fond of the terrible, especially noticeable in *Spalatro's Vision, Saul and the Witch of Endor*, and in the unfinished *Belshazzar's Feast*.

CHARLES ROBERT LESLIE was born in London, 1794. He was American by descent, his father and mother having been natives of Maryland, counting kin with original British settlers. Robert Leslie, the father, was engaged as a painter, and clock and watchmaker, in Philadelphia, but had taken a voyage to England on business, accompanied by his family. On the occasion of their visit, which was of several years' duration, Charles Leslie was born. The watchmaker and his family returned to Philadelphia, and after a voyage of more than seven months, he found that his affairs had fallen into great disorder, a discovery which caused his death, leaving Leslie, not yet ten years of age, under the charge of a widowed mother. The widow opened a boarding house for the support of her family, while her eldest daughter went out as a drawing teacher. The professors of the college at Philadelphia admitted the young Leslie lads to the college classes at reduced fees, and uncles and aunts, who had comfortable and pleasant farmers' and millers' homesteads on the Brandywine, welcomed the boys with homely kindness, for the summer holidays.

At fourteen years of age, Charles Leslie was bent on being a painter, but by the anxious care of his mother he was apprenticed to a firm of booksellers and publishers, to the head of which his apprentice's ineradicable propensity for art at first gave little satisfaction. Eventually, however, the man of business afforded liberal assistance to his subordinate.

The occasion of the visit of Cooke the tragedian to Philadelphia, when the bookseller's apprentice was able to make a telling sketch of the actor, caused the kindly conversion of the master to the lad's art-interest. By the aid of the business men who attended the Exchange Office House, Leslie was enabled to proceed to Europe to prosecute his studies. He went to England in 1811, when he was seventeen years of age, taking, of course, letters of introduction to his countryman, West.

Leslie and another American lad, two years older, took lodgings together, and started, by devoting "their days to painting, and their evenings to the Royal Academy," to which Leslie was admitted a student in 1813, when he was in his twentieth year. As a farther advantage the studios of West, and of the American painter, Allston, then in London, were open to Leslie. He was permitted to see his seniors' work in progress, and was encouraged and helped by their advice and friendship, for the lonely lad had taken with him the cheerful, amiable temper, as well as the enthusiasm for his profession, which had so speedily broken down opposition, and procured him influential friends beyond the Atlantic. He studied the Townley Marbles in the British Museum, and rose at six in the morning to accompany his American companion to Burlington House, to join him in the study of the Elgin Marbles then lodged there. For Leslie put little value on any outside help, which was not supplemented by personal diligence; indeed, he went so far as to deprecate all education save self-education, and was wont to speak of the "wise neglect" of Fuseli which made such men as Wilkie, Mulready, Etty, Landseer, and Haydon, and did not render them "all alike by teaching."

In order to gain an immediate livelihood, Leslie practised portrait painting; he was also induced, probably by the example of West, to try high art, in *Saul and the Witch of Endor;* but he very soon, almost as soon as Wilkie, found his proper vocation in genre painting. In 1817, when Leslie was twenty-three years of age, he visited Paris, Brussels, and Antwerp, studying the old masters. This was one of Leslie's few visits to the continent; like Mulready, he never went to Italy.

As early as 1819, when Leslie was no more than twenty-five years of age, he painted for an American merchant, and exhibited in the Academy, his *Sir Roger de Coverley going to Church*, which was at once received with great approbation—making his way clear. This was the first of a long series of pictures peculiarly acceptable to the public, because they were spirited and lovely illustrations of popular subjects, and both illustrations and subjects, while they were certainly not below, were, with equal certainty, not far above, the general intelligence of a fairly cultivated public. A list of Leslie's best-known subjects will show our meaning: *May-day in the Reign of Queen Elizabeth; Sancho Panza and the Duchess; Lady Jane Grey prevailed on to accept the Crown* (in this instance there is a slight departure from the usual rôle, for it will be observed that Leslie's subjects, while moderately intellectual, are for the most part cheerful as his own temper, and not even darkened by the shadow of a tragedy); *Dinner at Page's House; Uncle Toby and the Widow;* and *The Taming of the Shrew.** Leslie's intimacy with his countryman Washington Irving, whose Sketch Book Leslie illustrated, is judged, probably with perfect correctness, to have been the influence which directed the painter to the pages of Addison—greatly admired by Washington Irving—for inspiration, since Leslie drew his inspiration mainly from books.

Leslie corresponded regularly with his American relations, and for a time looked forward to his return to America, but his art friends and his good prospects in England proved too strong for this intention. In 1821, when he was twenty-seven years of age, Leslie was elected an associate of the Academy, and five years later he became a full member. The accident of his taking the place of another painter summoned hurriedly to sketch the features of a dying child introduced Leslie to the pictorial glories of Petworth, and the friendly patronage of Lord Egremont, for whom he painted *Sancho Panza in the apartment of the Duchess*, one of the most admired of Leslie's pictures, and one which secured his worldly success, enabling him to make in 1824, at thirty years of age, a happy marriage with a young English beauty, belonging to a bevy of six sisters, named Stone, whose personal charms provoked their grotesque classification by some would-be wit of the circle, as " the six precious Stones."

But though Leslie was settled in England and married to an English wife, he did not lose his American sympathies. He was given throughout his life to fast friendships, which even influenced his art, and his greatest friends for years were his countrymen—the pleasant, witty author, Washington Irving, and the clever, vain, hare-brained painter, Newton, to whose ability in colouring Leslie's inferiority in that respect owed improvement. The three young Americans seem to have been

---

* See Steel Engraving.

inseparable, visiting together in a circle of Americans resident in England, frequenting the two studios, running off in a trio on light-hearted expeditions, dining many a time frugally, but merrily, at the York Chop House, in Wardour Street, which Mr. Redgrave tells us is, or was till lately, still extant, and where generations of young painters have, in succession, been served.

But Leslie did not need to go beyond his own home for peace and relaxation. He was a man of domestic tastes and warm affections, and in his wife, with their children, to whom he was tenderly attached, rising round him, he found the sweetest solace after work, as well as one of the best incentives to honourable ambition. But the interests of these children, and the strength of old ties, broke up this English home for a time, and tempted Leslie to revive his old project of returning to America.

In 1833, when the painter was nearly forty years of age, he accepted the appointment offered to him by the American Government of Professor of Drawing to the Military Academy of West Point, on the Hudson, and made the somewhat rash venture of resigning his known and fair opportunities in England, for a return to long-left interests and new and untried resources. The experiment did not prove successful. His duties were irksome, his English wife did not like America, the very climate seemed to the naturalized Englishman to have undergone a change from the days of his hardy boyhood, and within the short space of six months Leslie returned with his family to his adopted country. The brief leave-taking and going back, form two of the principal events in Leslie's happy and prosperous career. Short as the interval was during which they occurred, it included the catastrophe of the declared insanity of poor Newton the painter. In the room of the regard whose object had passed beyond its reach, Leslie developed a faithful friendship—not the less affectionate on account of the ruggedness of the friend, for Constable the painter, who in his turn exerted a marked effect on the sympathetic mind of Leslie, and thenceforth Constable's cool greys and vivid greens became prominent where Newton's brilliant rainbow hues had prevailed in the chosen interpreter of Cervantes, Sterne, and Shakespeare, in their lighter scenes.

Before Leslie took his trial trip to America, he had painted for the Marquis of Westminster a family picture known as the *Grosvenor family*. A few years later he painted another portrait-piece for Lord Holland, *The Library at Holland House*, introducing portraits of Lord and Lady Holland. In 1838, Leslie painted for the Queen her *Coronation*, in which the maiden Queen, and the fair young members of the English aristocracy, figure very gracefully. In 1841, he executed a similar commission, with the *Christening of the Princess Royal* for his subject.

Leslie was elected Professor of Painting to the Royal Academy in 1848, and held the appointment till failing health forced him to resign it in 1851. Leslie's much-loved children, both while young and after they had grown to manhood and womanhood, are said to have supplied him with many a hint for childish playfulness, girlish shyness, and the elastic vigour of young manhood. The death of one of these children, a cherished daughter and young bride, who faded suddenly and died in her early prime, is said to have proved at last Leslie's death-blow. She died in March, 1859. Her father, after struggling in vain with his depression, sank of a complaint,

from which no fatal result had at first been apprehended, and died in his house in St. John's Wood, London, in the May of the same year, 1859, aged sixty-four years. On a slip of paper attached to his will Leslie had written, "I trust I may die as I now am, in the entire belief of the Christian religion, as I understand it from the books of the New Testament, that is, as a direct revelation of the will and goodness of God towards the world by Jesus Christ, the Saviour and Judge of the world."

Leslie has left a successor to his name and art, whose nymph-like maidens are a farther development of the love of the beautiful.

GILBERT STUART NEWTON, who was born at Halifax, Nova Scotia, in 1795, studied under his uncle, Gilbert Stuart, went to Europe in 1817, and paid one short visit to America in 1832. He died in London in 1835.

HENRY INMAN, who was born at Utica, New York, in 1801, studied for some time in New York under Jarvis, a good artist of the period. On the completion of his term, Inman after several years spent in New York, married, in 1832, and settled at Philadelphia, where he became famous as a painter of portraits, and occasionally of landscapes and genre pictures. In 1843, he went to England, where he remained for two years, much esteemed by the artist-circle in London of the time. Inman died in New York, in 1846, the year after his return.

The works of this artist are commonly seen in the public and private galleries of America. The City Hall, New York, has some good portraits by him; noteworthy among these is that of *Governor Van Buren*. His landscapes and genre pictures are best seen in private galleries. Of the former class, we may notice, a view of *Dundrennan Abbey*, in the possession of Mr. James Lenox, New York; and the *Newsboy*, belonging to Mr. Sturges, of the same city; and *Mumble the Peg*, in Mr. Carey's collection at Philadelphia.

Inman is more famous from the fact that he was equally good in three branches of art—portraiture, landscapes, and genre—than for any particular merit in his works.

J. B. WHITE, whose celebrated picture of *General Marion inviting a British Officer to Dinner in his Swamp Encampment*,* is an American artist of whom very little is known. He worked in New York about the year 1842, but his record has not been kept. The excellence apparent in this fine historical painting causes us to regret that the artist has done so little. This episode of the colonial war is well told. The native courtesy of Marion has prompted an invitation to dinner, which the British officer has accepted, only to discover that sweet potatoes roasted in wood ashes is his "bill of fare."

JOHN JAMES AUDUBON, who was born in Louisiana, in 1782, studied in Paris under David. On his return to America he devoted himself to portraying birds, just in the same manner as Catlin gave himself up to the painting of American Indians. Audubon's perseverance must have been great, for it is said that after he had collected several thousand sketches of birds, they were accidentally destroyed and the work had to be recommenced. When published in Edinburgh, the book contained more than one thousand birds' portraits, the originals of which are now in the possession of the

* See Steel Illustration.

New York Historical Society. Having exhausted the feathered tribe, Audubon was engaged on a work on the quadrupeds of America, when he died in 1851.

REMBRANDT PEALE, the son of Charles Wilson Peale, was born in Bucks County, Pennsylvania, in 1787. After a short career as a portrait painter in Charleston, South Carolina, he went to London and studied under West. Peale also resided for some time in Paris, where he painted, among other pictures, portraits for his father's museum. Rembrandt Peale died at Philadelphia in 1860. His works are common in America.

THOMAS COLE, the landscape painter, was born at Bolton-le-Moor, Lancashire, in 1801, went when eighteen years of age to Steubenville, Ohio. After travelling about the country for some time, he visited New York, where he was patronized by Trumbull and other artists. Cole made two journeys to Europe, and stayed chiefly in Italy and England, the scenery of which countries furnished him with subjects for many of his best works. He died among his "own dear Catskills," as he calls them; for with all the magnificent scenery of the Alps and elsewhere in Europe he remained true to his first love. Of Cole's works we may notice, in the possession of the New York Historical Society, the *Course of Empire*—five landscape scenes; lately in the Taylor Johnston Collection of New York, his famous series of *The Voyage of Life*, the *Mountain Ford*, and *Kenilworth Castle*. Many of his works are in the private and public galleries of America.

WILLIAM SYDNEY MOUNT, born in Long Island, near New York, in 1807, studied painting at the School of the New York Academy of Design. He became eminent as a portrait painter, and highly appreciated as a painter of humorous subjects, of which we furnish an example in *The Noon-day Rest*.* He died at Setauket, Long Island, 1868.

EMMANUEL LEUTZE, who was born at the village of Emingen in Würtemberg in 1816, went, when still young, with his father to America. He at first maintained himself by portrait painting, but his favourite subjects were of a historic nature. His earliest work of note is an *Indian gazing on the setting sun*. In 1841, Leutze determined to visit Europe. He arrived at Amsterdam early in the year, and thence went to Düsseldorf, where he studied under Lessing. His *Columbus before the council of Salamanca* was purchased by the Art Union of that city. From Düsseldorf Leutze went to Munich, and became the disciple of Cornelius and Kaulbach. After his *Wanderjahre* through Italy and Switzerland, he returned to America in 1859 and became justly famed as a painter of historic subjects. He subsequently paid a second visit to Europe, to bring home a wife, whom he had married at Düsseldorf on his first journey. Leutze died in 1868.

Of the pictures of Leutze which are chiefly seen in New York and other Eastern cities, we may notice in the Capitol at Washington the *Western Emigration*—with the motto "Westward the course of Empire takes its way"—which is considered one of his best works; also *Columbus in chains*, and *Columbus before the Queen;* the *Landing of the Norsemen in America;* and *John Knox admonishing Mary Queen of Scots*, in the possession of Mr. M. O. Roberts, of New York.

* See Steel Engraving.

CHARLES LORING ELLIOT, who was born at Scipio, New York, in 1812, was at first intended for a merchant, and then for an architect, his father's profession, but his love of painting prevailed, and he entered the studio of Trumbull in New York. On the completion of his studies, he established himself as a painter in that city, where, with the exception of several years spent in the western part of the State, he chiefly resided. He died in 1868. Elliot is said to have executed nearly seven hundred portraits. Of these the acknowledged masterpiece is that of *Fletcher Harper*, which was selected to represent American portraiture in the Paris Exhibition. Portraits by Elliot are in the possession of the Historical Society, and in the City Hall, New York, and also in private galleries in America. One of his best is the portrait of Mr. Corcoran in the Corcoran Gallery at Washington.

His portraits are noteworthy for vigour of drawing and colouring, and more especially for life-like representation.

LOUIS RÉMY MIGNOT, who was born in 1831, lived some part of his life in New York; he then removed to South Carolina, and subsequently took up his residence in England, though he paid various visits to his native land. He exhibited in the Royal Academy from time to time. In 1863 appeared *Lagoon of Guayaquil, South America*, and a *Winter Morning;* in 1865, an *Evening in the Tropics;* he was also a contributor to the exhibitions of 1866 and 1867. In 1870 appeared his last work, a *Sunset off Hastings*, " of genuine poetical treatment." Mignot died at Brighton, on the 22nd of September, 1870, in his fortieth year.

"His pictures show talent above the average order, and are characterized by much feeling for the picturesque beauty of nature, and great skill in handling."

THOMAS SULLY was born in England, but came to America with his parents (who were actors) when a child. He studied portrait painting in the South, and painted Jefferson and Lafayette, and on a visit to England had the honour of painting Queen Victoria. He settled finally in Philadelphia, where he applied himself to a wide range of subjects—Shakespeare, Robinson Crusoe, and others. We illustrate his *Bed-fellows*.*

JAMES and WILLIAM HART, both eminent American painters, were born in Scotland, in 1828 and 1823 respectively. They came to America in their childhood, and studied art at the Academy of Design, New York. They have both been famous for many years—William Hart for landscape, and James Hart for landscape and cattle. Few of the best galleries in America are without examples of the Harts'.

James Hart exhibited several pictures at the Centennial Exhibition, 1876, at Philadelphia, and was awarded a first class medal.

We have illustrated *The Watering-place*,† a fair example of James Hart's most excellent style.

W. T. RICHARDS was born in Philadelphia, in 1833. He studied painting under Paul Weber, who was then esteemed Philadelphia's best master. Richards went to Europe in 1855, and alternated between Paris and Düsseldorf for nearly three years, when he returned to Philadelphia much improved in ability, and with one or two

* See Steel Engraving.   † See Steel Engraving.

important commissions. His sea-side paintings are by many considered his best; but in both marine and landscape he is considered one of America's foremost painters. His works grace the best galleries of America, and some have been sold to Europe; they bring high prices.

ROBERT SWAIN GIFFORD was born in the State of Massachusetts, and was educated at New Bedford. He had the advantage of a clever tutor in Van Beest, who was an eminent art instructor in Boston during the last generation. Gifford opened a studio in Boston in 1864, but removed to New York in 1866, where he has been ever since. He went to Europe in 1872, and then visited Northern Africa, whence he returned with the glow of the Mediterranean sun in his eye, which he has embodied in his pictures. At home and abroad Gifford is ranked among the great living artists.

G. R. BONFIELD, a resident of Philadelphia, whose success as a marine painter earned for him the proud title of "The Van de Velde of America," is a native of England, but in early life made America his home as an adopted citizen. He studied first as a portrait painter, but soon found his *forte* to be marine painting. While in practice his pictures found a ready sale; but of late years Bonfield has been employed by Mr. James L. Claghorn as adviser in his great collection of engravings—a position for which Bonfield is eminently qualified as a tasteful and acute judge—and, for a retired artist, we could not imagine a more delightful position.

Bonfield's paintings are in the best galleries in America, and are distinguished by a soft breezy dash and subdued colouring. Bonfield is nearly seventy years (1878).

His son, VAN DE VELDE BONFIELD, gives great promise of success as a landscape painter, especially in his winter scenes.

FRANK BRISCOE, another Philadelphian, not over twenty-five years of age, has already made his mark as an accomplished painter. Briscoe exhibited at the Philadelphia Centennial *A Breezy Day Off Dieppe*, which would have passed as one of the best productions of the Belgian or the French school. This may be due to his French education; but, as one of the New York critics wrote of it, "It is a capital picture of amphibious life, and the painter's manipulation of forms is such that every object is in its right place, and would unhinge the composition if removed, shows a mastery of scenic effect."

P. T. ROTHERMEL, the best living American figure colourist, has been famous for nearly a generation, and neither his physical nor artistic capacity show signs of decay.

Born and educated in Philadelphia, he has made his name a household word in art throughout wide America.

He was, in 1870, commissioned by the legislature of Pennsylvania to paint the *Battle of Gettysburgh*, for which he was paid in the neighbourhood of $25,000. This splendid painting was exhibited at the Centennial celebration in 1876, together with *Trial of Sir Harry Vane*, and one or two others of his works. His paintings grace many of the best collections in America and Canada. We illustrate one of his earlier works, *January and May*.*

---

* See Steel Engraving.

THE RETURN OF THE MAYFLOWER.
(From the original painting by G. H. Boughton.)

JAMES HAMILTON, whose recent death cast a cloud over the art lovers of America, was a Philadelphian by residence and education, though we believe born in the North of Ireland. Self-educated in nearly every sense of the word, he achieved a success as a marine painter which placed his pictures in favourable comparison with the most accomplished marine painters of any school or time.

He, unfortunately, painted too many pictures, and sold the fruits of his great genius too cheap; but we venture to predict that now his pictures will advance in price. He was also a good landscape painter, but his sunset marines earned him the title of the "American Turner."

THE MORAN FAMILY—PETER, EDWARD, and TOM—all born in Philadelphia, and all men of high capacity. Tom Moran has achieved the greatest celebrity from his pictures of the *Yellowstone Country* and his *Mountain of the Holy Cross*. Edward Moran, now living in New York, and a member of the National Academy, is versatile in his excellence, but we like best his marine subjects. His *New York Harbour by Moonlight* and *The Leading Yacht* were exhibited at the Centennial Exhibition, 1876, and were awarded a first-class medal.

Peter Moran is noted for his excellence as an animal painter and an etcher, in both of which his success is very decided. He exhibited *Cattle in a Storm* at Philadelphia, 1876, and was awarded a first-class medal. A sister of the Morans is married to S. J. FERRIS, a rising artist and accomplished etcher in Philadelphia; and Mrs. Ferris has a little son of about ten years, who already has etched some copies of Meissonier and Fortuny that are simply wonderful. We believe that Mr. Edward Moran also has one or two children who have shown marked ability as artists, and who are at present being educated in Paris for an art career; so we may truly say "the Morans are an artistic family."

CHRISTEN SCHEUSSELE, who has for many years filled the chair of Professor and Director of the Academy of Fine Arts at Philadelphia, is a German by birth and education. He has painted some pictures that are well known throughout America, such as *The Ironworker, Clear the Track*, and *Daniel Webster at the Grave of Shakespeare*.* Scheussele has suffered for the last ten years from paralysis, but nevertheless continues his valuable position of instructor with unabated zeal. He was awarded a first class medal at the Centennial Exhibition of 1876.

ALBERT F. BELLOWS, was born in New York in 1834, he was apprenticed to a lithographer in Boston, he always had shown artistic talent, and was enabled in 1855, to visit Paris and other European cities, where he soon became known as an accomplished *genre* painter; among his works which are well known, are *City Cousins* and *The First Pair of Boots*. He returned to America in 1859, and was elected a member of the National Academy, New York. He now turned his attention to water-colour painting, with eminent success. He again visited England and has marked his visit by exquisite pictures of *Country Lanes, Devonshire Cottages, Country Orchards*, seductive in their green leafiness,—rivaling Birket Foster's chosen subjects.

E. WOOD TERRY, was born in Boston in 1832, after having early determined on

* See Steel Engraving.

ultimately becoming an artist; after the usual school education he took a situation in New Orleans as clerk in a commission house, and set himself to save money in order to educate himself in Europe for an artist's career. In 1833 he had saved what he deemed sufficient for his purpose, and went at once to Europe; when he reached Düsseldorf he put himself under the tuition of Leutz and worked for two years, showing marked improvement; he then returned to America and journeyed over the United States painting portraits. He settled for a time in San Francisco, and on his way home in 1864, he painted Brigham Young full length, and several of his family and elders. He has since settled in New York, and by his choice of home-like American subjects, coupled with excellent execution, has become a great favourite with all lovers of art. He exhibited several pictures at the Philadelphia Exhibit of 1876, and was awarded a first-class medal.

E. D. LEWIS, the great landscape artist, was born in Philadelphia, of wealthy parents, possessing many advantages; he has, however, been a hard worker all his life, (he is still quite a young man). Mr. Lewis is a painter who has been described by one of our best art critics as "a workman who makes his picture luminous," and although a rapid worker and a producer of many pictures he never duplicates his subjects, and his work has all the evidence of minute care and finish.

Some time ago Mr. Lewis went to Cuba, and painted many views from the tropical "Queen of the Antilles," and the magic of the tropics seems to have clung to his brush ever since.

Many of the best galleries throughout America have one or more of Mr. Lewis' paintings. We engrave one of his recent works, *A Scene on the Schuylkill.**

JAMES K. BEARD, the best American painter of domestic animals, in some respects rivaling even Landseer and Rivére, was born at Buffalo, New York, in 1814. While a child his parents removed to Painesville, Ohio, where he attended school; while yet a boy he commenced painting portraits of his neighbours at prices ranging from five to fifteen dollars. After a career of great adventure in the West he settled in New York, where he took high rank as an artist, which he maintains to the present day.

JOHN W. CASILEAR, who has achieved a world-wide reputation as a landscape painter, was born in New York in 1813; he was apprenticed to an engraver and worked at that trade till 1854. He had, however, in his occupation full opportunity of studying the sister art of painting, and in 1840 made a tour of Europe for the purpose of better advancing his knowledge of art. Kensett, the Baltimore artist, was his companion, and together they sketched and studied. On Casilear's return to New York he commenced painting landscapes and achieved immediate success. He again visited England in 1862, and sold his paintings not only to American visitors but to the best collectors in Europe. On his return to New York he settled himself permanently with success. His paintings are generally small, seldom exceeding 24x 36 inches; of recent years he has not painted much and his pictures—rarely for sale —when offered bring high prices.

* See Steel Engraving.

TOBY ROSENTHAL, born in San Francisco, California, but practicing art in Paris, is certainly one of the most promising young artists of the present day; his picture of *Elaine* * from Tennyson's "Idyls of the Kings," was exhibited at Philadelphia Centennial 1876, and obtained for its painter a first-class medal. Rosenthal's pictures command high prices.

GEORGE INNES, of Boston, on whose masterly work the influence of the French School is probably more apparent than in those of any other American painter, was born in New York State in 1825. Like many other American artists, portrait painting was the "crutch" that helped him to better things. When 21 he entered the studio of Regis Gignoux, in New York, where he adopted the style which he has since worked to such perfection. Innes has visited Europe several times, and every time on his return shows marked improvement. The wealthy gentlemen of New England and New York hold nearly all his pictures. Among his latest are, *On the Saco in Maine*, and *Scenes on the Compagna near Rome*.

JERVIS McENTEE, whose autumn and winter landscapes have become such favourites with American art-lovers, was born at Rondout, New York, in 1830; he became a pupil of Mr. Frederick Church in New York, in 1857; he visited Europe in 1869 in company with S. R. Gifford, studying art collections but chiefly filling his portfolio with sketches mostly from Switzerland and the more quiet landscapes of sunny Italy. McEntee is capable of other work besides landscapes, as witness his *Danger Signal*, which was exhibited in New York in 1872, and received universal admiration.

GEO. H. BOUGHTON, like Leslie and West, is a gift from America to England; he has developed without seriously changing the style he formed in this country, and is now pleasing, with the results of American art lessons, the most cultured classes of the old world. His youth was passed at Albany, New York, and already during his early life he impressed upon the American public a conviction that a painter of uncommonly delicate and refined powers had arisen. One of his early patrons was Mr. August Belmont, who now exhibits in his gallery in New York, *The Lake of the Dismal Swamp*. He left America in 1869, being then 25 years of age, and after studying in France for two years settled in London, where he now resides. Boughton has painted many pictures illustrative of the lives of the Pilgrim Fathers. *The March of Miles Standish*, *The Departure of the Mayflower*,* *New England Puritans going to Church*; he exhibited the latter and *Going to Seek his Fortune* at the Philadelphia Exhibition of 1876.

WHISTLER, an American painter, a native of Baltimore, early signalized himself by his experiments in colours. He received a French art training before he established himself in England. He is known both for his etchings and paintings; the former receive nearly unqualified praise, the latter have been alternately abused and lauded. But even his severest critics seem inclined, in these later days, to allow Whistler exceptional achievements, however fitful or marred, in colour. Mr. Rossetti assigns to the stranger from beyond the Atlantic, and from Parisian studios, with his preference for "shore-life, river-life, barge-life, for everything which hints of

* See Illustration.

old wherries, jetties, piers, rigging, bow-windows overlooking reaches of the peopled stream," an intuitive possession of the scenery of the Thames. "Never before," writes the critic of Whistler's picture of *Wapping*, "was that familiar scene so triumphantly painted ;" and he cites a similar picture, *Old Battersea Bridge*, and says of it, "with a mud shore and a river-side group, boats ready for launching, a grey sky, and greyer river, the side-long bridge crossed by carts and passengers, shows one way of treating these simple materials to perfection, whether composition, tone, truth, or originality is in demand." The painter is not always thus subdued in colour, neither is he always as blank as in the two pictures, entitled, oddly, *The White Girl* and *The Little White Girl*. He exhibited lately three pictures of river and coast scenes, named respectively, *A Nocturne in crimson and gold, A Nocturne in blue and silver*, and a *Symphony in grey and green*.

DANIEL HUNTINGTON was born in 1816, in New York. Mr. Tuckerman writes that more than thirty years ago—"within a stone's throw of the glorious old elms of New Haven, a slight-built youth with a green shade over his eyes, used to study the Odes of Horace at three o'clock in the morning," and that this lad thus fascinated by the old poet's wit, and oblivious of time, was the painter Daniel Huntington.

After studying in various American studios, Huntington went abroad in 1839, when he was twenty-three years of age, visiting Italy, and residing in turn at Florence and Rome. After his first return to America he painted portraits, and began an elaborate illustration of the *Pilgrim's Progress*, but was stopped in his work by an affection of the eyes. In 1844, when he was twenty-eight years of age, he repaired again to Italy, making Rome his head-quarters. In 1846 he was back once more in New York, painting portraits, with an occasional historical and genre picture.

Huntington is said to be a thoughtful, quiet painter, and a sincere, unassuming man, not without a considerable appreciation of humour. His aim is represented as sober and manly, rejecting alike violent efforts at dramatic effect and minute drudgery of elaboration. In historic and genre pictures he is understood to rely on his intelligent and sometimes highly-wrought transfer of a scene to canvas. In his portraits, truth and simplicity are reckoned his conspicuous merits. His execution is considered good, though subdued. In 1850, when Huntington was thirty-four years of age, there was an exhibition of his works in his native city of New York. Among his best pictures are *The Dream of Mercy, The Communion of the Sick, Shepherd Boy of the Compagna, Ichabod Crane and Katrina Von Tressel*, and *Sowing the Word*.

One of Huntington's later pictures, which chanced to be finished at the date of the outbreak of the Southern rebellion, was a pleasant commemoration of an old republican gala—*A Reception given by Mrs. Washington during her Husband's Presidency*. Sixty figures were introduced into the eight feet of canvas. There were grouped the patriotic, intrepid men, and the high-spirited, tender-hearted woman, who saw and lived through the struggle for independence. Old portraits, miniatures, and family descendants, who were supposed to retain family features with family names were faithfully sought out, to give the personages in the picture truth and living character.

Huntington's portraits include those of the late *President Lincoln, Agassiz, Bryant, Earl of Carlisle* and *Sir C. Eastlake*.

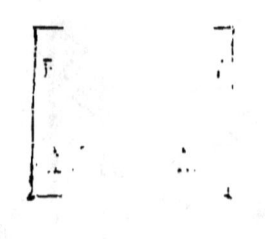

WILLIAM PAGE was born in 1811, at Albany. When eleven years of age he gained a premium from the American Institute for an India-ink drawing, but at a later stage of his youth he proposed to renounce art for theology, and went to Andover to study divinity. He soon resumed his artist life, while retaining his strong religious convictions. He soon found sitters as a portrait painter, and proposed to visit Europe in the prosecution of his art, but an early attachment, and a marriage before he was twenty-one, established him in New York. In spite of the want of a European training, so much coveted and so frequently secured by American painters, Page prospered and attracted notice—above all, by his successful colouring. His marriage proved unhappy. He was divorced from his wife, married again, removed to Boston, and soon proceeded to Europe, remaining abroad many years, and residing principally in Rome, where he had the reputation of being the first American portrait painter.

Page's love of colour, and possibly his speculative disposition, which has latterly led him to adopt the opinions of Swedenborg, have caused him to indulge in extensive experiments in colour, some of them proving fortunate, some unsuccessful in results. Many Americans think that Page, at his best, approaches the excellence of the Venitian school in colouring, and tell that "one of his copies of Titian was stopped by the authorities of Florence as an original."

Page has not been equally happy with his ideal subjects; his admirers acknowledge that their superior colouring is balanced by odd, incongruous composition. Among Page's best portraits are those of *Robert Browning*, *Mrs. Crawford*, and *Lowell*. After his return to America Page delivered a course of lectures on painting.

FREDERIC EDWIN CHURCH, the great American landscape painter, was born in 1826, at Hartford, Connecticut. He showed an early taste for art, sought the society of Bartholomew the sculptor, and entered as a pupil the studio of Cole the painter. Unlike so many of the American painters, Church did not seek to complete his art education in Europe, but set himself to study nature (at first in the home scenery of the Catskill mountains) in those atmospheric effects, the love of which has been a passion with him, while they seem to have been missed by the earlier American landscape painters. Church's pictures must have been distinguished from the beginning by originality and independence, and by genuine devotion to nature, while his drawing was held in advance of his colouring. His vividly conceived, vigorously portrayed skies at once attracted notice, in such early pictures as *The Lifting of a Storm Cloud*, *Evening after a Storm*. He was not contented with learning by heart nature cultivated and tamed; he turned with longing instinct to nature in the virgin charm of her wildest, most savage haunts, whether she broke forth in the gorgeous luxuriance and burning volcanos of the tropics, or stood arrested and frozen with a ghastly steel-blue gleam over her dead whiteness, in polar seas.

In 1853, when Church was twenty-seven years of age, he sailed for South America, where he travelled and made many sketches, residing, while in the vicinity of Quito, beneath the same roof and in the same family which fifty years before had received Humboldt, whose portrait as a lad in Prussian uniform is still preserved on the wall of one of the rooms. On Church's return home his picture of *The Great*

Mountain Chain of New Granada was welcomed with so much interest and admiration that he paid another visit to South America, bringing back new stores of sketches, worked up later into his famous pictures *The Heart of the Andes, Cotopaxi* (in eruption), *Chimborazo*, and *The Rainy Season in the Tropics*.

After his second expedition to South America, Church painted his well-known picture of the *Falls of Niagara*, in an oblong seven feet by three, where the Horseshoe Fall is given as seen from the Canadian shore near Table Rock. This picture added greatly to his reputation, as, while it dealt with a very difficult subject, it was regarded "as the first satisfactory delineation by art of one of the greatest natural wonders of the western world." In the mean time the fate of Sir John Franklin's expedition, and the adventures of the gallant men—among them Elisha Kane, who went in vain to the rescue of the "Erebus" and "Terror"—had taken a deep hold of the public mind, and fired the imagination of the painter of wild nature.

Church set himself to become familiar with the northern regions through the travels and the conversation of Arctic explorers, and at last chartered a vessel and set sail for Labrador to see with his own eyes the marvels of icebergs. The chief fruit of his voyage was *The Icebergs*, remarkable alike for its subject and its treatment, exhibited in London in 1863. Eventually the picture was destined for London, having become the property of Mr. Watson, M. P.

In 1866 a domestic affliction induced Church to seek change of scene in Jamaica, where he spent the summer, studying not only "sunset, storm, and mists," outlines of hills, mountain-gorges, lines of coast, but "the most minute and elaborate details of palms, ferns, cane-brakes, flowers, grasses, and lizards."

A curious work by Church was painted in anticipation of the civil war, and was circulated widely in the form of a coloured lithograph. It was called *Our Banner in the Sky*, and represented, by means of a genuine though fantastic study of a sky, cloudy "stripes" and "stars" shining through the clouds, with the leafless trunk of a tree standing for a flagstaff.

ALBERT BIERSTADT was born in 1829, at Düsseldorf. His father, a German soldier, who had seen service in the Peninsular war, emigrated to America two years after the birth of his son Albert, and the family have resided for many years at New Bedford, Massachusetts. There young Bierstadt received his education. While the lad turned from the first to art, he was dissuaded from making it his profession, till he was in his twenty-third year, when he painted a picture in oils, and resolved on earning the means to visit his native Düsseldorf with its German School of Art, and to cultivate the friendship of his cousin Hasenclever, a German genre painter popular in America. In 1853, when Bierstadt was in his twenty-fifth year, he sailed for Europe, and proceeded to Düsseldorf, when he had the disappointment of finding that Hasenclever was just dead. However, Bierstadt entered the Düsseldorf Academy as a student, and went during the summer months on a sketching tour in Germany and Switzerland, making, in the mean time, in the room of his kinsman Hasenclever, valuable friends in "Lessing, Achenbach, Leutze, and Whitteridge." During his student days Bierstadt gave no great proof of ability. His first good picture was *The Old Mill*, painted on a walking tour in Westphalia; and his next—which had sufficient merits to lay the foundation of his name as a landscape painter—was a picture called *Sunshine and Shadow*, taken on a tour in Hesse Cassel, and representing only the fine effect of light and shade "on the mossy, massive front and low-arched door of a quaint mediæval church, with a wide-spreading, venerable tree beside the wall, and an old woman seated under the gateway.

Bierstadt spent a winter in Rome along with Whitteridge, went on a pedestrian tour through the Apennines with another friendly artist, made a sojourn in Switzerland and on the Rhine, still with brother artists, before he returned home in 1857, when he was in his twenty-ninth year.

Bierstadt had, in the four years which he had spent abroad, become an accomplished artist, and needed but to show in proof of his attainments, his *Sunshine and Shadow*, *Bay of Sorento*, *Street Scene in Rome*, etc., etc. He took his next tour in America among the White Mountains, and a little later, in 1858, he joined the late General Lander's exploring party to the Rocky Mountains. On this long and adventurous expedition Bierstadt travelled with his companions in a spring wagon, or on Indian ponies, in pursuit of sport as well as art, shooting grouse, antelope, sage hens, and "sleeping in blankets under the open sky, waking with the dew on their faces."

Bierstadt's great picture of *The Rocky Mountains* represents a vast plain, over which groups of Indians in their primitive condition, and their wigwams are scattered; huge cotton-wood trees, oaks, and pines, occupy a portion of the foreground; beyond flows a river, on the opposite shore of which rise beetling cliffs, and lofty snow-crowned mountains—the highest peak Mount Lander. The picture made a great impression.

Among Bierstadt's later pictures which rank with the *Rocky Mountains—Mount Lander*, are *A Storm among the Rocky Mountains*, and *Mount Hood* in the Oregon Territory. Having received a government commission Bierstadt went again to Europe in 1867, in his thirty-ninth year, to make studies for a picture of the discovery of the North River by Henry Hudson. Bierstadt has his home on the banks of the Hudson, his studio commanding an extensive view of the noble river in the vicinity of the Tappan Zee.

Bierstadt represents the Düsseldorf school in landscape painting. High praise is awarded to his drawing and composition, but his colouring is objected to as hard and dry. In the style of the modern school of German painters, there is more pure intellect than fancy and feeling in his pictures, and where sentiment appears it tends to sensationalism. Mr. Tuckerman attributes Bierstadt's great success in America in part to the fact that Düsseldorf landscape painting has been until lately a novelty there. With some points in common, Bierstadt is a more scholarly and "finished" painter than Church, while the latter is probably the more original of the two, with more true poetry in his exclusive devotion to nature than exists in the exceeding cleverness of the master of the most learned modern school.

Bierstadt exhibited *Western Kansas* and the *Landing of Columbus*, at the Centennial exhibition, Philadelphia, 1876.

Among other well-known American landscape painters are CROPSEY, whose *Corfe Castle* was exhibited in the Royal Academy, and his *Autumn on the Hudson*

River at the International Exhibition, 1862; Kensett, lately dead, the greatest Præ-raphaelite of American artists, and held in special esteem among modern Belgian painters; Heade, famous for tropical birds and blossoms, and in his *Apple Blossoms* for the flower of home orchards.

We must say a word of the little colony of American artists in Rome, which has become a distinct feature of the Eternal City. Of these artists, Story the sculptor is to the English world the centre. Of the painters, Chapman is "the Nestor," and is famous in design and etching, though grave fault is found with his colouring. Among his most popular illustrations of books have been his drawings for Harper's Illustrated Bible, and Schmidt's Tales. He received a government commission to paint for the Rotunda of the Capitol, Washington, *The Baptism of Pocahontas*. He has resided in Rome for upwards of twenty years. Among his last pictures are, *A Sunset in the Campagna*, and *Stone Pines in the Barberini Valley*.

FREEMAN is another genre painter, and an old resident in Rome. His *Beggars, Crusaders' Return, Savoyard Boy in London*, and *Young Italy*, are among his well-known pictures. He ranks high among American artists. VEDDER is a third genre painter, one of the most original of American painters, distinguished specially for his quaintness, alike in his subjects and their treatment. The very names of some of his pictures have a quaint ring. Among them are—*The Arab listening with his ear to the Great Sphinx, The Lair of the Sea Serpent, The Lost Mind* ("wandering among the waste places of the earth"). YEWELL paints landscapes and interiors, the latter with great fidelity and delicacy. His *First Communion* is a procession of young girls from the door of the fine old church of Moret, France. HEALY, whose historical picture of *Franklin urging the claims of the American colonies before Louis XVI.* was exhibited at the Paris Exhibition in 1855, is one of the best American portrait painters of the French school. His portraits are said to be vigorous in character, but deficient in delicacy. Among his portraits are those of Louis Philippe, Marshal Soult, M. Guizot, Webster, Patrick Jackson, Lowell, Peabody, Longfellow, &c., &c. TILTON, with great merits and great defects, paints landscapes which require a strong light by which to see their beauties. The painter is great in atmospheric effects, but is accused of sacrificing to the gossamer veil or sunny haze—in which he is given to shrouding his objects—the solid details. His *Bays of Baiæ and Naples, Bernese Alps, Fishing Boats of Venice, Grand Canal of Venice*, and his views in Egypt, are among his best works. HASELTINE of the Düsseldorf school, DIX the marine painter, whose landscape in the Channel Islands was exhibited at the Royal Academy, London, in 1866.

GEORGE LORING BROWN was born in Boston in 1814, and at the age of fourteen was apprenticed to a wood engraver. His first painting was purchased by an art collector of repute in Boston, and on the strength of this success and the faith of some friends who advanced him the necessary means he sailed for Europe, and after various adventures became the pupil of the great Isaby. On his return to America he found ready sale for his pictures, at prices hitherto unknown to native talent. He painted the great cities of Europe, Rome, Florence, Genoa, Venice, &c., and in his own particular line is without a rival in America.

HORSES ALARMED BY WOLVES.
(From the original painting by A. Schreyer.)

In recording the remaining artists of the American School, we find that our space will not allow of more than an imperfect list of the more distinguished. WHITTREDGE, EASTMAN JOHNSON, J. G. BROWN, VAN ELTON, DE HAAS, J. B. IRVING, (deceased), BRIDGEMAN, WINSLOW, HORNER, MAYNARD, COLEMAN, SMILLIE, of New York. HERZOG, LAMBDIN, DE BERG RICHARDS, J. L. STEWART, TOM EAKINS, EMILY SARTAIN, WAUGH, DE CRANO, WEISMAN, KNIGHT, GEO. WRIGHT, WINNER, COOPER, J. H. BROWN, and CARISS, of Philadelphia. HILL, of San Francisco; FORBES, of Toronto; HEALY, of Chicago; MACHEN, of Toledo; BEIMER, of Louisville; JONES, of Baltimore; THOMPSON and WEIR, of New Haven; FALCONER, of Brooklyn; the two CHAMPNEYS, MILLETT, WATERMAN, BRACKETT, BILLINGS, THOMPSON and W. E. NORTON, who exhibited at Philadelphia, a marine painting of high merit, *A fog on the Grand Banks*; HUNT and PORTER, of Boston.

But, as a poetic critic wrote of poets, we may quote, applying the same to artists:

> "As lamps set high upon some earthly eminence,
> And to gazer brighter seem than the sphere stars they flout,
> Dwindle in distance and die out
> While no star waneth yet,
> So through the *past's* long searching night
> Only the *soul-stars* keep their light."

When the present becomes the past, it would at this time be hazardous to predict which of the artists of the present will be shining "*soul-stars*" in the future.

CHAPTER VII.

CONCLUSION.—CONTEMPORARY ART IN EUROPE.

N the preceding chapter we closed with a mere list of some of the more distinguished artists who complete the American School. In the present chapter we will treat with nearly the same brevity the contemporary painters of the European Schools—merely writing at somewhat greater length those whose names are most famous and most favorably known in America.

FRANCE.

HENRI FREDERICK SCHOPIN was born in Paris, in 1804. He achieved a great success a generation ago; but though still alive (1878), he has not painted anything for a long time.

Four of his paintings, which were made extremely popular by fine engravings, were illustrations of the story of "*Paul and Virginia.*"*

LEO HERMANN, of German descent, but painting in Paris, has recently achieved praise and profit from his treatment, in a slightly humourous natural style, of the clergy of France. We engrave one of his latest paintings, *A Pause in the Argument.*†

JOHN LEO GÉRÔME was born at Vesoul, in 1824. He was a pupil in the school of Paul Delaroche, and was admitted to the school of the Fine Arts when he was in his nineteenth year. In 1847, when Gérôme was in his twenty-fourth year, he exhibited his first picture which drew public attention—that of *a young Greek man and woman setting cocks to fight.* The subject was, thus early in his history, characteristic of Gérôme, who has shown a decided preference for incidents either in themselves painful or morally repulsive. The merits of the picture were also characteristic of Gérôme, being excellent of style and close imitation of the substances which were represented. After visiting Turkey and Egypt, and showing the influence of eastern travel on his art, Gérôme exhibited at the French Exhibition of 1855, when he was thirty-one years of age, the picture which gave him his place among

* See Steel Engraving. † See Illustration.

the leading painters of France. It was a picture of great size, and was named *The Age of Augustus, and the Birth of Jesus Christ*, the intention of the painter being to figure the decline of paganism and the rise of Christianity. The work is said to have displayed grandeur in design and care in execution. It was bought by the French government, and procured for Gérôme the Cross of the Legion of Honour. He has painted pictures still more famous—notably his *Duel after a Masked Ball*, the original of which is now in the Gallery of Mr. W. T. Walters, of Baltimore, his *Gladiators*, and his *Slave Market*, in the Louvre. Gérôme is represented as pleasant in manners while indomitable in will. As an artist his fine skill as a draughtsman is considered superior to his art as a colourist. He is believed to have great dramatic power, which he can hold under complete control; indeed, one of the fascinations of his pictures is said to be the absolute coolness with which he treats his impassioned or terrible subjects. The instances adduced by Mr. Hamerton are the merchants examining the teeth of the slave-girl; and the sentinel smoking his pipe beside the severed heads of the boys at the door of the Cairo Mosque. We illustrate his celebrated painting from the Salon of 1875, *A begging Monk at the door of a Mosque*.[*]

The following example of M. Gérôme's work is not open to the charge of repulsiveness:

Street Scene in Cairo.—Here we have architecture in sunlight and shadow, booths or shops, a long vista of broken pavement; half a score of dogs dozing; deep shadows in the recesses. The chief human figures are two superbly-armed and mounted Arabs, sitting in conference with a merchant who hands to one of them a bottle of cool water; a third Arab leans idly against a bulk; a tall woman, clad in dark blue, and veiled from head to foot in black, bears at her hip a basket filled with oranges, like globes of gold; astride on her shoulder, his flesh making delicious "colour" with her blue robe, sits a lively and entirely naked boy; she grasps his ankle and makes nothing of her double load. This is a charming group, exhibiting some of the noblest qualities of M. Gérôme's art. Before the mother trots an elder boy, who is naked but for a green veil streaming from his head; he bears a fresh branch of palm. Clad in light-blue, and walking behind the last, goes a tall negress, bearing a great water-jar on her head. Beyond these, two women, muffled in white from head to foot, are bargaining with the owner of a booth; men are chaffering just on the verge of the gloom which obscures more than half the interior of a nearer shop; a boy donkey-driver and his beast have brought to the door of a private house a lady, who, having knocked, is reconnoitred from an upper window by a servant. There is abundance of incident in this work; but one feels that it lacks movement, and that the design would be better if it had a dominant element. However this may be, it is a precious example of delicate and elaborate workmanship; its careful drawing will be enjoyed by all lovers of form, who will also like its sound and profoundly-studied modelling, and the faithfulness which is everywhere observable in the rendering of textures and light and shade; it has less of a certain metallic defect than is usual in this master's paintings.

Gérôme is regarded as unsurpassed in the present day in his drawing of dogs, and

---

[*] See Illustration.

perhaps in his studies of animals generally. He exhibited no less than ten of his finest pictures at the Paris Exhibition of 1878.

ROBERT-FLEURY was born at Cologne, of French parents in 1787. He was in youth a pupil of Horace Vernet's, a friend of Géricault's, and an art-student in Rome. He shows traces of these antecedents as a historical painter in clearness, force, and "fine technical knowledge," though his colour is commented upon as "hot and dirty" and his power of expression as that of a positivist. Robert-Fleury is a member of the Academy of Fine Arts and an officer of the Legion of Honour. His *Scene from St. Bartholomew's Eve*, *Procession of the League*, *Charles V. at the Monastery of St. Juste*, and *Colloquy of Poissy in 1651*, are all well-known pictures.

ROBERT TOREY FLEURY, son of Robert Fleury, promises to surpass his father.

GUSTAVE COURBET was born at Ornans in the Valley of the Doubs, in 1819. He was destined for the bar, and sent to Paris to prosecute his studies, but soon abandoned law for art. He had no regular art-education, working in a desultory manner in various ateliers, and depending chiefly on self-culture; one result was the opposition which he provoked from the masters of the great ateliers, in consequence of which, together with the objection of Courbet's irregular work, he was for six years rejected as a candidate for the exhibition. A farther and more injurious result was the sense of Ishmaelitism produced in the painter, who is now regarded as the chief of the realist painters of France, for Courbet was neither to be crushed nor turned from his course. At last his original power won its way, and he is, possibly, now in as much danger of being over-estimated as he was once of being undervalued. Courbet was a plain man, without affectation in his plainness, but with such a horror of mere prettiness that it approaches to a glorification of ugliness. (He is described, however, as having been, in person an exceptionally handsome man.) He was a great lover of Nature, and a resolute painter of what came before his own eyes, eschewing the classical, the historical, and the high ideal in painting. Almost inevitably he was said to be a narrow-minded artist, dogged in his narrowness—having the vigour of concentration, but wanting all true proportions in the more delicate details of greater breadth and refinement. He was spoken of as fond of painting massive muscular strength in men, and even in women. One of Courbet's most famous pictures is his *Stone Cutters*, a willing rendering of homely yet honest toil. Another work which has met at once with great admiration and severe criticism, is his *Woman with the Parrot*.

Offended by the place which was assigned to him in the Universal Exhibition of 1855, Courbet opened a separate exhibition of his own works; while, at the exhibition of 1860 at Munich, the jury reserved an entire room for Courbet's pictures, among which his *Deer Hunt* and *Hind forced to take to the Water*, were especially noticed.

Courbet won disgraceful distinction as a member of the Commune and was sentenced to death for his share in that affair, but pardoned (simply because he was such a great artist) on condition of paying a very large fine to go towards the re-construction of the Column Vendome, which he had helped to destroy. He died in 1877 before he had paid any of the fine.

JEAN LOUIS HAMON, pupil of Paul Delaroche. "From Gustave Courbet to Jean Louis Hamon," writes Mr. Rossetti, "is the stride from one pole of art to another;

from a digger's tent to a lady's boudoir; from the clenched fist whose knuckles are yet red with knocking down a bullock, to a long, white, consumptive hand. Hamon is one of the most delicious of idyllic painters; the most charming of French classicists; the most child-like and child-loving of Parisians. There is just a touch in him of dandyism, which one has scarcely heart to condemn." *My Sister is not at home, A Girl in Charge of Children*, and *The Orphans*, are famous and characteristic pictures by Hamon.

EDOUARD FRÉRE, the younger brother of a less distinguished painter, was born at Paris in 1819. In his eighteenth year he became a pupil of Paul Delaroche, and at the same time entered the school of the Fine Arts. From the first Edouard Frére has been a genre painter, choosing even specially rustic and simple subjects, and working almost always on a small canvas. He exhibited first in the Salon in 1843, when he was in his twenty-fourth year, and continued to rise in rank as a painter, receiving among other tokens of recognition, the Cross of the Legion of Honour, after the Exhibition of 1855.

Although Frére's subjects are simple, they are by no means treated in a petty manner or overloaded with accessories; he is rather reproached with the heaviness of his colouring, and the rigid exclusion of a multitude of details, along with the complete subordination of those which he introduces to his main purpose. His merits are the truth and tenderness and exceeding freshness of his pictures.

F. C. COMPTE-CALIX, born at Lyons, 1820, one of the bright modern French school, was educated at the School of Fine Arts, Lyons, and exhibited at the French Academy as early as 1844, where he was awarded a medal. He exhibited *Youth and Age*[*] at the French Exhibition, 1867, where the picture was purchased by the Countess of Bonneville.

A. CABANEL, a native of Montpellier, exhibited first in Paris in 1825, and received the Grand Medal of Honour, 1865. This artist, who like Gérôme and Meissonier, has received all the honours and decorations in the power of France to bestow, has several of his very choicest examples in American galleries. *Venus Rising from the Sea* is in the gallery of Mr. Henry C. Gibson, of Philadelphia ; Mr. August Belmont, of New York, has *Paradise Lost ;* and there is another painting of Cabanel's in the Corcoran Gallery at Washington. M. Cabanel exhibits this year at Paris, 1878. We illustrate his picture, *The Annunciation*,[†] painted in 1876.

J. A. BRETON is another great French artist, who has achieved the highest distinction. He was born at Couvriers in 1832, and as a figure painter, combined with landscape, we question whether he has an equal to-day. We illustrate one of his most recent pictures, *The Eve of St. John's Day*,[†] which was at the Exhibition at Philadelphia, 1876, and obtained for its painter a first-class medal.

JEAN LOUIS ERNEST MEISSONIER was born at Lyons in 1811. He is a genre painter, like Frére, and paints in still smaller compass, his pictures being not so much cabinet as miniature versions of subjects rendered with an "exquisite finish," which has been likened to that of Terburg and Metzu. But not only is there finish, there

---

[*] See Steel Engraving.   [†] See Illustration.

is great fidelity and "a large grasp" of a subject in small, which is supposed to have been attained by Meissonier from his wise habit of continuing to sketch his subjects life-size; as, according to the painter's dictum, no artist can paint well small what he cannot give with equal correctness large. Unfortunately Meissonier is considered to be deficient not only in what constitutes high art, but in the tenderness which distinguishes Frére's work. Meissonier's claims to fame rest on his fineness of observation, and skill of hand; and so marked are these qualities, and so uncommon the degree of excellence to which he has brought them in his very small pictures, that he has a high place of his own in modern French art. His *Chess-players*, and his *Little Messenger*, were his first very successful works. His *Lecture chez Diderot* and his *Smoker* are quoted by Mr. Hamerton for their great superiority in their kind. His *Dream* was bought by the late Emperor for twenty thousand francs, and presented to the late Prince Albert. We illustrate one of his latest works, *The Flute-player*.*

Meissonier was created a knight of the Legion of Honour in 1846, and a Member of the Institute in 1863.

PAUL GUSTAVE DORÉ, whose canvasses are as huge as Meissonier's are minute, and who has had the misfortune to be hailed in the beginning of his career with extravagant praise—to be followed, in the reaction which was nearly certain to come, with well-nigh unmitigated censure, was born at Strasbourg in 1832, and is therefore more than forty years of age. He went to Paris at the age of thirteen years, and pursued his studies in art at the Charlemagne Lyceum. In 1848, when he was but sixteen years of age, he contributed sketches to the *Journal pour Rire*, which may answer, in a fashion, to the English *Punch*, and exhibited pen sketches which attracted attention in the Salon. At the Exhibition in 1855, when he was twenty-two years of age, he exhibited his *Battle of the Alma*, and *Battle of Inkermann*. But he made his fame by his woodcuts and illustrations of books, especially the illustrations of Dante's *Inferno*, though he has never ceased to aspire to eminence as a painter, and not only rents "two large studios in Paris which are crowded with canvasses," but has a well-known "gallery" of his paintings open to the public in New Bond Street, London.

Doré, who has been accused of having exhausted his original resources, is declared to be among artists one of the most productive as well as assimilative (that is, capable of imbibing and reproducing in a fresh and almost individual form, the ideas of others); nevertheless, he may have drawn upon his powers to the verge of exhaustion. It is charitably allowed with regard to Doré, that if he had devoted his hours to painting, in place of being tempted aside to grow rich by woodcuts, he might by this time have done something remarkable as a painter.

Mr. Hamerton holds that Doré's best pictures are his early *Famille de Saltimbouque*, and his *Néophyte, or young Monk seated among his elder brethren*, of 1868, while the same critic believes Doré to have "a true landscape gift," and even "a sense of the sublimity of landscape very rare in France, but his landscape painting is wanting in refinement." Possibly refinement is wanting in more than his landscape

* See Illustration.

painting, at least that subdued moderation, which belongs to power tutored and regulated, is not found in the vividly-conceived, energetically-executed work of Doré. In "the science of art," he is said to be deficient; he is charged with being "false" in chiaro-scuro, and not possessed of more than "elementary" knowledge in form—defects which the great scale of his pictures make conspicuous; while as an exceptional and peculiar genius working after his own methods, he gets "as much science as he needs for his usual business of book illustration." We illustrate one of his recent paintings, *Alexander the Great weeping over the body of Darius.**

ROSALIE OR ROSA BONHEUR was born at Bordeaux, in 1822. She is the daughter of a painter, who was her first teacher in art, and one of a family of more or less distinguished artists—her brother Auguste being a painter, another brother, Isodor, a sculptor, and her sister Juliette, wife of M. Peyrol, a painter. Rosa Bonheur has kept steadfastly to animal and landscape painting. She exhibited in 1841, when she was nineteen years of age, two small pictures, entitled *Two Rabbits*, and *Sheep and Goats*. Her first great work exhibited in 1849—the year of her father's death, when she was twenty-seven years of age,—was her *Ploughing in the Nivernois*. This picture was placed in the Luxembourg. Four years later she won still greater fame by her *Horse Fair*, which was engraved by Landseer.

Rosa Bonheur, assisted by her sister, acts as directress of a gratuitous School of Design for girls, committed to her charge by the City of Paris in 1849.

When a girl Rosa Bonheur kept a sheep in a Parisian apartment, and as a distinguished woman she maintains "offices" full of animals which are not only associated with her name, but are her familiar friends. We have read anecdotes of visits to her studio, which include tours of this city farm-yard.

Rosa Bonheur has been, from youth to middle life, a devoted student, absorbed in her art. In order to prosecute it without obstacle or interruption, she has broken through many of the restraints of society, and indulged in a thousand eccentricities. She has gone in a man's clothes to study anatomy in the shambles, and to make adventurous and dangerous excursions, when she has had to lodge for weeks in the huts of herdsmen and muleteers. She has been so careless of ordinary forms as to go with a friend to the theatre after having painted to the last moment, "in a kind of dressing-gown, all spotted with drops of oil, and an old pair of yellow slippers; her hair, too, loose like a man's hair, when it is allowed to grow rather long." But however we may take exception to those liberties, and question whether they are absolutely necessary in the interest of art, we must at least rejoice that Rosa Bonheur, "the most accomplished female artist who has ever lived," is a woman of perfectly pure and unsullied character, in many respects very estimable, simple in her personal habits, kind, generous, and helpful to her neighbours.

Rosa Bonheur is a very prosperous artist, loaded with commissions, and paid sometimes as much as $4,000 for a slight water-colour sketch. One element of her success is said to have been the use which a crafty picture-dealer made once of the combination of her talent and industry with her sex. (It was so wonderful that such

---

* See Illustration.

work should be done by a woman!) Thus beyond a certain point the womanhood, which is so often brought forward either as an accusation of, or as a plea for, weakness, may operate advantageously in the assertion of a marvel. But the true worker, whether man or woman, wants only a fair field and no favour.

Here is Mr. Hamerton's enthusiastic reference to the *Ploughing in Nivernois*:—
"I hear as I write the cry of the ox-drivers—incessant, musical, monotonous. I hear it not in imagination, but coming to my open window from the fields. The morning air is fresh and pure, the scene is wide and fair, and the autumn sunshine filters through an expanse of broken, silvery cloud. They are ploughing not far off, with two teams of six oxen each—white oxen of the noble Charolais breed, sleek, powerful beasts, whose moving muscles show under their skins like the muscles of trained athletes. Where the gleams of sunshine fall on these changing groups I see in nature that picture of Rosa Bonheur's, *Ploughing in the Nivernois*."

Madame HENRIETTE BROWNE was born in Paris, and was a pupil of M. Chaplin. She received third and second class medals in acknowledgment of her work as a painter, in 1855, 1857, 1858, 1859, 1861, and as an engraver in 1863. We cannot tell more of her personal history, we can only write of her work as that of a gifted and accomplished contemporary painter, holding—not indeed so high a place as Rosa Bonheur, but an honourable place among her brother artists, and becoming well known and appreciated in this country. Her *Sick Boy tended by Sisters of Charity* was exhibited in England, and was deservedly admired for its tender and touching sentiment and good painting. We have before us a photograph copy of her *Saying Grace*. A simple young girl, with great black eyes looking from under the brow shaded by stray locks of her short-cut hair, and surmounted by her white cap, crosses decorously the hands, one of which poises a fork minus a prong. The whole air of the picture is innocent and loveable.

MILLET, in his *Moon-light*, COROT, ROUSSEAU, and DIAZ, have taken the place of Troyon as landscape painters, while FANTIN, with his perfect "white stocks" and his "lilac," is unsurpassed as a modern flower painter.

In closing a summary of the condition of art in France, we rejoice to say that it never was in such a prosperous state. Paris is decidedly the art capital of the world; every art sympathy centres there. It is said, on good authority, that the sale of paintings last year in Paris amounted to over $8,000,000, and that the average population of artists in Paris is 8,000. The Government is behind all this immense organization. There is in France a Minister of Fine Arts, appointed as much a matter of course as the American Government appoints a Secretary of the Interior or a Secretary of the Treasury. His portfolio is joined to that of Public Instruction, which means that proper education in the Fine Arts is considered by France the highest education of the highest civilization.

The famous names of the modern French school which we have not been able to embody at length in this work, but which names, in all instances, are richly deserving extended record, are as follows: CHINTREUIL, BONNAT, FROMENTIN, MERLE, LECOMPTE, DAUBIGNY, ZEIM, LALANNE, ALLONGÉ, JACQUES, REGNAULT (dead), LAMBINET, HARPIGNIES, ROUSSEAU, GIDE BERNIER, TOULMOUCHE, SCHENCK, DEFAUX, VAN MARKE,

THE ANNUNCIATION.

MAUVE, LEVY, CHAPLIN, DUBUFFE, CARLOS DURAN, TISSOT, DETAILLE, DE NEUVILLE, PROTAIS, PHILIPPOTEUX, PASINI, BELLY, VOLON, APPIAN, ANTIGNA, ARMAND, DUMERESQUE, BARON, BARRIAS, BAYARD, G. BECKER, BOUGEREAU, BOULANGER.

COMTE, (whose *Louis XI. and the Performing Pigs* attracted such attention in the Philadelphia Exhibition of 1876). CURZON, COT. FEYEN-PERRIN, GOUPIL, HEBERT, HENNER, HUEY, LAURENS, LECOMTE-DU-NOUY, MAZEROLLE, PERRAULT, PRIOU, PLASSAN, RIBOT, BIDA, VEYRASSAT, VIBERT, VIDAL, WORMS, YON, BERNE-BELLECOUR, J. LEWIS BROWN, LUMINAIS, MOREAU, P. BAUDRY (the decorator of the New Opera House) and GAVARNI.

We might have very considerably extended this list of distinguished French artists, because, as we have said, there are at least 8,000 artists and students of Painting in Paris to-day; and when we take into consideration the organized encouragement given by the French Government to art, we may cease to wonder at the multitude of great artists whose names we are enabled to enumerate, the large majority of whom have already been decorated with the cross of the Legion of Honor (in its various degrees); a distinction not lightly bestowed and only earned by the most undoubted merit.

BELGIUM AND THE NETHERLANDS.

Of contemporary Belgian painters, NICAISE DE KEYSER, who, like more than one of his great contemporaries, is said to have been originally a shepherd boy, fills a prominent place. His *Battle of Courtray*, and his *Battle of Woringen*, two of his best-known pictures, are in the Museum at Brussels. His *St. Elizabeth giving Alms* became the property of King Leopold. He and his school are said to be followers of Paul Delaroche.

Baron HENRI LEYS, officer of the Legion of Honour, officer of the order of Leopold, and Chevalier of the order of St. Michael, of Bavaria, is a native of Antwerp. While yet in his nineteenth year, he exhibited at Brussels, in 1833, a picture of *The Massacre at Antwerp in 1576*, which at once attracted notice, and he rapidly rose to eminence. He is considered to have trodden with ardour and diligence in the footsteps of the great Flemish masters, and he has gained great commendation for his fine colouring—rich and deep, and for his chiaro-scuro, as well as for his composition. A want of fire and fervour is hinted at, by his admirers, as a fault in the painter. His subjects have been drawn very frequently from mediæval times. Leys exhibited at the Paris Exhibition of 1855, and the English International Exhibition of 1862. Among his best works are *The Institution of the Golden Fleece*, *Margaret of Austria receiving the oaths of the Archers of Antwerp*, and *Young Luther singing hymns in the streets of Eisenach*.* His *Armourer* is in the Royal Collection, Windsor, and his *Mary of Burgundy giving Alms to the Poor*, brought at the sale of a well-known collection the sum of $5,000.

* See Illustration.

M. KAEMMERER, a Belgian, who recently came into notice, promises a great future. His first painting which attracted public notice was *Winter in Holland;* this was succeeded by *At the Sea Shore,** which we engrave. His touch is light and airy, and his colouring brilliant.

LOUIS GALLAIT, a native of Tourney, finished his art studies in Paris, and exhibited his pictures in the Paris Salon from 1835 to 1853, from his twenty-sixth to his forty-fourth year. From France he received the decoration of the Legion of Honour; in Belgium he was elected a member of the Royal Academy. He is fully recognized as an original and powerful historical painter. His *Job and his Friends* is in the Luxembourg Museum, his *Baldwin crowned Emperor at Constantinople* is in the Gallery at Versailles, and his *Montaigne visiting Tasso* was bought by the King of the Belgians, who also bought Gallait's *Temptation of St. Anthony*, and presented it to the Prince Consort. His *Murder of Counts Egmont and Horn* is in the Gallery of W. J. Walters, Baltimore.

WILLEMS is mentioned by Rossetti as a "dainty domestic painter," a definition warranted by Willems' *Interior of a Silk Mercer's Shop in 1660*, and his *La Prière Maternelle*, though perhaps his *Drinking the King's Health* scarcely comes under the same category. *I was There* is in Mrs. Wilstack's Gallery in Philadelphia.

The brothers ALFRED AND JOSEPH STEVENS—the latter an animal painter—are decided realists and naturalists in art, and are forcible and verging on violence as mannerists. Mr. Rossetti instances them as massive and intense colourists, and quotes with high praise Alfred Stevens' *Reading, Meditation*, and *What People call Vagrancy,* and Joseph Stevens' *Episode of the Dog Market at Paris*.

VERBOECKHOVEN, the great Belgian animal painter, is a native of Flanders. He is a Knight of the Legion of Honour and of the order of Leopold, and has immense popularity, though it is alleged by critics that his work, though clever, will by no means bear comparison with the work of Landseer and Rosa Bonheur. In 1834, Baron Rothschild gave Verboeckhoven ten thousand francs for a landscape painting, and he has not since painted a picture of the same size for less. Perhaps, partly as a natural result, he is employed far beyond one man's powers. Sheep is his speciality, but he includes horses, cattle, and indeed every quadruped and biped, in his long list.

Among Dutch painters ISRAELS exhibited in the London exhibition of 1862 *The Shipwreck*, which Mr. Rossetti describes as " solemn and dirge-like," and declares that it was unsurpassed by any piece of domestic tragedy in the Exhibition. Van Schendel, a native of Breda, an art student at Amsterdam and Antwerp, and at last settled in Brussels, is known for the masterly distribution of light and shade in his pictures. His *Market Scene by Moonlight*, and other market scenes, are examples of his peculiar skill. Some of his best pictures which have been bought by the King of Bavaria, are at Munich. He had three pictures at the Philadelphia Centennial Exhibition.

BERNARD CORNELIUS KOEKOEK, who died in 1862, was another eminent modern Dutch painter. He was the son of a marine painter also distinguished in art, and Bernard's surviving brothers, both good Dutch painters, make the name of Koekoek

---

* See Illustration.

a family name in Dutch art. Our painter was born at Middleburg, and ultimately resided at Cleves. As a landscape painter he was famous for his fidelity to nature, naïveté, and feeling. For a *Landscape in Autumn* and a *Wood Scene in Winter*, exhibited at the Universal Exhibition of 1855, Koekoek was awarded a first-class medal.

Of the other great names of Belgium and the Netherlands we may record PORTAELS, SELINGMEYER, JEAN VERHAS, FELIX COGEN, T. WEBER, BOSSUET, (whose view of *The Tiber at Rome* was at the Philadelphia Exhibition), WULFFAERT, GEMPT, (whose *Cat feigning death* was at the Philadelphia Exhibition, 1876), TEN-KATE, S. ALTMANN, HENRIETTA RONER, (whose *Last Hope* was at the Philadelphia Exhibition, 1876), BISCHOPP, MESDAG, PAUL WEBER and BARON WAPPERS.

ENGLAND.

Of the English School we must note OULESS, a young pupil of Millais, who already receives as much as $5,000 for a portrait; JOHN TENNEIL, the gifted artist of the Cartoons of Punch; R. ANSDELL, SIR FRANCIS GRANT, President of the Royal Academy; SIR JOHN GILBERT, ELMORE, EDWARD ARMITAGE, MRS. JOPLING, E. J. POYNTER, DOBSON, E. BURNE JONES, MCWHIRTER, R. W. MACBETH, PETTIE, CROWE, HERKOMER, FRANK HALL, S. LUKE FILDES, (whose *Casual Ward* caused such a sensation at the Philadelphia Centennial Exhibition); ORCHARDSON, SANT, PRINSEP, A. C. GOW, and RICHARD BEAVIS, CARL HAAG, C. W. COPE, ELIZABETH THOMPSON, (whose *Roll Call* was the sensation of the Academy years ago); VICAT COLE, HODGSON, HORSLEY, A. JOHNSTON, RIVIERE, ANSOLON, and the marine painters HAYES, COOKE, and DAWSON; all these painters are *giants*, and each deserving a chapter or more, but in this work it cannot be given. One notable circumstance is that very few of the paintings of the best English artists reach the shores of America. This has been variously attempted to be accounted for by the theory that French, Belgian, and German art has been more the fashion in America, but it is also said that Englishmen are very proud of their artists and almost invariably outbid the Americans who attempt to purchase from their favourites—to the latter theory we are rather inclined from facts which have come to our knowledge.

Art in England, notwithstanding the commercial depression, is in a very prosperous condition, and her school at the present moment is more glorious in talent than it ever was.

GERMANY.

H. RICHTER, is a professor and fellow of the Royal Academy of Berlin, and is probably one of the best known German artists in America. He is an artist of very decided ability, and among the highest, if not the highest, as a portrait painter. His poetic rendering of Oriental subjects is rich and highly prized. We have illustrated one of his earlier works, *The Tight Shoe;* * but the successful interpretation of "the pinch" is so eloquently set forth that we need not dwell on it, as it speaks for itself. Richter is still in his prime.

* See Steel Engraving.

LUDWIG KNAUS, also a professor of the Royal Academy of Berlin, was born at Düsseldorf. The humourous and pathetic are his specialties, witness his world-renowned pictures *In a Thousand Anxieties*, *A Country Funeral*, and *On the Heights*, in the Gallery of James L. Claghorn, Philadelphia. He also paints sacred subjects. *The Holy Family* is quite a success. His pictures are popular in America, and bring high prices.

FUERBACH and MAKART were both educated at Munich, and though the latter has achieved the greater reputation in America from his *Abundantia* and *Catherine Cornaro*, the former in the New York Metropolitan Museum, and the latter in the Austrian Department at Philadelphia Exhibition of 1876, yet Fuerbach's *Iphigenia at Aulis* is a superior composition, which we would rather have than the best of Makart's. Both artists are young, but promise to advance art in every way.

OSWALD and ANDREAS ACHENBACH, of the Düsseldorf school, have many of their fine landscapes and coast scenes in this country. VAUTIER is also a Düsseldorf artist and has come prominently forward recently with well executed *genre* subjects. A brilliant colourist and an excellent draughtsman of the Munich school, WILLIAM DIEZ, professor, is noted for his horses and landscapes; EDWARD GRÜTZNER for his interiors and sporting scenes, wine cellars and their visitors, a sort of refined HASSENCLEVER, and evidently a student of the great Düsseldorf painter.

STAMMEL, another of the present Düsseldorf school, whose excellent rendering of soldiers, has earned for him the title of the "German Meissonier," though he has far more natural jollity than the Frenchman. Many of his pictures are in America, bought years ago; but very few now leave Germany. We engrave one of his finely conceived, finely finished pictures, *The Connoisseur*.* His latest picture, *Hochheimer*, makes a beholder's lips water to behold it.

The Austrian division of the German school contains many able modern names—the result of the care the State bestows on art education—GABRIEL MAX, celebrated for his *Lion's Bride*, being among the chief. MUNKACSY, the Hungarian, with his grand historical successes, may be also called an Austrian.

MEYER VON BREMEN, who sprang from the Munich school, has so plentifully supplied the American market with his works, that we could tell of nearly thirty of his high-priced pictures here. He is a careful painter, choosing his subjects from every-day German peasant life, and deservedly popular.

FREDERICK CHARLES HAUSMANN, born at Hanau, near Frankfort, in 1825, holds an honourable place among German historical painters. His *Galileo before the Council of Constance*, exhibited, like Piloty's *Nero*, in the London Exhibition of 1862, won much admiration.

WINTERHALTER may be chronicled as a portrait painter, largely patronized by royal sitters. A native of Baden, he received his art education at Munich and Rome, and finally settled in Paris. He has painted the portraits of the leaders of two French dynasties, Louis Philippe and Queen Amalie, Napoleon III. and the Empress Eugénie, and he is well known in England as the painter, on more than one occasion, of the Queen, the Prince Consort, and the younger members of the royal family.

* See Illustration.

But the great leader of the modern naturalistic school in Germany is PILOTY of Munich, who in his energy and intensity of treatment is accused of coarseness, and, like the French artist Courbet, of a bizarre preference for uncouthness. Piloty exhibited his large picture of *Nero walking through the streets of Rome during the Burning of the City*, in the International Exhibition of 1861.

ADOLPH SHREYER, born at Frankfort-on-the-Main in 1829, is an animal painter of eminent excellence. Horses, wolves, dogs, sheep, goats, in all moods—happiness, fear, misery, or danger—are from his brush, like poetic realities. Many of his paintings have found their way to America, and bring good prices. We engrave his *Horses alarmed by Wolves*.*

We have only space to name among the remaining Germans of the present day as follows: C. BECKER, BODENMÜLLER, BRAITH, BRANDT, CAMPHAUSEN, DEFFREGGER, GEBHARDT, GUSSON, MENZEL, MÜLLER, MUNDT, NEUMAN, VOLTZ, WOLFF; these painters are all men who have achieved distinction, and are likely to increase that distinction.

RUSSIA.

In Russia there are promising artists, among them Moller, who exhibited in England in 1862.

H. SEMIRADSKY who exhibited his *Living Torches of Nero* at the Exhibition of Vienna, in 1873, and his *Amulet Seller* at Philadelphia in 1876, is another high example of what Russia is doing for painting.

NICHOLAS ZAGORSKY exhibited at Philadelphia more than one fine painting, notably the *Old Russian Couple*, on which an able art critic wrote as follows: "He is occupied in breaking lump sugar, from the original mass on the floor by his side, but for this purpose he uses the pinchers, with prongs terminating in balls. At his elbow sits his good wife at the *samovar*, whence she draws the family tea, not into cups but into tumblers.

"The cat awaits expectant, with a vigilance that would almost seem to be unspoiled by selfish aims, for the tea and sugar will not do her much good. It is a pretty piece of Darby and Joan life from the banks of the Neva."

SPAIN.

MARIANO FORTUNY, who was born at Barcelona about the year 1839, received his first instruction in art from a pupil of the great German master, Overbeck. He afterwards went to Madrid to study the works of Velazquez and Goya; but although he carefully examined the paintings of these masters, Fortuny never servilely copied them. In fact, his chief claim to renown as a painter is based on his originality. While in Madrid, he was commissioned by the Spanish Government to paint a repre-

---

* See Illustration.

sentation of the *Battle of Tetuan*; the price, 6000 francs, was to be paid on condition that the picture should equal the *Smala* of Horace Vernet. Soon after the completion of this picture, Fortuny visited Rome, and then went to Paris, where he soon became celebrated. Returning to the Papal capital, he died there in 1874, and was buried with much honour. In his own country, at Rome, and at Paris, Fortuny was very popular, and his works were much sought for; but in London, although several of his best pictures were exhibited, he scarcely met with the same success. We engrave his *Prayer in an Arabian Mosque*.*

EDUARDO ZAMACOIS, who was born in Bilbao, in the early half of the nineteenth century, studied painting under M. Meissonier. Many of his best pictures have been exhibited in the Paris Salon; two are especially worthy of mention, *Buffen au sixteenth Siècle*, exhibited in 1867, in which year he gained the medal of the society, and *L'éducation d'un Prince* in 1870. Zamacois died at Madrid on the 14th of January, 1874.

There are exhibiting at Paris in the present year, 1878, several Spanish painters of rare promise, chief among whom is Madrazo, equal to the best of any country's exhibit there; his *Coming out from the Ball* has created quite a stir in Paris.

TIDEMAND, a Norwegian landscape and genre painter, is a Knight of the Norwegian order of St. Olave's, and a member of the Academies at Berlin, Copenhagen, Stockholm, and Amsterdam. He finished his art studies at Düsseldorf. He paints the wild ffiords and primitive customs of his native country with such effect that by a picture, named *A Funeral in the Country parts of Norway, with Costumes of the Last Century*, exhibited at the Paris Universal Exhibition of 1855, he won a first-class medal. He is painter to the Crown, and has painted the interior of the Castle of Oscarshall, near Christiania.

In Sweden, Jernberg and Amelia Lindegren are able and accomplished painters.

In Denmark a good painter died in 1873. Vilhelm Marstrand was born in Copenhagen in 1810. He went while young to Rome, and worked there till 1841 in company with Thorwaldsen and a group of talented contemporaries. He became the first colourist among Scandinavian artists. His best pictures, some of which are mentioned as "bouquets of bright and sunny colour, dewy and sparkling," include *The Visit* (in the Danish National Gallery) illustrations of Don Quixote, and of the Comedies of Holberg, and *A Sunday at Lake Siljan*. Between 1864 and 1866 Marstrand was employed in painting the walls of the chapel of Christian IV., at Roeskilde Cathedral with frescoes, the subjects of which were taken from the heroic life of the Danish king.

Marstrand's successor in Danish art is Constantin Hansen, "the great realist," of whom Mr. Rossetti remarks that he is "one of the choicest painters of old interiors in Europe." Two of Hansen's best pictures are in the Gallery of Mr. Henry C. Gibson of Philadelphia.

J. E. C. RASMUSSEN, whose painting of the *Discovery of Greenland in the year A.D. 1000, by Red Erich*, was exhibited at Philadelphia in 1876, is now the foremost name in art in Denmark.

* See Illustration.

Another excellent Danish artist is Elizabeth Jerichau.

A. ANDERSEN, of Copenhagen, has a European reputation for winter landscapes.

C. ECKHARDT and H. J. HAMMER, of Copenhagen, exhibit coast marines of merit at the Paris Exhibition of 1878.

Besides RASMUSSEN in marine painting, may be mentioned BILLÉ, Professor SÖRENSEN, LOCHER and ANTON MELBY, who has been fitly named "the Stanfield of Scandinavia."

ITALY.

We recorded in the beginning of this work the history of the *renaissance* of art in Italy, and we close with a reference to the hope of another *renaissance* in Italy in our own time.

Since the days of Carlo Dolci which we have already indicated as marking the decline of Italian art, Italy has been as inert as though she had had no history, no traditions, examples or ambition.

But Italy, who has lived so long on the memories of her greatness, now that she is restored to unity and political existence, may see a renaissance in her art also. Of her recent painters, not copyists, PIETRO BENVENUTI—who died at Florence in 1844, and whose *Judith* at Arezzo, his *Head of our Saviour* in the cathedral at Sienna, and his cupola of the chapel of the Medici at Florence, painted with eight subjects taken from the Old and the New Testament, noble and pure, if cold, are not unworthy of Italian art—has been regarded as the chief painter of the modern Florentine school. USSI's *Expulsion of the Duke of Athens*, exhibited in London in 1862, received some praise. MORELLI's *Iconoclasts* Mr. Rossetti mentions as much admired in the Florentine Exhibition of 1861, but he finds it not above respectability as a work of art. He gives greater praise to three pen-and-ink designs from "Dante," by GOZZOTTO, and to the wonderful engraving by SCHAVONE from Titian's *Assumption*, as exhibited in London in 1862.

But in the exhibitions of Vienna in 1873, Philadelphia in 1876, and now in Paris in 1878, we have a glimpse and a hope of a restoration of her glory. With such landscapes as VERTUNIO's, and the dramatic subjects of GASTALDI and FARUFFINI, and the audacious colouring of the New Roman School (of which we may say that the Spaniard, Fortuny, was the founder) and BOLDINI, SIMONETTI, JORIS, and PASINI the present exponents.

REHO MICHES and ROBERT FONTANA of Milan, both exhibited at Philadelphia and Paris and have both received medals. Among other promising names we may record: BARTESAGO, BOMPIANI, CASTIGLIONI, CRESPI, DE NITTIS, and INDUNO. Whether Italy will, in the future, have another Raphael, Michael Angelo, Lionardi, or Titian among her sons,—who can tell?

The lesson which all the schools of Art, ancient and modern, should teach Americans, is so admirably summed up in Mr. Benjamin's recent work on "Contemporary Art in Europe," that we cannot do better than close with a quotation:

"If, therefore, we desire to see a worthy national school of art spring up in our land, let us first of all be true to ourselves. By all means let the study of foreign contemporary and ancient art be pursued; but the notion that our native methods and native ideas and culture can never equal those of the Old World should be frowned upon as not only unpatriotic, but unreasonable, until proved by a longer experience. What foreign or antique art had the Greeks to study when they produced the most perfect architecture and sculpture ever created? It is by depending upon their own native resources that the English, French, and German schools have ever achieved anything in art. It is by not being ashamed of home art that the governments and art patrons of Europe have given art the stimulus it required to raise it from a low, struggling condition, to the point where it has become a source of wealth to a people and a crown of glory."

ALEXANDER THE GREAT WEEPING OVER THE DYING DARIUS.
(From the original painting by Gustave Doré.)

DESCRIPTION OF THE STEEL AND WOOD ENGRAVINGS WHICH ILLUSTRATE THIS WORK.

FRONTISPIECE.—WILKIE'S *The Blind Fiddler,*

ILLUSTRATES a phase of life common in Scotland and Ireland fifty years ago. There were then certain privileged tramps who were looked upon as part of the social system of the rural districts—the shrewd gaberlunzie, as described by Scott in his "Eddie Ochiltree" in *The Antiquary;* the cripple who was carried from house to house —the last receiver being obliged to bestow alms and carry him or her (for there were cripples of both sexes), to the next neighbour, and so on. And the most welcome of them all (for the routine visits of those poor people was not looked upon as the nuisance which we in this country look upon the tramp), was the Blind Fiddler. He was not unfrequently accompanied by his wife, and, as in the case which Wilkie has painted, by his whole family, bag and baggage.

The Blind Fiddler brought his welcome with him in the Fiddle, which, by its dance-inspiring sounds, set lads and lasses capering as only country people can. Many an evening was thus made merry by the music of a fiddle, and young folks for miles around would gather to "shake a foot" to the music; and they were all kind to the blind man.

The painter has succeeded in immortalizing, in a happy manner, a very impressive picture of real life. The enthusiasm of the "guidman," who, snapping fingers to the tune, has worked the baby up to a tumult of unwonted hilarity; the appreciative audience which he has in the two bairns, who have deserted their play and stand spell-bound, drinking in the melody of sweet sound; the bye play of the "bad boy," who, secure in knowing that the fiddler is blind, mimics him to his face with tongs and bellows, to the evident delight of a maiden, who appreciates the humourist; the solid, business-like air of the fiddler's wife, who doubtless is thinking, not of the music, but of what the music will produce, all make up a picture of contrasts happy, skillful and unsurpassable.

MICHAEL ANGELO'S *The Cumean Sibyl.* (Page 2.)

There were, according to tradition, ten sibyls; the most famous was Almathea of Cumea, who offered her nine books to Tarquin the Proud. The offer was rejected; she burnt three of them, and after the lapse of twelve months, offered the remaining six at the same price. Again being refused she burnt three more, and after a similar interval asked the same price for the remaining three. The sum demanded was now given and the Cumean sibyl never made her appearance again.

The books referred to were Sibylline prophecies written in Greek upon palm leaves.

RAPHAEL'S *The Cartoons.* See description in the text, page 55. (Page 6.)

TITIAN'S *Daughter.* (Page 10.)

This ripe and blooming beauty, one of the four great portraits of the world, was doubtless a labour of love from Titian's easel; the other three great portraits are Raphael's Fornarina, Rubens' Straw Hat, and Lionardo's Joconde, all referred to in this work.

TERBURG'S *Refreshment.* (Page 14.)

It may be milk or water from the sober appearance of the pitcher, but the tell-tale glass suggests wine or even schnaps. However, her bedstead is not far to reach if it be the most potent "refreshment," and the lady's sober face does not suggest any habitual intemperance.

DÜRER'S *Samson and the Lion.* (Page 18.)

Judges xiv. 5th and 6th verses.—Then went Samson down, and his father and his mother, to Timnath, and came to the vineyards of Timnath : and behold, a young lion roared against him.

And the Spirit of the Lord came mightily upon him, and he rent him as he would have rent a kid, and he had nothing in his hand: but he told not his father or his mother what he had done.

BERGHEM'S *The Wayside Fountain.* (Page 22.)

A Dutch pastoral scene not requiring description.

RUBENS' *Descent from the Cross.* (Page 26.)

Luke xxiii. 50, 52 and 53.—And, behold, there was a man named Joseph, a counsellor; and he was a good man, and a just man.

This man went unto Pilate, and begged the body of Jesus.

And he took it down, and wrapped it in linen, and laid it in a sepulchre that was hewn in stone, wherein never man before was laid.

WEST'S *Healing the Sick.* (Page 30.)

Matthew xix. 1 and 2.—And it came to pass, that when Jesus had finished these sayings, he departed from Galilee, and came into the coasts of Judæa beyond Jordan; And great multitudes followed him; and he healed them there.

REMBRANDT'S *Adolphus Threatening his Father the Duke de Guildre*. (Page 34.)
Adolphus, impatient at his father's longevity, accused him falsely to the government and was awarded his estates. Adolphus then proceeded to prison and reviled and menaced his father, whereupon the judges reversed their decision.—*History of the Netherlands, 1450.*

TRUMBULL'S *The Declaration of Independence*. (Page 38.)
On the 4th of July, the Congress at Philadelphia agreed on a Declaration of Independence, thereby absolving the colonies from every allegiance to the crown of England. The motion for this purpose first made on the 7th of June by Richard Henry Lee, of Virginia, and seconded by John Adams, of Massachusetts, in conformity with the particular instruction of their constituents and the general voice of all the States, was decided by an almost unanimous vote.—*American History*.

CARAVAGGIO'S *Card-Players*. (Page 42.)
The poor lad who thinks he can play cards, and unaware of the cheats likely to be met with in the game, sits innocently studying his best to play his hand well, whilst his opponent is being made aware of the contents of the youth's hand, by a series of signals from a confederate, thus enabling the cheat to win the game from his unsuspecting victim.

REYNOLDS' *Coquette*. (Page 46.)
A painting in the Royal collection at Windsor is a fine piece of portrait painting, though we cannot see much coquetry in the high-bred, lady-like face before us.

THE SECOND PLATE IN HOGARTH'S SERIES OF *Marriage a la Mode*. (See page 50.)
This represents a Reception Room in the young nobleman's house, not long after the breaking up of a party. The clock shows us it is noon. We are to suppose, then, by the candles being still burning, that the day has been shut out, and converted into night—a circumstance not a little characteristic of the irregularity and disorder that reigns within the house—and that, after an hour or two's sleep, madam is just risen to breakfast; whose rising has occasioned that of the family in general. This is intimated by one of the servants in the background of this picture, who, we are to understand, though scarce awake, has hurried on his clothes, in order to set the house, in some measure, to rights. By the treatise of Hoyle's Games upon the floor, we are taught the idle study of people of distinction. With respect to the attitudes of the two principal figures, the fineness of the thought, and the particular exactness of the expressions, they must be allowed to be extremely beautiful. They are, at the same time, well introduced, as from the indifference that gives rise to them springs the destruction of this unhappy family. On the one hand, we are to suppose the lady totally neglected by her husband; on the other, by way of contrast, that the husband is just returned from the apartments of some woman, fatigued, exhausted and satiated. And as pleasures of this sort are seldom without interruption, we are shown, by the female cap in his pocket, and his broken sword, that he has been engaged in some

riot or uproar. An old, faithful steward, who has a regard for the family, seems to have taken this opportunity (not being able to find a better,) to settle his accounts; but the general disorder of the family, and the indisposition of his master and mistress, render it impossible. See him, then, returning in an attitude of concern, dreading the approaching ruin of them both. As a satire on the extravagance of the nobility, Mr. Hogarth has humourously put into this man's hands a number of unpaid bills, and placed upon the file only one receipt, intimating the general bad pay of people of quality.

Led, then, from one act of dissipation to another, the hero of this piece meets his destruction in hunting after pleasure. Little does he imagine what misery awaits him, and what dreadful consequences will be the result of his proceedings; but, determined to embrace the trifling happiness in view, he runs heedlessly on in his dissipated career, until he seals his unhappy fate.

It has been justly remarked, that "the figure of the young libertine, who, on his return home from his debaucheries, after daybreak, has thrown himself into a chair, is so admirable for its attitude, expression, drawing and colouring, as alone utterly to refute the assertion of Lord Oxford, that Hogarth, however great as an author or inventor, possessed as a painter but little merit."

GAINSBOROUGH'S *The Village Beau*. (Page 54.)

Is another of those episodes of every-day life which can be comprehended without a word of explanation, whether in America, Europe, Asia, or Africa. Under certain circumstances like those before us, "Two's company and three's none;" or rather as Gay puts it from the mouth of Captain Macheath in the Beggar's Opera:

> "How happy I could be with either
> Were the t'other dear charmer away."

The landscape is in Gainsborough's best style, and the two dogs are introduced to illustrate what is passing in the rural girls' minds, for the dogs are saying as plainly as dogs can look, "what are you doing here?"

HAYDON'S *Quintus Curtius*. (Page 58.)

The Roman legend which the painter Haydon has illustrated, is dated 362 B. C., and tells how a gulf suddenly appeared in the forum, according to one account, riven by a thunderbolt,—and the oracle declared that it would never close till what was dearest to Rome was thrown therein. At this announcement a noble youth, Quintus Curtius, came forward, declaring that her citizens were the most valuable possessions of the city; and, armed and on horseback, he leapt into the chasm, which forthwith closed over his head.

> "In the proud forum's central space
> Earth yawned a gulf profound,
> And then, with awe on every face,
> Rome's bravest gathered round;
> Each seeming, yet with startled ear,
> The oracle's dread voice to hear.

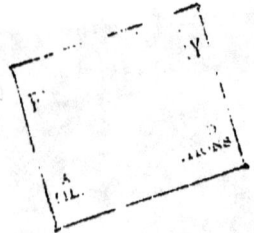

> Young Curtius on his war-horse sprung,
> 'Mid plaudits deep—not loud,
> For admiration checked each tongue
> In all the circling crowd;—
> He gave his noble steed the rein—
> Earth's closing gulf entombed the twain."

LESLIE'S *Taming of the Shrew*, Act iv., Scene 3. (Page 62.)

> *Petruchio;* Thy gown? Why ay:—come, tailor, let us see't!
> Oh mercy, God, what masking stuff is here!
> What's this? a sleeve? 'tis like a demi-cannon.
> What up and down, carved like an apple-tart?
> Here's snip and nip, and cut, and slish, and slash,
> Like to a censer in a barber's shop?
> Why, what, o' devil's name, call'st thou this?

CONSTABLE'S *Wheatfield*. (Page 66.)

A delicious English landscape, suggestive of shady lanes and rural retreats.

DELAROCHE'S *The Young Princes in the Tower*. For description see page 160. (Page 70.)

TURNER'S *Wreck of the Minotaur*. (Page 74.)

> At half-past eight o'clock, booms, hen-coops, spars,
> And all things, for a chance, had been cast loose
> That still could keep afloat the struggling tars,
> For yet they strove, although of no great use;
> There was no light in heaven but a few stars.
> The boats put off o'ercrowded with their crews;
> She gave a heel, and then a lurch to port,
> And, going down head foremost—sunk, in short.
>
> Then rose from sea to sky the wild farewell,—
> Then shrieked the timid, and stood still the brave,—
> Then some leaped overboard with dreadful yell,
> As eager to anticipate their grave;
> And the sea yawned around her like a hell,
> And down she sucked with her the whirling wave,
> Like one who grapples with his enemy,
> And strives to strangle him before he die.
>
> And first one universal shriek there rushed,
> Louder than the loud ocean, like a crash
> Of echoing thunder; and then all was hushed,
> Save the wild wind and the remorseless dash
> Of billows; but at intervals there gushed,
> Accompanied with a convulsive splash,
> A voluntary shriek, the bubbling cry
> Of some strong swimmer in his agony.—*Byron.*

WHITE'S *General Marion and the British Officer.* (Page 78.)

A British officer, having been sent from Georgetown, to negotiate an exchange of prisoners, was conducted into Marion's encampment. When the business was concluded, the officer took up his hat to retire——"Oh no!" said Marion, "it is now our time for dining; and I hope, Sir, you will give us the pleasure of your company to dinner." On mention of the word dinner, the British officer looked around him, but could see no indications of preparation. "Come, Tom," said the General to one of his men, "give us our dinner." The dinner to which he alluded was no other than a few sweet potatoes roasting under the embers, and which Tom, with his pine stick soon drew from their concealment, then having cleansed them from the ashes, partly by blowing them, and partly by brushing them with the sleeve of his old cotton shirt, he placed them before the General and the British officer.

FAED'S *Jeanie Deans and the Duke of Argyle.* (Page 82.)

"It was the other paper, sir," said Jeanie, somewhat abashed at the mistake.

"O, this is my unfortunate grandfather's hand, sure enough—'To all who may have friendship for the house of Argyle, these are to certify that Benjamin Butler, of Monk's regiment dragoons, of having been, under God, the means of saving my life from four English troopers who were about to slay me, I, having no other present means of recompense in my power, do give him this acknowledgment, hoping that it may be useful to him or his, during these troublesome times; and do conjure my friends, tenants, kinsmen, and whoever will do aught for me, either in the Highlands or Lowlands, to protect and assist the said Benjamin Butler and his friends or family, on their lawful occasions, giving them such countenance, maintenance, and supply, as may correspond with the benefit he hath bestowed on me; witness my hand, 'LORNE.'

"This is a strong injunction. This Benjamin Butler was your grandfather, I suppose? You seem too young to have been his daughter."

"He was nae akin to me, sir,—he was grandfather to ane—to a neighbour's son—to a sincere weel-wisher of mine, sir," dropping her little courtesy as she spoke.

"O, I understand," said the Duke, "a true-love affair. He was the grandsire of one you are engaged to?"

"One I was engaged to, sir," said Jeanie, sighing, "but this unhappy business of my poor sister—"

"What!" said the Duke, hastily,—"he has not deserted you on that account, has he?"

"No, sir; he wad be the last to leave a friend in difficulties," said Jeanie; "but I maun think for him, as weel as for mysel. He is a clergyman, sir, and it would not beseem him to marry the like of me, wi' this disgrace on my kindred."

"You are a singular young woman," said the Duke. "You seem to think of everyone before yourself. And have you really come up from Edinburgh on foot to attempt this hopeless solicitation for your sister's life?"

MOUNT'S *Noonday Rest.* (Page 86.)

"Sweet is rest after labour," and the dinner hour to the labourer is especially a sweet season for a brief *siesta.* The painter with a spirit of fun, for which he was noted, worthy of Wilkie, has introduced a boy full of mischief who tickles the sleeping negro's nose with a straw; the landscape is well painted, and the whole keeping of the picture is farm-like and rural.

CHALON'S *Hunt the Slipper.* (Page 90.)

The picture is "of high-born dames and courtly cavaliers," and the surroundings bespeak "wealth and pomp and palaces," but the game of Hunt the Slipper is as well known in the peasant's hut as in the baron's castle. But for the presence of the host and hostess and their grandchild, we could imagine the whole scene from the pages of Boccaccio.

SCHUESSELE'S *Daniel Webster at Stratford-on-Avon.* (Page 94.)

This is a good portrait of the great orator and statesman visiting the grave of the great poet.

ROBERTS' *Interior of the Greek Church, Constantinople.* (Page 98.)

The subjects of the Sultan number many Greeks, hence the policy of freedom of Christian worship in the very metropolis of Mahometanism. The church of our picture is one noted for its splendour, and Roberts has done his subject justice.

BURNETT'S *The Dancing Dolls.* (Page 102.)

Simple and home-like. A little Italian boy, with puppets, has "struck luck," in finding a grandfather and grandmother entertaining two grandchildren. Delight is universal, with the exception of a little girl at the window, who cannot see so well as her selfish brother, who has secured the best place for a stolen view.

JOHN LINNEL'S *Sunshine.* (Page 106.)

A fine English landscape. Warm, cloudy and sunshiny, as fine days in England are.

SULLY'S *Bed-Fellows.* (See page 110.)

"In my dim, fire-lighted chamber,
　Pussy purrs beneath my chair,
And my play-worn boy beside me
　Kneels to say his evening prayer;
　　*　　*　　*　　*　　*　　*
He is sleeping; soft and silken
　Lie the lashes long and meek,
Like caressing, clinging shadows
　O'er his plump and peachy cheek,
And I'm sitting silent weeping
　Thankful tears, oh!—undefiled—
For a mother's crown of glory,
　For the blessing of a child."

BIRKET FOSTER'S *The Race up the Hill.* (Page 114.)

Oh dear! and will the baby get first to the winning post? What a labour of love, and what a lovely scene!

Fleecy clouds, green fields and leafy woods; heath on the hill and flowers in among the bushes; white sheep dotting the gowany sward. The children have brought their dinner with them for a day's enjoyment—and they'll have it you may rest assured.

INGRES' *The Slave and her Slave.* (Page 118.)

Her hair's long auburn waves down to her heel
    Flowed like an Alpine torrent which the sun
Dyes with his morning light,—and would conceal
    Her person if allowed at large to run,
And still they seem resentfully to feel
    The silken fillet's curb, and sought to shun
Their bonds whene'er some Zephyr caught began
To offer his young pinion as her fan.

Round her she made an atmosphere of life,
    The very air seemed lighter from her eyes,
They were so soft, and beautiful, and rife
    With all we can imagine of the skies,
And pure as Psyche ere she grew a wife—
    Too pure even for the purest human ties;
Her overpowering presence made you feel
It would not be idolatry to kneel.—*Byron.*

BURR'S *The Peddler.* (Page 122.)

The scene represents one of those picturesque wayside cottages which are to be found all over England and Scotland. The peddler has called with his basket of wares; the mother is interested in a substantial earthenware dish, whilst the child points to some toys which she would like to have. The peddler, meanwhile, is holding forth in a general way on the cheapness of his merchandise.

FRITH'S *The Beau's Stratagem.* (Page 126.)

"Oh! love will venture in
    Where he daurna weel be seen."

So sang Robert Burns a hundred years ago, and so we may sing now, and a hundred years hence. The letter fixed on the arrow bespeaks a bowman not very far away, the startled look of the *duenna* betokens her surprise, while the quiet, puzzled look of the young lady shows that she knows all about it, and what is passing in her mind is how to get the letter before the old lady recovers from her surprise.

It is the old, old story, and a fine illustration of "Where there's a will there's a way."

DAVID'S *The Death of Socrates.* (Page 130.)

The servant of the Eleven entered at the same instant, and, having informed him that the time for drinking the hemlock was come (which was at sunset), the servant was so much affected with sorrow, that he turned his back and fell a-weeping.

A PAUSE IN THE ARGUMENT.

AT THE SEA-SHORE.
(From the original painting by M. Kemmerer.)

"See," said Socrates, "the good disposition of this man! Since my imprisonment he has often come to see me and to converse with me. He is more worthy than all his fellows. How heartily the poor man weeps for me!" This is a remarkable example, and might teach those in an office of this kind how they ought to behave to all prisoners, but more especially to persons of merit, if at any time they should happen to fall into their hands. The fatal cup was brought. Socrates asked what it was necessary for him to do. "Nothing more," replied the servant, "than as soon as you have drunk off the draught to walk about till you find your legs grow weary, and afterwards lie down upon your bed." He took the cup without any emotion or change in his colour or countenance, and, regarding the man with a firm and steady look, "Well," said he, "what say you of this drink; may one make a libation out of it?" Upon being told that there was only enough for one dose: "At least," continued he, "we may say our prayers to the gods, as it is our duty, and implore them to, make our exit from this world and our last stage happy; which is what I most ardently beg of them." After having spoken these words he kept silence for some time, and then drank off the whole draught with an amazing tranquility and a serenity of aspect not to be expressed or conceived.

*   *   *   *   *   *

In the meantime he kept walking to and fro, and when he felt his legs grow weary, he laid down upon his back, as he had been directed. The poison then operated more and more. When Socrates found it began to gain on the heart, uncovering his face, which had been covered without doubt to prevent anything from disturbing him in his last moments, "Crito," said he,—which were his last words,—"we owe a cock to Æsculapius; discharge that vow for me, and pray don't forget it;" soon after which he breathed his last. Crito drew near and closed his mouth and eyes. Such was the end of Socrates; in the first year of the 95th Olympiad, and the seventieth of his age. Cicero says he could never read the description of his death in Plato without tears.—*Plutarch's Lives.*

WILLIAM COLLINS' *Old Farm Gate.* (Page 134.)

'Twas here that the urchins would gather to play
In the shadows of twilight, or sunny mid-day,
For the stream running nigh and the hillocks of sand,
Were temptations no dirt-loving rogue could withstand;
But to swing on the gate rails, to clamber and ride
Was the utmost of pleasure, of glory, and pride;
And the car of the victor, or carriage of state,
Never carried such hearts as that old farm gate.

SCHEFFER'S *Temptation.* St. Luke iv. 5, 6, 7. (Page 138.)

5. And the devil, taking him up into an high mountain, shewed unto him all the kingdoms of the world in a moment of time.

6. And the devil said unto him, All this power will I give thee, and the glory of them: for that is delivered unto me; and to whomsoever I will I give it.

7. If thou wilt therefore worship me, all shall be thine.

8. And Jesus answered and said unto him, Get thee behind me, Satan: for it is written, Thou shalt worship the Lord thy God, and him only shalt thou serve.

CALLCOTT'S *Crossing the Stream*. (Page 142.)

This picture is a lovely landscape which requires no commentary; the landscape is a lovely one, common to England.

FORTUNY'S *Prayer in an Arabian Mosque*. (Page 146.)

Fortuny has a more cleanly subject to deal with than Gerome, giving good opportunity for his great display of colour; the Arab on his gorgeous mat, and his weapons, guns, sword and pistols, bristling like a walking arsenal—only think; this man is lifting his voice in prayer to "the Prince of Peace."

TSCHAGGENNY'S *The Cow Doctor*. (Page 150.)

Tells its own story. The Doctor is evidently on his rounds and has made a central farm-house his rendezvous, as the departing man and cow seen in the picture would indicate that the cow has been brought to the Doctor, not the Doctor to the cow. His cavalier air and fine clothes, and the traveling trunk, behind him, from which his boy is taking out medicines, all bespeak the itinerant.

The cow looks sick enough, poor beast! and the anxiety of the old couple who have brought her for prescription, could not be more intense if the life of a child were in question, in place of a cow; and who knows, perhaps to them the cow was as important in all results as the child would have been?

We hope however that the Doctor's confident air, which seems to say, "we'll soon set that all to rights," is not assumed, but that his medicine will set "crummie" all right.

LEWIS' *Arab Scribe*. (Page 154.)

Nobody in the Arab social circle is more powerful or important than the Scribe. Where few are so educated as to be able to write, it can easily be conceived how many secrets such a position implies. He must be the confidant of all the lovers, and all distant relatives must correspond through him. In the present instance he seems occupied on a love-letter for the swarthy beauties by his side.

JAMES HART'S *A Watering Place*. (Page 158.)

Is a scene in the neighbourhood of West Chester, but it would be equally pleasing as a natural pastoral scene were we to say it was in Holland, or Germany, or Scotland.

BARON LEYS' *Luther Singing in the Streets of Eisenach*. (Page 162.)

In his boyhood, Luther developed a capacity and a passion for music, and being of a magnetic character drew around him many enthusiastic companions. It is recorded in his biography, that he was wont to make an occasional tour of the streets of his native town Eisenach, in company with his musical comrades, and, as leader, delight the good burghers with his vocal accomplishment, in a manner equally novel and pleasing.

DESCRIPTION OF STEEL AND WOOD ENGRAVINGS.

NICOL'S *Kept In*. (Page 166.)

We may suppose that "we have all been there," and the picture will explain itself, each beholder making allowance for change of scene. This scene is in Ireland, and the same class schoolmasters and boys are there to-day.

GÉRÔME'S *Begging Monk at the Door of a Mosque*. (Page 170.)

The shoes left outside indicate the oriental custom referred to in the New Testament, "Take thy shoes from off thy feet, for the place whereon thou standest is holy ground." The worshipers in the mosque are on "holy ground." As regards "the monk" and his scant attire and unwholesome look, we would remark, as an Englishman said of a similar object, "he is a very disagreeable party."

TAYLOR'S *The Young Chief's First Ride*. (Page 174.)

Mounted on his Shetland pony, and accompanied by his father's plaided retainer and dogs, the young chief of a Highland clan has been gratified with his first ride.

The scene is a heathery, mossy moor, of the north of Scotland, and it is impossible to tell which is the most sagacious or careful, the great stag hound or the faithful game-keeper.

The delight of the young chief is successfully expressed, and as a model of happy childhood his face is a picture to behold and remember! and the coupled pair of Skye terriers, evidently his daily companions, are as much excited over the event as if they were to have the next ride.

ROSENTHAL'S *Elaine*. (Page 178.)

So those two brethren from the chariot took,
And on the black decks laid her in her bed,
Set in her hand a lily, o'er her hung
The silken case with braided blazonings,
And kiss'd her quiet brows, and saying to her
"Sister, farewell for ever," and again,
"Farewell, sweet sister," parted all in tears.

And the dead,
Oar'd by the dumb, went upward with the flood—
In her right hand the lily, in her left
The letter—all her bright hair streaming down—
And all the coverlid was cloth of gold
Drawn to her waist, and she herself in white
All but her face, and that clear-featured face
Was lovely, for she did not seem as dead,
But fast asleep, and lay as tho' she smiled.—*Tennyson.*

NOTE.—This picture is owned by Mrs. Johnson, of San Francisco.

LANDSEER'S *Caught*. (Page 182.)

Explains itself. Cats are fond of fish, and pussy has evidently meant to help herself, but her paw has got in a tight place—in the live lobster's claw. We can almost hear pussy's w–e–u–y!! and the hist! hist! w–e–u–y–y–y–y!!! as her starting eyeballs plainly show she is exclaiming; a tight place indeed!

BRETON'S *Eve of St. John's Day.* (Page 186.)

A curious custom prevalent in Ireland and the west coast of France and Portugal, is the custom illustrated in the Eve of St. John's Day. It may have originally been connected with the Druidical rites of Midsummer night, 22d of June, (being on the 27th of June, 5 days later) the custom is so old that the origin is lost in obscurity. The dance is only of maidens, and none but maidens dare join in the dance—so the superstition runs.

BELLANGE'S *The Old Soldier and his Family.* (Page 190.)

Safe and far from war's alarms, the old soldier has aroused within him a memory of former stirring times by the military wares of an Italian image boy. The pretty cottage, with its happy surroundings of wife and children, are skillfully contrasted with the scenes which are so easily to be seen passing before the backward-turned memory of the old soldier, who stands poseing the model of some old commander, and doubtless thinking of days of peril passed and comrades slain. His wife, with no such thoughts to disturb her, thinks, "Will they please the children?"

STAMMEL'S *The Connoisseur.* (Page 194.)

"In sooth a prosperous gentleman," and with tastes and education to correspond with his fortunate position, he has surrounded himself with every luxury and many articles of beauty, as the surest means of begetting a due regard for the ingenuity of his fellow-men.

In the picture he is evidently engaged in the scrutiny of a new purchase, either accomplished or contemplated, and we cannot doubt from his unmistakably pleased look that his verdict is favourable.

ALLOM'S *Constantinople.* (Page 198.)

* * * * * * * * *

Nor oft I've seen such sight, nor heard such song,
As wooed the eye, and thrilled the Bosphorus along.

Loud was the lightsome tumult on the shore,
   Oft Music changed, but never ceased her tone,
And timely echoed back the measured oar,
   And rippling waters made a pleasant moan;
The Queen of tides on high consenting shone,
   And when a transient breeze swept o'er the wave,
'Twas, as if darting from her heavenly throne,
   A brighter glance her form reflected gave,
Till sparkling billows seemed to light the banks they lave.—*Byron.*

[Of Constantinople, Byron says:—"I have seen the ruins of Athens, of Ephesus, and Delphi; I have traversed a great part of Turkey, and many other parts of Europe, and some of Asia; but I never beheld a work of nature or art which yielded an impression like the prospect on each side, from the Seven Towers to the end of the Golden Horn."]

DESCRIPTION OF STEEL AND WOOD ENGRAVINGS.

BOUGHTON'S *The Departure of the Mayflower.* (Page 202.)

    Long in silence they watched the receding sail of the vessel,
Much endeared to them all, as something living and human;
Then, as if filled with the spirit, and wrapt in a vision prophetic,
Baring his hoary head, the excellent Elder of Plymouth
Said, "Let us pray!" and they prayed and thanked the Lord and took courage.
Mournfully sobbed the waves at the base of the rock, and above them
Bowed and whispered the wheat on the hill of death, and their kindred
Seemed to awake in their graves, and to join in the prayer that they uttered.
Sun-illumined and white, on the eastern verge of the ocean,
Gleamed the departing sail, like a marble slab in a graveyard;
Buried beneath it lay forever all hope of escaping.
Lo! as they turned to depart, they saw the form of an Indian,
Watching them from the hill; but while they spake with each other,
Pointing with outstretched hands, and saying, "Look!" he had vanished.
So they returned to their homes; but Alden lingered a little,
Musing alone on the shore, and watching the wash of the billows
Round the base of the rock, and the sparkle and flash of the sunshine,
Like the spirit of God, moving visibly over the waters.

    Thus for a while he stood, and mused by the shore of the ocean,
Thinking of many things, and most of all of Priscilla;
And as if thought had the power to draw to itself, like the loadstone,
Whatsoever it touches, by subtle laws of its nature;
Lo! as he turned to depart, Priscilla was standing beside him.—*Longfellow.*

NOTE.—This painting is owned by Mr. Fairman Rogers of Philadelphia.

ROTHERMEL'S *January and May.* (Page 206.)

This picture illustrates the every day misalliance of youth and age—an old man and a young wife, which too frequently brings dissatisfaction to both.

Poets and painters have made this their favourite subject since the days of Chaucer, and long before then. We need not comment further on what is, after all, a matter of taste.

SCHREYER'S *Horses Alarmed by Wolves.* (Page 210.)

This is an admirable picture. The fine drawing of the animals, the terror of the horses so well depicted, the stealthy action of the wolves, and the dreary outlook of the landscape, and the miserable corral into which the horses have crowded, all combine in rendering the feeling of insecurity intense, which is the skilful artist's premeditated aim.

COMPTE-CALIX'S *Youth and Age.* (Page 214.)

"She grieves to think she may be burdensome
  Now feeble, old and tottering to the tomb."
"Oh hear me Heaven! and record my vow.
  Its non-performance let thy wrath pursue.
  I swear, of what thy providence may give
  My mother shall her due maintenance have.

> 'Twas hers to guide me through life's early day,
> To point out virtue's path and lead the way.
> Now, while her powers in frigid languor sleep,
> 'Tis mine to hand her down life's rugged steep;
> With all her little weaknesses to bear
> Attentive, kind, to soothe her every care.
> 'Tis Nature bids, and truest pleasure flows
> From lessening an aged parent's woes."

CABANEL'S *Annunciation*. (Page 218.)

Luke ii. 8–14.—And there were in the same country shepherds abiding in the field, keeping watch over their flock by night.

And, lo, the angel of the Lord came upon them, and the glory of the Lord shone round about them: and they were sore afraid.

And the angel said unto them, Fear not: for, behold, I bring you good tidings of great joy, which shall be to all people.

For unto you is born this day in the city of David a Saviour, which is Christ the Lord.

And this shall be a sign unto you: Ye shall find the babe wrapped in swaddling clothes, lying in a manger.

SCHOPIN'S *Paul and Virginia*. (Page 222.)

"Scarcely had they risen from prayer when they heard the barking of a dog. It is, said Paul, a dog belonging to some hunter, who comes at night to this lone place to lie in wait for the stags. Shortly they heard the dog bark louder. 'I think,' said Virginia, 'that is Fidele, our own dog. I surely recollect his voice. Can we be so near home, at the foot of our own mountain?' In an instant Fidele was at their feet, barking, howling, and almost overwhelming them with his caresses. They had not recovered from their surprise when they saw Domingo running towards them. At the sight of the good old negro, they were too much overcome to utter a word."—*Paul and Virginia*.

DORÉ'S *The Death of Darius*. (Page 226.)

After the battle of Issus, Darius'—king of the Persians—camp was plundered, and his wife, mother and children fell into the hands of Alexander, who treated them with the utmost consideration and care. Now that Susa, Persepolis and all his treasures had gone into the possession of the conqueror, Darius took refuge in Ecbatana, but was seized by Bessus, the governor of Bactria, who betrayed him in his misfortunes. Both the traitor and his prisoner fled before the march of Alexander, who hastened the pursuit till he came in sight of them, when they fled precipitately; and because Darius would not follow them, Bessus and those about him discharged their darts at him, and left him covered with blood at the mercy of the Macedonian. Alexander himself came up soon afterwards, and was much affected at seeing the king in such a deplorable state. He took off his own cloak and spread it over Darius, and when he died ordered the body to be embalmed and sent in a splendid coffin to Sisigambia, to be interred with the other monarchs of Persia.—*Plutarch's Lives*.

DESCRIPTION OF STEEL AND WOOD ENGRAVINGS.

RICHTER's *The Tight Shoe.* See text, page 221. (Page 230.)

J. T. LEWIS' *Scene on the Schuylkill below Grey's Ferry.* (Page 230.)

Before the Schuylkill joins the Delaware, the Schuylkill widens to noble proportions, and although not nearly so much frequented as above the Fairmount Dam, is often the resort of pleasure parties who wish to avoid a crowd.

LEO HERMANN's *A Pause in the Argument.* (Page 234.)

The discussion on some obscure point of theology, or it may be some question of politics has occupied the two priests for some time, and like armies in battle, they have declared a truce for a few minutes and exchange a pinch of snuff—"friends by their noses." The distant tower of the "Invalides" bespeaks the locality to be Paris which their clerical costume confirms.

KAEMMERER's *At the Seashore.* (Page 234.)

Where the sea waves ripple to the shore, and the air scene is charged with a *dolce far niente* feeling. The rich costumes of the ladies and the general impression of rest imparted by the whole scene, make it a picture fit to calm the nerves of the excited, or lull to peace the unduly disturbed. The scene is at *Boulogne sur mer* on the French coast.

MEISSONIER's *Flute-Player.* (Page 234.)

Needs no commentary. The "toot," "toot," of the flute-player is not a theme for eloquent description, but the correct drawing of the master Meissonier is simple and admirable.

INDEX.

	PAGE.
Ansolon, J.	221
Achenbach, A.,	221
Achenbach, O.,	222
Allan, David,	180
Allan, William,	182
Allegri, Antonio,	63
Allom, Thomas,	188
Allston, Washington,	195
Altmann, S.,	221
Andrea del Sarto,	41
Angelico, Fra,	29
Angelo, Michael,	48
Ansdell, R.,	221
Antigna, J. P. A.,	219
Appian,	219
Apelles,	9
Apollodorus,	6
Armand, Dumaresque,	219
Armytage, Edward,	221
Aristides,	9
Asclepiodorus,	10
Athenion,	8
Audubon, John J.,	199
Ayala, Bernabe de,	98
Barbarelli, Giorgio,	62
Baron, H. C. A.,	219
Barrias, Felix,	219
Barry, James,	135
Bartesago, E.	225

	PAGE.
Bartolommeo, Fra,	40
Bayard, A. E.,	219
Baudry, Paul,	219
Beard, J. K.,	204
Beavis, R.,	221
Becker, A. von,	219
Becker, Carl,	223
Bellangé, Jh. H.	163
Bellini, Gentile,	34
Bellini, Giovanni,	34
Bellini, Jacopo,	34
Belly, L. A. A.,	219
Bellows, A. F.,	203
Benvenuti, A.,	225
Berchem, (Claas), or Nicholas Berghem,	87
Berne—Bellecour,	219
Bida, Alex.,	219
Bierstadt, A.,	208
Billé,	225
Billings, A.,	211
Bischopp, H. C.,	221
Blake, William,	136
Bodenmüller,	223
Boldini, A.,	225
Bompiani, R.,	225
Bonfield, G. R.,	202
Bonnat, L.,	217
Bonheur, Rosa,	217
Bougereau, W.,	219
Bossuet, F. A.,	221

242

INDEX.

	PAGE
Boughton, G. H.,	205
Boulanger, G. R.,	219
Bracket, W.,	211
Braith,	223
Brandt,	223
Breton, J. A.,	215
Breughel, Jan,	82
Breughel, Pieter (the elder),	82
Breughel, Pieter (the younger),	82
Bridgeman, F. A.,	211
Briscoe, Frank,	202
Browne, H.,	218
Brown, J. G.,	211
Brown, J. L.,	219
Brown, G. L.,	210
Buonarroti, Michaelangelo,	48
Burnet, John,	174
Burr, John,	190
CABANEL, A.,	215
Cagliari, Paolo,	65
Callcott, A. W.,	171
Callot, Jacques,	107
Canaletto, (Antonio Canal),	120
Cano, Alonso,	98
Caravaggio, Mich. da,	71
Carracci, Agostino,	68
Carracci, Annibale,	68
Carracci, Lodovico,	67
Casilear, J. W.,	204
Castiglioni, G.,	225
Chalon,	172
Champhausen,	223
Champney,	211
Chapman,	210
Chaplin, G.,	219
Chintreuil, A.,	218
Church, Fred. E.,	207
Cimabue,	23
Claas, Nicholas (Berchem),	87
Claude Lorraine,	105
Claudius Pulcher,	13
Cogen, Felix,	221

	PAGE
Coello, Alonzo,	100
Cole, Vicat,	221
Cole, Thomas,	200
Coleman, C. C.,	211
Collins, William,	179
Cott, P. A.,	219
Comte, P. C.,	219
Compte, Calix, F. C.,	215
Constable, John,	151
Cooke, E. W.,	221
Cope, C. W.,	221
Cornelius, Peter von,	166
Corot, Jean Camille,	218
Correggio, (Allegri),	63
Cortona, Pietro da,	36
Courbet, Gustave,	214
Cox, David,	152
Crespi,	225
Creswick, Thomas,	190
Cropsey,	209
Cruikshank, Geo.,	187
Curzon,	219
Cuyp, Albert,	83
DAUBIGNY, C. F.,	218
David, Louis,	154
Dawson,	221
De Heem,	83
Deffregger,	223
Decamps, A. G.,	163
De Crano, F. F.,	211
De Haas,	211
De Keyser, N.,	219
Delaroche, Paul,	158
Delacroix, Eugène,	157
Defaux,	218
Diez,	222
De Neuville,	219
De Nittis, J.	225
Detaille,	219
Diaz de la Pina,	218
Dionysius, (of Colophon),	4
Dionysius, (of Rome),	13
Dobson, W. T. C.,	221

INDEX.

	PAGE.	
Dolci, Carlo,	73	Gavarni,
Domenichino, (Zampieri),	69	Gastaldi,
Doré, P. G.,	216	Gebhardt,
Dou, Gerard (or Dow),	86	Gelée, Claude,
Dubufe, Claude M.,	219	Gempt, B.te.,
Duran, Carolus,	219	Gérôme, J. L.,
Dürer, Albrecht,	60	Géricault, J. L. T. A.,
Dyce, William,	171	Ghiberti, Lorenzo,
		Ghirlandajo, (Corradi),
EAKINS, T.,	211	Gibbons, Grinling,
Eckhardt,	225	Gifford, R. S.,
Elliot, Charles L.,	201	Giorgione, (Barbarelli),
Elmore, A.,	221	Giotto,
Etty, William,	150	Gilbert, John,
Eupompus,	6	Goupil, Jules,
Euphranor,	7	Gow,
		Gossaert, Jan,
FABIUS Pictor,	12	Goya y Lucientes,
Faed, Thos.,	184	Grant, F.,
Faed, John,	184	Greuze, J. Baptiste,
Falconer, J. M.,	211	Grützner, E.,
Fantin,	218	Guercino, (di Curto),
Faruffini,	225	Gusson,
Ferris, S J.,	203	Guido, Reni,
Fildes, S. Luke,	221	
Flaxman, John,	139	HAAG, Carl,
Flandrin,	163	Hall, Frank,
Fleury, Robert,	214	Hals, Franz,
Fleury, T. R.,	214	Hamilton, James,
Fontana, R.,	225	Hammer,
Forbes,	211	Hamon, J. Louis,
Fortuny, Mariano,	223	Hansen, C.,
Foster, Birket,	189	Hart, James,
Francia, (Raibolini),	39	Hart, Wm.,
Freeman,	210	Harvey, George,
Frere, Edouard,	215	Harpignies, H.,
Frith, W. P.,	180	Hassenclever,
Fromentin, E.,	218	Haseltine,
Fuerbach, A.,	222	Hausmann,
Fuseli, Henry,	131	Haydon, Benjamin,
		Hayes,
GAINSBOROUGH, Thomas,	129	Healy,
Gallait, Louis,	220	Hebert,

INDEX.

	PAGE		PAGE
Henner, J. J.,	219	Knight, R.,	211
Herkomer, H.,	221	Kockkock, B. C.,	220
Hermann, Leo,	212		
Herzog, N. G.,	211	Laia, or Lala,	13
Hildebrandt,	169	Lambdin,	211
Hill,	211	Lance, George,	177
Hogarth, William,	124	Lambinet, E.,	218
Holbein, Hans, (the elder),	109	Landseer, Edwin,	175
Holbein, Hans, (the younger),	109	Lalanne,	218
Hook, J. C.,	183	Laurens, J. P.,	219
Homer, Winslow,	211	Lawrence, Thomas,	142
Horsley, J. G.,	221	Lebrun, Charles,	105
Huey,	219	Leech, John,	188
Hunt, B.,	211	Lecomte-du-Nouy,	219
Hunt, William H.,	176	Leighton, Frederick,	180
Hunt, Wm. Holman,	178	Lely, Peter, (Van der Faes),	119
Huntingdon, D.,	206	Leonardo da Vinci,	40
Huysum, Van,	87	Leslie, Charles Robert,	196
		Leutz, E.,	200
Induno, J.,	225	Levy, H. L.,	219
Ingres, Jean Dominique,	156	Lewis, E. D.,	204
Innes, Geo.,	205	Lewis, J. F.,	186
Inman, Henry,	199	Leys, Henri,	219
Israels, J.,	220	Linnel, John,	185
Irving, J. B.,	211	Linnel, J. T.,	186
Isaby, Jean Baptiste.	156	Linnel, T. G.,	185
		Linnel, W.,	186
Jacques,	218	Lippi, Fra Filippo,	28
Jerichau, H.,	225	Lindegren,	224
Jernberg,	224	Locher,	225
Jones, E. B.,	211	Luminais, E. V.,	219
Johnston, A.,	221	Ludius,	13
Johnson, E.,	211	Luke (St.),	19
Jopling, Mrs.,	221		
Joris, P.,	225	Machen,	211
		McEntee, J.,	205
Kæmmerer,	220	Maclise, Daniel,	172
Kate, M. Ten,	221	Madrazzo,	224
Kaufman, Angelica,	140	Makart, Hans,	222
Kaulbach, Wm. Von,	167	Mantegna, Andrea,	37
Kensett,	210	Marstrand,	224
Knaus, L.,	222	Masaccio,	27
Kneller, Godfrey,	120	Matsys, Quintin,	33

	PAGE.		PAGE.
Maynard, G. W.,	211	Nicomachus,	8
Mauve,	219	Northcote, James,	153
Mazerolle, A. J.,	219	Norton, W. E.,	211
Max, Gabriel,	222		
Memling, Hans,	32	OPIE, John,	133
Melby, A.,	225	Orcagna,	26
Melanthius,	8	Orchardson, W. Q.,	221
Menzel, A.,	223	Ouless, W. W.,	221
Messonier, J. L. E.,	215	Overbeck, Fredk.,	165
Mesdag,	221		
Metrodorus,	13	PACUVIUS, Marcus,	12
Merle, H.,	218	Page, Wm.,	207
Metsu, Gabriel,	84	Pamphilus,	7
Meyer von Bremen,	222	Panænus,	4
Micon,	6	Pasini, A.,	219
Miches, R.,	225	Parrhasius,	4
Mignot, L. Rémy,	201	Paton, Noel,	183
Millais, John E.,	180	Passini, Ludwig,	225
Millet, Francois,	164	Pausias,	8
Millet, F. D.,	211	Peale, Charles W.,	194
Morales, Luis de,	99	Peale, Rembrandt,	200
Moran, Edward,	203	Perugino,	41
Moran, Thomas,	203	Perrault, L. G. B.,	219
Moran, Peter,	203	Pettie, John,	221
More, Anthony,	119	Phillip, John,	174
Morelli,	225	Philoxenus,	10
Moreland, George,	134	Philippoteaux,	219
Moreau, G.,	219	Piloty, K.,	223
Mount, W. S.,	200	Pisano, Andrea,	26
Müller, William J.,	189	Pisano, Nicola,	22
Mulready, William,	170	Plassan,	219
Müller,	223	Polanco,	98
Mundt,	223	Polygnotus,	4
Munkacsy, Michel,	222	Pontormo, Jacopo da,	102
Murillo, Bartolomé,	92	Portaels, J. F.,	221
		Porter,	211
		Potter, Paul,	83
NASMYTH, Patrick,	157	Poussin, Gaspar, (Doughet),	102
Navarrete, Fernandez,	100	Poussin, Nicolas,	102
Neacles,	11	Poynter, E. J.,	221
Neumann, A.,	223	Priou, L.,	219
Newton, G. Stuart,	199	Protogenes,	8
Nicias,	7	Prout, Samuel,	152
Nicol, E.,	178	Protais, P. A.,	219

	PAGE.
Ramsay, Allan,	133
Rasmussen, C.,	224
Raphael, Sanzio,	53
Regnault, Henri,	164
Rembrandt van Rijn,	80
Reni, Guido,	69
Rethel,	169
Reynolds, Joshua,	127
Ribalta, Francisco de,	94
Ribalta, Juan de,	94
Ribera, Josef de,	95
Ribot, T.,	219
Richards, W. T.,	201
Richards, De Berg,	211
Richter, H.,	221
Riviere, B.,	221
Roberts, David,	176
Robert, Leopold,	162
Robusti, Jacopo,	64
Romney, George,	132
Ronner, Henrietta,	221
Rosa, Salvator,	70
Rosenthal, Toby,	204
Rousseau, P.,	218
Rothermel, P. T.,	202
Rubens, Peter Paul,	75
Ruysdael, Jacob,	84
Sandby, Paul,	153
Sant, J.,	221
Sartain, Emily,	211
Schenck, A. F.,	218
Scheffer, Ary,	212
Schopin, H. F.,	212
Scheussele, Christen,	203
Slingeneyer, E.,	221
Schreyer, A.,	223
Signorelli, Luca,	36
Simonetti, A.,	225
Simiradsky, H.,	223
Smillie, J. P.,	211
Smirke, Robert,	153
Snyders, Frans,	84

	PAGE.
Sörensen, C. F.,	225
Stanfield, Clarkson,	175
Stammel, E,	222
Steinle,	169
Stewart, J. L.,	211
Stone, Frank,	189
Stothard, Thomas,	139
Stuart, Gilbert,	193
Sully, Thomas,	201
Tadema, L. Alma,	183
Tayler, Frederick,	181
Teniers, David, (the elder),	82
Teniers, David, (the younger,)	82
Terburg, Gerard,	84
Terry, F. W.,	203
Tenniel, John,	221
Theon,	8
Thompson,	211
Thompson, Miss,	221
Thornhill, James,	124
Tidemand, A.,	224
Tilton, J. R.,	210
Timanthes (of Sicyon),	10
Timanthes (of Cythnos),	6
Timonachus,	10
Tissot, J.,	219
Tintoretto, Il,	64
Tintoretto, Marietta,	65
Titian,	58
Toulmouche, A.,	218
Tschaggeny, C.,	169
Troyon, Constantine,	218
Trumbull, John,	193
Turner, J. M. W.,	143
Ussi, E.,	225
Vanderlyn, John,	194
Van de Velde, Adriaan,	86
Van Dyck, Antony,	113
Van Elten, K.,	211
Van Eyck, Hubrecht,	31

	PAGE.		PAGE.
Van Eyck, Jan,	31	Wulffaert, H.,	
Van Huysum, Jan,	87	Waugh, S. B.,	
Van Marke, E.,	218	Weber, T.,	
Van Ostade, Adriaan,	86	Weber, Paul,	
Van Ostade, Isaac,	86	Weir, J. F.,	
Vanuccio, Pietro di,	41	Weisman, W. H.,	
Vanuche, Andre,	41	West, Benjamin,	
Vautier, B.,	222	Whistler,	
Vedder, E.,	210	White, J. B.,	
Velasquez de Silva,	88	Whittredge,	
Vernet, Emile J. Horace,	157	Willems, F.,	
Veronese, Paul, (Cagliari),	66	Wilkie, David,	
Vertunni, A.,	225	Wilson, Richard,	
Verboeckhoven, E. J.,	220	Winner,	
Verhas, Jean,	221	Winterhalter, F.	
Veyrassat, J. J.,	219	Wright, G.,	
Vibert, J. G.,	219	Wolff, A.,	
Vidal, V.,	219	Worms, J.,	
Vien, Marie J.,	154	Wouvermans, Jan,	
Volon, A.,	219	Wouvermans, Philip,	
Voltz, F.,	223	Wouvermans, Pieter,	
WALKER, FREDERICK,	189	YEWELL, G. H.,	
Walker, Robert,	187	Yon, E. C.,	
Walters,	213		
Wappers, G.,	221	ZAMACOIS, Eduardo,	
Ward, H.,	187	Zagorsky, N.,	
Ward, E. M.,	187	Zampieri, Domenico,	
Waterman, M.,	211	Zeim, F. P.,	
Watts, Geo. F.,	181	Zeuxis,	
Watteau, A.,	108	Zurbaran, Francisco,	

www.ingramcontent.com/pod-product-compliance
Lightning Source LLC
Chambersburg PA
CBHW030359230426
43664CB00007BB/659